OXFORD WORLD'S CLASSICS

THE PRAIRIE

JAMES FENIMORE COOPER (1789–1851) grew up at Otsego Hall, his father's large estate at the foot of Lake Otsego amid the newly developing farmlands of New York State. A son of the region's dominant land developer and politician, Cooper absorbed memories of the Iroquois Indians' habitation of his family's lands. At an Albany school for patricians' sons, he heard legends of the nearby battles of the two wars which had brought the new American Republic into existence: the French and Indian, or Seven Years War (1756–63), and the Revolutionary War (1776–83). After two years at Yale College, Cooper spent five years at sea, married into a prominent Westchester County family of former loyalists, and began the life of a gentleman farmer on family lands. Although literary and family legend contends that Cooper began writing his first novel *Precaution* (1820) in order to outdo a contemporary British woman novelist, recent research suggests that the loss of the Cooper family wealth had made a profitable career necessary.

Cooper's second novel *The Spy* (1821), a patriotic but politically complex novel about the Revolutionary War, was an immediate success. In *The Pioneers* (1823), Cooper introduced Natty Bumppo (Leatherstocking) and Indian John (Chingachgook), the paired heroes of the five Leatherstocking Tales, which would include *The Last of the Mohicans* (1826), *The Prairie* (1827), *The Pathfinder* (1840), and *The Deerslayer* (1841). *The Last of the Mohicans* secured Cooper an international reputation as a major writer of historical romance, America's counterpart to Sir Walter Scott. Testimonies to the lasting power of Cooper's fiction have been written by novelists as diverse as Balzac, Melville, George Sand, Joseph Conrad, and D. H. Lawrence.

DONALD A. RINGE is Professor of English at the University of Kentucky.

OXFORD WORLD'S CLASSICS

*For almost 100 years Oxford World's Classics have brought
readers closer to the world's great literature. Now with over 700
titles—from the 4,000-year-old myths of Mesopotamia to the
twentieth century's greatest novels—the series makes available
lesser-known as well as celebrated writing.*

*The pocket-sized hardbacks of the early years contained
introductions by Virginia Woolf, T. S. Eliot, Graham Greene,
and other literary figures which enriched the experience of reading.
Today the series is recognized for its fine scholarship and
reliability in texts that span world literature, drama and poetry,
religion, philosophy and politics. Each edition includes perceptive
commentary and essential background information to meet the
changing needs of readers.*

OXFORD WORLD'S CLASSICS

JAMES FENIMORE COOPER

The Prairie

With an Introduction and Notes by
DONALD A. RINGE

OXFORD
UNIVERSITY PRESS

OXFORD
UNIVERSITY PRESS

Great Clarendon Street, Oxford OX2 6DP

Oxford University Press is a department of the University of Oxford.
It furthers the University's objective of excellence in research, scholarship,
and education by publishing worldwide in

Oxford New York

Athens Auckland Bangkok Bogotá Buenos Aires Calcutta
Cape Town Chennai Dar es Salaam Delhi Florence Hong Kong Istanbul
Karachi Kuala Lumpur Madrid Melbourne Mexico City Mumbai
Nairobi Paris São Paulo Singapore Taipei Tokyo Toronto Warsaw

with associated companies in Berlin Ibadan

Oxford is a registered trade mark of Oxford University Press
in the UK and in certain other countries

Published in the United States
by Oxford University Press Inc., New York

British Library Cataloguing in Publication Data

Data available

Library of Congress Cataloging in Publication Data
Cooper, James Fenimore, 1789–1851.
The prairie/James Fenimore Cooper: edited with an introduction
and notes by Donald A. Ringe.
p. cm.—(Oxford world's classics)
Includes bibliographical references.
I. Ringe, Donald A. II. Title. III. Series.
PS1418.A2R56 1992 813'.2—dc20 91–45602

ISBN 0–19–283766–4

1 3 5 7 9 10 8 6 4 2

Printed in Great Britain by
Cox & Wyman Ltd.
Reading, Berkshire

CONTENTS

INTRODUCTION

WHEN James Fenimore Cooper sailed for Europe on 1 June 1826, he took with him the unfinished manuscript of *The Prairie*, a book he completed in Paris and published in the spring of 1827. The composition had presented him with at least two major problems. For the first time since his initial novel, *Precaution* (1820), he placed the entire setting in a locale with which he was not familiar, and he was very much aware that the book was to be the third and, as he thought at the time, the final volume of the Leatherstocking series. The new book had to be the logical sequel to those that had already been published. The first problem he solved by reading and absorbing two narratives of western exploration: *Account of an Expedition from Pittsburgh to the Rocky Mountains; Performed in the Years 1819 and '20 . . . Under the Command of Major Stephen H. Long* (Philadelphia, 1823), and *History of the Expedition Under the Command of Captains Lewis and Clark . . . Performed during the Years 1804-5-6* (Philadelphia and New York, 1814). Both provided his imagination with the materials he needed to create an artistically convincing—if not authentic—setting for his romance.

Cooper's second problem derived from the manner in which the Leatherstocking tales were written. The books had not been planned as a series but had simply developed as Cooper discovered the possibilities of his material. *The Pioneers* (1823), the first to be written, included Leatherstocking as an ageing hunter about to be displaced by the settlers who, in 1793-4, are establishing a town at the foot of Otsego Lake, New York. When the book was published, Cooper apparently had no plans to use the character again, and he turned to other subjects—the sea and the American Revolution—for his next two books. But when he conceived the idea for *The Last of the Mohicans* (1826), a narrative laid in upstate New York during the French and Indian War in 1757, he reintroduced the character, now called Hawkeye, as a frontier scout who, with his Delaware friends, Chingachgook and Uncas, saves his white companions from disaster in the wilderness. Cooper must soon have realized that a third book would be needed—*The Prairie*, set on the Great Plains in 1804–5—to provide a fitting conclusion both for the career of his hero and for the commentary on American society that had developed as he composed the novels.

To integrate the already published books into the series, Cooper had to tie them in closely with the one he was writing. In addition to the character of Leatherstocking, here called the trapper, who forms the obvious link among them, Cooper introduced Captain Duncan Uncas Middleton, grandson of Duncan Heyward and Alice Munro of *The Last of the Mohicans* and namesake of the young warrior who dies at the end of that book. During the course of the narrative, too, Cooper uses the trapper, now an aged man, to recall incidents from the past that were important elements in the earlier books: the fire on Mount Vision in *The Pioneers*, for example, or the episode in the caves at Glens Falls in *The Last of the Mohicans*. Just before he dies in *The Prairie*, moreover, the trapper asks Middleton to send his rifle, pouch, and horn to Oliver Effingham, who, as Oliver Edwards, was his young companion in *The Pioneers*. By these means, Cooper keeps before his readers a constant reminder that *The Prairie* is part of a trilogy and must be seen, if its fullest meaning is to be understood, in relation to the books that went before it.

More important than any of these devices, however, were the thematic connections that Cooper established with the earlier books. Since the westward movement of the American people had become the informing myth of the series, Cooper had to show in *The Prairie* that the issues he had raised in treating the earlier stages of the process had been brought to an appropriate resolution. The penetration of the wilderness by Europeans, the expulsion of the French from North America and the British from the United States, and the settlement of the West—all presented or alluded to in *The Last of the Mohicans* and *The Pioneers*—gave unprecedented opportunity for the American people to build a new society based on democratic principles. Yet experience had shown that the westward movement entailed some serious consequences, among them the despoliation of the wilderness and the displacement of the Indians. It had made apparent, too, the need for social restraint on individual freedom and thus for the establishment of law in the new territories if a just society were to be created. These issues, raised in the earlier books, had to be addressed again if Cooper was to bring the series to a satisfactory conclusion.

The despoliation of nature and the displacement of the Indians were, of course, closely related themes. When the settlers cut the trees and drove off the game, as Cooper had shown in *The Pioneers*, Indian culture could no longer survive. Indeed, because the tribes fought among themselves—Huron against Delaware in *The Last of the Mohicans*—the white man's invasion of the wilderness in that book foreshadowed the doom of the red men. Cooper returns to this theme in *The Prairie* when Mahtoree, the Sioux chief, makes an appeal to the Pawnee Hard-Heart similar to that of Magua, the Huron, in the camp of the Delawares. If Sioux and Pawnee fight each other, only the white man will triumph, and the western Indians will be supplanted as were those in the East. What happened in 1757, in other words, occurs again in 1804, and although the white characters return to the East at the end of the book, the implication is strong that the struggle is not over. The judgement that Tamenund makes at the end of *Mohicans* applies as well to *The Prairie*: 'The pale-faces are masters of the earth, and the time of the red-men has not yet come again.'

Because the westward movement entailed such serious consequences, Cooper makes much of the attitude that Americans should take towards the natural environment. In *The Pioneers* Leatherstocking condemns the 'wasty ways' of the settlers at Templeton, who cut the trees and destroy the birds and fish as if their resources were inexhaustible. In *The Prairie* he tells how he had observed the destruction of the forests on his journey westward, and he remains, as he was in the earlier book, the spokesman for the proper use as opposed to the abuse of nature. He takes from the natural world only what he needs for his subsistence. Opposed to him in this book are Ishmael Bush and his family, who destroy a grove of cottonwood trees for their camp, and even Paul Hover, who would waste the game by shooting a buffalo a day so that he might enjoy only the meat of the hump. Though all, including the trapper, would agree that nature was intended for man's use, Bush and Hover, like the settlers of Templeton, place no limits upon themselves, have no concern for the future, and make their desires of the moment the sole criteria for the exploitation of the natural world.

By setting *The Prairie* on the Great Plains, an area thought at that time to be the Great American Desert, Cooper was able to include the consequences that would ensue if Americans continued to ravage the landscape as so many of them were inclined to do. Their nation would suffer the same fate as those ancient civilizations that had perished and left only their ruined monuments scattered across the deserts of the Near East. Derived from a cyclical theory of history, the Ruins of Empire theme was a popular one at the time and found expression in poetry and painting as well as in fiction. Introduced by Cooper in Chapter XXII of *The Prairie*, it was intended to serve as a warning to modern Americans that their civilization could also be destroyed. The concept was made plausible to Americans of Cooper's generation by the presence of burial mounds scattered throughout the Middle West, evidence that America had had a pre-Columbian history and that a pre-Indian people, as the Mound Builders were then thought to be, had once flourished in the American landscape, only to be supplanted by the Indian tribes, who were now themselves being displaced by the white men.

In the great debate between the trapper and Doctor Bat in that chapter, Cooper gives the frontiersman an opponent who expresses a view towards nature that had not yet appeared in the Leatherstocking tales. Obed Bat is a child of the Enlightenment, a scientific rationalist who subscribes to a theory of progress. He believes that 'education might eradicate the evil principle' (p. 240), and that by the application of science, man might improve on nature. He places great faith in 'reasoning, learned, scientific, triumphant man' (p. 105), and he even suggests that 'if time and opportunity were given him, . . . he might become the Master of all learning, and consequently equal to the great moving principle' (p. 180). Bat is, of course, a gross caricature of the scientist, easily ridiculed for his narrow interest in recording and classifying, for his ambition to make a name for himself, and for his lack of vision, indicated by his name. But the attitude he represents is, to Cooper, a threatening one, as fraught with danger to the natural world as that of the exploiters. Both, in Cooper's view, are impelled by pride and assume that man can do as he pleases with the natural environment, subjecting it to his will.

To oppose so dangerous a belief, the trapper develops an argument based on a religious view of the natural world, one that he had developed, as he tells us, from having 'lived for seventy years in the very bosom of natur' . . . where he could at any instant open his heart to God, without having to strip it of the cares and wickednesses of the settlements' (p. 250). His belief has been given a Christian colouring by the Moravian missionaries whom he had heard while living among the Delawares, but he had already developed his fundamental belief by 'looking natur' steadily in the face, and in reasoning on what [he had] seen rather than on what [he had] heard in traditions' (p. 239). His experience in the wilderness has taught him to be humble before the power and majesty of God, who looks down on his creatures much as they look upon ants, and who views with sorrow their vanity and pride. In the trapper's opinion, the scientist looks at nature with myopic eyes and ignores those questions which fill the trapper's mind with wonder. Bat, he believes, can tell him nothing 'of the beginning and the end' of things, of the meaning of life and death, or why things are as they are (p. 181).

In developing so philosophic an argument, the trapper becomes a somewhat different character from what he had been in the earlier books. In *The Pioneers* he had, of course, assumed a similar view of the natural world as revealing the majesty of God, and he had, for the most part, practised those principles of humility and self-control that contrast so strongly with the pride and selfishness of the settlers at Templeton. His was a voice for conservation in that book as it is in this, but in *The Prairie* the character has been greatly elevated. He occupies a more central position in the development of both plot and theme, and he has been given a rhetorical voice far grander than any he had possessed in the previous novels. To introduce the reader to this altered conception of the character, Cooper depicts him in the opening chapter as almost a demigod. His appearance in the autumnal sunset, enlarged to colossal size, surrounded by an aura of light, 'musing and melancholy' in attitude, and directly in the path of the squatters (p. 15) suggests the important role he is to play as the intellectual centre of a book that is much more philosophic than either of its predecessors.

The image, however, is only a transient one. The brilliant sunset fades into 'a gray and more sober light' (p. 16), and the figure is revealed in its true proportions as only the aged trapper, who no longer possesses the physical prowess that distinguished him in the earlier books. He can, of course, employ his frontier skills in such matters as diverting the stampeding buffalo and escaping the prairie fire, but he is no match for Ishmael Bush and his clan. He remains, therefore, a rather passive character, strong in his affirmation of moral value, but ultimately incapable of thwarting the despoilers or changing the attitude of a scientific rationalist like Dr Bat. Though the trapper adopts the Pawnee Hard-Heart as his son, the Indian can provide no effective continuity for his vision. The whole movement of the Leatherstocking tales has made clear the fate of the Indians. Their elegy was spoken by Tamenund at the end of *The Last of the Mohicans*, Chingachgook lives as a pathetic remnant of his former self and dies in *The Pioneers*, and the doom of the Plains Indians is certainly suggested in the strife between Pawnee and Sioux in *The Prairie*.

The death of the trapper, therefore, suggests the passing as well of his philosophic view. Set in a second autumnal sunset that echoes his first appearance in the book, the scene provides a fitting end for Leatherstocking himself and brings both the book and the series to a rather sombre close. The tone, like that of the concluding chapter of *The Last of the Mohicans*, is elegiac. The despoliation of nature which

Leatherstocking had witnessed and protested in *The Pioneers* has continued westward to the Great Plains, where the arid desolation, emphasized in the descriptive passages of the novel, foreshadows the fate of the entire continent if Americans should fail to curb their wanton destruction of nature. There is no indication, however, that, left to themselves, they might adopt—or even be influenced by— the religious vision that Leatherstocking has professed. Nor are they likely to acquire the humility and self-control that would enable them to maintain a proper relation to their environment. Men being what they are, Cooper believed that some means for social control had to be established if Americans were to fulfill their promise and create a just society that was both ordered and free.

The solution to this problem gave Cooper his second major theme in the Leatherstocking tales, the function to be served by law in a democratic society. The first two books examine legal issues, and in both the law is upheld even in those cases in which circumstances might suggest that it should be subverted. In *The Last of the Mohicans* the evil Magua is allowed to take Cora out of the Delaware camp because she is his captive. According to Indian law she belongs to him and no one may interfere. Even Uncas controls his anger and allows Magua time to get away before he goes in pursuit. Similarly, in *The Pioneers* the settlers, who have cut the trees and killed masses of birds and fish with impunity because in doing so they broke no civil law, prosecute Leatherstocking for killing one deer a few days out of season and for resisting an unworthy magistrate, who obtains a warrant to search the hunter's cabin mainly to satisfy his own curiosity. Though Leatherstocking is the only character in the book who consistently respects nature, he is tried, found guilty, and severely punished because he has broken the law.

The issue of law is especially acute in *The Prairie* because of the setting Cooper chose for the novel, the trans-Mississippi West acquired by the United States in 1803 through the Louisiana Purchase. By this act, the size of the country was more than doubled, and questions arose as to whether the United States would be radically changed by the acquisition of so much wild and unsettled territory. Some questioned whether democracy could survive in so large a country, or whether the nature of the population would change because of the Latin inhabitants of Louisiana. There was even a question of whether the western expanses could ever be brought into submission to the Federal government or become the domain of barbarous nomadic tribes that would never conform to civilized standards of behaviour. That Cooper was aware of these questions is apparent from the opening paragraphs of the book, and although he believed in the wisdom of the purchase, he was also concerned that the rule of law be brought to the new territories, which in their wild and denuded state introduced a new aspect of nature to the experience of Americans and placed them in a new relation to their environment.

In contrast to the dense forest wilderness of *The Last of the Mohicans* and the rapidly domesticating landscape of *The Pioneers*, Cooper's third Leatherstocking novel takes place in a vast setting that dwarfs the human characters and leaves them naked to the elements. From the first pages of the novel, Cooper stresses the immensity of the landscape, the vast distance that separates the characters from the settled regions of the East, and their vulnerability both to the elements and to the bands of Indians that sweep across the prairies more like demons than like men. The forces of nature themselves are depicted as so powerful and uncontrolled that they threaten to overwhelm them. Masses of clouds whirl violently, driven by gusts of wind that blow 'across the wild and naked Prairies, with a violence that is seldom witnessed, in any section of the continent less open'. Although breaks in the clouds may occasionally 'admit transient glimpses of the bright and glorious sight of the heavens, dwelling in a magnificence by far too grand and durable, to be disturbed by the fitful efforts of the lower world' (p. 85), the earth appears to have been abandoned to violence and death.

Similar descriptions accompany the two darkest incidents in the book, the discovery of the murdered Asa Bush's body and the hanging of his uncle, Abiram White, for the crime, a deed that, taking place within the family, bespeaks a disorder that strikes at the very heart of society. In the former 'wild and striking' scene, flocks of screaming birds circle above the thicket where the body is concealed while lowering clouds whirl and roll 'over each other, in a terrific and yet grand disorder' (pp. 135–6). In the latter, the rising wind sweeps 'over the plain, in a manner that rendered it easy . . . to fancy strange and unearthly sounds were in the blasts'. The empty prairies 'assume the forms of illimitable and dreary wastes, and the rushing of the wind [sounds] like the whisperings of the dead' (p. 362). At length a shriek fills the air as Abiram White, left on a ledge with a rope, tied to a tree, around his neck, falls to his death. Gothic scenes like these serve an important function in the book, for they suggest that all order has been lost and the characters are struggling in a world that seems to have reverted to primeval chaos.

To emphasize the point Cooper describes the prairies as if they were the sea. 'The earth', he writes in his first description of them in the book, 'was not unlike the ocean, when its restless waters are heaving heavily, after the agitation and fury of the tempest have begun to lessen. There was the same waving and regular surface, the same absence of foreign objects, and the same boundless extent to the view.' Indeed, Cooper even imagines that other aspects of the landscape resemble what could be seen on the ocean. 'Here and there a tall tree rose out of the bottoms, stretching its naked branches abroad, like some solitary vessel; and, to strengthen the delusion, far in the distance, appeared two or three rounded thickets, looming in the misty horizon like islands resting on the waters' (p. 13). By equating prairie and sea, Cooper was able to suggest not only the expansiveness of the landscape, but also its inherent danger for the unwary. In the early nineteenth century, the sea could be a dangerous place where a ship was well advised to approach another with caution until the vessel was identified and its peaceful or warlike intentions were known.

Cooper further develops the figure by treating groups of characters as if they were ships at sea, well aware of the dangers they faced. When the trapper and his friends rescue Inez and Ellen from Bush's rock—itself depicted as a

Pharos—he shifts directions 'to elude pursuit, as a vessel changes her course in fogs and darkness, to escape from the vigilance of her enemies' (p. 177), and Bush and his sons approach the Sioux at one point 'as a squadron of cruisers is often seen to steer across the waste of waters towards the rich but well-protected convoy' (p. 214). Shortly thereafter, Bush and his sons, the Sioux, and Middleton's little band arrange themselves in defensive positions on the slight elevations. 'The three groupes', Cooper observes, 'now resembled so many fleets at sea, lying with their top-sails to the masts, with the commendable precaution of reconnoitring, before each could ascertain who among the strangers might be considered as friends, and who as foes' (p. 215). On the prairies, as on the sea, where the force of law is seldom felt, the only recourse available to anyone is the ability to defend himself against those who would do him harm.

In such an environment the absence of law is most acutely felt by the weak, who, unprotected by the restraints that society places on all, find themselves at the mercy of the ruthless and the strong. Even Leatherstocking comes to perceive this truth. As a skilled frontiersman and expert shot, he had always been able to maintain his independence, and even as an old man in *The Pioneers*, he was able to deny the authority of the civil law. But ten years later, in *The Prairie*, 'age and weakness' have brought him to a somewhat different view. When, early in the book, he meets Ellen Wade alone at night on the prairie and learns that she has no father to protect her, he asks her why she has ventured into 'a place where none but the strong should come'. By crossing the Mississippi, he tells her, she has left behind a friend—the law—'that is always bound to look to the young and feeble, like' herself. ' 'Tis bad to have it,' he observes, 'but, I sometimes think, it is worse to be entirely without it.' It is certainly needed 'when such as have not the gifts of strength and wisdom are to be taken care of' (p. 27).

Despite this concession, however, the trapper has not changed his fundamental attitude towards the law. He continues to follow his own understanding of right and wrong, to believe that the Indians follow a law that is suitable for their culture, and to maintain that the fruits of the earth are provided for all. These opinions put him both in opposition to, and in agreement with Ishmael Bush, whose basic values are the antithesis of his. When Bush asserts that he is 'as rightful an owner of the land [he stands] on, as any governor in the States', and asks the trapper 'where the law or the reason, is to [be] found, which says that one man shall have a section, or a town, or perhaps a county, to his use, and another have to beg for 'arth to make his grave in', the trapper 'cannot say that [he is] wrong'. He has 'often thought and said as much, when and where [he has] believed [his] voice could be heard' (p. 61). But if the trapper cannot contradict the squatter on this point, their opinions, though in singular agreement, are based on such different premises that the two men must be essentially at odds.

Unlike Leatherstocking, whose attitude towards the law derives from his humble submission to the God revealed through the natural landscape, Ishmael Bush is a man who acts as if he were a law unto himself. Though he considers the earth the common property of all, he would simply take whatever he wants and defend it with his power. His attitude is typified by the way he treats his family. He rules with an iron hand. His oldest son, Asa, puts it well. He protests that his father speaks 'of law, as if [he] knew of none'; yet he keeps his son down as if he 'had not life and wants of [his] own' (p. 90). When Asa strikes his uncle, Abiram White, moreover, Ishmael asserts his authority and assumes that he can distribute justice between them. Bush is able to maintain his authority, even though Asa has raised a 'spirit of insubordination' among his brothers, but it can be for only a little while. Bush is aware that sooner or later his sons will emulate their father, who had, 'in the wantonness of his youth and vigor', reversed 'the order of the brutes', and 'cast off his own aged and failing parents, to enter into the world unshackled and free' (p. 143).

Ishmael Bush and his family are just the kind of nomadic tribe that Americans feared might one day inhabit the trans-Mississippi West and pose a threat to American society. But if Cooper recognized the problem posed by the squatters, he does little more than suggest it before he brings them back again within the fold of civilization. Indeed, Bush is even made to assume the patriarchal role of judge while still on the prairie and to sit in judgment on the other characters. It is a role to which he is not accustomed, yet he manages to fulfill it with a considerable amount of dignity. Since he knows and respects no civil law, he can only turn to the sole code of which he is aware, the Old Testament rule which, as he puts it, 'is known unto all, and which teaches that an "eye must be returned for an eye" and "a tooth for a tooth" '. Bush sees 'reason in such a law that makes it a safe rule to journey by', and he solemnly declares, when he convenes his court, 'that this day shall I abide by it, and give unto all and each, that which is his due and no more' (p. 343).

But if Ishmael Bush succeeds in dispensing a rough kind of justice, his court is anything but legitimate. A self-appointed judge, he holds the other characters completely in his power and admits of no appeal from his decisions. Harsh in his judgment of others when he fancies himself wronged, he is quick to minimize his own crime. He shrugs off his role in the kidnapping of Inez as simply 'a mistake' (p. 344) which he is willing to rectify 'so far as it can be done, in safety' (p. 350), yet when he thinks the trapper is guilty of his son's murder, he is ready and willing to demand a life for a life. Only when he discovers that the trapper is innocent and Abiram White guilty of the crime is his mind troubled by second thoughts. As he and his wife Esther discuss the matter, it is plain that they have been trapped by their understanding of the law. Though Esther would show mercy, Ishmael reminds her that 'nothing was said of mercy' when the trapper was thought to have done the deed (p. 358). Bush can therefore render none to the man who is her brother, and Abiram White's judge becomes his executioner when he is left to die.

In his role of tribal patriarch sitting in judgment, Ishmael Bush becomes an impressive character, but his concept of law is that of the despot. The dispensing of justice in his court depends to a large extent on his personal power and will, a practice that cannot be tolerated in a democratic society. Cooper suggests what the basis of democratic law should be when he briefly describes the subsequent careers of Paul Hover and Duncan Middleton, both of whom eventually assume the role of lawmaker after they return to the settled regions east of the Mississippi. Hover, who abandons frontier life when he marries Ellen Wade, rises in society and becomes 'a member of the lower branch of the Legislature of the State where he' resides. There, his 'great practical knowledge' makes him a suitable lawmaker at that level of government. Middleton, on the other hand, whose education is much superior to Paul's, is elected to 'a far higher branch of Legislative Authority' (p. 376). In their histories, these two characters embody the essentials of Cooper's theory of democratic law, based, of course, on the people themselves, but put into practice by those whose virtue, talent, and education qualify them to be leaders in a democratic society.

Yet the social and political success that these characters attain is not emphasized in the book. Though Cooper had to affirm the rule of law, he was well aware, as he had shown in *The Pioneers*, that the law could be manipulated by unscrupulous men. Thus, although the civil law that Middleton and Hover will help to enact is superior to the kind of law maintained by Ishmael Bush, there is nothing in the book to suggest that they will be any more successful than Judge Temple was in *The Pioneers* in curbing the greed of selfish men and restraining them from the despoliation of nature. Though their future careers may suggest a degree of optimism concerning the rule of law, the book does not end on that note. It is, rather, the death of Leatherstocking, effectively depicted in the final chapter, that Cooper chooses for the conclusion to both the book and the series. The rule of law supported by Middleton and Hover may provide the only possible, if defective, hope for society, but an ideal is lost when Leatherstocking and all that he represents in humility, self-control, reverence for God, and respect for nature comes to an end on the prairie.

NOTE ON THE TEXT

THIS edition reprints the text of *The Prairie* established by
James P. Elliott for *The Writings of James Fenimore Cooper*,
published by the State University of New York Press. It
includes the footnotes, written for a European audience, that
Cooper provided for Richard Bentley's Standard Novels
edition of 1832 and reprints the prefaces that Cooper wrote
for the editions of 1827, 1832, and 1849.

SELECT BIBLIOGRAPHY

Cooper's Life and Work

Charles Hansford Adams, *'The Guardian of the Law': Authority and Identity in James Fenimore Cooper* (University Park, Pa., 1990).

Allan M. Axelrad, *History and Utopia: A Study of the World View of James Fenimore Cooper* (Norwood, Penn., 1978).

James F. Beard, ed., *The Letters and Journals of James Fenimore Cooper*, 6 vols. (Cambridge, Mass., 1960–8).

George Dekker, *James Fenimore Cooper, the Novelist* (London, 1967).

Wayne Franklin, *The New World of James Fenimore Cooper* (Chicago, 1982).

James Grossman, *James Fenimore Cooper* (New York, 1949).

Kay Seymour House, *Cooper's Americans* (Columbus, Oh., 1965).

William P. Kelly, *Plotting America's Past: Fenimore Cooper and the Leatherstocking Tales* (Carbondale and Edwardsville, Ill., 1983).

Robert Emmet Long, *James Fenimore Cooper* (New York, 1990).

John P. McWilliams, Jr., *Political Justice in a Republic: James Fenimore Cooper's America* (Berkeley and Los Angeles, 1972).

Warren Motley, *The American Abraham: James Fenimore Cooper and the Frontier Patriarch* (Cambridge and New York, 1987).

Blake Nevius, *Cooper's Landscapes: An Essay on the Picturesque Vision* (Berkeley and Los Angeles, 1976).

H. Daniel Peck, *A World by Itself: The Pastoral Moment in Cooper's Fiction* (New Haven, Conn., 1977).

Stephen Railton, *Fenimore Cooper: A Study of his Life and Imagination* (Princeton, NJ, 1978).

Donald A. Ringe, *James Fenimore Cooper*, updated edition (Boston, 1988).

Warren S. Walker, *James Fenimore Cooper: An Introduction and Interpretation* (New York, 1962).

James D. Wallace, *Early Cooper and his Audience* (New York, 1986).

Cooper's Place in American Literature

Richard Chase, *The American Novel and its Tradition* (Garden City, NY, 1957).

Robert Clark, *History and Myth in American Fiction, 1823–1852* (New York, 1984).

George Dekker, *The American Historical Romance* (Cambridge and New York, 1987).

Leslie A. Fiedler, *Love and Death in the American Novel* (New York, 1960).

Edwin Fussell, *Frontier: American Literature and the American West* (Princeton, NJ, 1965).

Harry B. Henderson III, *Versions of the Past: The Historical Imagination in American Fiction* (New York, 1974).

A. N. Kaul, *The American Vision: Actual and Ideal Society in Nineteenth-Century Fiction* (New Haven, Conn., 1963).

Annette Kolodny, *The Lay of the Land: Metaphor as Experience and History in American Life and Letters* (Chapel Hill, NC, 1975).

D. H. Lawrence, *Studies in Classic American Literature* (New York, 1923).

Joel Porte, *The Romance in America: Studies in Cooper, Poe, Hawthorne, Melville, and James* (Middletown, Conn., 1969).

Donald A. Ringe, *The Pictorial Mode: Space and Time in the Art of Bryant, Irving and Cooper* (Lexington, Ky., 1971).

Richard Slotkin, *Regeneration Through Violence: The Mythology of the American Frontier, 1600–1860* (Middletown, Conn., 1973).

Henry Nash Smith, *Virgin Land: The American West as Symbol and Myth* (Cambridge, Mass., 1950).

Jane Tompkins, *Sensational Designs: The Cultural Work of American Fiction, 1790–1860* (New York and Oxford, 1985).

The Prairie

Jesse Bier, 'Lapsarians on *The Prairie*: Cooper's Novel', *Texas Studies in Literature and Language*, 4 (1962), 49–57.

Gordon Brotherston, 'The Prairie and Cooper's Invention of the West', in Robert Clark, ed., *James Fenimore Cooper: New Critical Essays* (London and Totowa, NJ, 1985), 162–86.

François Brunet, 'Linguisters in the Prairie', *Revue française d'études américaines*, 37 (1988), 238–66.

James P. Elliott, 'Historical Introduction' to *The Prairie*, SUNY edn. (Albany, NY, 1985), pp. xv–xxxiii.

Eric Fassin, *'Théorie du language et idéologie dans La Prairie'*, *Revue française d'études américaines*, 37 (1988), 267–82.

Wayne Fields, 'Beyond Definition: A Reading of *The Prairie*', in Fields, ed., *James Fenimore Cooper: A Collection of Critical Essays* (Englewood Cliffs, NJ, 1979), 93–111.

John T. Flanagan, 'The Authenticity of Cooper's *The Prairie*', *Modern Language Quarterly*, 2 (1941), 99–104.

William H. Goetzmann, 'James Fenimore Cooper: *The Prairie*', in Hennig Cohen, ed., *Landmarks of American Writing* (New York and London, 1969), 66–78.

E. Soteris Muszynska-Wallace, 'The Sources of *The Prairie*', *American Literature*, 21 (1949), 191–200.

Carl Nelson, 'Cooper's Verbal Faction: The Hierarchy of Rhetoric, Voice, and Silence in *The Prairie*', *West Virginia University Philological Papers*, 24 (1977), 37–47.

Orm Överland, *The Making and Meaning of an American Classic: James Fenimore Cooper's 'The Prairie'* (Oslo and New York, 1973).

Donald A. Ringe, 'Man and Nature in Cooper's *The Prairie*', *Nineteenth-Century Fiction*, 15 (1961), 313–23.

Mary E. Rucker, 'Natural, Tribal, and Civil Law in Cooper's *The Prairie*', *Western American Literature*, 12 (1977), 215–22.

Francesca Sawaya, 'Between Revolution and Racism: Colonialism and the American Indian in *The Prairie*', in George A. Test, ed., *James Fenimore Cooper: His Country and His Art* (No. 7) (1991), 126–34.

Henry Nash Smith, 'Introduction' to *The Prairie*, Rinehart edn. (New York and Toronto, 1950), pp. v–xx.

A CHRONOLOGY OF
JAMES FENIMORE COOPER

1786 William Cooper establishes Cooperstown at the southern tip of Lake Otsego in New York State.

1789 James Cooper born in Burlington, New Jersey. William Cooper moves his family to Cooperstown the following year.

1803 Cooper matriculates at Yale College; dismissed for misconduct two years later.

1806–8 Sails before the mast to England and the continent aboard the *Stirling*; serves as a midshipman in the United States Navy at Fort Oswego on Lake Ontario.

1811 Marries Susan Augusta De Lancey.

1811–19 Lives as a gentleman farmer on family lands in Westchester County, New York and in Cooperstown.

1820 Writes his first novel, *Precaution*, and, in the following year, *The Spy* (1821).

1822–6 Moves to New York City and writes *The Pioneers* (1823), *The Pilot* (1824), *Lionel Lincoln* (1825), and *The Last of the Mohicans* (1826).

1826–33 Resides in Europe with his family. Lives most frequently in Paris but takes lengthy trips to England, the Low Countries, Switzerland, Germany, and Italy. Concern with, and involvement in, the European revolutionary movements of 1830. Writes *The Prairie* (1827), *The Red Rover* (1827), *Notions of the Americans* (1828), *The Wept of Wish-ton-Wish* (1829), and *The Water-Witch* (1830). After 1830, turns to novels that concern European politics: *The Bravo* (1831), *The Heidenmauer* (1832), and *The Headsman* (1833).

1833–6 Returns to America and resides in New York City. Political correspondent for the *Evening Post*. Writes *A Letter to His Countrymen* (1834) and *The Monikins* (1835).

1836 Returns to Cooperstown and remodels Otsego Hall, William Cooper's home.

1837–8   Publishes five volumes of sketches concerned with his European travels. Much publicized land controversy over the ownership and use of Three Mile Point on Lake Otsego. Writes *Homeward Bound* and *Home As Found* (1838). Lengthy libel suits against Whig editors begin. Writes *The American Democrat* (1838) and *History of the Navy of the United States* (1839).

1840   Resumes writing novels about the frontier and the sea: *The Pathfinder* (1840), *Mercedes of Castille* (1840), *The Deerslayer* (1841), *The Two Admirals* (1842), *The Wing-and-Wing* (1842), *Wyandotté* (1843).

1844–6   Defends the landowners' position in the Anti-Rent Wars occurring near Albany by writing a trilogy titled *The Littlepage Manuscripts: Satanstoe* (1845), *The Chainbearer* (1845), *The Redskins* (1846). Also writes *Afloat and Ashore* and *Miles Wallingford* (1844).

1847–9   Writes the first American Utopian novel, *The Crater* (1847). Last frontier and sea novels: *Jack Tier* (1848), *The Oak Openings* (1848), and *The Sea Lions* (1849).

1850   Prepares the Putnam Author's Revised Edition of his writings. Writes the Preface to the Leatherstocking Tales and a novel about criminal law, *The Ways of the Hour*.

1851   Dies in Cooperstown, leaving *The Towns of Manhattan* (also titled *New York*) unfinished.

1852   Memorial gathering for Cooper held in New York City, Daniel Webster presiding. Letters and tributes by Bancroft, Bryant, Emerson, Hawthorne, Irving, Longfellow, Melville, Parkman, Prescott, and Simms.

PREFACE

[1827]

The manner in which the writer of this book, came into possession of most of its materials is mentioned in the work itself. Any well bred reader will readily conceive that there may exist a thousand reasons, why he should not reveal any more of his private sources of information. He will only say, on his own responsibility, that the portions of the tale for which no authorities are given are quite as true as those which are not destitute of this peculiar advantage, and that all may be believed alike.

There is however to be found in the following pages an occasional departure from strict historical veracity which it may be well to mention. In the endless confusion of names, customs, opinions and languages which exists among the tribes of the West, the author, has paid much more attention to sound and convenience than to literal truth. He has uniformly called the Great Spirit, for instance, the Wahcondah,* though he is not ignorant that there are different names for that being in the two nations he has introduced. So in other matters he has rather adhered to simplicity than sought to make his narrative strictly correct at the expense of all order and clearness. It was enough for his purpose that the picture should possess the general features of the original. In the shading, attitude, and disposition of the figure a little liberty has been taken. Even this brief explanation would have been spared, did not the author know that there was a certain class of 'learned Thebans,' who are just as fit to read any thing which depends for its success on the imagination, as they are to write it.

It may be necessary to meet much graver and less easily explained objections in the minds of a far higher class of readers. The introduction of one and the same character, as a principal actor, in no less than three books, and the selection of a comparative desert,* which is aided by no historical recollections and embellished by so few or no poetical associations for the scene of a legend, in these times of perilous adventure in works of this description, may need more vindication. If the first objection can be removed, the latter must fall of course, as it clearly became the duty of a faithful chronicler, to follow his hero wherever he might choose to go.

It is quite probable that the narrator of these simple events has deceived himself as to the importance they may have in the eyes of other people. But he has seen or thought he has seen, something sufficiently instructive and touching in the life of a veteran of the forest, who, having commenced his career near the Atlantic had been driven, by the increasing and unparalleled advance of population, to seek a final refuge from society in the broad and tenantless plains of the West, to induce him to hazard the experiment of publication. That the changes, which might have driven a man so constituted to such an expedient, have actually occurred within a single life, is a matter of undeniable history;—that they did produce such an effect on the Scout of the Mohicans, the Leatherstocking of the Pioneers and the Trapper of the Prairie, rests on an authority no less imposing than these veritable pages, from which the reader shall no longer be detained, if he be disposed to peruse them, after this frank arrival of the poverty of their contents.

Introduction
[1832]

The geological formation of that portion of the American Union, which lies between the Alleghanies and the Rocky Mountains, has given rise to many ingenious theories. Virtually, the whole of this immense region is a plain. For a distance extending nearly 1500 miles east and west, and 600 north and south, there is scarcely an elevation worthy to be called a mountain. Even hills are not common; though a good deal of the face of the country has more or less of the "rolling" character, which is described in the opening pages of this work.

There is much reason to believe that the territory which now composes Ohio, Illinois, Indiana, Michigan, and a large portion of the country west of the Mississippi, lay formerly under water. The soil of all the former states has the appearance of an alluvial deposit; and isolated rocks have been found, of a nature and in situations which render it difficult to refute the opinion that they have been transfered to their present beds by floating ice. This theory assumes that the Great Lakes were the deep pools of one immense body of fresh water, which lay too low to be drained by the irruption that laid bare the land.

It will be remembered that the French, when masters of the Canadas and Louisiana, claimed the whole of the territory in question. Their hunters and advanced troops held the first communications with the savage occupants, and the earliest written accounts we possess of these vast regions, are from the pens of their missionaries. Many French words have, consequently, become of local use in this quarter of America, and not a few names given in that language have been perpetuated. When the adventurers, who first penetrated these wilds, met, in the centre of the forests, immense plains, covered with rich verdure or rank grasses, they naturally gave them the appellation of meadows. As the English succeeded the French, and found a peculiarity of nature, differing from all they had yet seen on the continent, already distinguished by a word that did not express any thing in their own language, they left these natural meadows in possession of their title of convention. In this manner has the word "Prairie" been adopted into the English tongue.

The American prairies are of two kinds. Those which lie east of the Mississippi are comparatively small, and exceedingly fertile, and are always surrounded by forests. They are susceptible of high cultivation, and are fast becoming settled. They abound in Ohio, Michigan, Illinois, and Indiana. They labour under the disadvantages of a scarcity of wood and water,—evils of a serious character, until art has had time to supply the deficiencies of nature. As coal is said to abound in all that region, and wells are generally successful, the enterprise of the emigrants is gradually prevailing against these difficulties.

The second description of these natural meadows lies west of the Mississippi, at a distance of a few hundred miles from that river, and is called the Great Prairies. They resemble the steppes of Tartary more than any other known portion of the world; being, in fact, a vast country, incapable of sustaining a dense population, in the absence of the two great necessaries already named. Rivers abound, it is true; but this region is nearly destitute of brooks and the smaller water courses, which tend so much to comfort and fertility.

The origin and date of the Great American Prairies form one of nature's most majestic mysteries. The general character of the United States, of the Canadas, and of Mexico, is that of luxuriant fertility. It would be difficult to find another portion of the world, of the same extent, which has so little useless land as the inhabited parts of the American Union. Most of the mountains are arable, and even the prairies, in this section of the republic, are of deep alluvion. The same is true between the Rocky Mountains and the Pacific. Between the two lies the broad belt, of comparative desert, which is the scene of this tale, appearing to interpose a barrier to the progress of the American people westward.

The Great Prairies appear to be the final gathering place of the red men. The remnants of the Mohicans, and the Delawares, of the Creeks, Choctaws, and Cherokees, are destined to fulfil their time on these vast plains. The entire number of the Indians, within the Union, is differently computed, at between one and five hundred thousand souls. Most of them inhabit the country west of the Mississippi. At the period of the tale, they dwelt in open hostility; national feuds passing from generation to generation. The power of the republic has done much to restore peace to these wild scenes, and it is now possible to travel in security, where civilized man did not dare to pass unprotected five-and-twenty years ago.

The reader, who has perused the two former works, of which this is the natural successor, will recognise an old acquaintance in the principal character of the story. We have here brought him to his end, and we trust he will be permitted to slumber in the peace of the just.

—Paris, June, 1832

Introduction
[1849]

In 1849, while revising for the Putnam Edition, Cooper interpolated the following sentence immediately after ". . . the progress of the American people westward."

Since the original publication of this book, however, the boundaries of the republic have been carried to the Pacific, and "the settler," preceded by the "trapper," has already established himself on the shores of that vast sea.

Cooper also cancelled the last paragraph of his 1832 "Introduction," and inserted the following two paragraphs in its place.

Recent events have brought the Grand Prairies into familiar notice, and we now read of journeys across them as, half a century since, we perused the narratives of the emigrants to Ohio and Louisiana. It is a singular commentary on the times that places for railroads across these vast plains are in active discussion, and that men have ceased to regard the project as chimerical.

This book closes the career of Leather-stocking. Pressed upon by time, he had ceased to be the hunter and the warrior, and has become a trapper of the great West. The sound of the axe has driven him from his beloved forests to seek a refuge, by a species of desperate resignation, on the denuded plains that stretch to the Rocky Mountains. Here he passes the few closing years of his life, dying as he had lived, a philosopher of the wilderness, with few of the failings, none of the vices, and all the nature and truth of his position.

The Prairie.

Chapter I.

"I pray thee, shepherd, if that love or gold
Can in this desert place buy entertainment,
Bring us where we may rest ourselves and feed."

As You Like It, II. iv. 71-73

MUCH was said and written, at the time, concerning the policy of adding the vast regions of Louisiana, to the already immense, and but half-tenanted territories of the United-States. As the warmth of the controversy however subsided, and party considerations gave place to more liberal views, the wisdom of the measure began to be generally conceded. It soon became apparent, to the meanest capacity, that, while nature had placed a barrier of desert to the extension of our population in the west, the measure had made us the masters of a belt of fertile country, which, in the revolutions of the day, might have become the property of a rival nation. It gave us the sole command of the great thoroughfare of the interior,* and placed the countless tribes of savages, who lay along our borders, entirely within our controul; it reconciled conflicting rights, and quieted national distrusts; it opened a thousand avenues to the inland trade, and to the waters of the Pacific; and, if ever time or necessity shall require a peaceful division of this vast empire, it assures us a neighbour that will possess our language, our religion, our institutions, and it is also to be hoped, our sense of political justice.

Although the purchase was made in 1803, the spring of the succeeding year was permitted to open, before the official prudence of the Spaniard, who held the province for his European master, admitted the authority, or even of the entrance, of its new proprietors. But the forms of the transfer were no sooner completed, and the new government acknowledged, than swarms of that restless people, which is ever found hovering on the skirts of American society, plunged into the thickets that fringed the right bank of the Mississippi, with the same careless hardihood, as had already sustained so many of them in their toilsome progress from the Atlantic states, to the eastern shores of the "Father of rivers."[1]

---

[1] The Mississippi is thus termed in several of the Indian languages. The reader will gain a more just idea of the importance of this stream, if he recall to mind the fact, that the Missouri and the Mississippi are properly the same river. Their united lengths cannot be greatly short of four thousand miles. [1832]

Time was necessary to blend the numerous and affluent colonists of the lower province with their new compatriots; but the thinner and more humble population, above, was almost immediately swallowed in the vortex which attended the tide of instant emigration. The inroad from the east was a new and sudden out-breaking of a people, who had endured a momentary restraint, after having been rendered nearly resistless by success. The toils and hazards of former undertakings were forgotten, as these endless and unexplored regions, with all their fancied as well as real advantages, were laid open to their enterprise. The consequences were such as might easily have been anticipated, from so tempting an offering, placed as it was before the eyes of a race long trained in adventure and nurtured in difficulties.

Thousands of the elders, of what were then called the *New*-States,[1] broke up from the enjoyment of their hard-earned indulgencies, and were to be seen leading long files of descendants, born and reared in the forests of Ohio and Kentucky, deeper into the land, in quest of that which might be termed, without the aid of poetry, their natural and more congenial atmosphere. The distinguished and resolute forester, who first penetrated the wilds of the latter state, was of the number. This adventurous and venerable patriarch was now seen making his last remove; placing the "endless river" between him and the multitude his own success had drawn around him, and seeking for the renewal of enjoyments which were rendered worthless in his eyes, when trammelled by the forms of human institutions.[2]

In the pursuit of adventures, such as these, men are ordinarily governed by their habits or deluded by their wishes. A few, led by the phantoms of hope, and ambitious of sudden affluence, sought the mines of the virgin territory; but by far the greater portion of the emigrants were satisfied to establish themselves along the margins of the larger water-courses, content with the rich returns that the generous alluvial bottoms of the rivers never fail to bestow on the most desultory industry. In this manner were communities formed with magical rapidity; and most of those who witnessed the purchase of

[1] All the states admitted to the American Union, since the revolution are called *New*-States, with the exception of Vermont that had claims before the war which were not, however, admitted until a later day. [1832]

[2] Col. Boon, the patriarch of Kentucky. This venerable and hardy pioneer of civilization emigrated to an estate three hundred miles west of the Mississippi, in his ninety second year, because he found a population of ten to the square mile, inconveniently crowded! [1832]

the empty empire, have lived to see already a populous and sovereign state, parcelled from its inhabitants, and received into the bosom of the national Union, on terms of political equality.

The incidents and scenes which are connected with this legend, occurred in the earliest periods of the enterprises which have led to so great and so speedy a result.

The harvest of the first year of our possession had long been passed, and the fading foliage of a few scattered trees was, already, beginning to exhibit the hues and tints of autumn, when a train of wagons issued from the bed of a dry rivulet, to pursue its course across the undulating surface of what, in the language of the country of which we write, is called a "rolling Prairie." The vehicles, loaded with household goods and implements of husbandry, the few straggling sheep and cattle that were herded in the rear, and the rugged appearance and careless mien of the sturdy men who loitered at the sides of the lingering teams, united to announce a band of emigrants seeking for the Eldorado of the West. Contrary to the usual practice of the men of their caste, this party had left the fertile bottoms of the low country, and had found its way, by means only known to such adventurers, across glen and torrent, over deep morasses and arid wastes, to a point far beyond the usual limits of civilized habitations. In their front were stretched those broad plains, which extend, with so little diversity of character, to the bases of the Rocky Mountains; and many long and dreary miles in their rear, foamed the swift and turbid waters of La Platte.

The appearance of such a train, in that bleak and solitary place, was rendered the more remarkable by the fact, that the surrounding country offered so little, that was tempting to the cupidity of speculation, and, if possible, still less that was flattering to the hopes of an ordinary settler of new lands.

The meagre herbage of the Prairie promised nothing, in favor of a hard and unyielding soil, over which the wheels of the vehicles rattled as lightly as if they travelled on a beaten road; neither wagons nor beasts making any deeper impression, than to mark that bruised and withered grass, which the cattle plucked, from time to time, and as often rejected, as food too sour, for even hunger to render palatable.

Whatever might be the final destination of these adventurers, or the secret causes of their apparent security in so remote and unprotected a situation, there was no visible sign of uneasiness, uncertainty, or alarm among them. Including both sexes, and every age, the number of the party exceeded twenty.

At some little distance in front of the whole, marched the individual who, by his position and air, appeared to be the leader of the band. He was a tall, sun-burnt man, past the middle age, of a dull countenance and listless manner. His frame appeared loose and flexible; but it was vast, and in reality of prodigious power. It was only at moments, however, as some slight impediment opposed itself to his loitering progress, that his person, which, in its ordinary gait seemed so lounging and nerveless, displayed any of those energies which lay latent in his system, like the slumbering and unwieldy, but terrible, strength of the elephant. The inferior lineaments of his countenance were coarse, extended and vacant; while the superior, or those nobler parts which are thought to affect the intellectual being, were low, receding and mean.

The dress of this individual was a mixture of the coarsest vestments of a husbandman, with the leathern garments, that fashion as well as use had in some degree rendered necessary to one engaged in his present pursuits. There was, however, a singular and wild display of prodigal and ill-judged ornaments blended with his motley attire. In place of the usual deer-skin belt, he wore around his body a tarnished silken sash of the most gaudy colours; the buck-horn haft of his knife was profusely decorated with plates of silver; the marten's fur of his cap was of a fineness and shadowing that a queen might covet; the buttons of his rude and soiled blanket-coat were of the glittering coinage of Mexico; the stock of his rifle was of beautiful mahogany, riveted and banded with the same precious metal, and the trinkets of no less than three worthless watches dangled from different parts of his person. In addition to the pack and the rifle which were slung at his back, together with the well-filled, and carefully guarded pouch and horn, he had carelessly cast a keen and bright wood-axe across his shoulder, sustaining the weight of the whole with as much apparent ease as if he moved, unfettered in limb, and free from incumbrance.

A short distance in the rear of this man, came a groupe of youths very similarly attired, and bearing sufficient resemblance to each other, and to their leader, to distinguish them as the children of one family. Though the youngest of their number could not much have passed the period, that, in the nicer judgment of the law, is called the age of discretion, he had proved himself so far worthy of his progenitors as to have reared already his aspiring person to the standard height of his race. There were one or two others, of different mould, whose descriptions must however be referred to the regular course of the narrative.

Of the females, there were but two who had arrived at womanhood; though several white-headed, olive-skinn'd faces were peering out of the foremost wagon of the train, with eyes of lively curiosity and characteristic animation. The elder of the two adults was the sallow and wrinkled mother of most of the party, and the younger was a sprightly, active girl of eighteen, who in figure, dress and mien, seemed to belong to a station in society several gradations above that of any one of her visible associates. The second vehicle was covered with a top of cloth so tightly drawn, as to conceal its contents, with the nicest care. The remaining wagons were loaded with such rude furniture and other personal effects as might be supposed to belong to one ready, at any moment to change his abode, without reference to season or distance.

Perhaps there was little in this train, or in the appearance of its proprietors, that is not daily to be encountered on the highways of this changeable and moving country. But the solitary and peculiar scenery, in which it was so unexpectedly exhibited, gave to the party a marked character of wildness and adventure.

In the little vallies which, in the regular formation of the land, occurred at every mile of their progress, the view was bounded, on two of the sides, by the gradual and low elevations, which give name to the description of Prairie we have mentioned; while on the others, the meagre prospect ran off in long, narrow, barren perspectives, but slightly relieved by a pitiful show of coarse, though somewhat luxuriant vegetation. From the summits of the swells, the eye became fatigued with the sameness and chilling dreariness of the landscape. The earth was not unlike the ocean, when its restless waters are heaving heavily, after the agitation and fury of the tempest have begun to lessen. There was the same waving and regular surface, the same absence of foreign objects, and the same boundless extent to the view. Indeed so very striking was the resemblance between the water and the land, that, however much the geologist might sneer at so simple a theory, it would have been difficult for a poet not to have felt that the formation of the one had been produced by the subsiding dominion of the other. Here and there a tall tree rose out of the bottoms, stretching its naked branches abroad, like some solitary vessel; and, to strengthen the delusion, far in the distance, appeared two or three rounded thickets, looming in the misty horizon like islands resting on the waters.* It is unnecessary to warn the practised reader, that the sameness of the surface, and the low stands of the spectators exaggerated the distances; but, as swell appeared after swell, and island succeeded island, there was a disheartening assurance that long, and seemingly interminable, tracts of territory must be passed, before the wishes of the humblest agriculturist could be realized.

Still the leader of the emigrants steadily pursued his way, with no other guide than the sun, turning his back resolutely on the abodes of civilization, and plunging, at each step, more deeply if not irretrievably, into the haunts of the barbarous and savage occupants of the country. As the day drew nigher to a close however, his mind, which was, perhaps, incapable of maturing any connected system of forethought, beyond that which related to the interests of the present moment, became, in some slight degree, troubled with the care of providing for the wants of the hours of darkness.

On reaching the crest of a swell that was a little higher than the usual elevations, he lingered a minute, and cast a half curious eye on either hand, in quest of those well-known signs, which might indicate a place, where the three grand requisites of water, fuel and fodder * were to be obtained in conjunction.

It would seem that his search was fruitless; for after a few moments of indolent and listless examination, he suffered his huge frame to descend the gentle declivity, in the same sluggish manner that an over-fatted beast would have yielded to the downward pressure.

His example was silently followed by those who succeeded him, though not until the young men had manifested much more of interest, if not of concern, in the brief inquiry which each, in his turn, made on gaining the same look-out. It was now evident, by the tardy movements both of beasts and men, that the time of necessary rest was not far distant. The matted grass of the lower land presented obstacles which fatigue began to render formidable, and the whip was becoming necessary to urge the lingering teams to their labour. At this moment, when, with the exception of the principal individual, a general lassitude was getting the mastery of the travellers, and every eye was cast, by a sort of common impulse, wistfully forward, the whole party was brought to a halt, by a spectacle as sudden as it was unexpected.

The sun had fallen below the crest of the nearest wave of the Prairie, leaving the usual rich and glowing train on its track. In the centre of this flood of fiery light a human form appeared, drawn against the gilded background, as distinctly, and seemingly as palpable, as though it would come within the grasp of any extended hand. The figure was colossal; the attitude musing and melancholy, and the situation directly in the route of the travellers. But embedded, as it was, in its setting of garish light, it was impossible to distinguish its just proportions or true character.

The effect of such a spectacle was instantaneous and powerful. The man in front of the emigrants came to a stand, and remained gazing at the mysterious object, with a dull interest, that soon quickened into superstitious awe. His sons, so soon as the first emotions of surprise had a little abated, drew slowly around him, and, as they who governed the teams gradually followed their example, the whole party was soon collected in one silent and wondering groupe. Notwithstanding the impression of a supernatural agency was very general among the travellers, the ticking of gun-locks was heard, and one of two of the bolder youths cast their rifles forward, in readiness for service.

"Send the boys off to the right," exclaimed the resolute wife and mother, in a sharp, dissonant voice; "I warrant me Asa or Abner will give me some account of the creature!"

"It may be well enough to try the rifle," muttered a dull looking man, whose features, both in outline and expression, bore no small resemblance to the first speaker, and who loosened the stock of his piece and brought it dexterously to the front, while delivering this opinion; "the Pawnee Loups are said to be hunting by hundreds in the plains; if so, they'll never miss a single man from their tribe."

"Stay!" exclaimed a soft-toned but alarmed female voice, which was easily to be traced to the trembling lips of the younger of the two women; "we are not all together; it may be a friend!"

"Who is scouting, now?" demanded the father, scanning, at the same time, the cluster of his stout sons, with a displeased and sullen eye. "Put by the piece, put by the piece;" he continued diverting the other's aim with the finger of a giant, and with the air of one it might be dangerous to deny. "My job is not yet ended; let us finish the little that remains in peace."

The man, who had manifested so hostile an intention, appeared to understand the other's allusion, and suffered himself to be diverted from his object. The sons turned their inquiring looks on the girl, who had so eagerly spoken, to require an explanation; but, as if content with the respite she had obtained for the stranger, she sunk back in her seat, and chose to affect a maidenly silence.

In the mean time the hues of the heavens had often changed. In place of the brightness, which had dazzled the eye, a gray and more sober light had succeeded, and, as the setting lost its brilliancy, the proportions of the fanciful form became less exaggerated, and finally distinct. Ashamed to hesitate, now that the truth was no longer doubtful, the leader of the party resumed his journey, using the precaution, as he ascended the slight acclivity, to release his own rifle from the strap, and to cast it into a situation more convenient for sudden use.

There was little apparent necessity, however, for such watchfulness. From the moment when it had thus unaccountably appeared, as it were, between the heavens and the earth, the stranger's figure had neither moved nor given the smallest evidence of hostility. Had he harboured any such evil intention, the individual who now came plainly into view, seemed but little qualified to execute them.

A frame, that had endured the hardships of more than eighty seasons, was not qualified to awaken apprehension in the breast of one as powerful as the emigrant. Notwithstanding his years, and his look of emaciation, if not of suffering, there was that about this solitary being however, which said that time, and not disease, had laid his hand heavily on him. His form had withered, but it was not wasted. The sinews and muscles, which had once denoted great strength, though shrunken, were still visible; and his whole figure had attained an appearance of induration, which, if it were not for the well-known frailty of humanity, would have seemed to bid defiance to the further approaches of decay. His dress was chiefly of skins, worn with the hair to the weather; a pouch and horn were suspended from his shoulders; and he leaned on a rifle of uncommon length, but which, like its owner exhibited the wear of long and hard service.

As the party drew nigher to this solitary being, and came within a distance to be heard, a low growl issued from the grass at his feet, and then a tall, gaunt, toothless hound arose lazily from his lair, and shaking himself made some show of resisting the nearer approach of the travellers.

"Down! Hector, down!" said his master, in a voice that was a little tremulous and hollow with age. "What have ye to do, pup, with men who journey on their lawful callings?"

"Stranger, if you ar' much acquainted in this country," said the leader of the emigrants, "can you tell a traveller where he may find necessaries for the night."

"Is the land filled on the other side of the Big River!" demanded the old man, solemnly, and without appearing to hearken to the other's question; " or why do I see a sight I had never thought to behold again?"

"Why there is country left, it is true, for such as have money, and ar' not particular in the choice," returned the emigrant; "but to my taste it is getting crowdy. What may a man call the distance from this place to the nighest point on the main river?"

"A hunted deer could not cool his sides, in the Mississippi, without travelling a weary five hundred miles."

"And what may you name the district, hereaway?"

"By what name," returned the old man pointing significantly upward, "would you call the spot, where you see yonder cloud?"

The emigrant looked at the other, like one who did not comprehend his meaning and who half suspected he was trifled with, but he contented himself by saying—

"You ar' but a new inhabitant, like myself, I reckon, stranger, otherwise you wouldn't be backward in helping a traveller to some advice; words cost but little, and sometimes lead to friendships."

"Advice is not a gift, but a debt that the old owe to the young. What would you wish to know?"

"Where I may 'camp for the night. I'm no great difficulty maker, as to bed and board, but all old journeyers, like myself, know the virtue of sweet water, and a good browse for the cattle."

"Come then with me, and you shall be master of both; and little more is it that I can offer on this hungry Prairie."

As the old man was speaking, he raised his heavy rifle to his shoulder, with a facility a little remarkable for his years and appearance, and without further words led the way over the acclivity into the adjacent bottom.

CHAPTER II.

"Up with my tent: here will I lie to night;
But where, to-morrow? — Well, all's one for that."

Richard III, V.iii. 7, 9.

THE travellers soon discovered the usual and unerring evidences, that the several articles necessary to their situation were not far distant. A clear and gurgling spring burst out of the side of the declivity, and joining its waters to those of other similar little fountains in its vicinity, their united contributions formed a run, which was easily to be traced, for miles along the Prairie, by the scattering foliage and verdure which occasionally grew within the influence of its moisture. Hither, then, the stranger held his way, eagerly followed by the willing teams, whose instinct gave them a prescience of refreshment and rest.

On reaching what he deemed a suitable spot, the old man halted, and with an enquiring look he seemed to demand if it possessed the needed conveniences. The leader of the emigrants cast his eyes understandingly about him, and examined the place with the keenness of one competent to judge of so nice a question, though in that dilatory and heavy manner which rarely permitted him to betray precipitation.

"Ay, this may do," he said, when satisfied with his scrutiny, "boys, you have seen the last of the sun; be stirring."

The young men manifested a characteristic obedience. The order, for such in tone and manner it was, in truth, was received with respect; but the utmost movement was the falling of an axe or two from the shoulder to the ground, while their owners continued to regard the place with listless and incurious eyes. In the mean time, the elder traveller, as if familiar with the nature of the impulses by which his children were governed, disencumbered himself of his pack and rifle, and, assisted by the man already mentioned as disposed to appeal so promptly to the rifle, he quietly proceeded to release the cattle from the gears.

At length the eldest of the sons stepped heavily forward, and, without any apparent effort, he buried his axe to the eye in the soft body of a cotton-wood tree. He stood, a moment, regarding the effect of the blow, with that sort of contempt with which a giant might be supposed to contemplate the puny resistance of a dwarf, and then flourishing the implement above his head, with the grace and dexterity with which a master of the art of offense would wield his nobler though less useful weapon, he quickly severed the trunk of the tree, bringing its tall top crashing to the earth, in submission to his prowess. His companions regarded the operation with indolent curiosity, until they saw the prostrate trunk stretch'd on the ground, when, as if a signal for a general attack had been given, they advanced in a body to the work, and in a space of time, and with a neatness of execution that would have astonished an ignorant spectator, they stripped a small but suitable spot of its burthen of forest, as effectually, and almost as promptly, as if a whirlwind had passed along the place.

The stranger had been a silent, but attentive observer of their progress. As tree after tree came whistling down, he cast his eyes upward, at the vacancies they left in the heavens, with a melancholy gaze, and finally turned away, muttering to himself with a bitter smile, like one who disdained giving a more audible utterance to his discontent. Pressing through the groupe of active and busy children, who had already lighted a cheerful fire, the attention of the old man became next fixed on the movements of the leader of the emigrants and of his savage looking assistant.

These two had already liberated the cattle, which were eagerly browsing the grateful and nutritious extremities of the fallen trees, and were now employed about the wagon, which has been described, as having its contents concealed with so much apparent care. Notwithstanding this particular conveyance appeared to be as silent, and as tenantless as the rest of the vehicles, the men applied their strength to its wheels, and rolled it apart from the others, to a dry and elevated spot, near the edge of the thicket. Here they brought certain poles, which had seemingly been long employed in such a service, and fastening their larger ends firmly in the ground, the smaller were attached to the hoops that supported the covering of the wagon. Large folds of cloth were next drawn out of the vehicle, and after being spread around the whole, were pegged to the earth in such a manner as to form a tolerably capacious and an exceedingly convenient tent. After surveying their work with inquisitive, and perhaps jealous eyes, arranging a fold here and driving a peg more firmly there, the men once more applied their strength to the wagon, pulling it, by its projecting tongue, from the centre of the canopy, until it appeared in the open air, deprived of its covering, and destitute of any other freight than a few light articles of furniture. The latter were immediately removed, by the traveller into the tent with his own hands, as though to enter it were a privilege to which even his bosom companion was not entitled.

Curiosity is a passion that is rather quickened than destroyed by seclusion, and the old inhabitant of the Prairies did not view these precautionary and mysterious movements, without experiencing some of its impulses. He approached the tent, and was about to sever two of its folds, with the very obvious intention of examining, more closely, into the nature of its contents, when the man, who had once already placed his life in jeopardy, seized him by the arm, and with a rude exercise of his strength threw him from the spot he had selected as the one most convenient for his object.

"It's an honest regulation, friend," the fellow drily observed, though with an eye that threatened volumes, "and sometimes it is a safe one, which says, mind your own business."

"Men seldom bring any thing to be concealed into these deserts," returned the old man, as if willing, and yet a little ignorant how to apologize for the liberty he had been about to take, " and I had hop'd no offence, in examining your comforts."

"They seldom bring themselves, I reckon though this has the look of an old country, to my eye it seems not to be overly peopled."

"The land is as aged as the rest of the works of the Lord, I believe; but you say true, concerning its inhabitants. Many months have passed since I have laid eyes on a face of my own colour, before your own. I say again, friend, I meant no harm; I did not know, but there was something behind the cloth, that might bring former days to my mind."

As the stranger ended his simple explanation, he walked meekly away, like one who felt the deepest sense of the right which every man has to the quiet enjoyment of his own, without any troublesome interference on the part of his neighbour; a wholesome and just principle, that he had, also, most probably imbibed from the habits of his secluded life. As he passed towards the little encampment of the emigrants, for such the place had now become, he heard the voice of the leader calling aloud, in its hoarse tones, the name of—

"Ellen Wade."

The girl, who has been already introduced to the reader, and who was occupied with the others of her sex, around the fires, sprang willingly forward at this summons, and passing the stranger with the activity of a young antelope, she was instantly lost behind the forbidden folds of the tent. Neither her sudden disappearance, nor any of the arrangements we have mentioned, seemed, however, to excite the smallest surprise among the remainder of the party. The young men, who had already completed their tasks with the axe, were all engaged after their lounging and listless manner; some in bestowing equitable portions of the fodder among the different animals; others in plying the heavy pestle of a moveable hommany-mortar,[1] and one or two, in wheeling the remainder of the wagons aside and arranging them in such a manner as to form a sort of outwork for their otherwise defenceless bivouac.

These several duties were soon performed, and, as darkness now began to conceal the objects on the surrounding Prairie, the shrill-toned termagant, whose voice since the halt had been diligently exercised among her idle and drowsy offspring, announced in tones that might have been heard at a dangerous distance, that the evening meal waited only for the approach of those who were to consume it. Whatever may be the other qualities of a border-man, he is seldom deficient in the virtue of hospitality. The emigrant no sooner heard the sharp call of his wife, than he cast his eyes about him in quest of the stranger, in order to offer him the place of distinction, in the rude entertainment to which they were so unceremoniously summoned.

"I thank you, friend," the old man replied to the rough invitation to take a seat nigh the smoking kettle; "you have my hearty thanks; but I have eaten for the day, and I am not one of them who dig their graves with their teeth. Well; as you wish it, I will take a place, for it is long sin' I have seen people of my colour eating their daily bread."

"You ar' an old settler, in these districts, then?" the emigrant rather remarked than inquired, with a mouth filled nearly to overflowing with the delicious hommany, prepared by his skillful, though repulsive spouse. "They told us below we should find settlers something thinnish, hereaway, and I must say, the report was mainly true; for, unless, we count the Canada traders on the big river, you ar' the first white face I have met, in a good five hundred miles; that is calculating according to your own reckoning."

"Though I have spent some years in this quarter, I can hardly be called a settler, seeing that I have no regular abode, and seldom pass more than a month, at a time, in the same range."

"A hunter, I reckon?" the other continued, glancing his eyes aside, as if to examine the equipments of his new acquaintance; "your fixen* seem none of the best, for such a calling."

---

[1] Hommany, is a dish composed chiefly of cracked corn, or maize. [1832]

"They are old, and nearly ready to be laid aside, like their master," said the old man regarding his rifle, with a look in which affection and regret were singularly blended; "and I may say they are but little needed, too. You are mistaken, friend, in calling me a hunter; I am nothing better than a trapper." [1]

"If you ar' much of the one, I'm bold to say you ar' something of the other; for the two callings go mainly together, in these districts."

"To the shame of the man who is able to follow the first be it so said!" returned the trapper, whom in future we shall choose to designate by his pursuit; "for more than fifty years did I carry my rifle in the wilderness, without so much as setting a snare for even a bird that flies the heavens;—much less a beast, that has nothing but legs, for its gifts."

"I see but little difference whether a man gets his peltry by the rifle or by the trap," said the ill-looking companion of the emigrant, in his rough manner. "The 'arth was made for our comfort; and, for that matter, so ar' its creatur's."

"You seem to have but little plunder, [2] stranger, for one who is far abroad," bluntly interrupted the emigrant, as if he had a reason for wishing to change the conversation. "I hope you ar' better off for skins."

"I make but little use of either," the trapper quietly replied. "At my time of life, food and clothing be all that is needed, and I have little occasion for what you call plunder, unless it may be, now and then, to barter for a horn of powder or a bar of lead."

"You ar' not, then, of these parts, by natur', friend?" the emigrant continued, having in his mind the exception which the other had taken to the very equivocal word, which he himself, according to the custom of the country, had used for "baggage" or "effects."

---

[1] It is scarcely necessary to say, that this American word means one who takes his game in a trap. It is of general use on the frontiers. The beaver, an animal too sagacious to be easily killed, is oftener taken in this way than in any other. [1832]

[2] The cant word for luggage in the western States is "plunder." The term might easily mislead one as to the character of the people, who, notwithstanding their pleasant use of so expressive a word, are, like the inhabitants of all new settlements hospitable and honest. Knavery of the description conveyed by "plunder," is chiefly found in regions more civilized. [1832]

"I was born on the sea-shore, though most of my life has been passed in the woods."

The whole party now looked up at him, as men are apt to turn their eyes on some unexpected object of general interest. One or two of the young men, repeated the words "sea-shore," and the woman tendered him one of those civilities with which, uncouth as they were, she was little accustomed to grace her hospitality, as if in deference to the travelled dignity of her guest. After a long, and seemingly a meditating silence, the emigrant, who had, however, seen no apparent necessity to suspend the functions of his masticating powers, resumed the discourse.

"It is a long road, as I have heard, from the waters of the west to the shores of the main sea?"

"It is a weary path, indeed, friend; and much have I seen, and something have I suffered in journeying over it."

"A man would see a good deal of hard travel in going its length?"

"Seventy and five years I have been upon the road, and there are not half that number of leagues in the whole distance, after you leave the Hudson, on which I have not tasted venison of my own killing. But this is vain boasting! of what use are former deeds, when time draws to an end!"

"I once met a man, that had boated on the river he names," observed the eldest son, speaking in a low tone of voice, like one who distrusted his knowledge, and deemed it prudent to assume a becoming diffidence in the presence of a man who had seen so much; "from his tell, it must be a considerable stream, and deep enough for a keelboat, from top to bottom."

"It is a wide and deep water-course, and many sightly towns are there growing on its banks," returned the trapper; "and yet it is but a brook, to the waters of the endless river!"

"I call nothing a stream, that a man can travel round," exclaimed the ill-looking associate of the emigrant; "a real river must be crossed; not headed, like a bear in a county hunt." [1]

---

* There is a practice, in the new countries, to assemble the men of a large district, sometimes of an entire county, to exterminate the beasts of prey. They form themselves into a circle of several miles in extent, and gradually draw nearer, killing all before them. The allusion is to this custom, in which the hunted beast is turned from one to another. [1832]

"Have you been far towards the sun-down, friend?" interrupted the emigrant, as if he desired to keep his rough companion, as much as possible out of the discourse. "I find it is a wide tract of clearing, this, into which I have fallen."

"You may travel weeks, and you will see it the same. I often think the Lord has placed this barren belt of Prairie, behind the States, to warn men to what their folly may yet bring the land! Ay, weeks if not months, may you journey in these open fields, in which there is neither dwelling, nor habitation for man or beast. Even the savage animals travel miles on miles to seek their dens. And yet the wind seldom blows from the east, but I conceit the sounds of axes, and the crash of falling trees are in my ears."

As the old man spoke with the seriousness and dignity that age seldom fails to communicate even to less striking sentiments, his auditors were deeply attentive, and as silent as the grave. Indeed the trapper was left to renew the dialogue, himself, which he soon did by asking a question, in the indirect manner so much in use by the border inhabitants.

"You found it no easy matter to ford the water-courses, and to make your way so deep into the Prairies, friend, with teams of horses, and herds of horned beasts?"

"I kept the left bank of the main river," the emigrant replied, "until I found the stream leading too much to the north, when we rafted ourselves across, without any great suffering. The woman lost a fleece or two from the next year's sheering, and the girls have one cow less to their dairy. Since then, we have done bravely, by bridging a creek every day or two."

"It is likely you will continue west, until you come to land more suitable for a settlement?"

"Until I see reason to stop, or to turn ag'in," the emigrant bluntly answered, rising at the same time, and cutting short the dialogue, by the suddenness of the movement. His example was followed by the trapper, as well as the rest of the party, and then, without much deference to the presence of their guest, the travellers proceeded to make their dispositions to pass the night. Several little bowers, or rather huts, had already been formed of the tops of trees, blankets of coarse country manufacture, and the skins of buffaloes,* united without much reference to any other object than temporary comfort. Into these covers the children with their mother soon drew themselves, and where, it is more than possible, they were all speedily lost in the oblivion of sleep. Before the men, however, could seek their rest, they had sundry little duties to perform; such as completing their works of defence; carefully concealing the fires; replenishing the fodder of their cattle, and setting the watch that was to protect the party, in the approaching hours of night.

The former was effected by dragging the trunks of a few trees into the intervals left by the wagons, and along the open space, between the vehicles and the thicket, on which, in military language, the encampment would be said to have rested; thus forming a sort of chevaux-de-frise on three sides of the position. Within these narrow limits (with the exception of what the tent contained), both man and beast were now collected; the latter being far too happy in resting their weary limbs, to give any undue annoyance to their scarcely more intelligent associates. Two of the young men took their rifles, and, first renewing the priming and examining the flints with the utmost care, they proceeded, the one to the extreme right and the other to the left of the encampment, where they posted themselves, within the shadows of the thicket, but in such positions, as enabled each to overlook a portion of the Prairie.

The trapper loitered about the place, declining to share the straw of the emigrant, until the whole arrangement was completed; and then, without the ceremony of an adieu, he slowly retired from the spot.

It was now in the first watch of the night, and the pale, quivering, and deceptive light, from a new moon, was playing over the endless waves of the Prairie, tipping the swells with gleams of brightness, and leaving the interval land in deep shadow. Accustomed to scenes of solitude like the present, the old man, as he left the encampment proceeded alone into the waste, like a bold vessel leaving its haven to enter on the trackless field of the ocean. He appeared to move for some time, without object, or indeed, without any apparent consciousness, whither his limbs were carrying him. At length, on reaching the rise of one of the undulations, he came to a stand, and for the first time, since leaving the band, who had caused such a flood of reflections and recollections to crowd upon his mind, the old man became aware of his present situation. Throwing one end of his rifle to the earth, he stood leaning on the other, again lost in deep contemplation for several minutes, during which time his hound came and crouched at his feet. A deep, menacing growl from the faithful animal, first aroused him from his musing.

"What now, dog?" he said, looking down at his companion, as if he addressed a being of an intelligence equal to his own, and speaking in a voice of great affection. "What is it, pup? ha! Hector; what is it noseing, now? It won't do, dog; it won't do; the very fa'ns play in open view of us, without minding so worn out curs, as you and I. Instinct is their gift, Hector; and they have found out how little we are to be fear'd, they have!"

The dog stretched his head upward, and responded to the words of his master by a long and plaintive whine, which he even continued after he had again buried his head in the grass, as if he held an intelligent communication with one who so well knew how to interpret his dumb discourse.

"This is a manifest warning, Hector!" The trapper continued, dropping his voice, to the tones of caution and looking warily about him. "What is it, pup; speak plainer, dog; what is it?"

The hound had, however, already laid his nose to the earth, and was silent; appearing to slumber. But the keen quick glances of his master, soon caught a glimpse of a distant figure, which seemed, through the deceptive light, floating along the very elevation on which he had placed himself. Presently its proportions became more distinct, and then an airy, female form appeared to hesitate, as if considering whether it would be prudent to advance. Though the eyes of the dog were now to be seen glancing in the rays of the moon, opening and shutting lazily, he gave no further signs of displeasure.

"Come nigher; we are friends," said the trapper, associating himself with his companion by long use, and, probably, through the strength of the secret tie that connected them together; "we are your friends; none will harm you."

Encouraged by the mild tones of his voice, and perhaps led on by the earnestness of her purpose, the female approached, until she stood at his side; when the old man perceived his visiter to be the young woman, with whom the reader, has already become acquainted by the name of Ellen Wade.

"I had thought you were gone," she said, looking timidly and anxiously around. "They said you were gone; and that we should never see you again. I did not think it was you!"

"Men are no common objects in these empty fields," returned the trapper, "and I humbly hope, though I have so long consorted with the beasts of the wilderness, that I have not yet lost the look of my kind."

"Oh! I knew you to be a man, and I thought I knew the whine of the hound, too," she answered hastily, as if willing to explain she knew not what, and then checking herself, like one fearful of having already said too much.

"I saw no dogs among the teams of your father," the trapper remarked.

"Father!" exclaimed the girl, feelingly, "I have no father! I had nearly said no friend."

The old man, turned towards her, with a look of kindness and interest, that was even more conciliating than the ordinary, upright, and benevolent expression of his weather-beaten countenance.

"Why then do you venture in a place where none but the strong should come?" he demanded. "Did you not know that, when you crossed the big river, you left a friend behind you that is always bound to look to the young and feeble, like yourself."

"Of whom do you speak?"

"The law — 'Tis bad to have it, but, I sometimes think, it is worse to be entirely without it. Age and weakness have brought me to feel such weakness, at times. Yes — yes, the law is needed, when such as have not the gifts of strength and wisdom are to be taken care of. I hope, young woman, if you have no father, you have at least a brother."

The maiden felt the tacit reproach conveyed in this covert question, and for a moment she remained in an embarrassed silence. But catching a glimpse of the mild and serious features of her companion, as he continued to gaze on her with a look of interest, she replied, firmly, and in a manner that left no doubt she comprehended his meaning:

"Heaven forbid that any such as you have seen, should be a brother of mine, or any thing else near or dear to me! But, tell me, do you then actually live alone, in this desert district, old man; is there really none here besides yourself?"

"There are hundreds, nay, thousands of the rightful owners of the country, roving about the plains; but few of our own colour."

"And have you then met none who are white, but us?" interrupted the girl, like one too impatient to await the tardy explanation of age and deliberation.

"Not in many days — Hush, Hector, hush," he added in reply to a low, and nearly inaudible growl from his hound. "The dog scents mischief in the wind! The black bears from the mountains sometimes make their way, even lower than this. The pup is not apt to complain of the harmless game. I am not so ready and true with the piece as I used-to-could-be, yet I have struck even the fiercest animals of the Prairie, in my time; so, you have little reason for fear, young woman."

The girl raised her eyes, in that peculiar manner which is so often practised by her sex, when they commence their glances, by examining the earth at their feet, and terminate them by noting every thing within the power of human vision; but she rather manifested the quality of impatience, than any feeling of alarm.

A short bark from the dog, however, soon gave a new direction to the looks of both, then the real object of his second warning became dimly visible.

CHAPTER III.

"Come, come, thou art as hot a Jack in thy
mood, as any in Italy; and as soon mov'd to be
moody, and as soon moody to be moved."

Romeo and Juliet, III.i. 12-14.

THOUGH the trapper manifested some surprise when he perceived that another human figure was approaching him, and that,
too, from a direction opposite to the place where the emigrant had
made his encampment, it was with the steadiness of one long accustomed to scenes of danger.

"This is a man," he said; "and one who has white blood in his veins,
or his step would be lighter. It will be well to be ready for the worst, as
the half-and-halfs,[1] that one meets in these distant districts, are altogether more barbarous than the real savage."

He raised his rifle while he spoke, and assured himself of the state
of its flint, as well as of the priming by manual examination. But his
arm was arrested, while in the act of throwing forward the muzzle of
the piece, by the eager and trembling hands of his companion.

"For God's sake, be not too hasty," she said; "it may be a friend—an
acquaintance—a neighbour!"

"A friend!" the old man repeated, deliberately releasing himself, at
the same time, from her grasp. "Friends are rare in any land, and less
in this, perhaps, than in another; and the neighbourhood is too thinly
settled to make it likely, that he who comes towards us is even an
acquaintance."

"But though a stranger, you would not seek his blood!"

The trapper earnestly regarded her anxious and frightened features, and then he dropped the butt of his rifle on the ground, like
one whose purpose had undergone a sudden change.

"No," he said, speaking rather to himself, than to his companion.
"she is right; blood is not to be spilt, to save the life of one so useless,
and so near his time. Let him come on; my skins, my traps, and even
my rifle shall be his, if he sees fit to demand them."

"He will ask for neither—He wants neither," returned the girl; "if

---

[1] Half-breeds; men born of Indian women by white fathers. This race has much of
the depravity of civilization without the virtues of the savage. [1832]

he be an honest man, he will surely be content with his own, and ask for nothing that is the property of another."

The trapper had not time to express the surprise he felt at this incoherent and contradictory language, for the man who was advancing, was, already, within fifty feet of the place where they stood.—In the mean time Hector had not been an indifferent witness of what was passing. At the sound of the distant footsteps, he had arisen, from his warm bed at the feet of his master; and now, as the stranger appeared in open view, he stalked slowly towards him, crouching to the earth like a panther about to take his leap.

"Call in your dog," said a firm, deep, manly voice, in tones of friendship, rather than of menace; "I love a hound, and should be sorry to do an injury to the animal."

"You hear what is said about you, pup?" the trapper answered; "come hither, fool. His growl and his bark are all that is left him now; you may come on, friend; the hound is toothless."

The stranger profited by the intelligence. He sprang eagerly forward, and at the next instant stood at the side of Ellen Wade. After assuring himself of the identity of the latter, by a hasty but keen glance, he turned his attention, with a quickness and impatience that proved the interest he took in the result, to a similar examination of her companion.

"From what cloud have you fallen, my good old man?" he said in a careless, off-hand, heedless manner that seemed too natural to be assumed: "Or do you actually live, hereaway, in the Prairies?"

"I have been long on earth, and never I hope nigher to Heaven than I am at this moment," returned the trapper; "my dwelling, if dwelling I may be said to have, is not far distant. Now may I take the liberty with you, that you are so willing to take with others? Whence do you come, and where is your home?"

"Softly, softly; when I have done with my catechism it will be time to begin with yours. What sport is this, you follow by moonlight? You are not dodging the buffaloes at such an hour!"

"I am, as you see, going from an encampment of travellers, which lies over yonder swell in the land, to my own wigwam; in doing so I wrong no man."

"All fair and true. And you got this young woman to show you the way, because she knows it so well and you know so little about it yourself."

"I met her, as I have met you, by accident. For ten tiresome years have I dwelt on these open fields, and never, before to-night, have I found human beings with white skins on them at this hour. If my presence here gives offence, I am sorry; and will go my way. It is more than likely that when your young friend has told her story, you will be better given to believe mine."

"Friend!" said the youth, lifting a cap of skins from his head, and running his fingers leisurely through a dense mass of black and shaggy locks, "if I ever laid eyes on the girl before to night, may I—"

"You've said enough, Paul," interrupted the female, laying her hand on his mouth with a familiarity that gave something very like the lie direct to his intended asseveration. "Our secret will be safe with this honest old man. I know it by his looks and kind words."

"Our secret! Ellen, have you forgot—"

"Nothing. I have not forgotten any thing I should remember. But still I say we are safe with this honest trapper."

"Trapper! is he then a trapper! Give me your hand, father; our trades should bring us acquainted."

"There is little call for handicrafts in this region," returned the other, examining the athletic and active form of the youth, as he leaned carelessly and not ungracefully on his rifle; "the art of taking the creatur's of God, in traps and nets is one that needs more cunning than manhood; and yet am I brought to practise it in my age! But it would be quite as seemly, in one like you, to follow a pursuit better becoming your years and courage."

"I! I never took even a slinking mink or a paddling musk-rat in a cage; though I admit having peppered a few of the dark-skin'd devils, when I had much better have kept my powder in the horn and the lead in its pouch. Not I, old man; nothing that crawls the earth is for my sport."

"What then may you do for a living, friend; for little profit is to be made in these districts, if a man denies himself his lawful right in the beasts of the fields."

"I deny myself nothing. If a bear crosses my path he is soon the mere ghost of Bruin. The deer begin to nose me; and as for the buffaloe, I have kill'd more beef, old stranger, than the largest butcher in all Kentucky."

"You can shoot, then!" demanded the trapper, with a glow of latent fire glimmering about his eyes; "is your hand true, and your look quick?"

"The first is like a steel-trap, and the last nimbler than a buck-shot. I wish it was hot noon, now, grand'ther; and that there was an acre or two of your white swans or of black feathered ducks going south, over our heads; you, or Ellen here, might set your heart on the finest in the flock, and my character against a horn of powder, that the bird would be hanging head downwards in five minutes, and that too with a single ball. I scorn a shotgun! No man can say he ever knew me carry one, a rod."

"The lad has good in him! I see it plainly by his manner;" said the trapper turning to Ellen with an encouraging air; "I will take it on myself to say that you are not unwise in meeting him as you do. Tell me, lad; did you ever strike a leaping buck atwixt the antlers? Hector; quiet, pup; quiet. The very name of venison quickens the blood of the cur;—did you ever take an animal in that fashion, on the long leap?"

"You might just as well ask me, did you ever eat? There is no fashion, old stranger, that a deer has not been touched by my hand, unless it was when asleep."

"Ay, ay; you have a long, and a happy—ay, and an honest life afore you! I am old, and I suppose I might also say, worn out and useless; but, if it was given me to choose my time and place, again,—as such things are not and ought not ever to be given to the will of man—though, if such a gift was to be given me, I would say, twenty and the wilderness! But, tell me; how do you part with the peltry?"

"With my pelts! I never took a skin from a buck, nor a quill from a goose, in my life! I knock them over, now and then, for a meal, and sometimes to keep my finger true to the touch; but when hunger is satisfied, the Prairie wolves get the remainder. No—no—I keep to my calling; which pays me better, than all the fur I could sell on the other side of the big river."

The old man appeared to ponder a little; but shaking his head, he soon continued—

"I know of but one business that can be followed here with profit—"

He was interrupted by the youth, who raised a small cup of tin, which dangled at his neck, before the other's eyes, and springing its lid, the delicious odour of the finest flavoured honey diffused itself over the organs of the trapper.

"A bee-hunter!" observed the latter, with a readiness that proved he understood the nature of the occupation, though not without some little surprise at discovering one of the other's spirited mien engaged in so humble a pursuit. "It pays well in the skirts of the settlements, but I should call it a doubtful trade in the more open districts."

"You think a tree is wanting for a swarm to settle in! But I know differently; and so I have stretched out a few hundred miles farther west, than common, to taste your honey. And now I have bated your curiosity, stranger, you will just move aside, while I tell the remainder of my story to this young woman."

"It is not necessary, I'm sure it is not necessary, that he should leave us," said Ellen, with a haste that implied some little consciousness of the singularity if not of the impropriety of the request. "You can have nothing to say that the whole world might not hear."

"No! well, may I be stung to death by drones if I understand the buzzings of a woman's mind! For my part, Ellen, I care for nothing nor any body; and am just as ready to go down to the place where your uncle, if uncle you can call one who I'll swear is no relation, has hoppled his teams, and tell the old man my mind now, as I shall be a year hence. You have only to say a single word, and the thing is done; let him like it or not."

"You are ever so hasty and so rash, Paul Hover, that I seldom know when I am safe with you. How can you, who know the danger of our being seen together, speak of going before my uncle and his sons?"

"Has he done that of which he has reason to be ashamed?" demanded the trapper, who had not moved an inch from the place he first occupied.

"Heaven forbid! But there are reasons why he should not be seen, just now, that could do him no harm if known, but which may not yet be told. And so if you will wait, father, near yonder willow bush, until I have heard what Paul can possibly have to say, I shall be sure to come and wish you a good-night, before I return to the camp."

The trapper drew slowly aside, as if satisfied with the somewhat incoherent reason Ellen had given why he should retire. When completely out of ear-shot of the earnest and hurried dialogue, that instantly commenced between the two he had left, the old man again paused, and patiently awaited the moment when he might renew his conversation with beings in whom he felt a growing interest, no less from the mysterious character of their intercourse, than from a natural sympathy in the welfare of a pair so young, and who, as in the simplicity of his heart he was also fain to believe, were also so deserving. He was accompanied by his indolent but attached dog, who once more made his bed at the feet of his master, and soon lay slumbering as usual, with his head nearly buried in the dense fog of the Prairie grass.

It was so unusual a spectacle to see the human form amid the solitude in which he dwelt, that the trapper bent his eyes on the dim figures of his new acquaintances, with sensations to which he had long been a stranger. Their presence awakened recollections and emotions, to which his sturdy but honest nature had latterly paid but little homage, and his thoughts began to wander over the varied scenes of a life of hardships, that had been strangely blended with scenes of wild and peculiar enjoyment. The train taken by his thoughts had already conducted him, in imagination, far into an ideal world, when he was once more suddenly recalled to the reality of his situation, by the movements of the faithful hound.

The dog who, in submission to his years and infirmities, had manifested such a decided propensity to sleep, now arose, and stalked from out the shadow cast by the tall person of his master, and looked abroad into the Prairie, as if his instinct apprised him of the presence of still another visiter. Then, seemingly content with his examination, he returned to his comfortable post, and disposed of his weary limbs with the deliberation and care of one who was no novice in the art of self-preservation.

"What; again, Hector!" said the trapper in a soothing voice, which he had the caution, however, to utter in an under tone; "what is it, dog? tell it all to his master, pup; what is it?"

Hector answered with another growl, but was content to continue in his lair. These were evidences of intelligence and distrust, to which one as practised as the trapper could not turn an inattentive ear. He again spoke to the dog. encouraging him to watchfulness by a low, guarded whistle. The animal, however, as if conscious of having already discharged his duty, obstinately refused to raise his head from the grass.

"A hint from such a friend is far better than man's advice!" muttered the trapper, as he slowly moved towards the couple, who were yet too earnestly and abstractedly engaged in their own discourse to notice his approach; "and none but a conceited settler would hear it and not respect it, as he ought. Children," he added, when near enough to address his companions, "we are not alone in these dreary fields; there are others stirring, and, therefore, to the shame of our kind be it said, danger is nigh."

"If one of the lazy sons of Skirting Ishmael is prowling out of his camp to night," said the young bee-hunter, with great vivacity, and in tones that might easily have been excited to a menace, "he may have an end put to his journey, sooner either than he or his father has calculated!"

"My life on it, they are all with the teams," hurriedly answered the girl. "I saw the whole of them asleep, myself, except the two on watch; and their natures have greatly changed, if they, too, are not both dreaming of a turkey-hunt, or a court-house fight,*at this very moment."

"Some beast, with a strong scent, has passed between the wind and the hound, father, and it makes him uneasy; or perhaps he too is dreaming. I had a pup of my own in Kentucky, that would start upon a long chase from a deep sleep; and all upon the fancy of some dream. Go to him, and pinch his ear that the beast may feel the life within him."

"Not so—not so," returned the trapper, shaking his head as one who better understood the qualities of his dog.—"Youth sleeps, ay, and dreams too; but age is awake and watchful. The pup is never false with his nose, and long experience tells me to heed his warnings."

"Did you ever run him upon the trail of carrion?"

"Why I must say that the ravenous beasts have sometimes tempted me to let him loose, for they are as greedy as men after the venison, in its season; but then I knew the reason of the dog would tell him the object!—No—no, Hector is an animal known in the ways of man, and will never strike a false trail when a true one is to be followed!"

"Ay, ay, the secret is out! you have run the hound on the track of a wolf, and his nose has a better memory than his master!" said the bee-hunter, laughing.

"I have seen the creatur' sleep for hours, with pack after pack, in open view. A wolf might eat out of his tray without a snarl, unless there was a scarcity; then, indeed, Hector would be apt to claim his own."

"There are panthers down from the mountains; I saw one make a leap at a sick deer, as the sun was setting. Go; go you back to the dog, and tell him the truth, father; in a minute I—"

He was interrupted by a long, loud, and piteous howl from the hound, which rose on the air of the evening like the wailing of some spirit of the place, and passed off into the Prairie, in cadences that rose and fell like its own undulating surface. The trapper was impressively silent, listening intently. Even the reckless bee-hunter was struck with the wailing wildness of the sounds. After a short pause the former whistled the dog to his side, and turning to his companions, he said, with the seriousness which, in his opinion, the occasion demanded—

"They who think man enjoys all the knowledge of the creatur's of God, will live to be disappointed, if they reach, as I have done, the age of fourscore years. I will not take upon myself to say what mischief is brewing, nor will I vouch that even the hound himself knows so much; but that evil is nigh, and that wisdom invites us to avoid it, I have heard from the mouth of one who never lies. I did think the pup had become unused to the footsteps of man, and that your presence made him uneasy; but his nose has been on a long scent the whole evening, and what I mistook as a notice of your coming, has been intended for something more serious. If the advice of an old man is, then, worth hearkening to, children, you will quickly go different ways to your places of shelter and safety."

"If I quit Ellen, at such a moment," exclaimed the youth, "may I—"

"You've said enough!" the girl interrupted, by again interposing a hand that might, both by its delicacy and colour, have graced a far more elevated station in life; "my time is out; and we must part, at all events—So good-night, Paul—father—good-night."

"Hist!" said the youth seizing her arm, as she was in the very act of tripping from his side—"Hist! do you hear nothing? There are buffaloes playing their pranks at no great distance—That sound beats the earth like a herd of the mad scampering devils!"

His two companions listened, as people in their situation would be apt to lend their faculties to discover the meaning of any doubtful noises, especially when heard after so many and such startling warnings. The unusual sounds were unequivocally though still faintly audible. The youth and his female companion had made several hurried and vacillating conjectures concerning their nature, when a current of the night air brought the rush of trampling footsteps too sensibly to their ears, to render mistake any longer possible.

"I am right!" said the bee-hunter; "a panther is driving a herd before him; or, may-be, there is a battle among the beasts."

"Your ears are cheats;" returned the old man, who, from the moment his own organs had been able to catch the distant sounds, stood like a statue made to represent deep attention—"The leaps are too long for the buffaloe, and too regular for terror. Hist; now they are in a bottom where the grass is high, and the sound is deadened! Ay, there they go on the hard earth! And now they come up the swell, dead upon us; they will be here afore you can find a cover."

"Come, Ellen," cried the youth seizing his companion by the hand, "let us make a trial for the encampment."

"Too late! too late!" exclaimed the trapper, "for the creatur's are in open view; and a bloody band of accursed Siouxes they are, by their thieving look and the random fashion in which they ride!"

"Siouxes or devils, they shall find *us* men!" said the bee-hunter, with a mien as fierce as if he led a party of superior strength, and of a courage equal to his own—"You have a piece, old man, and will pull a trigger in behalf of a helpless, Christian girl!"

"Down, down into the grass—down with ye both," whispered the trapper, intimating to them to turn aside to the tall weeds, which grew in a denser body than common near the place where they stood. "You've not the time to fly nor the numbers to fight, foolish boy. Down into the grass, if you prize the young woman or value the gift of life!"

His remonstrance, seconded as it was by a prompt and energetic action, did not fail to produce the submission to his order, which the occasion seemed, indeed, imperiously to require. The moon had fallen behind a sheet of thin, fleecy clouds, which skirted the horizon, leaving just enough of its faint and fluctuating light to render objects visible, dimly revealing their forms and proportions. The trapper, by exercising that species of influence over his companions, which experience and decision usually assert, in cases of emergency, had effectually succeeded in concealing them in the grass, and, by the aid of the feeble rays of the luminary, he was enabled to scan the disorderly party, which was riding like so many madmen directly upon them.

A band of beings, who resembled demons rather than men sporting in their nightly revels across the bleak plain, was in truth approaching, at a fearful rate, and in a direction to leave little hope that some one among them, at least, would not pass over the spot where the trapper and his companions lay. At intervals, the clattering of hoofs was borne along by the night wind quite audibly in their front, and then, again, their progress through the fog of the autumnal grass was swift and silent; adding to the unearthly appearance of the spectacle. The trapper, who had called in his hound, and bidden him crouch at his side, now kneeled in the cover, also, and kept a keen and watchful eye on the route of the band, soothing the fears of the girl, and restraining the impatience of the youth, in the same breath.

"If there's one, there's thirty of the miscreants!" he said, in a sort of episode to his whispered comments. "Ay, ay; they are edging towards the river—Peace, pup—pup—peace—no, here they come this-a-way again—the thieves dont seem to know their own errand! If there were just six of us, lad, what a beautiful ambushment we might make upon them, from this very spot—it wont do, it wont do, boy; keep yourself closer, or your head will be seen—besides, I'm not altogether strong in the opinion it would be lawful, as they have done us no harm— There they bend again to the river—no; here they come up the swell— now is the moment to be as still as if the breath had done its duty and departed the body."

The old man sunk into the grass while he was speaking, as if the final separation to which he alluded had in his own case actually occurred, and, at the next instant, a band of wild horsemen whirled by them, with the noiseless rapidity in which it might be imagined a troop of spectres would pass. The dark and fleeting forms were already vanished, when the trapper ventured again to raise his head to a level with the tops of the bending herbage, motioning at the same time to his companions, to maintain their positions and their silence.

"They are going down the swell, towards the encampment," he continued, in his former guarded tones; "no, they halt in the bottom, and are clustering together like deer in council. By the Lord they are turning again, and we are not yet done with the reptiles!"

Once more he sought his friendly cover, and at the next instant the dark troop were to be seen riding, in a disorderly manner, on the very summit of the little elevation on which the trapper and his companions lay. It was now soon apparent that they had returned to avail themselves of the height of the ground, in order to examine the dim horizon.

Some dismounted, while others rode to and fro, like men engaged in a local inquiry of much interest. Happily for the hidden party, the grass in which they were concealed not only served to skreen them from the eyes of the savages, but opposed an obstacle to prevent their horses, which were no less rude and untrained than their riders, from trampling on them, in their irregular and wild paces.

At length an athletic and dark-looking Indian, who, by his air of authority, would seem to be the leader, summoned his chiefs about him to a consultation, which was held mounted. This body was collected on the very margin of that mass of herbage in which the trapper and his companions were hid. As the young man looked up and saw the fierce aspect of the groupe, which was increasing at each instant by the accession of some countenance and figure, apparently more forbidding than any which had preceeded it, he drew his rifle, by a very natural impulse, from beneath him, and commenced putting it in a state for service. The female, at his side, buried her face in the grass, by a feeling that was, possibly, quite as natural to her sex and habits, leaving him to follow the impulses of his hot blood; but his aged and more prudent adviser whispered sternly in his ear.

"The tick of the lock is as well known to the knaves as the blast of a trumpet to a soldier! Lay down the piece—lay down the piece—should the moon touch the barrel, it could not fail to be seen by the devils, whose eyes are keener than the blackest snake's! The smallest motion, now, would be sure to bring an arrow among us."

The bee-hunter so far obeyed as to continue immoveable and silent. But there was still sufficient light to convince his companion, by the contracted brow and threatening eye of the young man, that a discovery would not bestow a bloodless victory on the savages. Finding his advice disregarded, the trapper took his measures accordingly, and awaited the result with a resignation and calmness that were characteristics of the individual.

In the mean time the Siouxes (for the sagacity of the old man was not deceived in the character of his dangerous neighbors) had terminated their council, and were again dispersed along the ridge of land as if they sought some hidden object.

"The imps have heard the hound!" whispered the trapper, "and their ears are too true to be cheated in the distance. Keep close, lad, keep close; down with your head to the very earth, like a dog that sleeps."

"Let us rather take to our feet, and trust to manhood," returned his impatient companion.

He would have proceeded, but feeling a hand laid rudely on his shoulder he turned his eyes upward, and beheld the dark and savage countenance of an Indian glooming full upon him. Notwithstanding the surprise and the disadvantage of his attitude, the youth was not disposed to become a captive so easily. Quicker than the flash of his own gun, he sprang upon his feet, and was throttling his opponent with a power that would soon have terminated the contest, when he felt the arms of the trapper thrown around his body, confining his exertions by a strength very little inferior to his own. Before he had time to reproach his comrade for this apparent treachery, a dozen Siouxes, were around them, and the whole party were compelled to yield themselves as prisoners.

CHAPTER IV.

— —"With much more dismay
I view the fight, than those that make the fray."

The Merchant of Venice, III.ii. 61-62.

THE unfortunate bee-hunter and his companions had become the captives of a people, who might, without exaggeration, be called the Ishmaelites of the American deserts. From time immemorial, the hands of the Siouxes had been turned against their neighbors of the Prairies, and even at this day, when the influence and authority of a civilized government are beginning to be felt around them, they are considered a treacherous and dangerous race. At the period of our tale, the case was far worse; few white men trusting themselves in the remote and unprotected regions where so false a tribe was known to dwell.

Notwithstanding the peaceable submission of the trapper, he was quite aware of the character of the band into whose hands he had fallen. It would have been difficult, however, for the nicest judge to have determined whether fear, policy or resignation formed the secret motive of the old man, in permitting himself to be plundered, as he did, without a murmur. So far from opposing any remonstrance to the rude and violent manner, in which his conquerors performed this customary office, he even anticipated their cupidity, by tendering to the chiefs, such articles as he thought might prove the most acceptable. On the other hand, Paul Hover, who had been literally a conquered man, manifested the strongest repugnance to submit to the violent liberties that were taken with his person and property. He, even, gave several exceedingly unequivocal demonstrations of his displeasure during the summary process, and would, more than once, have broken out into open and desperate resistance, but for the admonitions and intreaties of the trembling girl, who clung to his side, in a manner so dependant, as to show the youth, that her hopes were now placed, no less on his discretion, than on his disposition to serve her.

The Indians had, however, no sooner deprived the captives of their arms, and ammunition, and stript them of a few articles of dress of little use and perhaps of less value, than they appeared disposed to grant them a respite. Business of greater moment pressed on their hands, and required their attention. Another consultation of the chiefs was convened, and it was apparent, by the earnest and vehement manner of the few who spoke, that the warriors conceived their success, as yet, to be far from complete.

"It will be well," whispered the trapper, who knew enough of the language he heard, to comprehend perfectly the subject of the discussion, "if the travellers who lie near the willow brake, are not awoke out of their sleep by a visit from these miscreants. They are too cunning to believe that a woman of the pale faces is to be found so far from the settlements, without having a white man's inventions and comforts at hand."

"If they will carry the tribe of wandering Ishmael to the Rocky Mountains," said the young bee-hunter, laughing in his vexation with a sort of bitter merriment, "I may forgive the rascals!"

"Paul! Paul," exclaimed his companion in a tone of reproach, "you forget all! Think of the dreadful consequences!"

"Ay, it was thinking of what you call consequences, Ellen, that prevented me from putting the matter, at once, to yonder red-devil, and making it a real knock-down and drag out. Old trapper, the sin of this cowardly business lies on your shoulders! But it is no more than your daily calling, I reckon, to take men as well as beasts in snares!"

"I implore you, Paul, to be calm, to be patient."

"Well, since it is your wish, Ellen," returned the youth, endeavoring to swallow his spleen, "I will make the trial, though, as you ought to know, it is part of the religion of a Kentuckian, to fret himself, a little, at a mischance."

"I fear your friends, in the other bottom, will not escape the eyes of the imps," continued the trapper, as coolly as though he had not heard a syllable of the intervening discourse. "They scent plunder, and it would be as hard to drive a hound from his game, as to throw the varmints from its trail!"

"Is there nothing to be done?" asked Ellen, in an imploring manner which proved the sincerity of her concern.

"It would be an easy matter to call out, in so loud a voice, as to make old Ishmael dream that the wolves were among his flock," Paul replied, "I can make myself heard a mile in these open fields, and his camp is but a short quarter from us."

"And get knock'd on the head for your pains," returned the trapper— "No, no, cunning must match cunning, or the hounds, will murder the whole family."

"Murder! no — no murder. Ishmael loves travel, so well, there would be no harm in his having a look at the other sea, but the old fellow is in a bad condition to take the long journey. I would try a look myself, before he should be quite murdered!"

"His party is strong in number and well armed; do you think it will fight?"

"Look here, old trapper. Few men love Ishmael Bush and his seven sledge-hammer sons, less than one Paul Hover, but I scorn to slander even a Tennessee shot-gun. There is as much of the true stand-up courage among them, as there is in any family, that was ever raised in Kentuck, itself. They are a long-sided and double jointed breed, and let me tell you, that he, who takes the measure of one of them on the ground, must be a workman at a hug."

"Hist! The savages have done their talk, and are about to set their accursed devices in motion. Let us be patient, something may yet offer, in favor of your friends."

"Friends! call none of the race a friend of mine, trapper, if you have the smallest regard for my affection. What I say in their favor is less from love than honesty."

"I did not know but the young woman was of the kin," returned the other, a little drily. "But no offence should be taken where none was intended."

The mouth of Paul was again stopped by the hand of Ellen, who took on herself to reply, in her conciliating tones, "We should be all of a family, when it is in our power to serve each other. We depend entirely on your experience, honest old man, to discover the means to apprise our friends of their danger."

"There will be a real time of it," muttered the bee-hunter, laughing, "if the boys get at work, in good earnest, with these red-skins."

He was interrupted by a general movement which took place among the band. The Indians dismounted to a man, giving their horses in charge of three or four of the party, who were, also, entrusted with the safe keeping of the prisoners. They then, formed themselves in a circle around a warrior, who appeared to possess the chief authority, and at a given signal the whole array mov'd slowly, and cautiously from the centre, in straight, and consequently, in diverging lines. Most of their dark forms were soon blended with the brown covering of the Prairie, though the captives, who watched the slightest movements, of their enemies with vigilant eyes, were, now and then, enabled to discern a human figure drawn against the horizon, as some one more eager than the rest rose to his greatest height in order to extend the limits of his view. But it was not long, before even these fugitive glimpses of the moving and constantly increasing circle, were lost, and uncertainty and conjecture were added to apprehension. In this manner passed many anxious and weary minutes, during the close of which the listeners expected at each moment, to hear the whoop, of the assailants and the shrieks of the assailed, rising together on the stillness of the night. But it would seem, that the search which was so evidently making was without a sufficient object, for at the expiration of half an hour the different individuals of the band began to return singly, gloomy and sullen, like men who were disappointed.

"Our time is at hand," observed the trapper, who noted the smallest incident, or the slightest indication of hostility among the savages; "we are now to be questioned; and if I know any thing of the policy of our case, I should say it would be wise to choose one among us, to hold the discourse, in order that our testimony may agree. And furthermore if an opinion from one as old and as worthless as a hunter of fourscore is to be regarded, I would just venture to say, that man should be the one most skill'd in the natur' of an Indian, and that he should also, know something of their language. Are you acquainted with the tongue of the Siouxes, friend?"

"Swarm your own hive," returned the discontented bee-hunter. "You are good at buzzing, old trapper, if you are good at nothing else."

"'Tis the gift of youth to be rash and heady," the trapper calmly, retorted. "The day has been, boy, when my blood was like your own, too swift and too hot to run quietly in my veins. But what will it profit to talk of silly risks and foolish acts at this time of life! A gray head should cover a brain of reason and not the tongue of a boaster."

"True, true," whispered Ellen, "and we have other things to attend to now! here comes the Indian to put his questions."

The girl, whose apprehensions had quickened her senses was not deceived. She was yet speaking when a tall, half naked savage approached the spot where they stood, and after examining the whole party as closely as the dim light permitted, for more than a minute in perfect stillness,* he gave the usual salutation in the harsh and guttural tones of his own language. The trapper replied as well as he could, which it seems, was sufficiently well to be understood. In order to escape the imputation of pedantry we shall render the substance, and, so far as it is possible, the form of the dialogue that succeeded, into the English tongue.

"Have the pale faces eaten their own buffaloes, and taken the skins from all their own beavers," continued the savage, allowing the usual moment of decorum to elapse after the words of greeting, before he again spoke, "that they come to count how many are left among the Pawnees?"

"Some of us are here to buy and some to sell," returned the trapper, "but none will follow if they hear it is not safe to come nigh the lodge of a Sioux."

"The Siouxes are thieves, and they live in the snows, why do we talk of a people who are so far, when we are in the country of the Pawnees."

"If the Pawnees are the owners of this land, then white and red are here by equal right."

"Have not the Pale-faces stolen enough from the Red men, that you come so far to carry a lie! I have said that this is a hunting ground of my tribe."

"My right to be here is equal to your own," the trapper rejoined with undisturbed coolness: "I do not speak as I might—It is better to be silent. The Pawnees and the white men are brothers, but a Sioux dare not show his face in the village of the Loups."

"The Dahcotahs are men!" exclaimed the savage fiercely, forgetting, in his anger, to maintain the character he had assumed, and using the appellation of which his nation was most proud, "The Dahcotahs have no fear. Speak; what brings you so far from the villages of the Pale-faces?"

"I have seen the sun rise and set on many Councils, and have heard the words of wise men. Let your Chiefs come, and my mouth shall not be shut."

"I am a great Chief," said the savage, affecting an air of offended dignity. "Do you take me for an Assiniboine! Weucha* is a warrior often named, and much beloved!"

"Am I a fool not to know a 'burnt-wood Teton'!" demanded the trapper with a steadiness that did great credit to his nerves. "Go: it is dark, and you do not see that my head is gray."

The Indian, now, appeared convinced that he had adopted too shallow an artifice to deceive one so practised as the man he addressed, and he was deliberating what fiction he should next invent, in order to obtain his real object, when a slight commotion among the band, put an end at once, to all his schemes. Casting his eyes behind him, as if fearful of a speedy interruption, he said in tones much less pretending than those he had first resorted to—

"Give Weucha the milk of the Long-knives,* and he will sing your name in the ears of the great men of his tribe."

"Go," repeated the trapper motioning him away, with strong disgust. "Your young men are speaking of Mahtoree.* My words are for the ears of a chief."

The savage cast a look on the other which, notwithstanding the dim light, was sufficiently indicative of implacable hostility. He then stole away among his fellows, anxious to conceal the counterfeit he had attempted to practise, no less than the treachery he had contemplated against a fair division of the spoils, from the man named by the trapper, whom he now also knew to be approaching, by the manner in which his name passed from one to another in the band. He had hardly disappeared, before a warrior of powerful frame, advanced out of the dark circle, and placed himself before the captives with that high and proud bearing for which a distinguished Indian chief is ever so remarkable. He was followed by all the party, who arranged themselves around his person, in a deep and respectful silence.

"The earth is very large," the Chief commenced, after a pause of that true dignity, which his counterfeit had so miserably affected. "Why can the children of my Great White Father* never find room on it?"

"Some among them have heard, that their friends in the Prairies are in want of many things," returned the trapper, "and they have come to see if it be true. Some want, in their turns, what the red men are willing to sell, and they come to make their friends rich, with powder and blankets."

"Do traders cross the big river, with empty hands!"

"Our hands are empty because your young men thought we were tired, and they have lightened us of our loads. They were mistaken. I am old, but I am still strong."

"It cannot be. Your load has fallen in the Prairies. Show my young men the place, that they may pick it up, before the Pawnees find it."

"The path to the spot is crooked, and it is night. The hour is come for sleep," said the trapper with perfect composure—"bid your warriors go over yonder hill. There is water and there is wood; let them light their fires and sleep with warm feet. When the sun comes again I will speak to you."

A low murmur, but one that was clearly indicative of dissatisfaction passed among the attentive listeners, and served to inform the old man, that he had not been sufficiently wary in proposing a measure, that he intended should notify the travellers in the brake, of the presence of their dangerous neighbors. Mahtoree, however, without betraying, in the slightest degree, the excitement which was so strongly exhibited by his companions, continued the discourse in the same lofty manner, as before.

"I know that my friend is rich," he said, "that he has many warriors not far off, and that horses are plentier with him than dogs among the red skins."

"You see my warriors and my horses."

"What! has the woman the feet of a Dahcotah, that she can walk for thirty nights in the Prairies, and not fall! I know that the red men of the woods make long marches on foot, but we who live where the eye cannot see from one lodge to another, love our horses."

The trapper now hesitated, in his turn. He was perfectly aware that deception, if detected, might prove dangerous, and for one of his pursuits and character, he was strongly troubled with an unaccommodating regard for the truth. But recollecting that he controlled the fate of others as well as of himself, he determined to let things take their course, and to permit the Dahcotah Chief to deceive himself if he would.

"The women of the Siouxes and of the white men are not of the same wigwam," he answered evasively. "Would a Teton warrior make his wife greater than himself. I know he would not; and yet, my ears have heard that there are lands, where the Councils are held by squaws."

Another slight movement in the dark circle, apprised the trapper, that his declaration was not received without surprise, if entirely without distrust. The Chief, alone, seem'd unmoved, nor was he disposed to relax from the loftiness and high dignity of his air.

"My white Fathers who live on the Great Lakes have declared," he said, "that their brothers towards the rising sun are not men; and, now, I know they did not lie! Go. What is a nation, whose chief is a squaw! are you the dog and not the husband of this woman?"

"I am neither. Never did I see her face before this day. She came into the Prairies, because they had told her a great and generous nation called the Dahcotahs liv'd there, and she wish'd to look on men. The women of the pale-faces, like the women of the Siouxes, open their eyes to see things that are new; but she is poor, like myself, and she will want corn and buffaloe, if you take away the little that she and her friend still have."

"My ears listen to many wicked lies!" exclaimed the Teton warrior, in a voice so stern, that it startled even his red auditors. "Am I a woman! Has not a Dacotah eyes! Tell me, white hunter, who are the men of your colour, that sleep near the fallen trees!"

As he spoke, the indignant Chief pointed in the direction of Ishmael's encampment, leaving the trapper no reason to doubt that the superior industry and sagacity of this man had effected a discovery which had eluded the search of the rest of his party. Notwithstanding his regret at an event that might prove fatal to the sleepers, and some little vexation at having been so completely outwitted in the dialogue, just related, the old man continued to maintain his air of inflexible composure.

"It may be true," he answered, "that white men are sleeping on the Prairie. If my brother says it, it is true; but what men thus trust to the generosity of the Tetons, I cannot tell. If there be strangers asleep, send your young men to wake them up and let them say why they are here; every pale-face has a tongue."

The Chief shook his head with a wild and fierce smile, answering abruptly, as he turned away to put an end to the conference.

"The Dacotahs are a wise race, and Mahtoree is their Chief. He will not call to the strangers, that they may rise and speak to him, with their carabines. He will whisper softly in their ears. When this is done let the men of their own colour come and awake them!"

As he uttered these words and turned on his heel, a low, and approving laugh passed around the dark circle, which instantly broke its order and followed him to a little distance, from the stand of the captives, where those who might presume to mingle opinions with so great a warrior, again, gathered about him; in consultation. Weucha profited by the occasion to renew his importunities, but the trapper, who had discovered how great a counterfeit he was, shook him off, in displeasure. An end was, however, more effectually put to the annoyance of this malignant savage by a mandate for the whole party, including men and beasts, to change their position. The movement was made in dead silence, and with an order that would have done credit to more enlightened beings. A halt, however, was soon made, and when the captives had time to look about them, they found they were in view of the low, dark outline of the copse, near which lay the slumbering party of Ishmael.

Here another short but grave and deliberative consultation was held.

The beasts, which seem'd trained to such covert and silent attacks, were once more plac'd under the care of keepers, who, as before were

charged with the duty of watching the prisoners. The mind of the
trapper was in no degree relieved from the uneasiness, which was, at
each instant, getting a stronger possession of him, when he found that
Weucha was plac'd nearest to his own person, and, as it appeared by
the air of triumph and authority he assumed, at the head of the guard
also. The savage, however, who doubtless had his secret instructions,
was content, for the present, with making a significant gesture with
his tomahawk, which menaced death to Ellen. After admonishing in
this expressive manner his male captives of the fate that would instantly
attend their female companion, on the slightest alarm proceeding
from any of the party, he was content to maintain a rigid silence. This
unexpected forbearance, on the part of Weucha, enabled the trapper
and his two associates to give their undivided attention to the little
that might be seen of the interesting movements which were passing
in their front.

Mahtoree took the entire dispositon of the arrangements on himself. He pointed out the precise situation he wished each individual
to occupy, like one intimately acquainted with the qualifications of
his respective followers, and he was obeyed with the deference and
promptitude with which an Indian warrior is wont to submit to the
instructions of his chief, in moments of trial. Some he despatched to
the right, and others to the left. Each man departed with the noiseless
and quick step peculiar to the race, until all had assumed their allotted stations, with the exception of two chosen warriors, who remained
nigh the person of their leader. When the rest had disappeared,
Mahtoree turned to these select companions, and intimated by a sign,
that the critical moment had arrived, when the enterprise he contemplated was to be put in execution.

Each man laid aside the light fowling piece which, under the name
of a carabyne, he carried in virtue of his rank, and divesting himself
of every article of exterior or heavy clothing, he stood resembling a
dark and fierce looking statue, in the attitude and nearly in the garb
of nature. Mahtoree assured himself of the right position of his tomahawk, felt that his knife was secure in its sheath of skin, tightened his
girdle of wampum, and saw that the lacing of his fringed and ornamented leggings was secure and likely to offer no impediment to his
exertions. Thus prepared at all points, and ready for his desperate
undertaking, the Teton gave the signal to proceed.

The three advanced in a line with the encampment of the travellers, until, in the dim light by which they were seen, their dusky

forms were nearly lost to the eyes of the prisoners. Here they paused, looking around them like men who deliberate and ponder long on the consequences before they take a desperate leap. Then sinking together, they became lost in the grass of the Prairie.

It is not difficult to imagine the distress and anxiety of the different spectators of these threatening movements. Whatever might be the reasons of Ellen for entertaining no strong attachment to the family in which she has first been seen by the reader, the feelings of her sex, and, perhaps, some lingering seeds of kindness, predominated. More than once she felt tempted to brave the awful and instant danger that awaited such an offence, and to raise her feeble and in truth impotent voice in warning. So strong, indeed, and so very natural was the inclination, that she would most probably have put it in execution, but for the often-repeated though whispered remonstrances of Paul Hover. In the breast of the young bee-hunter himself, there was a singular union of emotions. His first and chiefest solicitude was certainly in behalf of his gentle and dependant companion; but the sense of her danger was mingled in the breast of the reckless woods-man with a consciousness of a high and wild, and by no means an unpleasant excitement. Though united to the emigrants by ties still less binding than those of Ellen, he longed to hear the crack of their rifles, and, had occasion offered, he would gladly have been among the first to rush to their rescue. There were in truth moments when he felt in his turn an impulse, that was nearly resistless, to spring forward and awake the unconscious sleepers; but a glance at Ellen would serve to recall his tottering prudence, and to admonish him of the consequences. The trapper, alone, remained calm and observant, as if nothing that involved his personal comfort or safety had occurred. His ever-moving, vigilant eyes, watched the smallest change, with the composure of one too long inured to scenes of danger to be easily moved, and with an expression of cool determination which denoted the intention he actually harboured, of profiting by the smallest oversight on the part of the captors.

In the mean time the Teton warriors had not been idle. Profiting by the high fog* which grew in the bottoms, they had worm'd their way, through the matted grass, like so many treacherous serpents stealing on their prey, until the point was gained, where an extraordinary caution became necessary to their further advance. Mahtoree, alone, had occasionally elevated his dark, grim countenance above the herbage, straining his eye balls to penetrate the gloom which skirted

the border of the brake. In these momentary glances he gained sufficient knowledge, added to that he had obtained in his former search,
to be the perfect master of the position of his intended victims, though
he was still profoundly ignorant of their numbers, and of their means
of defence.

His efforts to possess himself of the requisite knowledge concerning these two latter and essential points were, however, completely
baffled by the stillness of the camp, which lay in a quiet as deep as if it
were literally a place of the dead. Too wary and distrustful to rely, in
circumstances of so much doubt, on the discretion of any less firm
and crafty than himself, the Dahcotah, bade his companions remain
where they lay, and pursued the adventure alone.

The progress of Mahtoree was now slow, and to one less accustomed
to such a species of exercise, it would have proved painfully laborious.
But the advance of the wily snake itself is not more certain or noiseless,
than was his approach. He drew his form, foot by foot, through the
bending grass, pausing at each movement to catch the smallest sound
that might betray any knowledge, on the part of the travellers, of his
proximity. He succeeded, at length, in dragging himself, out of the
sickly light of the moon, into the shadows of the brake, where not
only his own dark person was much less liable to be seen, but where
the surrounding objects became more distinctly visible to his keen
and active glances.

Here the Teton paused long and warily to make his observations,
before he ventured further. His position enabled him to bring the
whole encampment, with its tent, wagons and lodges, into a dark but
clearly marked profile, furnishing a clue by which the practised warrior was led to a tolerably accurate estimate of the force he was about
to encounter. Still an unnatural silence pervaded the spot, as if men
suppressed even the quiet breathings of sleep, in order to render the
appearance of their confidence more evident. The chief bent his head
to the earth, and listened intently. He was about to raise it again, in
disappointment, when the long drawn and trembling respiration of
one who slumbered imperfectly met his ear. The Indian was too well
skilled in all the means of deception to become himself the victim of
any common artifice. He knew the sound to be natural, by its peculiar quivering, and he hesitated no longer.

A man of nerves less tried than those of the fierce and conquering
Mahtoree would have been keenly sensible of all the hazard he incurred. The reputation of those hardy and powerful white adven-

turers, who so often penetrated the wilds inhabited by his people, was well known to him; but while he drew nigher, with the respect and caution that a brave enemy never fails to inspire, it was with the vindictive animosity of a red man, jealous and resentful of the inroads of the stranger.

Turning from the line of his former route, the Teton dragged himself directly towards the margin of the thicket. When this material object was effected in safety, he arose to his seat, and took a better survey of his situation. A single moment served to apprise him of the place where the unsuspecting traveller lay. The reader will readily anticipate that the savage had succeeded in gaining a dangerous proximity to one of those slothful sons of Ishmael, who were deputed to watch over the isolated encampment of the travellers.

When certain that he was undiscovered, the Dahcotah raised his person again, and bending forward, he mov'd his dark visage above the face of the sleeper, in that sort of wanton and subtle manner with which the reptile is seen to play about its victim before it strikes. Satisfied at length, not only of the condition but of the character of the stranger, Mahtoree was in the act of withdrawing his head, when a slight movement of the sleeper announced the symptoms of reviving consciousness. The savage seized the knife which hung at his girdle, and in an instant it was poised above the breast of the young emigrant. Then changing his purpose, with an action as rapid as his own flashing thoughts, he sunk back behind the trunk of the fallen tree against which the other reclined, and lay in its shadow, as dark, as motionless and apparently as insensible as the wood itself.

The slothful sentinel opened his heavy eyes, and gazing upward for a moment at the hazy heavens, he made an extraordinary exertion and raised his powerful frame from the support of the log. Then he looked about him, with an air of something like watchfulness, suffering his dull glances to run over the misty objects of the encampment until they finally settled on the distant and dim field of the open Prairie. Meeting with nothing more attractive than the same faint outlines of swell and interval, which everywhere rose before his drowsy eyes, he changed his position so as completely to turn his back on his dangerous neighbour, and suffered his person to sink sluggishly down into its former recumbent attitude. A long and, on the part of the Teton, an anxious and painful silence succeeded, before the deep breathing of the traveller again announced that he was indulging in his slumbers. The savage was however far too jealous of a counterfeit to trust to the first appearance of sleep. But the fatigues of a day of unusual toil lay too heavy on the sentinel to leave the other long in doubt. Still the motion with which Mahtoree again raised himself to his knees was so noiseless and guarded, that even a vigilant observer might have hesitated to believe he stirred. The change was, however, at length effected, and the Dacotah chief, then bent again over his enemy, without having produced a noise louder than that of the cotton-wood leaf which fluttered at his side in the currents of the passing air.

Mahtoree now felt himself master of the sleeper's fate. At the same time that he scanned the vast proportions and athletic limbs of the youth, in that sort of admiration which physical excellence seldom fails to excite in the breast of a savage, he coolly prepared to extinguish the principle of vitality which could alone render them formidable. After making himself sure of the seat of life, by gently removing the folds of the intervening cloth, he raised his keen weapon, and was about to unite his strength and skill in the impending blow, when the young man threw his brawny arm carelessly backward, exhibiting in the action the vast volume of its muscles.

The sagacious and wary Teton paused. It struck his acute faculties that sleep was less dangerous to him, at that moment, than even death itself might prove. The smallest noise, the agony of struggling, with which such a frame would probably relinquish its hold of life, suggested themselves to his rapid thoughts, and were all present to his experienced senses. He looked back into the encampment, turned his head into the thicket, and glanced his glowing eyes abroad into the .wild and silent Prairies. Bending once more over the respited victim, he assured himself that he was sleeping heavily, and then abandoned his immediate purpose in obedience alone to the suggestions of a more crafty policy.

The retreat of Mahtoree was as still and guarded as had been his approach. He now took the direction of the encampment, stealing along the margin of the brake, as a cover into which he might easily plunge at the smallest alarm. The drapery of the solitary hut attracted his notice in passing. After examining the whole of its exterior, and listening with painful intensity, in order to gather counsel from his ears, the savage ventured to raise the cloth at the bottom, and to thrust his dark visage beneath. It might have been a minute before the Teton chief drew back, and seated himself with the whole of his form without the linen tenement. Here he sat, seemingly brooding over his discovery, for many moments, in rigid inaction. Then he resumed his crouching attitude, and once more projected his visage beyond the covering of the tent. His second visit to the interior was longer and, if possible, more ominous than the first. But it had, like every thing else, its termination, and the savage again withdrew his glaring eyes from the secrets of the place.

Mahtoree had drawn his person many yards from the spot, in his slow progress towards the cluster of objects which pointed out the centre of the position, before he again stopped. He made another pause, and looked back at the solitary little dwelling he had left, as if doubtful whether he should not return. But the chevaux-de-frise of branches now lay within reach of his arm, and the very appearance of precaution it presented, as it announced the value of the effects it encircled, tempted his cupidity, and induced him to proceed.

The passage of the savage, through the tender and brittle limbs of the cotton-wood, could be likened only to the sinuous and noiseless winding of the reptiles which he imitated. When he had effected his object, and had taken an instant to become acquainted with the nature of the localities within the enclosure, the Teton used the precaution to open a way through which he might make a swift retreat. Then raising himself on his feet, he stalked through the encampment, like the master of evil, seeking whom and what he should first devote to his fell purposes. He had already ascertained the contents of the lodge in which were collected the woman and her young children, and had passed several gigantic frames, stretched on different piles of brush, which happily for him lay in unconscious helplessness, when he reached the spot occupied by Ishmael in person. It could not escape the sagacity of one like Mahtoree that he had now within his power the principal man among the travellers. He stood long hovering above the recumbent and Herculean form of the emigrant, keenly debating in his own mind the chances of his enterprise, and the most effectual means of reaping its richest harvest.

He sheathed the knife which, under the hasty and burning impulse of his thoughts, he had been tempted to draw, and was passing on, when Ishmael turned in his lair, and demanded roughly who was moving before his half-opened eyes. Nothing short of the readiness and cunning of a savage could have evaded the crisis. Imitating the gruff tones and nearly unintelligible sounds he heard, Mahtoree threw his body heavily on the earth, and appeared to dispose himself to sleep. Though the whole movement was seen by Ishmael, in a sort of stupid observation, the artifice was too bold and too admirably executed to fail. The drowsy father closed his eyes, and slept heavily, with this treacherous inmate in the very bosom of his family.

It was necessary for the Teton to maintain the position he had taken, for many long weary minutes, in order to make sure that he was no longer watched. Though his body lay so motionless, his active mind was not idle. He profited by the delay to mature a plan which he intended should put the whole encampment, including both its effects and their proprietors, entirely at his mercy. The instant he could do so with safety, the indefatigable savage was again in motion. He took his way towards the slight pen which contained the domestic animals, worming himself along the ground in his former subtle and guarded manner.

The first animal he encountered among the beasts occasioned a long and hazardous delay. The weary creature, perhaps conscious, through its secret instinct, that in the endless wastes of the Prairies its surest protector was to be found in man, was so exceedingly docile as quietly to submit to the close examinaton it was doomed to undergo. The hand of the wandering Teton passed over the downy coat, the meek countenance, and the slender limbs of the gentle creature with untiring curiosity; but he finally abandoned the prize, as useless in his predatory expeditions, and offering too little temptation to the appetite. As soon however as he found himself among the beasts of burthen, his gratification was extreme, and it was with difficulty that he restrained the customary ejaculations of pleasure that were more than once on the point of bursting from his lips. Here he lost sight of the hazards by which he had gained access to his dangerous position, and the watchfulness of the wary and long practised warrior was momentarily forgotten in the exultation of the savage.

CHAPTER V.

"Why, worthy father, what have we to lose?"
— The law

Protects us not. Then why should we be tender
To let an arrogant piece of flesh threat us!
Play judge and executioner."

Cymbeline, IV.ii. 124-28.

WHILE the Teton thus enacted his subtle and characteristic part, not a sound broke the stillness of the surrounding Prairie. The whole band, lay at their several posts, waiting, with the well known patience of the Natives, for the signal which was to summon them to action. To the eyes of the anxious spectators, who occupied the little eminence, already described as the position of the captives, the scene presented the broad, solemn view, of a waste dimly lighted, by the glimmering rays of a clouded moon. The place of the encampment was marked by a gloom deeper than that which faintly shadowed out the courses of the bottoms, and here and there, a brighter streak tinged the rolling summits of the ridges. As for the rest, it was the deep, imposing quiet, of a desert.

But to those who so well knew, how much was brooding beneath this mantle of stillness and night, it was a scene of high and wild excitement. Their anxiety gradually increased, as minute after minute, passed away, and not the smallest sound of life arose out of the calm and darkness which enveloped the brake. The breathing of Paul grew louder and deeper, and more than once Ellen trembled at she knew not what, as she felt the quivering of his active frame, while she leaned dependantly on his arm, for support.

The shallow honesty, as well as the besetting infirmity of Weucha, have, already, been exhibited. The reader therefore will not be surprised to learn, that he was the first to forget the regulations he had himself imposed. It was at the precise moment, when we left, Mahtoree yielding to his nearly ungovernable delight, as he surveyed the number and quality of Ishmael's beasts of burthen, that the man he had selected to watch his captives, chose to indulge in the malignant pleasure of tormenting those it was his duty to protect. Bending his head nigh the ear of the trapper, the savage, rather muttered than whispered—

"If the Tetons lose their Great Chief, by the hands of the Long-knives,[1] old shall die, as well as young!"

"Life is the gift of the Wahcondah," was the unmov'd reply. "The burnt-wood warrior must submit to his laws, as well as his other children. Men only die when *he* chooses; and no Dahcotah can change the hour."

"Look!" returned the savage thrusting the blade of his knife before the face of his captive. "Weucha is the Wahcondah of a dog!"

The old man raised his eyes to the fierce visage of his keeper, and, for a moment, a gleam of honest and powerful disgust shot from their deep cells; but it instantly pass'd away, leaving in its place, an expression of commiseration, if not of sorrow.

"Why should one made in the real image of God, suffer his natur' to be provoked by a mere effigy of reason!" he said in English, and in tones much louder than those, in which Weucha had chosen to pitch the conversation. The latter profited by the unintentional offence of his captive, and seizing him, by the thin, gray locks that fell from beneath his cap, was on the point of passing the blade of his knife in malignant triumph around their roots, when a long, shrill yell rent the air, and was instantly echoed from the surrounding waste, as if a thousand demons opened their throats in common at the summons. Weucha relinquished his grasp, and uttered a cry of exultation.

"Now!" shouted Paul, unable to controul his impatience any longer, "now, old Ishmael, is the time to show the native blood of Kentucky! Fire, low, boys—Level into the swales, for the red-skins are settling to the very earth!"

His voice was however, lost, or rather unheeded, in the midst of the shrieks, shouts, and yells, that were, by this time, bursting from fifty mouths on every side of him. The guards still maintained their posts, at the side of the captives, but it was with that sort of difficulty with which steeds are restrained at the starting-post, when expecting the signal to commence the trial of speed. They toss'd their arms wildly in the air, leaping up and down, more like exulting children than sober men, and continued to utter the most frantic cries.

In the midst of this tumultuous disorder, a rushing sound was heard, similar to that which might be expected to precede the passage of a flight of buffaloes, and then came the flocks and cattle of Ishmael, in one confused and frightened drove.

"They have robbed the squatter of his beasts!" said the attentive

[1] The whites are so called by the Indians, from their swords. [1832]

trapper. "The reptiles have left him as hoofless as a beaver!" He was yet speaking, when the whole body of the terrified animals rose the little acclivity and swept by the place where he stood, followed by a band of dusky, and demon-like looking figures, who pressed madly on their rear.

The impulse was communicated to the Teton horses, long accustomed to sympathise in the untutored passions of their owners, and it was with difficulty that their keepers were enabled to restrain their impatience. At this moment, when all eyes were directed to the passing whirlwind of men and beasts, the trapper caught the knife, from the hands of his inattentive keeper, with a power that his age would have seemed to contradict, and, at a single blow, severed the thong of hide which connected the whole of the drove. The wild animals snorted with joy and terror, and tearing the earth with their heels, they dash'd away into the broad Prairies in a dozen different directions.

Weucha turned upon his assailant with the ferocity and agility of a tiger. He felt for the weapon of which he had been so suddenly deprived, fumbled, with impotent haste for the handle of his tomahawk, and at the same moment, glanced his eyes after the flying cattle, with the longings of a Western Indian. The struggle between thirst for vengeance and cupidity was severe but short. The latter quickly predominated in the bosom of one whose passions were proverbially grovelling, and scarcely a moment intervened between the flight of the animals and the swift pursuit of the guards. The trapper had continued calmly facing his foe, during the instant of suspense that succeeded his hardy act, and now that Weucha was seen following his companions, he pointed after the dark train, saying, with his deep and nearly inaudible laugh—

"Red-natur' is red-natur', let it show itself on a Prairie, or in a Forest. A knock on the head, would be the smallest reward to him, who should take such a liberty with a Christian sentinel, but there goes the Teton after his horses as if he thought two legs as good as four in such a race! And yet the imps will have every hoof of them afore the day sets in, because it's reason ag'in instinct. Poor reason, I allow; but still there is a great deal of the man in an Indian. Ah's me! your Delawares were the red-skins of which America might boast; but few and scattered is that mighty people now! Well! the traveller may just make his pitch where he is; he has plenty of water, though natur' has cheated him of the pleasure of stripping the 'arth of its lawful trees. He has seen the last of his four-footed creaturs or I am but little skilled in Sioux cunning!"

"Had we not better join the party of Ishmael," said the Bee-hunter. "There will be a regular fight about this matter, or the old fellow has suddenly grown chicken hearted."

"No, no, no," hastily exclaimed Ellen —

She was stopped by the trapper, who laid his hand gently on her mouth, as he answered —

"Hist — hist — the sound of voices, might bring us into danger. Is your friend," he added, turning to Paul, "a man of spirit, enough . . . ."

"Dont call the squatter a friend of mine!" interrupted the youth. "I never, yet, harbored with one, who could not show hand and seal for the land which fed him."

"Well, well, let it then be acquaintance. Is he a man to maintain his own, stoutly, by dint of powder and lead?"

"His own! ay, and that which is not his own, too! Can you tell me, old trapper, who held the rifle that did the deed for the sheriff's deputy, that thought to rout the unlawful settlers who had gathered nigh the Buffaloe Lick, in old Kentuck. I had lin'd a beautiful swarm that very day into the hollow of a dead beech, and there lay the People's Officer at its roots with a hole directly through the 'Grace of God', which he carried in his jacket pocket, covering his heart, as if he thought a bit of sheepskin was a breast plate, against a squatter's bullet. Now, Ellen, you need'n't be troubled, for it never strictly was brought home to him; and there were fifty others who had pitch'd in that neighbourhood with just the same authority from the law."

The poor girl shuddered, struggling powerfully to suppress the sigh, which arose, in spite of her efforts, as if from the very bottom of her heart.

Thoroughly satisfied that he understood the character of the emigrants by the short but comprehensive description conveyed in Paul's reply, the old man, raised no further question concerning the readiness of Ishmael to revenge his wrongs, but rather, followed the train of thought which was suggested to his experience, by the occasion.

"Each one knows the ties which bind him to his fellow creatur's best," he answered. "Though it is greatly to be mourned, that colour, and property, and tongue, and l'arning, should make so wide a difference in those who, after all, are but the children of one Father! Howsomever," he continued, by a transition, not a little characteristic of the pursuits and feelings of the man, "as this is a business in which there is much more likelihood of a fight than need for a sermon, it is best to be prepared for what may follow. Hush. There is a movement below, it is an equal chance that we are seen."

"The family is stirring," cried Ellen with a tremor that announced nearly as much terror at the approach of her friends as she had before manifested at the presence of her enemies. "Go, Paul, leave me. *You*, at least must not be seen!"

"If I leave you, Ellen, in this desert before I see you safe, in the care of old Ishmael at least, may I never hear the hum of another bee, or what is worse fail in sight, to line him to his hive!"

"You forget, this good old man. He will not leave me. Though I am sure, Paul, we have parted before, where there has been more of a desert than this."

"Never. These Indians may come whooping back, and then where are you? Half way to the Rocky Mountains before a man can fairly strike the line of your flight. What think you, old trapper? How long may it be before these Tetons, as you call them, will be coming for the rest of old Ishmael's goods and chattels!"

"No fear of them," returned the old man laughing in his own peculiar and silent manner, "I warrant me, the devils will be scampering after their beasts, these six hours yet! Listen, you may hear them in the willow bottoms, at this very moment, ay, your real Sioux cattle will run like so many long-legged Elks. Hist, crouch again into the grass, down with ye both; as I'm a miserable piece of clay, I heard the ticking of a gun-lock!"

The trapper did not allow his companions time to hesitate, but dragging them both after him, he nearly buried his own person in the fog of the Prairie, while he was speaking. It was fortunate that the senses of the aged hunter remained so acute, and that he had lost none of his readiness of action. The three were scarcely bowed to the ground, when their ears were saluted with the well known, sharp, short, reports of the western rifle, and instantly, the whizzing of the ragged lead was heard, buzzing within dangerous proximity of their heads.

"Well done young chips! well done old block!" whispered Paul, whose spirits no danger or situation could entirely depress. "As pretty a volley, as one would wish to hear on the wrong end of a rifle! What d'ye say, trapper! here is likely to be a three-cornered war, shall I give 'em as good as they send?"

"Give them nothing but fair words," returned the other, hastily, "or you are both lost."

"I'm not certain it would much mend the matter, if I were to speak with my tongue, instead of the piece," said Paul, in a tone half jocular, half bitter.

"For the sake of Heaven, do not let them hear you!" cried Ellen. "Go, Paul, go, you can easily quit us now!"

Several shots in quick succession, each sending its dangerous messenger, still nearer than the preceding discharge, cut short her speech, no less in prudence than in terror.

"This must end," said the trapper rising with the dignity of one bent only on the importance of his object. "I know not what need, ye may have, children, to fear those you should both love and honour; but something must be done to save your lives. A few hours more or less, can never be missed from the time of one, who has, already numbered so many days, therefore I will advance. Here is a clear space around you. Profit by it, as you need, and may God bless and prosper each of you as ye deserve."

Without waiting for any reply, the trapper walked boldly down the declivity in his front, taking the direction of the encampment, neither quickening his pace in trepidation nor suffering it to be retarded by fear. The light of the moon fell brighter for a moment, on his tall, gaunt, form, and served to warn the emigrants of his approach. Indifferent however, to this unfavorable circumstance, he held his way, silently and steadily towards the copse, until a threatening voice met him with the challenge of—

"Who comes. Friend or Foe?"

"Friend," was the reply, "one who has liv'd too long, to disturb the close of life with quarrels."

"But not so long as to forget the tricks of his youth," said Ishmael, rearing his huge frame from beneath the slight covering of a low bush, and meeting the trapper face to face. "Old man, you have brought this tribe of red devils upon us, and to-morrow you will be sharing the booty."

"What have you lost?" calmly demanded the trapper.

"Eight as good mares, as ever travelled in gears, besides a foal, that is worth thirty of the brightest Mexicans that bear the face of the King of Spain. Then the woman has not a cloven hoof for her dairy, or her loom, and I believe even the grunters, foot sore as they be, are ploughing the Prairie. And now, stranger," he added dropping the butt of his rifle on the hard earth with a violence and clatter that would have intimidated one less firm than the man he addressed. "how many of these creatures may fall to your lot?"

"Horses have I never craved, nor even used, though few have journeyed over more of the wide lands of America than myself, old and feeble as I seem. But little use is there for a horse among the hills and woods of York; that is as York was, but as I greatly fear York is no longer. As for woolen covering and cow's milk, I covet no such womanly fashions! The beasts of the field give me food and raiment. No, I crave no cloth better than the skin of a deer, nor any meat richer than his flesh."

The sincere manner of the trapper, as he uttered this simple vindication, was not entirely thrown away on the emigrant, whose dull nature was gradually quickening into a flame, that might speedily have burst forth, with dangerous violence. He listened like one who doubted, though not entirely convinced, and he muttered between his teeth, the denunciation, with which, a moment before, he intended to precede the summary vengeance he had certainly meditated.

"This is brave talking," he at length grumbled; "but to my judgement, too lawyer like for a straight forward, fair weather, and foul weather, hunter."

"I claim to be no better than a trapper," the other meekly answered.

"Hunter or trapper—There is little difference. I have come, old man, into these districts because I found the law sitting too tight upon me, and am not over fond of neighbors who cant settle a dispute without troubling a justice and twelve men; but I didn't come to be robbed of my plunder and then to say thank'ee to the man who did it!"

"He who ventures far into the Prairies, must abide by the ways of its owners."

"Owners!" echoed the squatter, "I am as rightful an owner of the land I stand on, as any governor in the States! Can you tell me, stranger, where the law or the reason, is to found, which says that one man shall have a section, or a town, or perhaps a county,* to his use, and another have to beg for 'arth to make his grave in. This is not natur and I deny that it is law. That is, your legal law."

"I cannot say that you are wrong," returned the trapper, whose opinions on this important topic, though drawn from very different premises were in singular accordance, with those of his companion, "and I have often thought and said as much, when and where I have believed my voice could be heard. But your beasts are stolen by them who claim to be masters of all they find in these deserts."

"They had better not dispute that matter with a man who knows better," said the other, in a portentous voice, though it seem'd deep and sluggish as he who spoke; "I call myself a fair trader, and one who gives to his chaps as good as he receives. You saw the Indians?"

"I did. They held me a prisoner, while they stole into your camp."

"It would have been more like a white-man and a christian to have let me known as much, in better season," retorted Ishmael, casting another ominous sidelong glance at the trapper, as if still meditating evil. "I am not much given to call every man, I fall in with, cousin, but colour should be something, when christians meet in such a place as this. But what is done, is done, and cannot be mended by words. Come out of your ambush, boys; here is no one but the old man: he has eaten of my bread, and should be our friend, though there is such good reason to suspect him of harboring with our enemies."

The trapper made no reply to the harsh suspicion which the other did not scruple to utter without the smallest delicacy, notwithstanding the explanations and denials to which he had just listened. The summons of the unnurtured squatter brought an immediate accession to their party. Four or five of his sons, made their appearance from beneath as many covers, where they had been posted under the impression that the figures they had seen on the swell of the Prairies, were a part of the Sioux band. As each man approached, and dropped his rifle into the hollow of his arm, he cast an indolent but inquiring glance at the stranger, though none of them expressed the least curiosity to know whence he had come or why he was there. This forebearance, however, proceeded only in part from the sluggishness of their common temper, for long and frequent experience in scenes of a similar character, had taught them the virtue of discretion. The trapper endured their sullen scrutiny with the steadiness of one as practised as themselves, and with the entire composure of innocence. Content with the momentary examination he had made, the eldest of the groupe, who was in truth the delinquent sentinel, by whose remissness the wily Mahtoree had so well profited, turned towards his father, and said bluntly—

"If this man is all that is left of the party I saw on the upland, yonder, we haven't altogether thrown away our ammunition."

"Asa, you are right," said the Father, turning suddenly on the trapper, a lost idea being recalled by the hint of his son. "How is it, stranger, there were three of you, just now, or there is no virtue in moonlight!"

"If you had seen the Tetons racing across the Prairies, like so many black-looking evil ones, on the heels of your cattle, my friend, it would have been an easy matter to have fancied them a thousand."

"Ay! for a town bred boy, or a skeary woman; though, for that matter, there is old Esther, she has no more fear of a red skin than of a crawling cub or of a wolf pup. I'll warrant ye, had your thievish devils made their push, by the light of the sun, the good woman would have been smartly at work among them, and the Siouxes would have found she was not given to part with her cheese and her butter without a price. But there'll come a time, stranger, right soon, when justice will have its dues, and that, too, without the help of what is called the law. We ar' of a slow breed, it may be said, and it is often said, of us, but slow is sure, and there ar' few men living who can say they ever struck a blow that they did not get one as hard in return from Ishmael Bush."

"Then has Ishmael Bush followed the instinct of the beasts, rather than the principle which ought to belong to his kind," returned the stubborn trapper. "I have struck many a blow, myself, but never have I felt the same ease of mind, that of right belongs to a man who follows his reason, after slaying, even, a fa'an when there was no call for his meat or hide, as I have felt at leaving a Mingo*unburied in the woods, when following the trade of open and honest warfare."

"What, you have been a soldier, have you, trapper! I made a forage or two among the Cherokees when I was a lad myself; and I followed Mad Anthony[1] one season, through the beeches, but there was, altogether, too much tatooing and regulating among his troops for me, so I left him, without calling on the Paymaster to settle my arrearages. Though as Esther afterward boasted, she had made such use of the pay-ticket, that the States gained no great sum, by the oversight. You have heard of such a man as Mad Anthony, if you tarried long among the soldiers?"

"I fout my last battle, as I hope, under his orders," returned the trapper, a gleam of sunshine shooting from his dim eyes, as if the event was recollected with pleasure, and then a sudden shade of sorrow succeeding, as though he felt a secret admonition against dwelling on the violent scenes in which he had so often been an actor. "I was passing from the states on the sea shore, into these far regions, when I cross'd the trail of his army and I fell in, on his rear, just as a looker-on, but when they got to blows, the crack of my rifle was heard among the

---

[1] Anthony Wayne, a Pennsylvanian distinguished in the war of the revolution, and subsequently against the Indians of the west, for his daring as a general, by which he gained from his followers the title of Mad Anthony. General Wayne was the son of the person mentioned in the life of West as commanding the regiment which excited his military ardor. [1832]

rest, though to my shame it may be said I never knew the right of the quarrel as well as a man of three score and ten, should know the reason of his acts afore he takes mortal life, which is a gift he never can return!"

"Come, stranger," said the Emigrant, his rugged nature a good deal softened when he found that they had fought on the same side in the wild warfare of the West. "It is of small account, what may be the ground-work of the disturbance, when it's a Christian ag'in a savage. We shall hear more of this horse-stealing to-morrow; to-night we can do no wiser or safer thing than to sleep."

So saying Ishmael deliberately led the way back towards his rifled encampment, and ushered the man, whose life a few minutes before had been in real jeopardy from his resentment, into the presence of his family. Here, with a very few words of explanation, mingled with scarce but ominous denunciations against the plunderers, he made his wife acquainted with the state of things on the Prairies, and announced his own determination to compensate himself for his broken rest, by devoting the remainder of the night to sleep.

The trapper gave his ready assent to the measure and adjusted his gaunt form on the pile of brush that was offered him, with as much composure as a Sovereign could resign himself to sleep, in the security of his Capital and surrounded by his armed protectors. The old man did not close his eyes, however, until he had assured himself, that Ellen Wade was among the females of the family, and that her relative, or lover, whichever he might be, had observed the caution of keeping himself out of view. After which he slept though with the peculiar watchfulness of one long accustomed to vigilance even in the hours of deepest night.

CHAPTER VI.

"He is too picked, too spruce, too affected, too odd,
As it were too peregrinate, as I may call it."

Love's Labours Lost, V.i. 14-16

THE Anglo-American is apt to boast, and not without reason, that his nation may claim a descent more truly honorable than that of any other people whose history is to be credited. Whatever might have been the weaknesses of the original colonists, their virtues have rarely been disputed. If they were superstitious, they were sincerely pious, and, consequently, honest. The descendants of these simple and single minded provincials have been content to reject the ordinary and artificial means by which honors have been perpetuated in families, and have substituted a standard which brings the individual himself to the ordeal of the public estimation, paying as little deference as may be to those who have gone before him. This forbearance, self denial, or common sense, or by whatever term it may be thought proper to distinguish the measure, has subjected the nation to the imputation of having an ignoble origin. Were it worth the inquiry, it would be found that more than a just proportion of the renowned names of the mother country are, at this hour, to be found in her ci-devant colonies, and it is a fact well known to the few who have wasted sufficient time to become the masters of so unimportant a subject, that the direct descendants of many a failing line, which the policy of England has seen fit to sustain by collateral supporters, are now discharging the simple duties of citizens in the bosom of this republic. The hive has remained stationary, and they who flutter around the venerable straw are wont to claim the empty distinction of antiquity, regardless alike of the frailty of their tenement and of the enjoyments of the numerous and vigorous swarms that are culling the fresher sweets of a virgin world. But as this is a subject which belongs rather to the politician and historian than to the humble narrator of the home-bred incidents we are about to reveal, we must confine our reflexions to such matters as have an immediate relation to the subject of the tale.

Although the citizen of the United States may claim so just an ancestry, he is far from being exempt from the penalties of his fallen race.

Like causes are well known to produce like effects. That tribute, which it would seem nations must ever pay, by way of a weary probation, around the shrine of Ceres before they can be indulged in her fullest favors, is in some measure exacted in America, from the descendant instead of the ancestor. The march of civilization with us, has a strong analogy to that of all coming events, which are known "to cast their shadows before." The gradations of society, from that state which is called refined to that which approaches as near barbarity as connexion with an intelligent people will readily allow, are to be traced from the bosom of the states, where wealth, luxury and the arts are beginning to seat themselves, to those distant, and ever-receding borders which mark the skirts, and announce the approach, of the nation, as moving mists precede the signs of day.

Here, and here only, is to be found that widely spread, though far from numerous class, which may be at all likened to those who have paved the way for the intellectual progress of nations, in the old world. The resemblance between the American borderer and his European prototype is singular, though not always uniform. Both might be called without restraint; the one being above, the other beyond the reach of the law—brave, because they were inured to dangers—proud, because they were independant, and vindictive, because each was the avenger of his own wrongs. It would be unjust to the borderer to pursue the parallel much farther. He is irreligious, because he has inherited the knowledge that religion does not exist in forms, and his reason rejects a mockery. He is not a knight, because he has not the power to bestow distinctions; and he has not the power, because he is the offspring and not the parent of a system. In what manner these several qualities are exhibited, in some of the most strongly marked of the latter class, will be seen in the course of the ensuing narrative.

Ishmael Bush had passed the whole of a life of more than fifty years on the skirts of society. He boasted that he had never dwelt where he might not safely fell every tree he could view from his own threshold; that the law had rarely been known to enter his clearing, and that his ears had never willingly admitted the sound of a church bell. His exertions seldom exceeded his wants, which were peculiar to his class, and rarely failed of being supplied. He had no respect for any learning except that of the leech; because he was ignorant of the application of any other intelligence, than such as met the senses. His deference to this particular branch of science had induced him to listen to the application of a medical man, whose thirst for natural

history had led him to the desire of profiting by the migratory pro-
pensities of the squatter. This gentleman he had cordially received
into his family, or rather under his protection, and they had journeyed together, thus far through the Prairies, in perfect harmony:
Ishmael often felicitating his wife on the possession of a companion,
who would be so serviceable in their new abode, wherever it might
chance to be, until the family were thoroughly "acclimated." The
pursuits of the naturalist frequently led him, however, for days at a
time, from the direct line of the route of the squatter, who rarely
seemed to have any other guide than the sun. Most men would have
deem'd themselves fortunate to have been absent on the perilous occasion of the Sioux inroad, as was Obed Bat, (or as he was fond of hearing
himself called, Battius) M.D. and fellow of several cis-atlantic learned
societies—the adventurous gentleman in question.

Although the sluggish nature of Ishmael was not actually awakened,
it was sorely pricked by the liberties which had just been taken with
his property. He slept, however, for it was the hour he had allotted to
that refreshment, and because he knew how impotent any exertions
to recover his effects must prove in the darkness of mid-night. He
also knew the danger of his present situation too well, to hazard what
was left, in pursuit of that which was lost. Much as the inhabitants of
the Prairies were known to love horses, their attachment to many
other articles, still in the possession of the travellers, was equally well
understood. It was a common artifice to scatter the herds, and to profit
by the confusion. But, Mahtoree had, it would seem in this particular,
undervalued the acuteness of the man he had assailed. The phlegm
with which the squatter learned his loss, has already been seen, and it
now remains to exhibit the results of his more matured determinations.

Though the encampment contained many an eye that was long
unclosed, and many an ear that listened greedily to catch the faintest
evidence of any new alarm, it lay in deep quiet, during the remainder
of the night. Silence and fatigue finally performed their accustomed
offices, and before the morning, all but the sentinels were again buried
in sleep. How well these indolent watchers discharged their duties
after the assault, has never been known, inasmuch as nothing occured
to confirm or to disprove their subsequent vigilance.

Just as day, however, began to dawn, and a gray light was falling
from the heavens on the dusky objects of the plain, the half-startled,
anxious, and yet blooming countenance of Ellen Wade was reared
above the confused mass of children, among whom she had clus-

tered, on her stolen return to the camp. Arising warily, she stepp'd lightly across the recumbent bodies, and proceeded, with the same caution to the utmost limits of the defences of Ishmael. Here, she listened, as if doubting the propriety of venturing further. The pause was only momentary, however, and long before the drowsy eyes of the sentinel, who overlooked the spot where she stood, had time to catch a glimpse of her active form, it had glided along the bottom, and stood on the summit of the nearest eminence.

Ellen now listened, intently anxious to catch some other sound, than the breathing of the morning air, which faintly rustled the herbage at her feet. She was about to turn, in disappointment, from the inquiry, when the tread of human feet, making their way, through the matted grass, met her ear. Springing eagerly forward, she soon beheld the outlines of a figure advancing up the eminence, on the side opposite to the camp. She had already uttered the name of Paul, and was beginning to speak in the hurried and eager voice with which female affection is apt to greet a friend, when drawing back, the disappointed girl, clos'd her salutations, by coldly adding—

"I did not expect, Doctor, to meet you, at this unusual hour."

"All hours, and all seasons are alike, my good Ellen, to the genuine lover of nature," returned a small, slightly made, but exceedingly active man dressed in an odd mixture of cloth and skins, a little past the middle age, and who advanced directly to her side, with the familiarity of an old acquaintance, "and he who does not know how to find things to admire by this gray light, is ignorant of a large portion of the blessings he enjoys."

"Very true," said Ellen, suddenly recollecting the necessity of accounting for her own appearance abroad, at that unseasonable hour, "I know many who think the earth has a pleasanter look, in the night, than when seen by the brightest sunshine."

"Ah! Their organs of sight must be too convex! But the man who wishes to study the active habits of the feline race or the variety, Albinos, must indeed be stirring at this hour. I dare say there are men, who prefer even looking at objects by twilight, for the simple reason, that they see better at that time of the day."

"And is this the cause why you are so much abroad, in the night?"

"I am abroad at night, my good girl, because the earth in its diurnal revolutions, leaves the light of the sun, but half the time on any given meridian, and because what I have to do, cannot be performed in twelve or fifteen consecutive hours. Now have I been off, two days from the family, in search of a plant, that is known to exist on the tributaries of La Platte, without seeing even a blade of grass that is not already enumerated and classed."

"You have been unfortunate, Doctor, but—"

"Unfortunate!" echoed the little man sideling nigher to his companion and producing his tabletts with an air, in which exultation struggled strangely with an affectation of self abasement. "No, no, Ellen, I am any thing but unfortunate. Unless indeed, a man may be so called, whose fortune is made—whose fame may be said to be established forever—whose name will go down to posterity with that of Buffon*—Buffon! a mere compiler! one who flourishes on the foundation of other men's labours—no, pari passu, with Solander*who bought his knowledge, with pain and privations!"

"Have you discovered a mine, Doctor Bat?"

"More than a mine; a treasure, coined, and fit for instant use, girl. Listen! I was making the angle, necessary to intersect the line of your uncle's march, after my fruitless search, when I heard sounds like the explosion produced by fire arms."

"Yes," exclaimed Ellen eagerly. "We had an alarm—"

"And thought I was lost," continued the man of science too much bent on his own ideas, to understand her interruption. "Little danger of that! I made my own base, knew the length of the perpendicular by calculation, and to draw the hypothenuse had nothing to do, but to work my angle. I supposed the guns were fired for my benefit, and changed my course for the sounds; not that I think the senses more accurate, or even as accurate as a mathematical calculation, but I feared, that some of the children might need my services."

"They are all happily—"

"Listen;" interrupted the other, already forgetting his affected anxiety for his patients, in the greater importance of the present subject. "I had crossed a large tract of Prairie, for sound is conveyed far, where there is little obstruction, when I heard the trampling of feet, as if Bisons, were beating the earth. Then I caught a distant view of a herd of quadrupeds, rushing up and down the swells, animals, which would have still remained unknown and undescribed, had it not been for a most felicitous accident. One, and he a noble specimen of the whole! was running a little apart from the rest. The herd made an inclination in my direction, in which the solitary animal coincided and this brought him, within fifty yards of the spot where I stood. I profited by the opportunity, and by the aid of steel and taper, I wrote his description on the spot. I would have given a thousand dollars, Ellen, for a single shot from the rifle of one of the boys."

"You carry a pistol, Doctor, why didn't you use it?" said the half inattentive girl, anxiously examining the Prairie, but still lingering where she stood, quite willing to be detained.

"Ay, but it carries nothing but the most minute particles of lead, adapted to the destruction of the larger insects and reptiles. No. I did better than to attempt waging a war, in which I could not be the victor. I recorded the event, noting each particular, with the precision necessary to science. You shall hear, Ellen, for you are a good and improving girl, and by retaining what you learn in this way, may yet be of great service to learning, should any accident occur to me. Indeed, my worthy Ellen, mine is a pursuit, which has its dangers as well as that of the warrior. This very night," he continued, glancing his eye behind him, "this awful night has the principle of life, itself, been in great danger of extinction!"

"By what?"

"By the monster I have discovered. It approached me, often, and ever as I receded it continued to advance. I believe nothing but the little lamp I carried was my protector. I kept it between us whilst I wrote, making it serve the double purpose of luminary and shield. But you shall hear the character of the beast, and you may then, judge of the risks we promoters of science run in behalf of mankind."

The naturalist raised his tabletts to the heavens and disposed himself to read as well as he could, by the dim light, they yet shed upon the plain, premising with saying—

"Listen, girl, and you shall hear, with what a treasure it has been my happy lot to enrich the pages of Natural History."

"Is it then a creature of your forming," said Ellen, turning away from her fruitless examination, with a sudden lighting of her sprightly blue eyes, that shewed she knew how to play with the foible of her learned companion.

"Is the power to give life to inanimate matter the gift of man; I would it were! You should speedily see a Historia Naturalis, Americana, that would put the sneering imitators of the Frenchman de Buffon to shame! A great improvement might be made in the formation of all quadrupeds; especially those in which velocity is a virtue. Two of the inferior limbs should be on the principle of the lever— wheels, perhaps as they are now formed, though I have not yet determined whether the improvement might be better applied to the anterior or posterior members, inasmuch as I am yet to learn whether dragging or shoving requires the greatest muscular exertion. A natural exudation of the animal, might assist in overcoming the friction, and a powerful momentum be obtained. But all this is hopeless; at least for the present," he added, raising his tabletts, again to the light and reading aloud. "Oct. 6, 1805,* that's merely the date which I dare say you know better than I, mem. *Quadruped;* seen by star-light, and by the aid of a pocket lamp, in the Prairies of North America, see journal for Latitude and Meridian. *Genus,* unknown, therefore named after the Discoverer, and from the happy coincidence of having been seen in the evening — *Vespertilio; Horribilis, Americanus. Dimensions* (by estimation). *Greatest length* eleven feet, *height,* six feet. *Head,* erect, *nostrils,* expansive, *eyes,* expressive and fierce, *teeth,* serrated and abundant. *Tail,* horizontal, waving, and slightly feline. *Feet,* large and hairy. *Talons,* long, arquated, dangerous. *Ears,* inconspicuous. *Horns,* elongated, diverging and formidable, *colour,* plumbeous-ashy, with fiery spots. *Voice,* sonorous, martial and appalling. *Habits,* gregarious, carnivorous, fierce, and fearless. There," exclaimed Obed, when he had ended this sententious but comprehensive description, "there is an animal, which will be likely to dispute with the Lion, his title to be called the King of the Beasts!"

"I know not the meaning of all you have said, Doctor Battius," returned the quick witted girl, who understood the weakness of the Philosopher, and often indulged him with a title he loved so well to hear, "but I shall think it dangerous to venture far from the camp, if such monsters are prowling over the Prairies."

"You may well call it prowling," returned the Naturalist nestling still closer to her side, and dropping his voice to such low, and undignified tones, of confidence, as conveyed a meaning, still more pointed than he had intended. "I have never before experienced such a trial of the nervous system; there was a moment I acknowledge when the *fortiter in re* faltered before so terrible an enemy; but the love of Natural Science, bore me up, and brought me off in triumph!"

"You speak a language so different from that we use in Tennessee," said Ellen, struggling to conceal her laughter, "that I hardly know, whether I understand your meaning. If I am right, you wish to say you were chicken-hearted."

"An absurd simile, drawn from an ignorance of the formation of the biped. The heart of a chicken, bears a just proportion to its other organs, and the domestic fowl is, in a state of nature, a gallant bird. Ellen," he added with a countenance so solemn as to produce an impression on the attentive girl, "I was pursued—hunted—and in a danger that I scorn to dwell on—what's that."

Ellen started, for the earnestness and simple sincerity of her companion's manner had produced a certain degree of credulity, even on her buoyant mind. Looking in the direction indicated by the Doctor, she beheld, in fact, a beast coursing over the Prairie, and making a straight and rapid approach to the spot they occupied. The day was not yet sufficiently advanced, to enable her to distinguish its form and character, though enough was discernible to induce her to imagine it a fierce and savage animal.

"It comes! it comes!" exclaimed the Doctor, fumbling, by a sort of instinct for his tablets, while he fairly tottered on his feet, under the powerful efforts he made to maintain his ground. "Now Ellen, has fortune given me an opportunity to correct the errors made by star-light, hold, ashey plumbeous, no ears. Horns, excessive—"

His voice, and hand, were both arrested, by a roar, or rather a shriek from the beast, that was sufficiently terrific to appal even a stouter heart, than that of the Naturalist. The cries of the animal passed over the Prairie in strange cadences, and then succeeded a deep and solemn silence, that was only broken by an uncontrolled fit of merriment from the more musical voice of Ellen Wade. In the mean time, the Naturalist stood like a statue of amazement, permitting a well grown Ass, against whose approach he no longer offered his boasted shield of light, to smell about his person, without comment or hindrance.

"It is your own ass!" cried Ellen, the instant she found breath for words, "your own patient, hard-working hack!"

The Doctor roll'd his eyes from the beast to the speaker, and from the speaker to the beast, but gave no audible expression of his wonder.

"Do you refuse to know an animal that has laboured so long in your service!" continued the laughing girl. "A beast, that I have heard you say a thousand times, has served you well, and whom you loved like a brother!"

"Asinus Domesticus!" ejaculated the Doctor, drawing his breath like one who had been near suffocation. "There is no doubt of the genus; and I will always maintain that the animal is not of the species, equus. This is undeniably Asinus himself, Ellen Wade; but this is not the Vespertilio Horribilis of the Prairies! Very different animals, I can assure you, young woman, and differently characterised in every important particular. That, carnivorous," he continued glancing his eye at the open page of his tablets; "this, granivorous; *habits,* fierce, dangerous; *habits,* patient, abstemious; *ears,* inconspicuous; *ears,* elongated; *horns,* diverging, etc. *horns,* none!"

He was interrupted by another burst of merriment from Ellen, which served, in some measure, to recall him to his recollection.

"The image of the Vespertilio was on the retina," the astounded enquirer into the secrets of nature observed, in a manner that seemed a little apologetic, "and I was silly enough to mistake my own faithful beast for the monster? Though even now I greatly marvel to see this animal running at large!"

Ellen then proceeded to explain, the history of the attack and its results. She described, with an accuracy that might have raised suspicions of her own movements in the mind of one less simple than her auditor, the manner in which the beasts burst out of the encampment and the headlong speed with which they had dispersed themselves over the open plain. Although she forbore to say as much in terms, she so managed as to present before the eyes of her listener the strong probability of his having mistaken the frightened drove for savage beasts, and then terminated her account by a lamentation for their loss, and some very natural remarks on the helpless condition in which it had left the family. The naturalist listened in silent wonder, neither interrupting her narrative nor suffering a single exclamation of surprise to escape him. The keen-eyed girl, however, saw that as she proceeded the important leaf was torn from the tablets, in a manner which shewed that their owner had got rid of his delusion at the same instant. From that moment the world has heard no more of the Vespertilio Horribilis Americanus, and the natural sciences have irretrieveably lost an important link in that great animated chain which is said to connect earth and heaven, and in which man is thought to be so familiarly complicated with the monkey.

When Dr. Batt was put in full possession of all the circumstances of the inroad, his concern immediately took a different direction. He had left sundry folios, and certain boxes well stored with botanical specimens and defunct animals, under the good keeping of Ishmael, and it immediately struck his acute mind, that marauders as subtle as the Siouxes would never neglect the opportunity to despoil him of these treasures. Nothing that Ellen could say to the contrary served to appease his apprehensions, and, consequently, they separated; he to relieve his doubts and fears together, and she to glide, as swiftly and silently as she had just before passed it, into the still and solitary tent.

CHAPTER VII.

"What, fifty of my followers, at a clap!"

King Lear, I.iv. 316.

THE day had now fairly opened on the seemingly, interminable waste of the Prairie. The entrance of Obed, at such a moment into the camp, accompanied, as it was, by vociferous lamentations over his anticipated loss, did not fail to rouse the drowsy family of the squatter. Ishmael and his sons, together with the forbidding looking brother of his wife, were all, speedily afoot; and then, as the sun began to shed his light on the place, they became gradually apprised of the extent of their loss.

Ishmael look'd round upon the motionless and heavily loaded vehicles, with his teeth firmly compressed, cast a glance at the amazed and helpless groupe of children which clustered around their sullen but desponding, mother, and walked out upon the open land, as if he found the air of the encampment, too confined. He was followed by several of the men, who were attentive observers, watching the dark expression of his eye, as the index of their own future movements. The whole proceeded in profound and moody silence to the summit of the nearest swell, whence they could command an almost boundless view of the naked plains. Here, nothing was visible, but a solitary buffaloe, that gleaned a meagre subsistence from the decaying herbage, at no great distance, and the Ass of the Physician, who profited by his freedom to enjoy a meal richer than common.

"Yonder is one of the creatures left by the villains to mock us!" said Ishmael, glancing his eye towards the latter, "and that the meanest of the stock. This is a hard country to make a crop in, boys; and yet food must be found to fill many hungry mouths!"

"The rifle, is better than the hoe in such a place as this," returned the eldest of his sons, kicking the hard and thirsty soil on which he stood, with an air of contempt. "It is good for such as they, who make their dinner better on beggar's beans, than on homminy. A crow would shed tears, if obliged by its errand to fly across this district!"

"What say you, trapper," resumed the Father, showing the slight impression his powerful heel, had made on the compact earth, and laughing with frightful ferocity. "Is this the quality of land a man would choose, who never troubles the County Clerk with Title deeds!"

"There is richer soil in the bottoms," returned the old man, calmly, "and you have passed millions of acres, to get to this dreary spot, where he who loves to till the 'arth might have received bushels in return for pints, and that too at the cost of no very grievous labour. If you have come in search of land, you have journeyed hundreds of miles too far, or as many leagues too little."

"There is, then, a better choice, towards the other Ocean?" demanded the squatter pointing in the direction of the Pacific.

"There is; and I have seen it all," was the answer of the other, who dropped his rifle to the earth, and stood leaning on its barrel like one who recalled the scenes he had witnessed, with melancholy pleasure. "I have seen the waters of the two seas. On one of them, was I born, and raised to be a lad, like yonder tumbling boy. America has grown, my man, since the days of my youth, to be a country larger than I once had thought the world itself to be. Near seventy years, I dwelt in York, Province and State, together. You've been in York, 'tis like?"

"Not I—not I, I never visited the towns; but often have heard the place you speak of named. 'Tis a wide clearing, there, I reckon!"

"Too wide! Too wide! They scourge the very 'arth with their axes. Such hills and hunting grounds as I have seen stripped of the gifts of the Lord; without remorse or shame! I tarried till the mouths of my hounds were deafened by the blows of the choppers, and then I came west, in search of quiet. It was a grievous journey, that I made; a grievous toil to pass through falling timber, and to breathe the thick air of smoky clearings week after week, as I did. 'Tis a far country too, that State of York, from this!"

"It lies ag'in the outer edge of old Kentuck I reckon; though what the distance may be, I never knew."

"A gull, would have to fan a thousand miles of air, to find the Eastern Sea. And yet it is no mighty reach to hunt across, when shade and game are plenty! The time has been, when I followed the deer in the mountains of the Delaware and Hudson, and took the beaver on the streams of the Upper Lakes in the same season; but my eye was quick and certain at that day, and my limbs were like the legs of a moose. The dam of Hector," dropping his look kindly to the aged hound that crouch'd at his feet, "was then a pup, and apt to open on the game, the moment she struck the scent. She gave me a deal of trouble, that slut; she did!"

"Your hound is old, stranger, and a rap on the head would prove a mercy to the beast."

"The dog is like his master," returned the trapper without appearing to heed the brutal advice the other gave, "and will number his days when his work amongst the game is over, and not before. To my eye, things seem ordered to meet each other, in this creation. Tis not the swiftest running deer that always throws off the hounds, nor the biggest arm that holds the truest rifle. Look around you, men; what will the Yankee choppers say, when they have cut their path from the eastern to the western waters, and find that a hand, which can lay the 'arth bare at a blow, has been here, and swept the country, in very mockery of their wickedness. They will turn on their tracks, like a fox that doubles, and then the rank smell of their own footsteps, will show them the madness of their waste. Howsom'ever, these are thoughts that are more likely to rise in him who has seen the folly of Eighty seasons, than to teach wisdom to men, still bent on the pleasures of their kind! You have need yet of a stirring time, if you think to escape the craft and hatred of the burnt-wood Indians. They claim to be the lawful owners of this Country, and seldom leave a white, more than the skin he boasts of, when once they get the power, as they always have the will, to do him harm."

"Old man," said Ishmael, sternly, "to which people do you belong? You have the colour and speech of a Christian, while it seems that your heart is with the red-skins."

"To me there is little difference in Nations. The people I lov'd most, are scattered as the sands of the dry river-beds fly before the Fall hurricanes, and life is too short, to make use and custom, with strangers, as one can do with such as he has dwelt amongst for years. Still am I a man, without the cross of Indian blood; and what is due from a warrior to his Nation, is owing by me to the people of the States; though little need, have they, with their militia and their armed boats, of help from a single arm of fourscore."

"Since you own your kin, I may ask a simple question. Where are the Siouxes who have stolen my cattle?"

"Where is the herd of Buffaloe, which was chased by the Panther across this plain, no later, than the morning of yesterday. It is as hard—"

"Friend," said Dr. Battius, who had hitherto been an attentive listener, but who, now, felt a sudden impulse to mingle in the discourse, "I am grieved when I find a venator or hunter of your experience and observation, following the current of vulgar error. The animal you describe, is in truth a species of the bos ferus or bos sylvestris, as he has been happily called by the poets, but, though of close affinity it is altogether distinct, from the common Bubulus. Bison is the better word, and I would suggest the necessity of adopting it in future, when you shall have occasion to allude to the species."

"Bison or Buffaloe, it makes but little matter. The creatur' is the same, call it by what name you will, and—"

"Pardon me, venerable venator; as classification is the very soul of the Natural Sciences, the animal or vegetable, must, of necessity, be characterised by the peculiarities of its species, which is always indicated by the name."

"Friend," said the trapper, a little positively, "would the tail of a beaver make the worse dinner, for calling it a mink? or could you eat of the wolf, with relish, because some bookish man, had given it the name of venison?"

As these questions were put with no little earnestness and some spirit, there was every probability that a hot discussion would have succeeded between two men, of whom one was so purely practical and the other so much given to theory, had not Ishamel, seen fit to terminate the dispute by bringing into view a subject that was much more important to his own immediate interests.

"Beavers' tails, and minks-flesh may do to talk about, before a maple fire and a quiet hearth," interrupted the squatter, without the smallest deference to the interested feelings of the disputants, "but, something more than foreign words, or words of any sort, is now needed. Tell me, trapper; where are your Siouxes, skulking?"

"It would be as easy to tell you the colours of the hawk, that is floating beneath yonder white cloud! When a red-skin strikes his blow, he is not apt to wait, until he is paid for the evil deed, in lead."

"Will the beggarly savages believe they have enough, when they find themselves master of all the stock?"

"Natur is much the same, let it be covered by what skin it may. Do you ever find your longings after riches less when you have made a good crop than before you were master of a kernel of corn. If you do, you differ from what the experience of a long life, tells me is the common cravings of man."

"Speak plainly, old stranger," said the squatter, striking the butt of his rifle heavily on the earth, his dull capacity finding no pleasure in a discourse that was conducted in so obscure allusions, "I have asked a simple question, and one I know well that you can answer."

"You are right, you are right, I can answer; for I have too often seen the disposition of my kind, to mistake it, when evil is stirring. When the Siouxes have gathered in the beasts, and have made sure that you are not upon their heels, they will be back nibbling like hungry wolves to take the bait they have left. Or it may be they'll show the temper of the Great Bears that are found at the falls of the Long River, and strike at once with the paw, without stopping to nose their prey."

"You have then, seen, the animals you mention!" exclaimed Dr. Battius, who had now been thrown out of the conversation quite as long as his impatience could well brook, and who approached the subject, with his tabletts ready opened, as a book of reference. "Can you tell me if what you encountered was of the species, Ursus Horribilis, with the *ears* rounded, *front,* arquated, *eyes,* destitute of the remarkable supplemental lid, with six insicores—one false, and four perfect molares—"

"Trapper, go on, for we are engaged in reasonable discourse," interrupted Ishmael; "you believe we shall see more of these robbers."

"Nay, nay, I do not call them robbers, for it is the usage of their people, and what may be called the Prairie law."

"I have come five hundred miles to find a place, where no man can ding the words of the Law, in my ears," said Ishmael, fiercely, "and I am not in a humour to stand quietly at a bar, while a red-skin sits in judgement. I tell you, trapper, if another Sioux is seen prowling around my camp, wherever it may be, he shall feel the contents of old Kentuck," slapping his rifle in a manner that could not be easily misconstrued, "though he wore the medal of Washington[1] himself. I call the man a robber who takes that which is not his own."

"The Teton and the Pawnee and the Konza, and men of a dozen other tribes claim to own these naked fields."

"Natur gives them the lie, in their teeth. The air, the water and the ground are free gifts to man, and no one has the power to portion them out in parcels. Man must drink, and breathe and walk, and therefore each has a right to his share of 'arth. Why do not the Surveyors of the States, set their compasses and run their lines over our heads, as well as beneath our feet? Why do they not, cover their shining sheep skins with big words, giving to this land-holder, or perhaps he should be called air-holder, so many rods of heaven, with the use of such a star for a boundary mark and such a cloud to turn a mill!"

[1] The American government creates chiefs among the western tribes, and decorates them with silver medals bearing the impression of the different Presidents. That of Washington is the most prized. [1832]

As the squatter uttered his wild conceit, he laughed from the very bottom of his chest, in scorn. The deriding but frightful merriment pass'd from the mouth of one of his ponderous sons to that of the other, until it had made the circuit of the whole family.

"Come, trapper," continued Ishmael in a tone of better humour, like a man who feels that he has triumphed, "neither of us, I reckon, has ever had much to do with title deeds or County Clerks, or blazed trees; therefore we will not waste words on fooleries. You ar' a man, that has tarried long in this clearing, and, now I ask your opinion, face to face, without fear or favor, if you had the lead in my business, what would you do."

The old man hesitated, and seem'd to give the required advice with deep reluctance. As every eye, however, was fastened on him, and whichever way he turned his face, he encountered a look rivetted on the lineaments of his own working countenance, he answered in a low, melancholy, tone.

"I have seen too much mortal blood, poured out in empty quarrels, to wish ever to hear an angry rifle, again. Ten weary years have I sojourned alone, on these naked plains, waiting for my hour, and not a blow have I struck ag'in an enemy more humanized than the grizzly bear."

"Ursus horribilis!" muttered the Doctor.

The speaker paused at the sound of the other's voice, but perceiving it was no more than a sort of mental ejaculation, he continued in the same strain—

"More humanized than the grizzly bear, or the Panther of the Rocky Mountains; unless the Beaver, which is a wise and knowing animal may be so reckoned. What would I advise! Even the female Buffaloe will fight for her young!"

"It never then shall be said, that Ishmael Bush, has less kindness for his children, than the bear for her cubs."

"And yet this is but a naked spot, for a dozen men to make head in, ag'in five hundred."

"Ay, it is so," returned the squatter glancing his eye towards his humble camp, "but something might be done, with the wagons and the cotton wood."

The trapper shook his head, incredulously, and pointed across the rolling plain in the direction of the west, as he answered.

"A rifle would send a bullet from these hills into your very sleeping-cabins; nay, arrows from the thicket in your rear would keep you, all, burrowed like so many Prairie dogs: it wouldn't do—it wouldn't do. Three long miles from this spot, is a place where, as I have often thought, in passing across this desert, a stand might be made, for days and weeks together, if there were hearts and hands ready to engage in the bloody work."

Another low, deriding laugh, passed among the young men, announcing in a manner sufficiently intelligible their readiness to undertake a task, even more arduous. The squatter himself, eagerly seized the hint, which had been so reluctantly extorted from the trapper, who by some singular process of reasoning had, evidently, persuaded himself that it was his duty to be strictly neutral. A few direct and pertinent inquiries, served to obtain the little additional information that was necessary, in order to make the contemplated movement, and then Ishmael, who was, on emergencies, as terrifically energetic, as he was sluggish in common, set about effecting his object without delay.

Notwithstanding the industry and zeal of all engaged, the task was one of great labor and difficulty. The loaded vehicles were to be drawn by hand across a wide distance of plain, without track, or guide of any sort, except that which the trapper furnished, by communicating his knowledge of the cardinal points of the compass. In accomplishing this object, the gigantic strength of the men was taxed to the utmost, nor were the females or the children spared a heavy proportion of the toil. While the sons distributed themselves about the heavily loaded wagons and drew them, by main strength up the neighboring swell, their mother and Ellen, surrounded by the amazed groupe of little ones, followed slowly in the rear, bending under the weight of such different articles, as were suited to their several strengths.

Ishmael, himself, superintended and directed the whole, occasionally applying his colossal shoulder to some lagging vehicle until he saw that the chief difficulty, that of gaining the level of their intended route, was accomplished. Then he pointed out the required course, cautioning his sons to proceed, in such a manner, that they should not lose the advantage they had with so much labour obtained, and beckoning to the brother of his wife, they returned, together, to the empty camp.

Throughout the whole of this movement, which occupied an hour of time, the trapper had stood apart, leaning on his rifle with the aged hound slumbering at his feet, a silent but attentive observer of all that passed. Occasionally, a smile, lighted his hard, muscular, but wasted features, like a gleam of sunshine, flitting across a ragged ruin, and betrayed the momentary pleasure he found, in witnessing from time to time the vast power the youths discovered. Then, as the train drew slowly up the ascent, a cloud of thought and sorrow threw all into the shade again, leaving the expression of his countenance, in its usual state of quiet melancholy. As vehicle, after vehicle left the place of the encampment, he noted the change, with increasing attention, seldom failing to cast an enquiring look at the little, neglected tent, which with its proper wagon, still remained, as before, solitary and apparently forgotten. The summons of Ishmael to his gloomy associate, had, however, as it would now seem, this, hitherto, neglected portion of his effects, for its object.

First casting a cautious and suspicious glance on every side of him, the squatter and his companion advanced to the little wagon, and caused it to enter within the folds of the cloth, much in the manner, that it had been extricated the preceding evening. They both then disappeared behind the drapery, and many moments of suspense succeeded, during which, the old man, secretly urged by a burning desire to know the meaning of so much mystery, insensibly drew nigh to the place, until he stood within a few yards of the proscribed spot. The agitation of the cloth, betrayed the nature of the occupation of those whom it concealed, though their work was conducted in rigid silence. It would appear that long practice had made each of the two, acquainted with his particular duty, for neither sign nor direction of any sort was necessary from Ishmael, in order to apprise his surly associate of the manner in which he was to proceed. In less time, than has been consumed in relating it, the interior portion of the arrangement was complete, when the men re-appeared without the tent. Too busy with his occupation to heed the presence of the trapper, Ishmael, began to release the folds of the cloth from the ground, and to dispose of them, in such a manner, around the vehicle, as to form a sweeping train to the new form the little pavillion had now assumed. The arch'd roof trembled with the occasional movement of the light vehicle, which, it was now apparent, once more supported its secret burthen. Just as the work was ended, the scowling eye of Ishmael's assistant caught a glimpse of the figure of the attentive observer of their movements. Dropping the shaft, which he had already lifted from the ground, preparatory to occupying the place, that was usually filled by an animal less reasoning, and perhaps less dangerous than himself, he bluntly exclaimed—

"I am a fool, as you often say! But look for yourself: if that man is not an enemy, I will disgrace father and mother, call myself an Indian, and go hunt with the Siouxes."

The cloud, as it is about to discharge the subtle lightning, is not more dark nor threatening, than the look with which Ishmael greeted the intruder. He turned his head on every side of him, as if seeking some engine sufficiently terrible to annihilate the offending trapper at a blow, and, then, possibly recollecting the further occasion he might have for his counsel, he forced himself, to say with an appearance of moderation that nearly choked him—

"Stranger, I did believe this prying into the concerns of others, was the business of women in the towns and settlements, and not the manner in which men, who are used to live where each has room for himself, deal with the secrets of their neighbors. To what lawyer or sheriff do you calculate to sell your news?"

"I hold but little discourse except with one; and, then, chiefly of my own affairs," returned the old man, without the least observable apprehension, and pointing imposingly upward, "a judge; and judge of all. Little does he need knowledge from my hands, and but little will your wish to keep any thing secret from him, profit you, even, in this desert."

The mounting tempers of his unnurtured listeners were rebuked by the simple, solemn, manner of the trapper. Ishmael stood, sullen and thoughtful; while his companion stole a furtive and involuntary glance at the placid sky which spread, so wide and blue above his head, as if he expected, to see, the Almighty eye, itself, beaming from the heavenly vault. But impressions of a serious character are seldom lasting on minds long indulged in forgetfulness. The hesitation of the squatter was consequently of short duration. The language, however, as well as the firm and collected air of the speaker, were the means of preventing much subsequent abuse if not violence.

"It would be shewing more of the kindness of a friend and comrade," Ishmael returned in a tone sufficiently sullen to betray his humour, though it was no longer threatening, "had your shoulder been put to the wheel of one of yonder wagons, instead of edging itself in here, where none are wanted, but such as are invited."

"I can put the little strength that is left me," returned the trapper, "to this as well as to another of your loads."

"Do you take us for boys!" exclaimed Ishmael, laughing half in ferocity and half in derision, applying his powerful strength at the same time, to the little vehicle, which rolled over the grass, with as much seeming facility, as if it were drawn by its usual team.

The trapper paused, and followed the departing wagon with his eye, marvelling greatly as to the nature of its concealed contents, until it had, also, gained the summit of the eminence, and, in its turn, disappeared behind the swell of the land. Then, he turned to gaze at the desolation of the scene around him. The absence of human forms would have scarce created a sensation in the bosom of one so long accustomed to solitude, had not the site of the deserted camp, furnished such strong memorials of its recent visiters, and, as the old man was quick to detect, of their waste also. He cast his eye upwards with a shake of the head, at the vacant spot in the heavens, which had so lately been filled by the branches of those trees, that now lay, stripped of their verdure, worthless and deserted logs at his feet.

"Ay!" he muttered to himself, "I might have know'd it! I might have know'd it! Often have I seen the same before, and yet I brought them to the spot myself,* and have now sent them to the only neighborhood of their kind, within many long leagues of the spot where I stand. This is man's wish, and pride, and waste, and sinfulness. He tames the beasts of the field, to feed his idle wants, and having robbed the brutes of their natural food, he teaches them to strip the 'arth of its trees, to quiet their hunger."

A rustling in the low bushes, which still grew, for some distance, along the swale that formed the thicket on which the camp of Ishmael had rested, caught his ear, at the moment, and cut short the soliloquy. The habits of so many years spent in the wilderness, caused the old man to bring his rifle to a poise with something like the activity and promptitude of his youth, but suddenly recovering his recollection, he dropped it into the hollow of his arm again, and resumed his air of melancholy resignation.

"Come forth, come forth," he said aloud, "be ye bird or be ye beast, ye are safe from these old hands. I have eaten and I have drunk, why should I take life, when my wants call for no sacrifice. It will not be long afore the birds will peck at eyes that shall not see them, and perhaps light on my very bones, for if things like these are only made to perish, why am I to expect to live forever. Come, forth. Come, forth! you are safe from harm at these weak hands."

"Thank you for the good word, old trapper," cried Paul Hover, springing actively forward from his place of concealment. "There was an air about you, when you threw forward the muzzle of the piece, that I did not like; for it seem'd to say that you were master of all the rest of the motions."

"You are right! you are right!" cried the trapper laughing, with inward self-complacency, at the recollection of his former skill. "The day has been, when few men knew the virtues of a long rifle, like this I carry, better than myself, old and useless as I now seem. You are right, young man, and the time was, when it was dangerous to move a leaf, within ear-shot of my stand, or," he added dropping his voice and looking serious, "for a red Mingo, to show an eye-ball from his ambushment. You have heard of the Red Mingos."

"I have heard of minks," said Paul, taking the old man by the arm, and gently urging him towards the thicket as he spoke, while at the same time, he cast quick and uneasy glances behind him, in order to make sure he was not observed. "Of your common black minks, but none of any other colour."

"Lord, Lord," continued the trapper, shaking his head and still laughing in his deep but quiet manner, "the boy mistakes a brute for a man. Though, a Mingo is little better than a beast, or, for that matter, he is worse, when rum and opportunity are placed before his eyes. There was that accursed Huron, from the Upper Lakes, that I knocked from his perch, among the rocks,* in the hills back of the Hori—"*

His voice was lost in the thicket, into which he had suffered himself to be led by Paul, while speaking, too much occupied by thoughts which dwelt on scenes and acts that had taken place, half a century earlier, in the History of the Country, to offer the smallest resistance.

CHAPTER VIII.

"Now they are clapper-clawing one another; I'll go look on.
That dissembling abominable varlet, Diomed, has got that same
scurvy, doting, foolish young knave in his helm."

Troilus and Cressida, V.iv. 1-5.

IT is necessary, in order that the thread of the narrative should
not be spun to a length which might fatigue the reader, that he should
imagine a week to have intervened between the scene, with which the
preceding chapter closed, and the events, with which it is our intention to resume its relation in this. The season was on the point of
changing its character, the verdure of summer giving place, more rapidly, to the brown and party coloured livery of the Fall.[1] The heavens
were clothed in driving clouds, piled in vast masses one above the
other, which whirled violently, in the gusts, opening, occasionally, to
admit transient glimpses of the bright and glorious sight of the heavens,
dwelling in a magnificence by far too grand and durable, to be disturbed
by the fitful efforts of the lower world. Beneath, the wind swept across
the wild and naked Prairies, with a violence that is seldom witnessed,
in any section of the continent less open. It would have been easy to
have imagined, in the ages of Fable, that the god of the winds had
permitted his subordinate agents to escape from their den, and that
they now rioted, in wantonness, across wastes, where neither tree, nor
work of man, nor mountain, nor obstacle of any sort opposed itself
to their gambols.

Though nakedness, might, as usual, be given as the pervading character of the spot, whither it is now necessary to transfer the scene of
the tale, it was not, entirely without the signs of human life. Amid the
monotonous rolling of the Prairies, a single, naked, and ragged rock
arose, on the margin of a little water course, which found its way,
after winding a vast distance through the plains, into one of the
numerous tributaries of the Father of Rivers. A swale of low land, lay
near the base of the eminence, and as it was still fringed with a thicket
of alders and sumack, it bore the signs of having once nurtured a
feeble growth of wood. The trees themselves, had been transferred,
however, to the summit and crags of the neighboring rocks. On this

---

[1] The Americans call the autumn the "fall," from the fall of the leaf. [1832]

elevation the signs of man to which this allusion just made applies were to be found.

Seen from beneath, there were visible a breast-work of logs and stones, intermingled in such a manner as to save all unnecessary labour, a few low roofs made of bark and boughs of trees, an occasional barrier, constructed like the defences on the summit, and placed on such points of the acclivity as were easier of approach than the general face of the eminence, and a little dwelling of cloth, perched on the apex of a small pyramid that shot up, on one angle of the rock, the white covering of which glimmered from a distance like a spot of snow, or to make the simile more suitable to the rest of the subject, like a spotless and carefully guarded standard, which was to be protected by the dearest blood of those who defended the citadel beneath. It is hardly necessary to add that this rude and characteristic fortress was the place, where Ishmael Bush had taken refuge, after the robbery of his flocks and herds.

On the day to which the narrative is advanced, the squatter was standing near the base of the rocks, leaning on his rifle, and regarding the sterile soil that supported him, with a look, in which contempt and disappointment were strongly blended.

"'Tis time to change our naturs," he observed to the brother of his wife, who was rarely far from his elbow, "and to become ruminaters instead of people used to the fare of Christians and free men. I reckon, Abiram, you could glean a living among the grasshoppers; you ar' an active man, and might outrun the nimblest skipper of them all."

"The country will never do," returned the other, who relished but little the forced humour of his kinsman; "and it is well, to remember that a lazy traveller, makes a long journey!"

"Would you have me draw a cart at my heels, across this desert, for weeks; ay, months!" retorted Ishmael, who like all of his class could labor with incredible efforts on emergencies, but who too seldom exerted continued industry on any occasion to brook a proposal that offered so little repose. "It may do for your people who live in settlements, to hasten on, to their houses. But thank Heaven, my farm is too big, for its owner ever to want a resting place."

"Since you like the Plantation, then, you have only to make your crop!"

"That is easier said than done, on this corner of the estate. I tell you, Abiram, there is need of moving for more reasons than one. You know I'm a man, that very seldom enters into a bargain, but who always fulfils his agreements better than your dealers in wordy contracts written on rags of paper. If there's one mile, there ar' a hundred still needed to make up the distance for which you have my honour."

As he spoke, the squatter glanced his eye upward at the little tenement of cloth, which crowned the summit of his ragged fortress. The look was understood and answered by the other, and by some secret influence, which operated either through their interests or feelings, it served to re-establish that harmony between them which had just been threatened with something like a momentary breach.

"I know it, and feel it, in every bone of my body. But I remember the reason why I have set myself on this accursed journey, too well, to forget the distance between me and the end. Neither you nor I, will ever be the better for what we have done, unless we thoroughly finish what is so well begun. Ay, that is the doctrine of the whole world, I judge: I heard a travelling Preacher, who was skirting it down the Ohio, a time since, say that if a man should live up to the faith, for a hundred years, and then fall from his work a single day, he would find the settlement was to be made for the finishing blow that he had put to his job, and that all the bad and none of the good would come into the final account."

"And you believed the hungry hypocrite?"

"Who said that I believed it!" retorted Abiram with a bullying look, that betrayed how much, his fears had dwelt on the subject he affected to despise. "Is it believing to tell what a roguish—and yet Ishmael, the man might have been honest after all. He told us that the world was, in truth, no better than a desert, and that there was but one hand that could lead the most learned man through all its crooked windings. Now, if this be true of the whole, it may be true of a part."

"Abiram, out with your grievances like a man," interrupted the squatter with a hoarse laugh. "You want to pray! But of what use will it be, according to your own doctrine, to serve God, five minutes and the Devil an hour. Harkee, friend, I'm not much of a husbandman, but this I know to my cost; that to make a right good crop even on the richest bottom, there must be hard labor, and your snufflers liken the 'arth to a field of corn, and the men who live on it, to its yield. Now I tell you, Abiram; that you are no better than a thistle or a mullen; yea, ye ar' wood, of too open a pore to be good even to burn."

The malign glance, which shot from the scowling eye of Abiram, announced the angry character of his feelings, but as the furtive look quailed, immediately before the unmoved, steady, countenance of the squatter, it also betrayed how much the bolder spirit of the latter had obtained the mastery over his craven nature.

Content with his ascendancy, which was too apparent, and had been too often exerted on similar occasions, to leave him in any doubt of its extent, Ishmael coolly continued the discourse, by adverting more directly to his future plans.

"You will own the justice of paying every one, in kind," he said. "I have been robbed of my stock; and I have a scheme to make myself as good as before, by taking hoof for hoof, or, for that matter, when a man is put to the trouble of bargaining for both sides, he is a fool if he dont pay himself, something in the way of commission."

As the squatter made this declaration in a tone, which was a little excited by the humour of the moment, four or five of his lounging sons, who had been leaning against the foot of the rock, came forward, with the indolent step, so common to the family.

"I have been calling Ellen Wade, who is on the rock keeping the look out, to know if there is any thing to be seen," observed the eldest of the young men; "and she shakes her head, for an answer. Ellen is sparing of her words for a woman; and might be taught manners, at least, without spoiling her good looks."

Ishmael cast his eye upward, to the place where the offending, but unconscious girl was holding her anxious watch. She was seated at the edge of the uppermost crag, by the side of the little tent, and, at least, two hundred feet, above the level of the plain. Little else was to be distinguished at that distance, but the outline of her form, her fair hair streaming, in the gusts beyond her shoulders, and the steady, and seemingly unchangeable look that she had rivetted on some remote point of the Prairie.

"What is it, Nell?" cried Ishmael, lifting his powerful voice a little above the rushing of the element. "Have you got a glimpse of any thing, bigger than a burrowing barker?"

The lips of the attentive Ellen parted, she rose to the utmost height her small stature admitted, seeming still to regard the unknown object, but her voice, if she spoke at all, was not sufficiently loud to be heard amid the wind.

"It ar' a fact, that the child sees something more uncommon than a buffaloe or a Prairie dog!" continued Ishmael. "Why, Nell; girl, ar' ye deaf? Nell, I say: I hope it is an army of red-skins she has in her eye; for I should relish the chance to pay them, for their kindness, under the favor of these logs and rocks!"

As the squatter accompanied his vaunt with corresponding gestures, and directed his eyes to the circle of his equally confident sons while speaking, he drew their gaze from Ellen to himself; but, now, when they turned together to note the succeeding movements of their female sentinel, the place which had, so lately, been occupied by her form, was vacant.

"As I am a sinner," exclaimed Asa, usually one of the most phlegmatic of the youths, "the girl is blown away by the wind!"

Something like a sensation was exhibited among them, which might have denoted that the influence of the laughing blue eyes, flaxen hair, and glowing cheeks of Ellen had not been lost on the dull natures of the young men, and looks of amazement mingled slightly with concern, passed from one to the other, as they gazed in dull wonder at the point of the naked rock.

"It might well be!" added another. "She sat on a slivered stone, and, I have been thinking, of telling her she was in danger, for more than an hour."

"Is that a ribband of the child, dangling from the corner of the hill below!" cried Ishmael, "Ha! who is moving about the tent! Have I not told you, all—"

"Ellen! tis Ellen!" interrupted the whole body of his sons in a breath; and at that instant she re-appeared to put an end to their different surmises, and, to relieve more than one sluggish nature from its unwonted excitement. As Ellen issued from beneath the folds of the tent, she advanced with a light and fearless step to her former giddy stand, and pointed, toward the Prairie, appearing to speak in an eager and rapid voice to some invisible auditor.

"Nell is mad!" said Asa, half in contempt, and yet not a little in concern. "The girl is dreaming with her eyes open; and thinks she sees some of them fierce creatures with hard names, with which the Doctor fills her ears."

"Can it be the child has found a scout of the Siouxes!" said Ishmael, bending his look towards the plain; but, a low, significant whisper from Abiram, drew his eyes quickly upward, again, where they were turned just in time, to perceive that the cloth of the tent, was agitated by a motion very evidently different from the quivering occasioned by the wind. "Let her, if she dare!" the squatter muttered, in his teeth. "Abiram; they know my temper too well, to play the prank with me."

"Look for yourself! if the curtain is not lifted, I can see no better than the owl, by day light."

Ishmael struck the breech of his rifle violently on the earth, and shouted, in a voice that might easily have been heard by Ellen, had not her attention still continued rapt on the object, which, so unaccountably attracted her eyes in the distance.

"Nell!" continued the squatter, "Away with you, fool! Will you bring down punishment on your own head. Why, Nell! She has forgotten her native speech; let us see, if she can understand another language."

Ishmael threw his rifle to his shoulder, and at the next moment it was pointed upward at the summit of the rock. Before time was given for a word of remonstrance, it had sent forth its contents, in its usual streak of bright flame. Ellen started like the frightened chamois, and uttering a piercing scream, she darted into the tent, with a swiftness, that left it uncertain, whether terror or actual injury, had been the penalty of her offence.

The action of the squatter was too sudden and unexpected to admit of prevention, but the instant it was done, his sons manifested, in an unequivocal manner the temper with which they witnessed the desperate measure. Angry and fierce glances were interchanged, and a murmur of disapprobation was uttered by the whole, in common.

"What has Ellen done, Father," said Asa, with a degree of spirit, which was the more striking from being unusual, "that she should be shot at, like a straggling deer or a hungry wolf!"

"Mischief," deliberately returned the squatter, but with a cool expression of defiance in his eye, that show'd, how little he was mov'd by the ill concealed humour of his children. "Mischief, boy; mischief. Take you heed, that the disorder dont spread."

"It would need a different treatment in a man, than in yon screaming girl."

"Asa, you ar' a man, as you have often boasted; but, remember I am your Father, and your better."

"I know it well—and what sort of a Father!"

"Harkee, boy: I more than half believe, that your drowsy head, let in the Siouxes. Be modest in speech, my watchful son, or you may have to answer yet for the mischief, your own bad conduct has brought upon us."

"I'll stay no longer to be hectored like a child in petticoats. You talk of law, as if you knew of none; and yet you keep me, down, as though I had not life and wants of my own. I'll stay no longer to be treated like one of your meanest cattle!"

"The world is wide, my gallant boy, and there's many a noble plantation, on it, without a tenant. Go, you have title deeds, sign'd and seal'd to your hand. Few Fathers portion their children better than Ishmael Bush, you will say that for me, at least when you get to be a wealthy land holder."

"Look, Father, look!" exclaimed several voices at once, seizing with avidity, an opportunity to interrupt a dialogue, which threatened to become more violent.

"Look!" repeated Abiram, in a voice, which sounded hollow and warning. "If you have time for any thing but quarrels, Ishmael, look!"

The squatter turned slowly from his offending son, and cast an eye that still lowered with deep resentment upward, but, which, the instant it caught a view of the object that now attracted the attention of all around him, chang'd its expression to one of astonishment and dismay.

A female stood on the spot, from which Ellen had been so fearfully expelled. Her person, was of the smallest size that is believed to comport with beauty, and which poets and artists have chosen as the beau idéal of female loveliness. Her dress was of a dark and glossy silk, and fluttered like gossamer, around her form. Long, flowing, and curling tresses of hair, still blacker and more shining than her robe, fell at times about her shoulders, completely enveloping the whole of her delicate bust in their ringlets, or at others, streamed long and waving in the wind. The elevation at which she stood prevented a close examination of the lineaments of a countenance, which, however, it might be seen was youthful, and, at the moment of her unlooked for appearance eloquent with feeling. So young indeed, did this fair and fragile being appear, that it might be doubted whether the age of childhood was entirely passed. One small and exquisitely moulded hand was pressed on her heart, while with the other she made an impressive gesture, which seem'd to invite Ishmael, if further violence was meditated, to direct it against her bosom.

The silent wonder with which the groupe of borderers gazed upward at so extraordinary a spectacle, was only interrupted, as the person of Ellen was seen, emerging with timidity from the tent, as if equally urged by apprehensions in behalf of herself, and the fears which she felt on account of her companion to remain concealed and to advance. She spoke; but her words were unheard by those below, and unheeded by her, to whom they were addressed. The latter, however, as if content with the offer she had made of herself as a victim to the resentment of Ishmael, now, calmly retired, and the spot she had so lately occupied became vacant, leaving a sort of stupid impression on the spectators beneath, not unlike that which it might be supposed would have been created, had they just been gazing at some supernatural vision.

More than a minute of profound silence succeeded, during which the sons of Ishmael, still continued gazing at the naked rock, in stupid wonder. Then as eye met eye, an expression of novel intelligence passed from one to the other, indicating that to them at least the appearance of this extraordinary tenant of the pavilion was as unexpected as it was incomprehensible. At length, Asa, in right of his years, and moved by the rankling impulse of the recent quarrel, took on himself the office of interrogator. Instead, however, of braving the resentment of his father, of whose fierce nature, when roused, he had had too frequent evidence, to excite it wantonly, he turned upon the cowering person of Abiram, observing with a sneer—

"This then is the beast, you were bringing into the Prairies for a decoy! I know you to be a man who seldom troubles truth, when any thing worse may answer, but I never knew you to outdo yourself, so thoroughly, before. The news-papers of Kentuck have called you a dealer in black flesh, a hundred times, but little did they reckon that you drove the trade into white families."

"Who is a kidnapper!" demanded Abiram, with a blustering show of resentment. "Am I to be called to account for every lie, they put in print, throughout the States! Look to your own family, boy; look to yourselves. The very stumps, of Kentucky and Tennessee, cry out ag'in ye! Ay, my tonguey gentleman, I have seen, Father and Mother, and three children, yourself for one, published on the logs and stubs of the settlements with dollars enough for reward to have made an honest man rich, for—"

He was interrupted by a back handed, but violent blow on the mouth, that caused him to totter, and which left the impression of its weight in the starting blood, and swelling lips.

"Asa!" said the Father, advancing with a portion of that dignity with which the hand of Nature seems to have invested the parental character. "You have struck the brother of your Mother!"

"I have struck the abuser of the whole family," returned the angry youth, "and unless he teach his tongue a wiser language, he had better part with it, altogether, as the unruly member. I'm no great performer with the knife, but, on an occasion, could make out, myself, to cut off a slande—"

"Boy; twice have you forgotten yourself to-day. Be careful that it does not happen the third time. Where the law of the land is weak, it is right that the law of natur should be strong. You understand me, Asa, and you know me. As for you, Abiram, the child has done you wrong, and it is my place to see you righted. Remember; I tell you, justice shall be done; it is enough. But you have said hard things ag'in me and my family. If the hounds of the law have put their bills on the trees and stumps of the clearings, it was for no act of dishonesty, as you know, but because we maintain the rule that 'arth is common property. No, Abiram; could I wash my hands, of things done by your advice, as easily as I can of the things done by the whisperings of the devil, my sleep would be quieter at night, and none, who bear my name, need blush to hear it mentioned. Peace, Asa, and you too, man; enough has been said. Let us all think well, before any thing is added, that may make what is already so bad still more bitter."

Ishmael wav'd his hand, with authority, as he ended, and turned away with the air of one, who felt assured, that those he addressed would not have the temerity to dispute his commands. Asa, evidently struggled with himself to compel the required obedience, but his heavy nature quietly sunk into its ordinary repose, and he soon appeared, again, the being he really was; dangerous, only, at moments, and one whose passions were too sluggish to be long maintained at the point of ferocity. Not so with Abiram. While there was an appearance of a personal conflict between him and his colossal nephew, his mien had expressed the infallible evidences of engrossing apprehension, but, now, that the authority, as well as gigantic strength of the Father were interposed, between him and his assailant, his countenance changed from paleness to a livid hue, that bespoke how deeply, the injury he had received, rankled in his breast. Like Asa, however, he acquiesced in the decision of the squatter, and the appearance, at least, of harmony was restored again among a set of beings who were restrained, by no obligations more powerful, than the frail web, of authority, with which Ishmael had been able to envelope his children.

One effect of the quarrel, had been to divert the thoughts of the young men, from their recent visiter. With the dispute, that succeeded the disappearance of the fair stranger, all recollection of her existence appeared to have vanished. A few ominous and secret conferences, it is true were held apart, during which the direction of the eyes of the different speakers betrayed their subject; but these threatening symptoms soon disappeared, and the whole party, was again seen broken into its usual, listless, silent, and lounging groupes.

"I will go upon the rock, boys, and look abroad for the savages," said Ishmael, shortly after advancing towards them, with a mien which he intended should be conciliating, at the same time that it was authoritative. "If there is nothing to fear, we will go out on the plain; the day is too good to be lost in words, like women in the towns wrangling over their tea and sugared cakes."

Without waiting for approbation or dissent, the squatter advanced to the base of the rock, which formed a sort of perpendicular wall, nearly twenty feet high, around the whole acclivity. Ishmael, however, directed his footsteps to a point, where an ascent might be made, through a narrow cleft, which he had taken the precaution to fortify, with a breast-work of cotton wood logs, and which in its turn was defended by a chevaux de frieze of the branches of the same tree. Here, an armed man was usually kept, as at the key of the whole position, and here one of the young men, now stood, indolently leaning against the rock, ready to protect the pass, if it should prove necessary until the whole party, could be mustered at the several points of defence.

From this place the squatter found the ascent still difficult, partly by nature, and partly by artificial impediments, until he reach'd a sort of terrace, or to speak more properly the plain of the elevation, where he had established the huts, in which the whole family dwelt. These tenements were, as already mentioned, of that class, which are so often seen on the borders, and such as belong'd to the infancy of architecture, being simply formed of logs, bark, and poles. The area on which they stood contained several hundred square feet, and was sufficiently elevated above the plain, greatly to lessen if not to remove all danger from Indian missiles. Here Ishmael, believed he might leave his infants in comparative security, under the protection of their spirited mother, and here he, now, found Esther, engaged, at her ordinary domestic employments, surrounded by her daughters, and lifting her voice in declamatory censure, as one or another of the idle fry incurred her displeasure, and far too much engrossed with the tempest of her own conversation to know any thing of the violent scene which had been passing below.

"A fine windy place, you have chosen for the camp, Ishmael!" she commenced, or rather continued, by merely, diverting the attack from a sobbing girl of ten at her elbow, to her husband. "My word, if I haven't to count the young ones, every ten minutes, to see, they are not flying away among the buzzards, or the ducks. Why do ye all keep hovering round the rock, like lolloping reptiles in the spring, when the heavens are beginning to be alive with birds, man? D'ye think mouths can be fill'd, and hunger satisfied, by laziness and sleep!"

"You'll have your say, Eester," said the husband, using the provincial pronunciation of America for the name, and regarding his noisy companions with a look of habitual tolerance rather than of affection. "But the birds you shall have, if your own tongue dont frighten them, to take too high a flight. Ay, woman," he continued, standing on the very spot whence he had so rudely banished Ellen, which he had, by this time, gained, "and buffaloe too, if my eye can tell the animal, at the distance of a Spanish league."*

"Come down; come down and be doing instead of talking. A talking man is no better than a barking dog. Nell shall hang out the cloth, if any of the red-skins show themselves, in time to give you notice. But, Ishmael, what have you been killing, my man, for it was your rifle, I heard a few minutes agone, unless I have lost my skill in sounds."

"Poh! 'twas to frighten the hawk you see, sailing above the rock."

"Hawk, indeed! at your time of day, to be shooting at hawks and buzzards, with eighteen open mouths to feed! Look at the bee, and at the beaver, my good man, and learn to be a provider. Why, Ishmael! I believe my soul," she continued, dropping the tow she was twisting on a distaff, "the man is in that tent ag'in! More than half his time is spent about that worthless, good-for-nothing—"

The sudden re-appearance of her husband closed the mouth of the wife, and as the former descended to the place where Esther had resumed her employment, she was content to grumble forth her dissatisfaction, instead of expressing it, in more audible terms.

The dialogue that now took place between the affectionate pair was sufficiently succinct and expressive. The woman was at first a little brief and sullen in her answers, but care for her family soon rendered her more complaisant. As the purport of the conversation was merely an engagement to hunt during the remainder of the day, in order to provide the chief necessary of life, we shall not stop to record it.

With this resolution, then, the squatter descended to the plains, and divided his forces, into two parts; one of which was to remain as a guard with the fortress, and the other to accompany him to the field. He warily included, Asa and Abiram in his own party, well knowing that no authority short of his own was competent to repress the fierce disposition of his head-strong son, if fairly awakened. When these arrangements were completed, the hunters sallied forth, separating, at no great distance from the rock in order to form a circle about the distant herd of Buffaloes.

CHAPTER IX.

"Priscian a little scratch'd;
'Twill serve."

Love's Labour's Lost, V.i. 31-32.

Having made the reader acquainted with the manner in which Ishmael Bush had disposed of his family, under circumstances that might have proved so embarrassing to most other men, we shall again shift the scene a few short miles from the place last described, preserving, however, the due and natural succession of time. At the very moment that the squatter and his sons departed in the manner mentioned in the preceding chapter, two men were intently occupied in a swale that lay along the borders of a little run, just out of cannon-shot from the encampment, discussing the merits of a savoury bison's hump, that had been prepared for their palates with the utmost attention to the particular merits of that description of food. The choice morsel had been judiciously separated from the adjoining and less worthy parts of the beast, and, enveloped in the hairy coating provided by nature, it had duly undergone the heat of the customary subterraneous oven,* and was now laid before its proprietors in all the culinary glory of the Prairies. So far as richness, delicacy, and wildness of flavour, and substantial nourishment were concerned, the viand might well have claimed a decided superiority over the meretricious cookery and laboured compounds of the most renowned artist; though the service of the dainty was certainly achieved in a manner far from artificial. It would appear that the two fortunate mortals, to whose happy lot it fell to enjoy a meal in which health and appetite lent so keen a relish to the exquisite food of the American deserts, were far from being insensible of the advantage they possesed.

The one, to whose knowledge in the culinary art the other was indebted for his banquet, seemed the least disposed of the two to profit by his own skill. He ate, it is true, and with a relish; but it was always with the moderation with which age is apt to temper the appetite. No such restraint, however, was imposed on the inclination of his companion. In the very flower of his days and in the vigour of manhood, the homage that he paid to the work of his more aged friend's hands was of the most profound and engrossing character. As one delicious morsel succeeded another he rolled his eyes towards his companion, and seemed to express that gratitude which he had not speech to utter, in looks of the most benignant nature.

"Cut more into the heart of it, lad," said the trapper, for it was the venerable inhabitant of those vast wastes, who had served the bee-hunter with the banquet in question; "cut more into the centre of the piece; there you will find the genuine riches of natur'; and that without need from spices, or any of your biting mustard to give it a foreign relish."

"If I had but a cup of metheglin,"*said Paul, stopping to perform the necessary operation of breathing, "I should swear this was the strongest meal that was ever placed before the mouth of man!"

"Ay, ay, well you may call it strong!" returned the other, laughing after his peculiar manner, in pure satisfaction at witnessing the infinite contentment of his companion; "strong it is, and strong it makes him who eats it! Here, Hector," tossing the patient hound, who was watching his eye with a wistful look, a portion of the meat, "you have need of strength, my friend, in your old days as well as your master. Now, lad, there is a dog that has eaten and slept wiser and better, ay, and that of richer food, than any king of them all! and why? because he has used and not abused the gifts of his Maker. He was made a hound, and like a hound has he feasted. Them did He create men; but they have eaten like famished wolves! A good and prudent dog has Hector proved, and never have I found one of his breed false in nose or friendship. Do you know the difference between the cookery of the wilderness and that which is found in the settlements? No; I see plainly you don't, by your appetite; then I will tell you. The one follows man, the other natur'. One thinks he can add to the gifts of the Creator, while the other is humble enough to enjoy them; therein lies the secret."

"I tell you, trapper," said Paul, who was very little edified by the morality with which his associate saw fit to season their repast, "that, every day while we are in this place, and they are likely to be many, I will shoot a buffaloe and you shall cook his hump!"

"I cannot say that, I cannot say that. The beast is good, take him in what part you will, and it was to be food for man that he was fashioned; but I cannot say that I will be a witness and a helper to the waste of killing one daily."

"The devil a bit of waste shall there be, old man. If they all turn out as good as this, I will engage to eat them clean myself, even to the hoofs—how now, who comes here! some one with a long nose I will answer; and one that has led him on a true scent, if he is following the trail of a dinner."

The individual who interrupted the conversation, and who had elicited the foregoing remark of Paul, was seen advancing along the margin of the run, with a deliberate pace, in a direct line for the two revellers. As there was nothing formidable nor hostile in his appearance, the bee-hunter, instead of suspending his operations, rather increased his efforts, in a manner which would seem to imply that he doubted whether the hump would suffice for the proper entertainment of all who were now likely to partake of the delicious morsel. With the trapper, however, the case was different. His more tempered appetite was already satisfied, and he faced the new comer with a look of cordiality, that plainly evinced how very opportune he considered his arrival.

"Come on, friend," he said waving his hand, as he observed the stranger to pause a moment, apparently in doubt. "Come on, I say: if hunger be your guide it has led you to a fitting place. Here is meat, and this youth can give you corn, parch'd till it be whiter than the upland snow; come on, without fear. We are not ravenous beasts, eating of each other, but Christian men, receiving thankfully that which the Lord hath seen fit to give."

"Venerable hunter," returned the Doctor, for it was no other than the naturalist on one of his daily exploring expeditions, "I rejoice greatly at this happy meeting; we are lovers of the same pursuits, and should be friends."

"Lord, lord!" said the old man laughing, without much deference to the rules of decorum, in the philosopher's very face, "it is the man who wanted to make me believe that a name could change the natur' of a beast! Come, friend; you are welcome, though your notions are a little blinded with reading too many books. Sit ye down, and after eating of this morsel, tell me, if you can, the name of the creatur' that has bestowed on you its flesh for a meal?"

The eyes of Dr. Battius (for we deem it decorous to give the good man the appellation he most preferred), the eyes of Dr. Battius sufficiently denoted the satisfaction with which he listened to this proposal. The exercise he had taken, and the sharpness of the wind, proved excellent stimulants, and Paul himself had hardly been in better plight to do credit to the trapper's cookery, than was the lover of nature, when the grateful invitation met his ears. Indulging in a small laugh, which his exertions to repress reduced nearly to a simper, he took the indicated seat by the old man's side, and made the customary dispositions to commence his meal without further ceremony.

"I should be ashamed of my profession," he said, swallowing a morsel of the hump with evident delight, slily endeavouring at the same time to distinguish the peculiarities of the singed and defaced skin, "I ought to be ashamed of my profession were there beast, or bird, on the continent of America that I could not tell by some one of the many evidences which science has enlisted in her cause. This—then—the food is nutritious and savoury—a mouthful of your corn, friend, if you please?"

Paul, who continued eating with increasing industry, looking askaunt not unlike a dog when engaged in the same agreeable pursuit, threw him his pouch, without deeming it at all necessary to suspend his own labours.

"You were saying, friend, that you have many ways of telling the creatur'?"—observed the attentive trapper.

"Many; many and infallible. Now, the animals that are carnivorous are known by their incisores."

"Their what!" demanded the trapper.

"The teeth with which nature has furnished them for defence, and in order to tear their food. Again—"

"Look you then for the teeth of this creatur'," interrupted the trapper, who was bent on convicting a man who had presumed to enter into competition with himself, in matters pertaining to the wilds, of gross ignorance; "turn the piece round and find your inside-overs."

The doctor complied, and of course without success; though he profited by the occasion to take another fruitless glance at the wrinkled hide.

"Well, friend, do you find the things you need, before you can pronounce the creatur' a duck or a salmon?"

"I apprehend the entire animal is not here?"

"You may well say as much," cried Paul, who was now compelled to pause from pure repletion; "I will answer for some pounds of the fellow, weighed by the truest steel-yards west of the Alleghanies. Still you may make out to keep soul and body together, with what is left," reluctantly eyeing a piece large enough to feed twenty men, but which he felt compelled to abandon from satiety; "cut in nigher to the heart, as the old man says, and you will find the riches of the piece."

"The heart!" exclaimed the doctor, inwardly delighted to learn there was a distinct organ to be submitted to his inspection. "Ay, let me see the heart—it will at once determine the character of the animal—certes this is not the cor—ay, sure enough it is—the animal must be of the order belluae, from its obese habits!"

He was interrupted by a long and hearty, but still a noiseless fit of merriment, from the trapper, which was considered so ill-timed by the offended naturalist, as to produce an instant cessation of speech, if not a stagnation of ideas.

"Listen to his beasts' habits and belly orders," said the old man delighted with the evident embarrassment of his rival; "and then he says it is not the core! Why, man, you are farther from the truth than you are from the settlements, with all your bookish l'arning and hard words; which I have once for all, said cannot be understood by any tribe or nation east of the Rocky Mountains. Beastly habits or no beastly habits, the creatur's are to be seen cropping the Prairies, by tens of thousands, and the piece in your hand is the core of as juicy a buffaloe-hump as stomach need crave!"

"My aged companion," said Obed, struggling to keep down a rising irascibility, that he conceived would ill comport with the dignity of his character, "your system is erroneous from the premises to the conclusion, and your classification so faulty, as utterly to confound the distinctions of science. The buffaloe is not gifted with a hump at all. Nor is his flesh savoury and wholesome, as I must acknowledge it would seem the subject before us may well be characterized—"

"There I'm dead against you, and clearly with the trapper," interrupted Paul Hover. "The man who denies that buffaloe beef is good, should scorn to eat it!" [1]

The Doctor, whose observation of the bee-hunter had hitherto been exceedingly cursory, stared at the new speaker with a look which denoted something like recognition.

"The principal characteristics of your countenance, friend," he said, "are familiar; either you, or some other specimen of your class, is known to me."

"I am the man you met in the woods east of the big river, and whom you tried to persuade to line a yellow hornet to his nest: as if my eye was not too true to mistake any other animal for a honey-bee, in a clear day! we tarried together a week, as you may remember; you at your toads and lizards, and I at my high holes and hollow trees.

[1] It is scarcely necessary to tell the reader, that the animal so often alluded to in this book, and which is vulgarily called the buffaloe, is in truth the bison; hence so many contre tems between the man of the Prairies and the man of science. [1832]

And a good job we made of it, between us! I filled my tubs with the sweetest honey I ever sent to the settlements, besides housing a dozen hives; and your bag was near bursting with a crawling museum. I never was bold enough to put the question to your face, stranger, but I reckon you are a keeper of curiosities?"[1]

"Ay! that is another of their wanton wickednesses!" exclaimed the trapper. "They slay the buck, and the moose, and the wild cat, and all the beasts that range the woods, and stuffing them with worthless rags, and placing eyes of glass into their heads, they set them up to be stared at, and call them the creatur's of the Lord; as if any mortal effigy could equal the works of his hand!"

"I know you well," returned the Doctor, on whom the plaint of the old man produced no visible impression. "I know you," offering his hand cordially to Paul; "it was a prolific week, as my herbal and catalogues shall one day prove. Ay, I remember you well, young man. You are of the *class*, mammalia; *order*, primates; *genus*, homo; *species*, Kentucky." Pausing to smile at his own humour, the naturalist proceeded. "Since our separation, I have journeyed far, having entered into a compactum or agreement with a certain man, named Ishmael—"

"Bush!" interrupted the impatient and reckless Paul. "By the Lord, trapper, this is the very blood-letter that Ellen told me of!"

"Then Nelly has not done me credit for what I trust I deserve;" returned the single-minded Doctor, "for I am not of the phlebotomizing school at all; greatly preferring the practice which purifies the blood instead of abstracting it."

"It was a blunder of mine, good stranger; the girl called you a skilful man."

"Therein she may have exceeded my merits," Dr. Battius continued, bowing with sufficient meekness. "But Ellen is a good, and a kind, and a spirited girl, too. A kind and a sweet girl I have ever found Nelly Wade to be!"

"The devil you have!" cried Paul, dropping the morsel he was sucking, from sheer reluctance to abandon the hump, and casting a fierce

[1] The pursuit of a bee-hunter is not uncommon on the skirts of American society, though it is a little embellished here. When the bees are seen sucking the flowers, their pursuer contrives to capture one or two. He then chooses a proper spot, and suffering one to escape, the insect invariably takes its flight towards the hive. Changing his ground to a greater or less distance, according to circumstances the bee-hunter then permits another to escape. Having watched the courses of the bees, which is technically called "lining," he is enabled to calculate the intersecting angle of the two lines, which is the hive. [1832]

and direct look into the very teeth of the unconscious physician. "I reckon, stranger, you have a mind to bag Ellen, too!"

"The riches of the whole vegetable and animal world united, would not tempt me to harm a hair of her head! I love the child, with what may be called amor naturalis—or rather paternus.—The affection of a father."

"Ay—that indeed is more befitting the difference in your years," Paul coolly rejoined, stretching forth his hand to regain the rejected morsel. "You would be no better than a drone at your time of day, with a young hive to feed and swarm."

"Yes, there is reason, because there is natur', in what he says," observed the trapper: "But friend, you have said you were a dweller in the camp of one Ishmael Bush?"

"True; it is, in virtue of compactum—"

"I know but little of the virtue of packing, though I follow trapping, in my old age, for a livelihood. They tell me that skins are well kept, in the new fashion, but it is long since I have left off killing more than I need for food and garments. I was an eye-witness, myself, of the manner in which the Siouxes broke into your encampment, and drove off the cattle; stripping the poor man you call Ishmael of his smallest hoofs, counting even the cloven feet."

"Asinus excepted;" muttered the Doctor, who by this time was discussing his portion of the hump, in utter forgetfulness of all its scientific attributes. "Asinus domesticus Americanus excepted."

"I am glad to hear that so many of them are saved, though I know not the value of the animals you name; which is nothing uncommon, seeing how long it is that I have been out the settlements. But can you tell me, friend, what the traveller carries under the white cloth, he guards with teeth as sharp as a wolf that quarrels for the carcass the hunter has left?"

"You've heard of it!" exclaimed the other, dropping the morsel he was conveying to his mouth, in manifest surprise.

"Nay, I have heard nothing; but I have seen the cloth, and had like to have been bitten for no greater crime than wishing to know what it covered."

"Bitten! then after all the animal must be carnivorous! It is too tranquil for the ursus horridus; if it were the canis latrans, the voice would betray it. Nor would Nelly Wade be so familiar with any of the *genus,* feræ. Venerable hunter! the solitary animal confined in that wagon by day, and in the tent at night, has occasioned me more perplexity of mind than the whole catalogue of quadrupeds besides: and for this plain reason; I did not know how to class it."

"You think it a ravenous beast?"

"I know it to be a quadruped: your own danger proves it to be carnivorous."

During this broken explanation, Paul Hover sat silent and thoughtful, regarding each speaker with deep attention. But, suddenly moved by the manner of the Doctor, the latter had scarcely time to utter his positive assertion, before the young man bluntly demanded—

"And pray, friend, what may you call a quadruped?"

"A vagary of nature, wherein she has displayed less of her infinite wisdom than is usual. Could rotary levers be substituted for two of the limbs, agreeably to the improvement in my new order of phalanga-crura, which might be rendered into the vernacular as lever-legged, there would be a delightful perfection and harmony in the construction. But, as the quadruped is now formed, I call it a mere vagary of nature; no other than a vagary."

"Harkee, stranger! in Kentucky we are but small dealers in dictionaries. Vagary is as hard a word to turn into English as quadruped."

"A quadruped is an animal with four legs—a beast."

"A beast! Do you then reckon that Ishmael Bush travels with a beast caged in that wagon?"

"I know it, and lend me your ear—not literally, friend," observing Paul to start and look surprised, "but figuratively, through its functions, and you shall hear. I have already made known that, in virtue of a compactum I journey with the aforesaid Ishmael Bush; but though I am bound to perform certain duties while the journey lasts, there is no condition which says that the said journey shall be sempiternum, or eternal. Now, though this region may scarcely be said to be wedded to science, being to all intents a virgin territory as respects the inquirer into natural history, still it is greatly destitute of the treasures of the vegetable kingdom. I should therefore have tarried some hundreds of miles more to the eastward, were it not for the inward propensity that I feel to have the beast in question inspected and suitably described and classed. For that matter," he continued, dropping his voice, like one who imparts an important secret, "I am not without hopes of persuading Ishmael to let me dissect it."

"You have seen the creature?"

"Not with the organs of sight; but with much more infallible instruments of vision: the conclusions of reason, and the deductions of scientific premises. I have watched the habits of the animal, young man; and can fearlessly pronounce, by evidence that would be thrown away on ordinary observers, that it is of vast dimensions, inactive, possibly torpid, of voracious appetite, and, as it now appears by the direct testimony of this venerable hunter, ferocious and carnivorous!"

"I should be better pleased, stranger," said Paul, on whom the Doctor's description was making a very sensible impression, "to be sure the creature was a beast at all."

"As to that, if I wanted evidence of a fact, which is abundantly apparent by the habits of the animal, I have the word of Ishmael, himself. A reason can be given for my smallest deductions. I am not troubled, young man, with a vulgar and idle curiosity, but all my aspirations after knowledge, as I humbly believe, are, first, for the advancement of learning, and secondly, for the benefit of my fellow-creatures. I pined greatly in secret to know the contents of the tent, which Ishmael guarded so carefully, and which he had covenanted that I should swear, (jurare per deos) not to approach nigher than a defined number of cubits, for a definite period of time. Your jus-jurandum, or oath, is a serious matter, and not to be dealt in lightly; but, as my expedition depended on complying, I consented to the act, reserving to myself at all times the power of distant observation. It is now some ten days since Ishmael, pitying the state in which he saw me, a humble lover of science, imparted the fact that the vehicle contained a beast, which he was carrying into the Prairies as a decoy, by which he intends to entrap others of the same genus, or perhaps species. Since then my task, has been reduced simply to watch the habits of the animal, and to record the results. When we reach a certain distance where these beasts are said to abound, I am to have the liberal examination of the specimen."

Paul continued to listen, in the most profound silence, until the Doctor concluded his singular but characteristic explanation; then the incredulous bee-hunter shook his head, and saw fit to reply, by saying—

"Stranger, old Ishmael has burrowed you in the very bottom of a hollow tree, where your eyes will be of no more use than the sting of a drone. I, too, know something of that very wagon, and I may say that I have lined the squatter down into a flat lie. Harkee, friend; do you think a girl, like Ellen Wade, would become the companion of a wild beast?"

"Why not! why not!" repeated the naturalist; "Nelly has a taste, and often listens with pleasure to the treasures that I am sometimes compelled to scatter in this desert. Why should she not study the habits of any animal, even though it were a rhinoceros!"

"Softly, softly," returned the equally positive, and, though less scientific, certainly, on this subject, better instructed bee-hunter; "Ellen is a girl of spirit, and one too that knows her own mind, or I'm much mistaken; but with all her courage and brave looks, she is no better than a woman after all. Haven't I often had the girl, crying—"

"You are an acquaintance, then, of Nelly's?"

"The devil a bit. But I know woman is woman; and all the books in Kentucky couldn't make Ellen Wade go into a tent alone with a ravenous beast!"

"It seems to me," the trapper calmly observed, "that there is something dark and hidden in this matter. I am a witness that the traveller likes none to look into the tent, and I have a proof more sure than what either of you can lay claim to, that the wagon does not carry the cage of a beast. Here is Hector, come of a breed with noses as true and faithful as a hand that is all-powerful has made any of their kind, and had there been a beast in the place, the hound would long since have told it to his master."

"Do you pretend to oppose a dog to a man! brutality to learning! instinct to reason!" exclaimed the Doctor in some heat. "In what manner, pray, can a hound distinguish the habits, species, or even the genus of an animal, like reasoning, learned, scientific, triumphant man!"

"In what manner!" coolly repeated the veteran woodsman. "Listen; and if you believe that a schoolmaster can make a quicker wit than the Lord, you shall be made to see how much you're mistaken. Do you not hear something move in the brake? it has been cracking the twigs these five minutes. Now tell me what the creatur' is?"

"I hope nothing ferocious!" exclaimed the Doctor, who still retained a lively impression of his rencounter with the vespertilio horribilis. "You have rifles, friends; would it not be prudent to prime them; for this fowling-piece of mine is little to be depended on."

"There may be reason in what he says," returned the trapper, so far complying as to take his piece from the place where it had lain during the repast, and raising its muzzle in the air. "Now tell me the name of the creatur'?"

"It exceeds the limits of earthly knowledge! Buffon himself could not tell whether the animal was a quadruped, or of the *order*, serpens! a sheep, or a tiger!"

"Then was your buffoon a fool to my Hector! Here; pup!—What is it, dog!—Shall we run it down, pup—or shall we let it pass?"

The hound, which had already manifested to the experienced trapper, by the tremulous motion of his ears, his consciousness of the proximity of a strange animal, lifted his head from his fore paws and slightly parted his lips, as if about to shew the remnants of his teeth. But, suddenly abandoning his hostile purpose, he snuffed the air a moment, gaped heavily, shook himself, and peaceably resumed his recumbent attitude.

"Now, Doctor," cried the trapper, triumphantly, "I am well convinced there is neither game nor ravenous beast in the thicket; and that I call substantial knowledge to a man who is too old to be a spendthrift of his strength, and yet who would not wish to be a meal for a panther!"

The dog interrupted his master by a growl, but still kept his head crouched to the earth.

"It is a man!" exclaimed the trapper rising. "It is a man, if I am a judge of the creatur's ways. There is but little said atwixt the hound and me, but we seldom mistake each other's meaning!"

Paul Hover sprang to his feet like lightning, and, throwing forward his rifle, he cried in a voice of menace—

"Come forward, if a friend; if an enemy, stand ready for the worst!"

"A friend, a white man, and I hope a Christian," returned a voice from the thicket; which opened at the same instant, and at the next, the speaker made his appearance.

CHAPTER X.

"Go apart, Adam, and thou shalt hear
How he will shake me up."

As You Like It, I.i. 29-30.

IT is well known, that even long before the immense regions of
Louisiana changed their masters, for the second, and, as it is to be
hoped for the last time, its unguarded territory was by no means, safe
from the inroads of white adventurers. The semi-barbarous hunters
from the Canadas, the same description of population, a little more
enlightened from the States, and the metiffs or half breeds who claimed
to be ranked in the class of white men, were scattered, among the
different Indian tribes or gleaned a scanty livelihood, in solitude,
amid the haunts of the beaver and the bison; or, to adopt the popular
nomenclature of the country, of the buffaloe.[1]

It was, therefore, no unusual thing for strangers to encounter each
other in the endless wastes of the West. By signs which an unpractised
eye would pass unobserved, a borderer, knew when one of his fellows
was in his vicinity, and he avoided or approached the intruder, as best
comported with his feelings or his interests. Generally, these interviews were pacific, for the whites had a common enemy to dread in
the ancient, and perhaps more lawful, occupants, of the country, but
instances were not rare, in which jealousy and cupidity, had caused
them to terminate in scenes of the most violent and ruthless treachery.
The meeting of two hunters on the American desert, as we find it
convenient, sometimes, to call this region, was, consequently, somewhat in the suspicious and wary manner in which two vessels draw
together in a sea, that is known to be infested with pirates. While
neither party is willing to betray its weakness by exhibiting distrust,
neither is disposed to commit itself, by any acts of confidence from
which it may be difficult to recede.

Such, was, in some degree, the character of the present interview.
The stranger drew nigh, deliberately, keeping his eyes steadily fastened

---

[1] In addition to the scientific distinctions which mark the two species, it may be added,
with due deference to Dr. Battius, that a much more important particular is, the fact,
that while the former of these animals is delicious and nourishing food, the latter is
scarcely edible. [1827]

on the movements of the other party, while he purposely created little difficulties to impede an approach which might prove too hasty. On the other hand, Paul stood, playing with the lock of his rifle, too proud to let it appear that three men could manifest any apprehension of a solitary individual, and yet too prudent, to omit, entirely, the customary precautions. The principal reason of the marked difference which the two legitimate proprietors of the banquet, made in the receptions of their guests, was to be explained by the entire difference which existed in their respective appearances.

While the exterior of the Naturalist was decidedly pacific, not to say, abstracted, that of the new comer was distinguished by an air of vigour, and a front and step, which it would not have been difficult to have at once pronounced to be military. He wore a forage cap, of fine blue cloth, from which depended a soiled tassel in gold, and which was nearly buried, in a mass of exuberant, curling, jet-black hair. Around his throat, he had, negligently, fastened a stock of black silk. His body was enveloped in a hunting shirt, of dark green, trimmed with the yellow fringes and ornaments that were sometimes seen among the border-troops of the Confederacy. Beneath this, however, were visible the collar and lapels of a jacket, similar in colour and cloth to the cap. His lower limbs were protected by buckskin leggings, and his feet, by the ordinary Indian moccasins. A richly ornamented, and exceedingly dangerous, straight dirk was stuck in a sash of red-silk, net-work; another girdle, or rather belt, of uncolored leather, contained a pair of the smallest sized pistols, in holsters nicely made to fit, and across his shoulder was thrown a short, heavy, military rifle; its horn and pouch occupying the usual places, beneath his arms. At his back he bore, a knapsack, marked by the well known initials, that have since, gained for the Government of the United States, the good humoured and quaint appellation of Uncle Sam.

"I come in amity," the stranger said, like one too much accustomed to the sight of arms, to be startled at the ludicrously belligerent attitude which Doctor Battius had seen fit to assume. "I come as a friend; and am one, whose pursuits and wishes will not at all interfere with your own."

"Harkee, stranger," said Paul Hover, bluntly, "do you understand lining a bee, from this open place, into a wood, distant, perhaps a dozen miles."

"The bee is a bird, I have never been compelled to seek," returned the other, laughing, "though I have too, been something of a fowler, in my time."

"I thought as much," exclaimed Paul, thrusting forth his hand, frankly, and with the true freedom of manner, that marks an American borderer. "Let us cross fingers. You and I will never quarrel about the comb, since you set so little store, by the honey. And, now, if your stomach has an empty corner, and you know how to relish a genuine dew drop when it falls into your very mouth, there lies the exact morsel to put into it. Try it, stranger; and having tried it, if you dont call it as snug a fit, as you have made since— How long ar' you from the settlements, pray?"

"'Tis many weeks, and I fear, it may be as many more, before I can return. I will however gladly profit by your invitation; for I have fasted since the rising of yesterday's sun, and I know too well the merits of a bison's hump, to reject the food."

"Ah! you ar' acquainted with the dish! Well, therein, you have the advantage of me, in setting out, though I think, I may say we could now, start on equal grounds. I should be the happiest fellow, between Kentuck and the Rocky Mountains, if I had a snug cabin, near some old wood that was filled with hollow trees, just such a hump every day as that for dinner; a load of fresh straw for hives, and little El—"

"Little what?" demanded the stranger, evidently amused with the communicative and frank disposition of the bee-hunter.

"Something that I shall have one day, and which concerns no body so much as myself," returned Paul, pecking the flint of his rifle, and beginning very cavalierly to whistle an air well known on the waters of the Mississippi.

During this preliminary discourse the stranger had taken his seat by the side of the hump, and was already making a serious inroad on its relicks. Dr. Battius however watch'd his movements, with a jealousy, still more striking than the cordial reception which the open hearted Paul had just exhibited.

But the doubts, or rather apprehensions, of the naturalist, were of a character altogether different from the confidence of the bee-hunter. He had been struck with the stranger's using the legitimate instead of the perverted name of the animal off which he was making his repast, and as he had been among the foremost, himself, to profit by the removal of the impediments which the policy of Spain had plac'd in the way of all explorers of her Trans-Atlantic dominions; whether bent on the purposes of commerce, or like himself on the more laudable pursuits of science, he had a sufficiency of every day philosophy to feel, that the same motives which had so powerfully urged himself to his present undertaking, might produce a like result on the mind of some other student of Nature. Here, then, was the prospect of an alarming rivalry, which bade fair to strip him of, at least, a moiety of the just rewards of all his labors, privations and dangers. Under these views of his character, therefore, it is not at all surprising that the native meekness of the naturalist's disposition was a little disturbed, and that he watch'd the proceedings of the other, with such a degree of vigilance, as he believed best suited to detect his sinister designs.

"This is, truly, a delicious repast," observed the unconscious young stranger; for both young and handsome, he was fairly entitled to be considered, "either hunger has given a peculiar relish to the viand, or the bison may lay claim to be the finest of the ox family!"

"Naturalists, sir, are apt, when they speak familiarly, to give the cow the credit of the genus," said Doctor Battius, swelling with secret distrust, and clearing his throat before speaking, much in the manner that a duellist examines the point of the weapon he is about to put into the body of his foe. "The figure is more perfect, as the bos, meaning the ox, is unable to perpetuate his kind; and the bos, in its most extended meaning, or vacca, is altogether the nobler animal of the two."

The Doctor uttered this opinion with a certain air, that he intended should express his readiness to come, at once, to any of the numerous points of difference, which he doubted not existed between them, and he now awaited the blow of his antagonist, intending that his next thrust should be still more vigorous. But the young stranger appeared much better disposed to partake of the good cheer with which he had been so providently provided, than to take up the cudgels of argument on this or on any other of the knotty points, which are so apt to furnish the lovers of science, with the materials of a mental joust.

"I dare say, you are very right, sir," he replied, with a most provoking indifference to the importance of the points he conceded. "I dare say, you are quite right, and that vacca, would have been the better word."

"Pardon me, sir; you are giving a very wrong construction to my language, if you suppose I include, without many and particular qualifications, the bibulus Americanus, in the family of the vacca. For as you well know, sir—or, as I presume I should say, Doctor—you have the Medical Diploma, no doubt?"

"You give me credit for an honour I can not claim," interrupted the other.

"An under-graduate! or perhaps your degrees have been taken in some other of the liberal sciences?"

"Still wrong, I do assure you."

"Surely, young man, you have not entered on this important—I may say this awful service, without some evidence of your fitness for the task!—some commission by which you can assert an authority to proceed, or by which you may claim, an affinity and a communion with your fellow-workers, in the same beneficent pursuits!"

"I know not, by what means, or for what purposes, you have made yourself master of my objects!" exclaimed the youth, reddening, and rising with a quickness, which manifested how little he regarded the grosser appetites, when a subject nearer his heart was approached. "Still, sir, your language is incomprehensible. That pursuit which in another might perhaps be justly called beneficent, is, in me a dear and cherished duty; though why a commission should be demanded or needed, is, I confess, no less a subject of surprise."

"It is customary to be provided with such a document," returned the Doctor gravely, "and, on all suitable occasions to produce it, in order that congenial and friendly minds, may at once, reject unworthy suspicions, and stepping over, what may be called the elements of discourse, come at once, to those points which are desiderata, to both."

"It is a strange request!" the youth muttered, turning his frowning eye, from one to the other, as if examining the characters of his companions, with a view to weigh their physical powers. Then, putting his hand into his bosom he drew forth a small box and extending it, with an air of dignity towards the Doctor, he continued—"you will find by this, sir, that I have some right, to travel in a country, which is now the property of the American States."

"What have we here!" exclaimed the Naturalist, opening the folds of a large parchment. "Why, this is the sign manual of the Philosopher Jefferson! The seal of State! Countersigned, by the Minister of War! Why this is a commission, creating Duncan Uncas Middleton* a Captain of Artillery."

"Of whom! of whom!" repeated the trapper, who had sat regarding the stranger, during the whole discourse, with eyes that seem'd greedily to devour each lineament. "How is the name! did you call him Uncas? Uncas! was it, Uncas?"

"Such is my name," returned the youth, a little haughtily. "It is the appellation of a native chief, that both my uncle and myself, bear with pride; for it is the memorial of an important service done my family, by a warrior, in the old wars of the Provinces!"

"Uncas! did ye call him, Uncas!" repeated the trapper, approaching the youth, and parting the dark curls which clustered over his brow, without the slightest resistance on the part, of their wondering owner. "Ah! my eyes are old, and not so keen as when I was a warrior, myself, but I can see the look of the father in the son! I saw it, when he first came nigh, but so many things have, since, passed before my failing sight, that I could not name, the place, where I had met his likeness! Tell me, lad, by what name is your father known?"

"He was an officer of the States in the war of the revolution, of my own name of course; my mother's brother was called Duncan Uncas Heyward."

"Still Uncas! still, Uncas!" echoed the other, trembling with eagerness. "And *his* father?"

"Was called the same, without the appellation of the native chief. It was to him and to my grandmother, that the service of which I have just spoken was rendered."

"I know'd it! I know'd it!" shouted the old man, in his tremulous voice, his rigid features working, powerfully, as if the names the other mentioned, awakened some long dormant emotions, connected with the events of an anterior age. "I know'd it! son or grandson, it is all the same, it is the blood, and 'tis the look! Tell me, is he they call'd Duncan, without the Uncas, is he living."

The young man shook his head sorrowfully as he replied in the negative.

"He died full of days, and of honours. Beloved, happy and bestowing happiness."

"Full of days!" repeated the trapper looking down at his own meagre, but still muscular hands. "Ah! he liv'd in the settlements, and was wise, only, after their fashions. But you have often seen him, and you have heard him discourse of Uncas, and of the wilderness?"

"Often! He was then an Officer of the King; but when the war took place between the Crown and her Colonies, my grandfather did not forget his birth-place, but threw off the empty allegiance of names, and was true to his proper country; he fought on the side of Liberty."

"There was reason in it; and what is better, there was Natur. Come, sit ye down, beside me lad; sit ye down and tell me of what your grand'ther used to speak, when his mind dwelt on the wonders of the wilderness."

The youth smiled, no less at the importunity than at the interest manifested by the old man, but, as he found that there was no longer, the least appearance of any violence being contemplated, he unhesitatingly complied.

"Give it all, to the trapper, by rule and by figures of speech," said

Paul, very coolly taking his seat on the other side of the young soldier. "It is the fashion of old age to relish these ancient traditions, and, for that matter, I can say, that I dont dislike to listen to them, myself."

Middleton smiled, again, and perhaps with a slight air of derision; but good naturedly turning to the trapper, he continued—

"It is a long, and might prove a painful story. Blood-shed and all the horrors of Indian cruelty and of Indian warfare, are fearfully mingled in the narrative."

"Ay, give it all to us, stranger," continued Paul; "we are used to these matters in Kentuck; and I must say, I think a story none the worse, for having a few scalps in it!"

"But he told you of Uncas, did he!" resumed the trapper, without regarding the slight interruptions of the bee hunter, which amounted to no more than a sort of by-play. "And, what thought he, and said he, of the lad, in his parlour, with the comforts and ease of the settlements at his elbow?"

"I doubt not, he used a language similar to that he would have adopted in the woods, and had he stood face to face with his friend—"

"Did he call the savage his friend! the poor, naked, painted warrior; he was not too proud then, to call the Indian his friend?"

"He even boasted of the connexion; and as you have already heard, bestowed a name on his first-born, which is likely to be handed down, as an heir loom among the rest of his descendants."

"It was well done! Like a man, ay! and like a christian too! He used to say the Delaware was swift of foot—did he remember that?"

"As the antelope. Indeed he often spoke of him, by the appellation of Le Cerf Agile, a name he had obtained by his activity."

"And bold and fearless, lad!" continued the trapper looking up into the eyes of his companion, with a wistfulness that bespoke the delight he received in listening to the praises of one, whom it was so very evident, he had once, tenderly lov'd.

"Brave as a blooded hound! Without fear. He always quoted Uncas and his father, who from his wisdom, was called the Grand Serpent, as models of heroism and constancy."

"He did them justice! He did them justice! Truer men, were not to be found in tribe or nation, be their skins of what colour they might. I see your grand'ther was just; and did his duty, too, by his offspring. 'Twas a perilous time he had of it, among them hills, and nobly did he play his own part. Tell, me, lad, or, officer, I should say, since officer, you be, was this all?"

"Certainly not; it was as I have said a fearful tale, full of moving incidents, and the memories both of my grandfather and of my grandmother."

"Ah!" exclaimed the trapper tossing a hand into the air, as his whole countenance lighted with the recollections the name revived. "They called her Alice! Elsie or Alice, 'tis all the same. A laughing, playful, child she was, when happy, and tender and weeping in her misery. Her hair was shining and yellow as the coat of the young fawn, and her skin clearer than the purest water that drips from the rocks. Well do I remember her! I remember her right well!"

The lip of the youth slightly curled, and he regarded the old man, with an expression, which might easily have been construed into a declaration that such were not his own recollections of his venerable and revered ancestor, though it would seem he did not think it necessary to say as much in words. He was content to answer:—

"They both retained impressions of the dangers they had passed, by far too vivid easily to lose the recollection of any of their fellow actors."

The trapper look'd aside, and seem'd to struggle with some deeply innate feeling; then turning again, towards his companion, though his honest eyes no longer dwelt with the same open interest, as before, on the countenance of the other, he continued—

"Did he tell you of them *all?* were they *all* red-skins, but himself and the daughters of Munro?"

"No. There was a white man, associated with the Delawares. A scout of the English Army, but a native of the Provinces."

"A drunken, worthless, vagabond, like most of his colour who harbor with the savages, I warrant you!"

"Old man, your gray hairs, should caution you against slander. The man, I speak of, was of great simplicity of mind, but of sterling worth. Unlike most of those who live a border life, he united the better, instead of the worst qualities of the two people. He was a man, endowed with the choicest and perhaps rarest gift of nature, that of distinguishing, good from evil, his virtues were those of simplicity, because such were the fruits of his habits, as were, indeed, his very prejudices. In courage, he was the equal of his red associates, in war-like skill, being better instructed, their superior. In short, he was a noble shoot from the stock of human nature, which never could attain its proper elevation and importance, for no other reason, than because it grew in the forest: such, old hunter, were the very words of my grandfather, when speaking of the man, you imagine so worthless."

The eyes of the trapper had sunk to the earth as the stranger delivered this character in the ardent tones of generous youth. He play'd with the ears of his hound, fingered his own rustic garment, and open'd and shut the pan of his rifle, with hands that trembled in a manner, that would have implied their total unfitness to wield the weapon. When the other had concluded he hoarsely added—

"Your grand'ther didn't then entirely forget the white man!"

"So far from that, there are already three, among us, who have also names derived from that scout."

"A name, did you say!" exclaimed the old man, starting, "what, the name, of the solitary, unl'arned hunter! Do the great, and the rich, and the honored, and what is better, still, the just, do they bear his very actual name!"

"It is borne, by my brother, and by two of my cousins, whatever may be their titles to be described by the terms you have mentioned."

"Do you mean, the actual name itself: spelt with the very same letters; beginning with an N. and ending with an L."*

"Exactly the same," the youth smilingly replied. "No, no, we have forgotten nothing that was his; I have at this moment a dog brushing a deer, not far from this, who is come of a hound, that very scout sent as a present after his friends, and which was of the stock he always used himself: a truer breed in nose and foot, is not to be found in the wide Union."

"Hector!" said the old man, struggling to conquer an emotion that nearly suffocated him, and speaking to his hound, in the sort of tones he would have used to a child, "do ye hear that, Pup. Your kin and blood, are on the Prairies! A name! it is wonderful! very wonderful!"

Nature could endure no more. Overcome by a flood of unusual and extraordinary sensations, and stimulated by tender and long dormant recollections strangely and unexpectedly revived, the old man had just self command enough to add, in a voice that was hollow and unnatural, through the efforts he made to command it—

"Boy, I am that scout; a warrior once, a miserable trapper now!" when the tears broke over his wasted cheeks out of fountains that had long been dried and, sinking his face between his knees, he covered it decently, with his buckskin garment, and sobb'd aloud.

The spectacle produced correspondent emotions in his companions. Paul Hover had actually swallowed each syllable of the discourse as they fell, alternately, from the different speakers, his feelings keeping equal pace with the increasing interest of the scene. Unused to such strange sensations, he was turning his face on every side of him, to avoid he knew not what, until he saw the tears and heard the sobs of the old man, when he sprang to his feet, and grappling his guest fiercely by the throat, he demanded, by what authority he had made his aged companion weep. A flash of recollection crossing his brain, at the same instant, he released his hold, and stretching forth an arm in the very wantonness of gratification, he seized the Doctor by the hair, which instantly revealed its artificial formation, by cleaving to his hand, leaving the white and shining poll of the Naturalist with a covering no warmer than the skin.

"What think you of that, Mr. Bug-gatherer!" he rather shouted, than cried, "is not this a strange bee to line into his hole!"

"'Tis remarkable! wonderful! edifying!" returned the lover of nature, good humouredly recovering his wig, with twinkling eyes and a husky voice. "'Tis rare and commendable! Though I doubt not in the exact order of causes and effects."

With this sudden outbreaking, however, the commotion instantly subsided, the three spectators clustering around the trapper with a species of awe, at beholding the tears of one so aged.

"It must be so, or how could he be so familiar with a history that is little known beyond my own family," at length the youth observed, not ashamed to acknowledge how much he had been affected by unequivocally drying his own eyes.

"True!" echoed Paul: "If you want any more evidence I will swear to it! I know every word of it, myself, to be true as the gospel!"

"And yet we had long supposed him dead!" continued the soldier. "My grandfather had filled his days, with honor, and we had believed him the junior of the two."

"It is not often that youth, has an opportunity of thus looking down on the weakness of age!" the trapper observed, raising his head, and looking around him with composure and dignity. "That I am still here, young man, is the pleasure of the Lord, who has spared me, until I have seen fourscore long and laborious years, for his own secret ends. That I am the man I say, you need not doubt, for why should I go to my grave with so cheap a lie in my mouth?"

"I do not hesitate to believe, I only marvel that it should be so. But why do I find you, venerable and excellent friend of my parents in these wastes so far from the comforts and safety of the lower country?"

"I have come into these plains to escape the sound of the axe, for, here, surely the choppers can never follow. But, I may put the like question to yourself. Are you of the party which the States have sent into their new purchase to look after the natur of the bargain they have made?"

"I am not. Lewis*is working his way up the river, some hundreds of miles from this. I come on a private adventure."

"Though it is no cause of wonder that a man whose strength and eyes have failed him as a hunter, should be seen nigh the haunts of the beaver, using a trap instead of a rifle, it is strange, that one so young and prosperous, and bearing the commission of the Great Father, should be moving among the Prairies, without even a camp-colour-man to do his biddings!"

"You would think my reasons sufficient did you know them, as know them you shall, if you are disposed to listen to my story. I think you all, honest, and men who would rather aid than betray one, bent on a worthy object."

"Come, then, and tell us at your leisure," said the trapper, seating himself, and beckoning to the youth to follow his example. The latter willingly complied, and after Paul and the Doctor, had disposed of themselves to their several likings, the new-comer, entered into a narrative of the singular reasons which had led him so far into the deserts.

CHAPTER XI.

"So foul a sky clears not without a storm."

King John, IV.ii. 108.

In the mean time the industrious and irreclaimable hours continued their labours. The sun, which had been struggling through such masses of vapor throughout the day, fell slowly into a streak of clear sky, and thence sunk, gloriously, into the gloomy wastes, as he is wont to settle into the waters of the ocean. The vast herds, which had been grazing among the wild pastures of the Prairies, gradually disappeared, and the endless flocks of aquatic birds, that were pursuing their customary annual journey from the virgin Lakes of the North towards the Gulf of Mexico, ceased to fan that air, which had now become loaded with dew and vapour. In short, the shadows of night, fell upon the rock, adding the mantle of darkness to the other dreary accompanyments of the place.

As the light began to fail, Esther collected her younger children at her side, and placing herself on a projecting point of her insulated fortress, she sat patiently awaiting the return of the hunters. Ellen Wade was at no great distance, seeming to keep a little aloof from the anxious circle, as if willing to mark the distinction which existed in their characters.

"Your uncle is, and always will be a dull calculator, Nell," observed the mother, after a long pause in a conversation that had turned on the labors of the day; "A lazy hand at figures, and foreknowledge is that said Ishmael Bush! Here he sat, lolloping about the rock from light till noon, doing nothing, but scheme—scheme—scheme, with seven as noble boys at his elbows, as woman ever gave to man, and what's the upshot! why, night is setting in, and his needful work not yet ended."

"It is not prudent, certainly, aunt," Ellen replied, with a vacancy in her air, that proved how little she knew what she was saying; "and it is setting a very bad example to his sons."

"Hoity toity, girl, who has reared you up as a judge over your elders, ay! and your betters, too! I should like to see the man on the whole frontier, who sets a more honest example to his children than this same Ishmael Bush! Show me if you can, Miss fault-finder, but not fault-mender, a set of boys who will, on occasion, sooner chop a piece of logging, and dress it for the crop, than my own children, though I say it, myself, who, perhaps should be silent; or a cradler that knows better how to lead a gang of hands through a field of wheat leaving a cleaner stubble, in his track, than my own good man! Then as a father, he is as generous as a Lord; for his sons have only to name the spot where they would like to pitch, and he gives 'em a deed of the Plantation, and no charge for papers, is ever made."

As the wife of the squatter concluded, she raised a hollow taunting laugh, that was echoed from the mouths of several juvenile imitators, whom she was training to a life as shiftless and lawless as her own, but which notwithstanding its uncertainty was not without its secret charms.

"Holla! old Eester;" shouted the well known voice of her husband from the plain beneath; "ar' you keeping your junketts, while we ar' finding you in venison and buffaloe beef. Come down, come down, old girl, with all your young and lend us a hand to carry up the meat! why what a frolick, you ar' in, woman! Come down, come down; for the boys are at hand, and we have work here for double your number."

Ishmael might have spared his lungs, more than a moiety of the effort they were compelled to make, in order that he should be heard. He had hardly uttered the name of his wife, before the whole of the crouching circle rose in a body, and tumbling over each other, they precipitated themselves down the dangerous passes of the rock, with ungovernable impatience. Esther followed the young fry, with a more measured gait, nor did Ellen deem it wise, or rather discreet, to remain behind. Consequently, the whole were soon assembled at the base of the citadel, on the open plain.

Here the squatter was found, staggering under the weight of a fine fat buck, attended by one or two of his younger sons. Abiram quickly appeared, and before many minutes had elapsed most of the hunters dropped in, singly and in pairs, each man bringing with him some fruits of his prowess in the field.

"The plain is free from red-skins to night, at least," said Ishmael, after the bustle of reception had a little subsided: "for I have scoured the Prairie, for many long miles, on my own feet, and I call myself a judge of the print of an Indian moccasin. So, old woman, you can give us a few steaks of the venison, and then we will sleep on the day's work."

"I'll not swear there are no savages near us," said Abiram. "I, too, know something of the trail of a red-skin, and unless my eyes have lost some of their sight, I would swear, boldly, that there ar' Indians at hand. But wait till Asa, comes in. He pass'd the spot where I found the marks, and the boy knows something of such matters too."

"Ay, the boy, knows too much of many things," returned Ishmael, gloomily. "It will be better for him, when he thinks he knows less. But what matters it, Hetty, if all the Sioux tribes west of the big river, are within a mile of us; they will find it no easy matter to scale this rock in the teeth of ten bold men."

"Call 'em twelve, at once, Ishmael, call 'em twelve," cried his termigant assistant. "For if your moth gathering, bug hunting friend, can be counted a man, I beg you will set me down as two. I will not turn my back to him, with the rifle or the shot-gun, and for courage, the yearling heifer that them skulking devils the Tetons stole, was the biggest coward among us all, and after her comes your drivelling Doctor. Ah! Ishmael, you rarely attempt a regular trade, but you come out the loser; and this man, I reckon, is the hardest bargain among them all. Would you think it, the fellow ordered me a blister around my mouth, because I complained of a pain in the foot!"

"It is a pity, Eester," the husband, coolly answered, "that you did not take it, I reckon, it would have done considerable good. But, boys, if it should turn out as Abiram thinks, that there are Indians near us, we may have to scamper up the rock, and lose our suppers after all. Therefore we will make sure of the game, and talk over the performances of the Doctor, when we have nothing better to do."

The hint was taken, and in a few minutes, the exposed situation in which the family was collected, was exchanged for the more secure elevation of the rock. Here Esther busied herself, working and scolding with equal industry, until the repast was prepared, when she summoned her husband to his meal, in a voice as sonorous as that with which the Imaum reminds the Faithful of a more important duty.

When each had assumed his proper and customary place around the smoking viand, the squatter set the example, by beginning to partake of a delicious venison steak, prepared like the hump of the bison, with a skill, that rather increased than concealed its natural properties. A painter would gladly have seized the moment, to transfer the wild and characteristic scene to the canvass.

The reader will remember that the citadel of Ishmael, stood insulated, lofty, ragged, and nearly inaccessible. A bright, flashing fire, that was burning on the centre of its summit, and around which the busy groupe was clustered, lent it the appearance of some tall Pharos, placed in the centre of the deserts, to light such adventurers as wandered through their broad wastes. The flashing flame, gleamed from one sun burnt countenance to another, exhibiting every variety of expression, from the juvenile simplicity of the children, mingled as it was with a shade of the wildness peculiar to their semi-barbarous lives, to the dull and immovable apathy that dwelt on the features of the squatter, when unexcited. Occasionally a gust of wind, would fan the embers, and as a brighter light shot upward, the little solitary tent, was seen, as it were suspended in the gloom of the upper air. All beyond was enveloped as usual at that hour in an impenetrable body of darkness.

"It is unaccountable that Asa, should choose to be out of the way, at such a time as this," Esther pettishly observed. "When all is finished and to rights, we shall have the boy coming up grumbling for his meal, and hungry as a bear after his winter's nap. His stomach is as true as the best clock in Kentucky, and seldom wants winding up, to tell the time, whether of day, or night. A desperate eater, is Asa, when a-hungered by a little work!"

Ishmael look'd, sternly, around the circle of his silent sons, as if to see whether any among them would presume to say aught in favour of the absent delinquent. But, now, when no exciting cause existed to arouse their slumbering tempers, it seemed to be too great an effort to enter on the defence of their rebellious brother. Abiram, however, who since the pacification either felt or affected to feel a more generous interest in his late adversary, saw fit to express an anxiety, to which the others were strangers.

"It will be well if the boy has escaped the Tetons!" he muttered. "I should be sorry to have Asa, who is one of the stoutest of our party, both in heart and hand, fall into the power of the red devils."

"Look to yourself, Abiram; and spare your breath if you can use it only to frighten the woman and her huddling girls. You have whitened the face of Ellen Wade, already, who looks as pale, as if she was staring to-day at the very Indians you name, when I was forced to speak to her through the rifle, because I couldn't reach her ears with my tongue. How was it, Nell; you have never given the reason of your deafness?"

The colour of Ellen's cheek changed, as suddenly as the squatter's piece had flash'd, on the occasion to which he alluded, the burning glow, suffusing her features, until even her throat mantled with its fine healthful tinge. She hung her head abashed, but, did not seem to think it necessary to reply.

Ishmael, too sluggish to pursue the subject, or content with the pointed allusion he had just made, rose from his seat on the rock, and stretching his heavy frame, like a well fed and fattened ox, he announced his intention to sleep. Among a race who liv'd chiefly for the indulgence of the natural wants, such a declaration, could not fail of meeting with sympathetic dispositions. One after another disappeared each seeking his or her rude dormitory, and before many minutes, Esther, who by this time had scolded the younger fry to sleep, found, herself, if we except the usual watchman below, in solitary possession of the naked rock.

Whatever less valuable fruits had been produced, in this uneducated woman, by her migratory habits, the great principle of female nature was too deeply rooted ever to be entirely eradicated. Of a powerful, not to say fierce temperament, her passions, were violent and difficult to be smothered. But, however she might and did abuse the accidental prerogatives of her situation, love for her offspring, while it often, slumbered, could never be said to become extinct. She lik'd not the protracted absence of Asa. Too fearless herself to have hesitated, an instant, on her own account about crossing the dark abyss, into which she now sat looking with longing eyes, her busy imagination, in obedience to this inextinguishable sentiment, began to conjure nameless evils on account of her son. It might be true, as Abiram had hinted, that he had become a captive to some of the tribes who were hunting the buffaloe in that vicinity, or even a still more dreadful calamity might have befallen. So thought the mother, while silence and darkness lent their aid to the secret impulses of nature.

Agitated by these reflections, which put sleep at defiance, Esther, continued at her post, listening with that sort of acuteness, which is termed instinct in the animals a few degrees below her in the scale of intelligence, for any of those noises which might indicate the approach of footsteps. At length, her wishes had an appearance of being realized, for the long desired sounds were distinctly audible, and presently she distinguished the dim form of a man, at the base of the rock.

"Now, Asa, richly do you deserve to be left with an earthen bed this blessed night!" the woman began to mutter, with a revolution in her feelings that will not be surprising to those who have made the contradictions that give variety to the human character a study. "And a hard one, I've mind it shall be. Why Abner; Abner; you Abner, do you sleep? Let me not see you dare to open the hole, till I get down. I will know who it is that wishes to disturb a peaceable, ay, and an honest family too, at such a time, in the night, as this!"

"Woman! exclaimed a voice, that intended to bluster, while the speaker was manifestly, a little apprehensive of the consequences; "Woman, I forbid you, on pain of the Law to project any of your infernal missiles. I am a citizen, and a freeholder, and a graduate of two universities, and I stand upon my rights. Beware of malice prepense — of chance medley and of man-slaughter. It is I — your amicus, a Friend and inmate, I — Doctor Obed Battius!"

"Who!" demanded Esther in a voice that nearly refused to convey her words to the ears of the anxious listener beneath. "Did you say it was not Asa?"

"Nay, I am neither Asa nor Absolem, nor any of the Hebrew Princes; but Obed, the root and stock of them all. Have I not said, woman, that you keep one, in attendance, who is entitled, to a peaceable as well as an honorable admission. Do you take me for an animal of the class Amphibia, and that I can play with my lungs, as a blacksmith does with his bellows!"

The naturalist might have expended his breath much longer, without producing any desirable result, had Esther been his only auditor. Disappointed and alarmed, the woman had already sought her pallet, and was preparing with a sort of desperate indifference, to compose herself to sleep. Abner, the sentinel below, however, had been aroused from an exceedingly equivocal situation, by the outcry, and as he had now regained sufficient consciousness to recognize the voice of the Physician, the latter was admitted, with the least possible delay. Doctor Battius bustled through the narrow entrance, with an air of singular impatience, and was already beginning to mount the difficult ascent, when catching a view of the porter, he paused to observe with an air that he intended should be impressively admonitory —

"Abner, there are dangerous symptoms of somnolency about thee! It is sufficiently exhibited in the tendency to hiation, and may prove dangerous not only to yourself, but to all thy father's family!"

"You never made a greater mistake, Doctor," returned the youth, gaping like an indolent lion; "I haven't a symptom, as you call it, about any part of me, and as to father and the children, I reckon, the small-pox, and the measles, have been thoroughly through the breed these many months ago."

Content with his brief admonition, the Naturalist, had surmounted half the difficulties of the ascent, before the deliberate Abner ended his justification. On the summit, Obed fully expected to encounter Esther, of whose linguacious powers, he had too often been furnished with the most sinister proofs, and of which he stood in an awe too salutary to covet a repetition of the attacks. The reader can foresee that he was to be agreeably disappointed. Treading lightly, and looking timidly over his shoulder as if he apprehended a shower of something, even more formidable than words, the Doctor, proceeded to the place, which had been allotted to himself, in the general disposition of the dormitories.

Instead of sleeping the worthy naturalist sat ruminating over what he had both seen and heard that day, until the tossing and mutterings which proceeded from the cabin of Esther, who was his nearest neighbor, advertised him of the wakeful situation of its inmate. Perceiving the necessity of doing something to disarm this female Cerberus, before his own purpose could be accomplished, the Doctor, reluctant as he was to encounter her tongue, found himself compelled, to invite a colloquial communication.

"You appear not to sleep, my very kind and worthy Mrs. Bush," he said, determined to commence his applications with a plaister that was usually found to adhere; "you appear to rest badly, my excellent hostess. Can I administer to your ailings?"

"What would you give me, man," grumbled Esther. "A blister to make me sleep!"

"Say, rather a cataplasm.* But if you are in pain, here are some cordial drops, which, taken in a glass of my own Cogniac, will give you rest, if I know aught of the Materia Medica."

The Doctor, as he very well knew, had assailed Esther on her weak side; and as he doubted not of the acceptable quality of his prescription he set himself at work, without unnecessary delay, to prepare it. When he made his offering, it was received in a snappish and threatening manner, but swallowed with a facility that sufficiently proclaimed how much it was relished. The woman muttered her thanks, and her leech re-seated himself, in silence, to await the operation of the dose. In less than half an hour, the breathing of Esther became so profound, and as the Doctor himself, might have termed it, so very abstracted, that, had he not known how easy it was to ascribe this new instance of somnolency to the powerful dose of opium with which he had garnished the brandy, he might have seen reason to distrust his own prescription. With the sleep of the restless woman, the stillness became profound and general.

Then Dr. Battius saw fit, to arise, with the silence and caution, of the midnight robber, and to steal out of his own cabin, or rather kennel, for it deserved no better name, towards the adjoining dormitories. Here he took time to assure himself that all his neighbors were buried in deep sleep. Once advised of this important fact, he hesitated no longer, but commenced the difficult ascent which led to the upper pinnacle of the rock. His advance, though abundantly guarded, was not entirely noiseless, but while he was felicitating himself on having successfully effected his object, and he was in the very act of placing his foot on the highest ledge, a hand was laid upon the skirts of his coat, which as effectually put an end to his advance, as if the gigantic strength of Ishmael had pinned him to the earth.

"Is there sickness in the tent," whispered a soft voice in his very ear, "that Doctor Battius, is called to visit it at such an hour!"

So soon as the heart of the Naturalist had returned from its hasty expedition into his throat, as one less skilled than Dr. Battius in the formation of the animal, would have been apt to have accounted for the extraordinary sensation with which he received this unlook'd for interruption, he found resolution to reply, using, as much in terror as in prudence, the same precaution in the indulgence of his voice.

"My worthy Nelly, I am greatly rejoiced to find it is no other than thee! Hist! child, hist! Should Ishmael gain a knowledge of our plans, he would not hesitate to cast us both, from this rock, upon the plain beneath. Hist, Nelly, hist."

As the Doctor delivered his injunctions between the intervals of his ascent, by the time they were concluded, both he and his auditor had gained the upper level.

"And now, Doctor Battius," the girl gravely demanded, "may I know the reason why you have run so great a risk of flying from this place, without wings, and at the certain expense of your neck?"

"Nothing shall be concealed from thee, worthy and trusty Nelly—but are you certain, that Ishmael will not awake."

"No fear of him; he will sleep until the sun scorches his eye lids. The danger is from my aunt."

"Esther sleepeth," the Doctor sententiously replied. "Ellen, you have been watching, on this rock, to-day?"

"I was ordered to do so."

"And you have seen the bison, and the antelope, and the wolf, and the deer, as usual; animals of the *orders,* pecora, belluæ and feræ."

"I have seen the creatures you nam'd in English; but I know nothing of the Indian languages."

"There is still an *order* that I have not named, which you have also seen. The Primates—is it not true?"

"I cannot say. I know no animal by that name."

"Nay, Ellen, you confer with a friend. Of the *genus,* homo, child."

"Whatever else I may have had in view, I have not seen the ves-pertilio horribi—"

"Hush, Nelly, thy vivacity will betray us. Tell me, girl; have you not seen certain *bipeds,* called, *men,* wandering about the Prairie."

"Surely. My uncle and his sons, have been hunting the buffaloe since the sun began to fall."

"I must speak in the vernaculár to be comprehended! Ellen, I would say of the *species,* Kentucky."

Though Ellen reddened like the rose, her blushes were concealed by the darkness. She hesitated an instant, and then summoned suffi-cient spirit to say, decidedly—

"If you wish to speak in parables, Doctor Battius, you must find another listener. Put your questions plainly, in English, and I will answer them honestly in the same tongue."

"I have been journeying in this desert, as thou knowest, Nelly, in quest of animals, that have been hidden from the eyes of science, until now. Among others, I have discovered a Primates, of the *genus* homo; *species,* Kentucky; which I term Paul—"

"Hist, for the sake of mercy!" said Ellen, "speak lower, Doctor, or we shall be ruined."

"Hover, by profession a collector of the Apes, or Bee," continued the other. "Do I use the vernacular now—am I understood."

"Perfectly, perfectly," returned the girl, breathing with difficulty in her surprise. "But what of him—did he tell you to mount this rock—he knows nothing, himself, for the oath I gave my uncle, has shut my mouth."

"Ay, but there is one, that has taken no oath, who has revealed all. I would that the mantle which is wrapped around the mysteries of nature, were as effectually withdrawn from its hidden treasures! Ellen. Ellen, the man with whom I have unwittingly formed a compactum, or agreement, is sadly forgetful of the obligations of honesty! Thy uncle, child."

"You mean, Ishmael Bush, my father's brother's widow's husband," returned the offended girl, a little proudly—"Indeed, indeed, it is cruel to reproach me with a tie, that chance has formed, and which I would rejoice so much to break for ever."

The humbled Ellen could utter no more, but sinking on a projec-tion of the rock, she began to sob in a manner that rendered their situation doubly critical. The Doctor muttered a few words, which he intended as an apologetic explanation, but before he had time to complete his laboured vindication, she arose and said with decision—

"I did not come here to pass my time in foolish tears, nor you to try to stop them. What then has brought you hither?"

"I must see the inmate of that tent."

"You know what it contains?"

"I am taught to believe I do; and I bear a letter, which I must deliver with my own hands. If the animal prove a quadruped, Ishmael is a true man—if a biped, fledged or unfledged, I care not, he is false, and our compactum at an end!"

Ellen made a sign for the Doctor to remain where he was, and to be silent. She then glided into the tent, where she continued many minutes, that proved exceedingly weary and anxious to the expectant without, but the instant she returned, she took him by the arm, and together they entered beneath the folds of the mysterious cloth.

CHAPTER XII.

"Pray God the Duke of York excuse himself!"

Henry VI, Part II, I.iii.181.

THE mustering of the borderers on the following morning, was silent, sullen and gloomy. The repast of that hour, was wanting in the inharmonious accompanyment, with which Esther ordinarily enlivened their meals, for the effects of the powerful opiate the Doctor had administered, still muddled her intellects. The young men brooded over the absence of their elder brother, and the brows of Ishmael, himself, were knit, as he cast his scowling eyes from one to the other, like a man preparing to meet and to repel an expected assault on his authority. In the midst of this family distrust, Ellen and her midnight confederate, the Naturalist, took their usual places, among the children, without awakening suspicion or exciting comment. The only apparent fruits of the adventure in which they had been engaged, were occasional upliftings of the eyes, on the part of the Doctor, which were mistaken by the observers for some of his scientific contemplations of the heavens, but which, in reality, were no other than furtive glances at the fluttering walls of the proscribed tent.

At length the squatter, who had waited, in vain for some more decided manifestation of the expected rising among his sons, resolved to make a demonstration of his own intentions.

"Asa shall account to me, for this undutiful conduct!" he observed. "Here has the live-long night gone by, and he out-lying on the Prairie, when his hand and his rifle might both have been wanted in a brush with the Siouxes, for any right he had to know the contrary."

"Spare your breath, good man;" retorted his wife, "be saving of your breath; for you may have to call long enough for the boy before he will answer."

"It ar' a fact, that some men be so womanish, as to let the young master the old! But you, old Eester, should know better, than to think such will ever be the natur of things, in the family of Ishmael Bush."

"Ah! you ar' a hectorer with the boys, when need calls! I know it, well, Ishmael, and one of your sons, have you driven from you, by your temper; and that, too, at a time when he is most wanted."

"Father," said Abner, whose sluggish nature had, gradually, been stimulating itself to the exertion of taking so bold a stand, "the boys and I have pretty generally concluded, to go out on the search of Asa. We are disagreeable, about his camping on the Prairie, instead of coming in to his own bed, as we all know, he would like to do—"

"Pshaw!" muttered Abiram; "the boy, has killed a buck, or, perhaps a buffaloe, and he is sleeping by the carcass to keep off the wolves 'till day; we shall soon see him, or hear him, bawling for help to bring in his load."

"Tis little help, that a son of mine will call for, to shoulder a buck or to quarter your wild beef!" returned the Mother. "And you, Abiram, to say so uncertain a thing! you, who said yourself, that the red skins had been prowling around this place, no later than the yesterday."

"I!" exclaimed her brother, hastily, as if anxious to retract an error. "I said it then, and I say it now, and so you will find it to be. The Tetons are in our neighborhood, and happy will it prove for the boy, if he is well shut of them."

"It seems to me," said Doctor Battius, speaking with the sort of deliberation and dignity one is apt to use, after having thoroughly ripened his opinions by sufficient reflection, "it seems to me, a man but little skilled in the signs and tokens of Indian warfare, especially as practised in these remote plains, but one, who I may say without vanity has some insight into the mysteries of nature; it seems, then, to me thus humbly qualified, that when doubts exist, in a matter of moment, it would, always be the wisest course to appease them."

"No more of your doctoring for me," cried the grum Esther, "no more of your quiddities in a healthy family, say I. Here, was I doing well, only a little out of sorts with over instructing the young, and you dos'd me with a drug, that hangs about my tongue, like a pound weight on a humming bird's wing."

"Is the medicine out?" drily demanded Ishmael: "it must be a rare dose that gives a heavy feel to the tongue of old Eester!"

"Friends," continued the Doctor, waving his hand for the angry wife to maintain the peace, "that it cannot perform all that is said of it, the very charge of good Mrs. Bush is a sufficient proof. But to speak of the absent, Asa. There is doubt, as to his fate, and there is a proposition to solve it. Now in the natural sciences, truth is always a desideratum, and I confess it would seem to be equally so, in the present case of domestick uncertainty, which may be called a vacuum, where, according to the laws of physick, there should exist some pretty palpable proofs of materiality."

"Don't mind him, don't mind him," cried Esther, observing that the rest of his auditors listened with an attention which might proceed, equally, from acquiescence in his proposal or ignorance of its meaning. "There is a drug in every word he utters."

"Doctor Battius wishes to say," Ellen modestly interposed, "that as some of us, think Asa is in danger, and some think otherwise, the whole family might pass an hour or two, in looking for him."

"Does he," interrupted the woman, "then Dr. Battius has more sense in him, than I believed. She is right, Ishmael; and what she says shall be done. I will shoulder a rifle myself, and woe betide, the red-skin, that crosses my path! I have pulled a trigger before to day, ay, and heard an Indian yell, too, to my sorrow."

The spirit of Esther diffused itself, like the stimulus which attends a war-cry, among her sons. They arose in a body and declared their determination to second so bold a resolution. Ishmael prudently yielded to an impulse that he could not resist, and in a few minutes, the woman appeared, shouldering her arms, prepared to lead forth in person, such of her descendants as chose to follow.

"Let them stay with the children that please," she said, "and them follow me who ar' not chicken-hearted."

"Abiram, it will not do to leave the huts without some guard," Ishmael whispered glancing his eye upward.

The man whom he address'd started, and betrayed extraordinary eagerness in his reply.

"I will tarry and watch the camp."

A dozen voices were instantly raised in objections to this proposal. He was wanted to point out the places where the hostile tracks had been seen, and his termagant sister openly scouted at the idea, as unworthy of his manhood. The reluctant Abiram was compelled to yield, and Ishmael, made a new disposition for the defence of the place, which was admitted, by every one, to be all important to their security and comfort.

He offered the post of Commandant to Dr. Battius, who, however peremptorily and somewhat haughtily declined the doubtful honor, exchanging looks of intelligence with Ellen as he did so. In this dilemma the squatter was obliged to constitute the girl, herself, castellan; taking care, however, in deputing this important trust to omit no words of caution and instruction. When this preliminary point was settled, the young men, proceeded to arrange certain means of defence, and signals of alarm, that were adapted to the weakness and character of the garrison. Several masses of rock were drawn to the edge of the upper level, and, so placed, as to leave it at the discretion of the feeble Ellen and her associates to cast them or not, as they might choose, on the heads of any invaders, who would, of necessity, be obliged to mount the eminence, by the difficult and narrow passage already so often mentioned. In addition to this formidable obstruction, the barriers were strengthened, and rendered nearly impassable. Smaller missiles, that might be hurled even by the hands of the younger children, but which would prove, from the elevation of the place, exceedingly dangerous, were provided in profusion. A pile of dried leaves and splinters, was placed as a beacon on the upper rock, and then even in the jealous judgment of the squatter, the post was deemed competent to maintain a creditable siege.

The moment the rock was thought to be in a state of sufficient security, the party who composed what might be called the sortie, sallied forth, on their anxious expedition. The advance was led by Esther in person, who, attired in a dress half-masculine, and bearing a weapon like the rest, seem'd no unfit leader for the groupe of wildly clad frontier-men, that followed in her rear.

"Now, Abiram," cried the Amazon in a voice that was cracked and harsh, for the simple reason of being used too often on a strained and unnatural key, "now, Abiram, run with your nose low, show yourself a hound of the true breed, and do some credit to your training. You it was, that saw the prints of the Indian moccasin, and it behoves you, to let others be as wise as yourself. Come; come to the front, man, and give us a bold lead."

The brother, who appeared, at all times, to stand in awe of his sister's authority, complied, though it was with a reluctance so evident, as to excite sneers, even among the unobservant and indolent sons of the squatter. Ishmael, himself, mov'd among his tall children like one who expected nothing from the search, and who was indifferent, alike to its success or failure. In this manner the party proceeded until their distant fortress had sunk so low, as to present an object no larger nor more distinct than a hazy point, on the margin of the Prairie. Hitherto their progress, had been silent, and somewhat rapid, for as swell after swell, was mounted and passed, without varying, or discovering a living object to enliven the monotony of the view, even the tongue of Esther was hushed in increasing anxiety. Here, however,

Ishmael chose to pause; and casting the butt of his rifle from his shoulder to the ground, he observed—

"This is enough. Buffaloe signs, and deer signs, ar' plenty; but where ar' thy Indian footsteps, Abiram?"

"Still farther West," returned the other pointing in the direction he named. "This was the spot where I struck the tracks of the buck; it was after I took the deer, that I fell upon the Teton trail."

"And a bloody piece of work you made of it, man," cried the squatter, pointing tauntingly to the soiled garments of his kinsman, and then directing the attention of the spectators to his own, by the way of a triumphant contrast. "Here have I cut the throat of two lively does, and a scampering fawn without spot or stain, while you, blundering dog as you ar', have made as much work for Eester and her girls, as though butchering was your regular calling. Come, boys: it is enough. I am too old, not to know the signs of the frontiers; no Indian has been here since the last fall of water. Follow me, and I will make a turn that shall give us at least the beef of a fallow cow, for our trouble."

"Follow *me!*" echoed Esther, stepping undauntedly forward. "I am leader to day, and I *will* be followed—who so proper, let me know, as a mother to head a search for her own lost child!"

Ishmael regarded his untractable mate with a smile of indulgent pity. Observing that she had already struck out a path for herself, different both from that of Abiram and the one he had seen fit to choose, and being unwilling to draw the cord of authority too tight, just at that moment, he submitted to her will. But Doctor Battius, who had hitherto, been a silent and thoughtful, attendant on the woman, now, saw fit to raise his feeble voice, in the way of remonstrance.

"I agree with thy partner in life, worthy and gentle Mrs. Bush," he said, "in believing that some ignuus fatuus of the imagination, has deceived Abiram, in the signs or symptoms of which he has spoken."

"Symptoms, yourself!" interrupted the termagant. "This is no time for bookish words, nor is this a place to stop, and swallow medicines. If you ar' a-leg weary say so, as a plain-speaking man should; then seat yourself on the Prairie, like a hound that is foot-sore, and take your natural rest."

"I accord in the opinion," the Naturalist calmly replied, complying literally with the opinion of the deriding Esther, by taking his seat, very coolly by the side of an indigenous shrub, the examination of which he commenced, on the instant, in order, that science might not lose any of its just and important dues. "I honor your excellent advice, Mistress Esther, as you may perceive. Go thou in quest of thy offspring, while I tarry here, in pursuit of that which is better; viz, an insight into the arcana of nature's volume."

The woman answered with a hollow, unnatural and scornful laugh, and even her heavy sons, as they slowly passed the seat of the already abstracted naturalist, did not disdain to manifest their contempt in smiles. In a few minutes, the train mounted the nearest eminence, and as it turned the rounded acclivity, the Doctor was left to pursue his profitable investigations in entire solitude.

Another half-hour passed during which Esther, continued to advance on her, seemingly, fruitless search. Her pauses, however, were becoming frequent and her looks wandering and uncertain, when footsteps, were heard, clattering through the bottom, and at the next instant, a buck was seen to bound up the ascent, and to dart from before their eyes, in the direction of the naturalist. So sudden and unlooked-for had been the passage of the animal, and so much had he been favored by the shape of the ground, that, before any one of the foresters had time to bring his rifle to his shoulder, it was already beyond the range of a bullet.

"Look out for the wolf!" shouted Abner, shaking his head, in vexation at being a single moment too late. "A wolf's skin, will be no bad gift, in a winter's night. Ay, yonder the hungry devil comes."

"Hold!" cried Ishmael, knocking up the levelled weapon of his too eager son. "'Tis not a wolf; but a hound of thorough blood and bottom! Ha! we have hunters nigh. There ar' two of them!"

He was still speaking when the animals in question, came leaping, on the track of the deer, striving with noble ardor to outdo each other. One was an aged dog, whose strength seem'd to be sustained purely by generous emulation, and the other a pup, that gamboled, even, while he press'd most warmly on the chace. They both ran, however, with clean and powerful leaps, carrying their noses high, like animals of the most keen and subtle scent. They had passed; and in another minute, they would have been, running open-mouthed with the deer in view, had not the younger dog, suddenly bounded from the course, and uttered a cry of surprise. His aged companion, stopped also, and returned panting and exhausted, to the place where the other was whirling around in swift, and apparently in mad evolutions, circling the spot in his own footsteps and continuing his outcry, in a short, snappish barking. But when the elder hound, had reach'd the spot, he seated himself, and lifting his nose high into the air, he raised a long, loud, and wailing howl.

"It must be a strong scent," said Abner, who had been, with the rest of the family, an admiring observer of the movements of the dogs, "that can break off two such creaturs so suddenly from their trail."

"Murder them!" cried Abiram; "I'll swear to the old hound, 'tis the dog of the trapper, whom we now know to be our mortal enemy."

Though the brother of Esther gave so hostile advice, he appeared in no way ready to put it in execution, himself. The surprise which had taken possession of the whole party exhibited itself, in his own vacant, wondering stare, as strongly as in any of the admiring visages, by whom he was surrounded. His denunciation, therefore, notwithstanding its dire import was disregarded, and the dogs were left to obey the impulses of their mysterious instinct, without let or hindrance.

It was long before any of the spectators broke the silence; but the squatter, at length, so far recollected his authority, as to take on himself the right to controul the movements of his children.

"Come away, boys; come, away and leave the hounds to sing their tunes for their own amusement," Ishmael said in his coldest manner. "I scorn to take the life of a beast because its master has pitch'd himself too nigh my clearing—come, away, boys; come away; we have enough of our own work before us, without turning aside to do that of the whole neighbourhood."

"Come *not,* away!" cried Esther, in tones that sounded like the admonitions of some Sybil. "I say, come, *not* away, my children. There is a meaning and a warning in this; and as I am a woman and a mother, will I know the truth of it all."

So saying, the awakened wife brandished her weapon with an air, that was not without its wild and secret influence, and led the way, towards the spot, where the dogs, still remained, filling the air with their long drawn and piteous complaints. The whole party, followed in her steps, some too indolent to oppose, others obedient to her will, and all more or less excited by the uncommon character of the scene.

"Tell me, you Abner—Abiram—Ishmael—" the woman cried, standing over a spot where the earth was trampled and beaten, and plainly sprinkled with blood; "tell me, you who ar' hunters, what sort of animal, has here met his death?—Speak!—ye ar' men, and used to the signs of the plains; is it the blood of wolf or panther?"

"A buffaloe, and a noble and powerful creatur has it been," returned the squatter, who look'd down calmly on these fatal signs, which so strangely affected his wife. "Here are the marks of the spot, where he has struck his hoofs into the earth in the death-struggle, and yonder he has plunged and torn the ground with his horns. Ay, a buffaloe bull, of wonderful strength and courage has he been!"

"And who has slain him!" continued Esther; "man! where—are the offals?—wolves!—they devour not the hide. Tell me, ye men and hunters, is this the blood of a beast?"

"The creatur, has plunged over the hillock," said Abner, who had proceeded a short distance beyond the rest of the party. "Ah! there you will find it, in yon swale of alders. Look! a thousand carrion birds, ar' hovering, above the carcass."

"The animal has still life in him," returned the squatter, "or the buzzards would settle upon their prey! By the action of the dogs, it must be something ravenous, I reckon it is the white bear from the upper falls. They are said to cling desperately to life."

"Let us go back," said Abiram; "there may be danger, and there can be no good, in attacking a ravenous beast. Remember, Ishmael, 'twill be a risky job, and one of small profit."

The young men smil'd at this new proof of the well known pusil-animity of their uncle. The oldest even proceeded, so far as to express his contempt, by bluntly saying—

"It will do, to cage with the other animal we carry. Then we may go back double-handed into the settlements, and set up for showmen around the court-houses and gaols of Kentuck."

The threatening frown which gathered on the brow of his father admonished the young man to forbear. Exchanging looks that were half-rebellious with his brethren, he saw fit to be silent. But instead of observing the caution recommended by Abiram, they proceeded in a body until, they, again, came to a halt within a few yards of the matted cover of the thicket.

The scene had, now, indeed, become wild and striking enough, to have produced a powerful effect on minds better prepared than those of the unnurtured family of the squatter, to resist the impressions of so exciting a spectacle. The heavens were as usual at the season covered with dark driving clouds, beneath which interminable flocks of aquatic birds, were again on the wing, holding their toilsome and heavy way, towards the distant waters of the south. The wind had risen, and was once more sweeping over the Prairie in gusts, which it was often vain to oppose, and then again the blasts would seem to mount into the upper air, as if to sport with the drifting vapour, whirling and rolling, vast masses of the dusky and ragged volumes over each other, in a terrific and yet grand disorder. Above the little brake, the flocks of birds, still held their flight, circling with heavy wings about the spot, struggling at times against the torrent of wind, and then, favored by their position and height, making bold swoops upon the thicket, away from which, however, they never fail'd to sail, screaming in terror, as if apprised, either by sight or instinct, that the hour of their voracious dominion had not yet fully arrived.

Ishmael stood for many minutes, with his wife and children clustered together, in an amazement with which awe was singularly mingled, gazing in death-like stillness on the sight. The voice of Esther, at length, broke the charm, and reminded the spectators of the necessity of resolving their doubts, in some manner more worthy of their manhood, than by dull and inactive observation.

"Call in the dogs!" she said, "call in the hounds, and put them into the thicket. There ar' men enough of ye, if ye have not lost the spirit, with which I know ye were born, to tame the tempers of all the bears, west of the big river. Call in the dogs, I say, you, Enoch—Abner, Gabriel, has wonder made ye deaf!"

One of the young men complied; and having succeeded in detaching the hounds from the place, around which, until then, they had not ceased to hover, he led them down to the margin of the thicket.

"Put them in, boy. Put them in," continued the woman; "and you, Ishmael and Abiram, if anything wicked or hurtful comes forth, show them the use of your rifles, like frontier-men. If ye ar' wanting in spirit, before the eyes of my children will I put ye both to shame!"

The youths who, until now, had detained the hounds, let slip the thongs of skin by which they had been held, and urged them to the attack, by their voices. But it would seem, that the elder dog, was restrained by some extraordinary sensation, or that he was much too experienced to attempt the rash adventure. After proceeding a few yards to the very verge of the brake, he made a sudden pause, and stood trembling in all his aged limbs, apparently as unable to recede as to advance. The encouraging calls of the young men were disregarded, or only answered by a low and plaintive whining. For a minute, the pup also was similarly affected; but less sage, or more easily excited, he was induced at length, to leap forward, and finally to dash into the cover. An alarmed and startling howl was heard, and at the next minute he broke out of the thicket, and commenced circling the spot in the same wild and unsteady manner as before.

"Have I a man among my children!" demanded Esther. "Give me, a truer piece than a childish shot-gun, and I will show ye, what the courage of a frontier woman can do!"

"Stay, mother," exclaimed Abner and Enoch; "if you *will* see the creatur, let *us* drive it into view."

This was quite as much, as the youths were accustomed to utter even on more important occasions, but having given a pledge of their intentions, they were far from being backward in redeeming it. Preparing their arms with the utmost care, they advanced with steadiness, to the brake. Nerves less often tried, than those of the young borderers might have shrunk before the dangers of so uncertain an undertaking. As they proceeded, the howls of the dogs, became more shrill and plaintive, the vultures and buzzards settled so low, as to flap the bushes with their heavy wings, and the wind came hoarsely sweeping along the naked Prairie, as if the spirits of the air, had, also descended, to witness the approaching developement.

There was a breathless moment, when the blood of the undaunted Esther, flowed backward to her heart, as she saw her sons push aside the matted branches of the thicket, and bury themselves in its labyrinth. A deep and solemn pause succeeded. Then arose two loud and piercing cries, in quick succession, which were followed by a quiet still more awful and appalling.

"Come back, come back, my children," cried the woman, the feelings of a mother getting the ascendancy.

But her voice, was hushed, and every faculty seem'd frozen with horror, as at that instant, the bushes once more parted, and the two adventurers reappeared, pale and nearly insensible themselves and laid at her feet, the stiff and motionless body of the lost Asa, with the marks of a violent death but too plainly stamp'd on every pallid lineament.

The dogs uttered a long and closing howl and then breaking off, together, they disappeared on the forsaken trail of the deer. The flight of birds, wheeled upward into the heavens, filling the air with their complaints at having been robbed of a victim, which, frightful and disgusting as it was, still bore too much of the impression of humanity to become the prey of their obscene appetites.

CHAPTER XIII.

"A pickaxe, and a spade, a spade.
For, — and a shrouding sheet:
O, a pit of clay for to be made
For such a guest is meet."

Hamlet, V.i.102-05.

STAND back! stand off, the whole of ye!" said Esther, hoarsely, to the crowd which press'd too closely on the corpse, "I am his mother, and my right is better than that of ye all. Who has done this! Tell, me, Ishmael, Abiram, Abner, open your mouths and your hearts, and let God's truth and no other issue from them. Who has done this bloody deed?"

Her husband made no reply but stood, leaning on his rifle, looking sadly, but with an unaltered eye, at the mangled remains of his son. Not so the mother: She threw herself on the earth, and receiving the cold and ghastly head into her lap, she sat contemplating those muscular features, on which the death-agony was still horridly impressed, in a silence, far more expressive than any language of lamentation could have proved.

The voice of the woman was frozen in grief. In vain Ishmael attempted a few words of rude consolation; she neither listened nor answered. Her sons gathered about her in a circle, and expressed after their uncouth manner, their sympathy in her sorrows, as well as their sense of their own loss; but she motioned them away, impatiently, with her hand. At times, her fingers play'd in the matted hair of the dead, and at others, they lightly attempted to smooth the painfully expressive muscles of its ghastly visage, as the hand of the mother, is seen lingering fondly about the features of her sleeping child. Then starting from their revolting office, her hands would flutter around her, and seem to seek some fruitless remedy against the violent blow, which had thus suddenly destroyed the child, in whom she had not only plac'd her greatest hopes, but so much of her maternal pride. While engaged in the latter incomprehensible manner, the lethargic Abner, turned aside, and swallowing the unwonted emotions which were rising in his own throat, he observed—

"Mother means, that we should look for the signs, that we may know in what manner, Asa has come by his end."

"We owe it to the accursed Siouxes," answered Ishmael. "Twice have they put me deeply in their debt! The third time, the score shall be cleared!"

But, not content with this plausible explanation, and perhaps secretly glad to avert their eyes from a spectacle which awakened so extraordinary and unusual sensations in their sluggish bosoms, the sons of the squatter turned away, in a body, from their mother and the corpse, and proceeded to make the enquiries, which they fancied the former had so repeatedly demanded. Ishmael, made no objections; but, though he accompanied his children, while they proceeded in the investigation, it was more with the appearance of complying with their wishes, at a time when resistance might not be seemly, than with any visible interest in the result. As the borderers, notwithstanding their usual dullness, were well instructed in most things connected with their habits of life, an inquiry, the success of which depended so much on signs and evidences that bore so strong a resemblance to a forest trail, was likely to be conducted, with skill and acuteness. Accordingly, they proceeded to the melancholy task with great readiness and intelligence.

Abner and Enoch, agreed in their accounts as to the position in which they had found the body. It was seated nearly upright, the back supported by a mass of matted brush, and one hand still grasping a broken twig of the alders. It was, most probably, owing to the former circumstance, that the body had escaped the rapacity of the carrion birds, which had been seen hovering above the thicket, and the latter prov'd that life had not yet entirely abandoned the hapless victim when he entered the brake. The opinion now became general that the youth had received his death wound in the open Prairie, and had dragged his enfeebled form into the cover of the thicket for the purpose of concealment. A trail through the bushes confirmed this opinion. It also appeared, on examination, that a desperate struggle had taken place on the very margin of the thicket. This was sufficiently apparent by the trodden branches, the deep impressions on the moist ground, and the lavish flow of blood.

"He has been shot in the open ground and come here for a cover," said Abiram, "these marks would clearly prove it. The boy has been set upon by the savages, in a body, and has fout like a hero as he was, until they have mastered his strength, and then drawn him to the bushes."

To this probable opinion there was now but one dissenting voice;

that of the slow-minded Ishmael who demanded that the corpse, itself, should be examined in order to obtain a more accurate knowledge of its injuries. On examination, it appeared, that a rifle bullet had passed directly through the body of the deceased, entering beneath one of his brawny shoulders and making its exit, by the breast. It required some knowledge in gun-shot wounds to decide this delicate point, but the experience of the borderers was quite equal to the scrutiny, and a smile of wild, and certainly of singular satisfaction passed among the sons of Ishmael, when Abner confidently announced that the enemies of Asa had assailed him in the rear.

"It must be so," said the gloomy but attentive squatter. "He was of too good a stock and too well trained, knowingly to turn the weak side to man or beast! Remember, boys, that while the front of manhood is to your enemy, let him be who or what he may, you ar' safe from cowardly surprise—Why Eester, woman! you ar' getting beside yourself, with picking at the hair and the garments of the child! Little good can you do him, now, old girl."

"See!" interrupted Enoch extricating from the fragments of cloth, the morsel of lead which had prostrated the strength of one so powerful. "Here is the very bullet!"

Ishmael took it in his hand, and eyed it long and closely.

"There's no mistake"—at length he muttered, through his compressed teeth. "It is from the pouch of that accursed trapper. Like many of the hunters, he has a mark in his mould in order to know the work his rifle performs, and here you see it plainly—six little holes laid crossways."

"I'll swear to it!" cried Abiram, triumphantly; "he show'd me his private mark, himself, and boasted of the number of deer he had laid upon the Prairies with these very bullets! Now, Ishmael, will you believe me, when I tell you the old knave is a spy of the red-skins."

The lead pass'd from the hand of one to that of another, and unfortunately for the reputation of the old man, several among them remembered also to have seen the aforesaid private bullet-mark, during the curious examination which all had made of his accoutrements. In addition to this wound, however, were many others of a less dangerous nature, all of which were deemed to confirm the supposed guilt of the trapper.

The traces of many different struggles were to be seen, between the spot, where the first blood was spilt and the thicket to which it was now generally believed Asa had retreated as a place of refuge. These were interpreted into so many proofs of the weakness of the murderer, who would have sooner dispatched his victim had not even the dying strength of the youth rendered him formidable to the infirmities of one so old. The danger of drawing some others of the hunters to the spot, by repeated firing, was deem'd a sufficient reason for not again resorting to the rifle after it had performed the important duty of disabling the victim. The weapon of the dead man, was not to be found, and had doubtless, together with many other less valuable and lighter articles, that he was accustomed to carry about his person, become a prize to his destroyer.

But what, in addition to the tell tale bullet, appeared to fix the ruthless deed with peculiar certainty on the trapper, was the accumulated evidence, furnished by the trail, which proved, notwithstanding his deadly hurt, that the wounded man had still been able to make a long and desperate resistance to the subsequent efforts of his murderer. Ishmael seemed to press this proof, with a singular mixture of sorrow and pride—sorrow at the loss of a son, whom in their moments of amity he highly valued; and pride at the courage and power he had manifested to his last and weakest breath.

"He died as a son of mine should die," said the squatter, gleaning a hollow consolation from so unnatural an exultation, "a dread to his enemy to the last, and without help from the law. Come, children; we have the grave to make, and then to hunt his murderer!"

The sons of the squatter set about their melancholy office in silence and in sadness. An excavation was made in the hard earth, at a great expense of toil and time, and the body was wrapped in such spare vestments as could be collected among the laborers. When these arrangements were completed, Ishmael approached the seemingly, unconscious Esther, and announced his intention to inter the dead. She heard him, and quietly relinquished her grasp of the corpse, rising in silence to follow it to its narrow resting place. Here she seated herself, again, at the head of the grave, watching each movement of the youths, with eager and jealous eyes. When a sufficiency of earth was laid upon the senseless clay of Asa, to protect it from injury, Enoch and Abner, entered the cavity, and trode it into a solid mass, by the weight of their huge frames, with an appearance of a strange, not to say savage mixture, of care and indifference. This well-known precaution was adopted to prevent the speedy exhumation of the body, by some of the carnivorous beasts of the Prairie, whose instinct was sure to guide them to the spot. Even the rapacious birds, appeared to comprehend the nature of the ceremony, for, mysteriously apprised that the miserable victim was now about to be abandoned by the human race, they once more began to make their airy circuits above the place, screaming, as if to frighten the kinsmen from their labour of caution and love.

Ishmael stood with folded arms, steadily watching the manner in which this necessary duty was performed, and when the whole was completed, he lifted his cap to his sons, to thank them for their services, with a dignity that would have become one much better nurtured. Throughout the whole of a ceremony, which is ever solemn and admonitory, the squatter had maintained a grave and serious deportment. His vast features were visibly stamp'd with an expression of deep concern, but at no time did they falter, until he turned his back, as he believed forever, on the grave of his first-born. Nature was then stirring powerfully within him, and the muscles of his stern visage began to work perceptibly. His children fastened their eyes on his, as if to seek a direction to the strange emotions which were moving their own heavy natures, when the struggle in the bosom of the squatter, suddenly ceased, and taking his wife by the arm he raised her to her feet as if she had been an infant, saying in a voice that was perfectly steady, though a nice observer would have discovered that it was kinder than usual—

"Eester, we have now done all that man and woman can do. We raised the boy, and made him such, as few others were like, on the frontiers of America; and, we have given him a grave. Let us go our way."

The woman turned her eyes slowly from the fresh earth, and laying her hands on the shoulders of her husband, stood looking him, anxiously in the eyes.

"Ishmael! Ishmael!" she said, "you parted from the boy, in your wrath!"

"May the Lord pardon his sins, as freely as I have forgiven his worst misdeeds," calmly returned the squatter; "woman, go you back to the rock, and read your bible, a chapter in that book always does you good. You *can* read, Eester; which is a privilege I never did enjoy."

"Yes, yes," muttered the woman yielding to his strength and suffering herself to be led, though with powerful reluctance, from the spot. "I *can* read; and how have I used the knowledge! But he, Ishmael, he has not the sin, of wasted l'arning to answer for. We have spared him *that*, at least, whether it be in mercy or in cruelty, I know not."

Her husband made no reply, but continued steadily to lead her in the direction of their temporary abode. When they reached the summit of the swell of land, which they knew, was the last spot, from which the situation of the grave of Asa could be seen, they all turned, as by common concurrence to take a farewell view of the place. The little mound itself, was not visible, but it was frightfully indicated by the flock of screaming birds, which hovered above. In the opposite direction, a low blue hillock, in the skirts of the horizon, pointed out the place where Esther had left, the rest of her young, and served as an attraction to draw her reluctant steps from the last abode of her eldest born. Nature quickened in the bosom of the mother at the sight, and she finally yielded the rights of the dead, to the more urgent claims of the living.

The foregoing occurrences had struck a spark from the stern tempers of a set of beings so singularly moulded in the habits of their uncultivated lives, which served to keep alive among them the dying embers of family affection. United to their parents by ties no stronger than those which use had created, there had been great danger, as Ishmael had foreseen, that the overloaded hive would swarm, and leave him, saddled with the difficulties of a young and helpless brood, unsupported by the exertions of those, whom he had, already, brought to a state of maturity. The spirit of insubordination, which emanated from the unfortunate Asa, had spread among his juniors, and the squatter had been made painfully to remember the time, when in the wantonness of his youth and vigor, he had, reversing the order of the brutes, cast off his own aged and failing parents, to enter into the world unshackled and free. But the danger had now abated, for a time at least, and if his authority was not restored with all its former influence, it was admitted to exist, and to maintain its ascendancy a little longer.

It is true, that his slow-minded sons, even while they submitted to the impressions of the recent event, had glimmerings of terrible distrusts, as to the manner in which their elder brother had met with his death. There were, faint and indistinct images in the minds of two or three of the oldest, which portrayed the father, himself, as ready to imitate the example of Abraham,* without the justification of the sacred authority, which commanded the holy man to attempt the revolting office. But, then, these images were so transient and so much obscured in intellectual mists as to leave no very strong impressions, and the tendency of the whole transaction, as we have already said, was rather to strengthen, than to weaken the authority of Ishmael.

In this disposition of mind, the party continued their route towards the place, whence, they had that morning issued on a search which had been crowned with so melancholy a success. The long and fruitless march, which they had made under the direction of Abiram, the discovery of the body and its subsequent interment had so far consumed the day, that by the time, their steps were retraced across the broad tract of waste which lay between the grave of Asa and the rock, the sun had fallen, far below his meridian altitude. The hill had gradually risen, as they approached, like some tower, emerging from the bosom of the sea, and when within a mile the minuter objects that crowned its height came, dimly into view.

"It will be a sad meeting for the girls!" said Ishmael, who, from time to time, did not cease to utter something which he intended should be consolatory to the bruised spirit of his partner. "Asa was much regarded, by all the young, and seldom failed to bring in from his hunts something, that they lov'd."

"He did, he did," murmured Esther, "the boy was the pride of the family—My other children are as nothing to him!"

"Say not so, good woman," returned the Father glancing his eye, a little proudly at the athletic train which followed at no great distance in their rear. "Say not so, old Eester for few fathers and mothers, have greater reason to be boastful than ourselves."

"Thankful, thankful," muttered the humbled woman; "ye mean thankful, Ishmael!"

"Then thankful, let it be, if you like the word better, my good girl— but what has become of Nelly and the young! The child has forgotten the charge I gave her, and has not only suffered the children to sleep, but I warrant you, is dreaming of the fields of Tennessee at this very moment. The mind of your niece is mainly fix'd on the settlements, I reckon."

"Ay, she is not for us. I said it, and thought it, when I took her, because death had stripped her of all other friends. Death is a sad worker in the bosom of families, Ishmael. Asa had a kind feeling to the child, and they might have come, one day, into our places, had things been so ordered."

"Nay, she is not gifted for a frontier wife if this is the manner she is to keep house, while the husband, is on the hunt. Abner, let off your rifle, that they may know we ar' coming. I fear Nelly, and the young, ar' asleep."

The young man complied with an alacrity, that manifested how gladly he would see, the rounded, active figure of Ellen, enliven the ragged summit of the rock. But the report was succeeded by neither signal nor answer of any sort. For a moment, the whole party stood in suspense, awaiting the result, and then a simultaneous impulse caused the whole to let off their pieces at the same instant, producing a noise, which might not fail to reach the ears of all within so short a distance.

"Ah! there they come at last!" cried Abiram, who was usually among the first to seize on any circumstance which promised relief from disagreeable apprehensions.

"It is a petticoat fluttering on the line," said Esther; "I put it there myself."

"You ar' right—but now she comes. The jade has been taking her comfort in the tent!"

"It is not so," said Ishmael, whose usually inflexible features were beginning to manifest the uneasiness he felt. "It is the tent, itself, blowing about, loosely, in the wind. They have loosened the bottom, like silly children as they ar', and unless care is had, the whole will come down!"

The words were scarcely uttered, before a rushing blast of wind, swept by the spot where they stood, raising the dust in little eddies, in its progress, and then, as if guided by a master hand, it quitted the earth and mounted, to the precise spot, on which all eyes were just then rivetted. The loosened linen felt its influence and tottered, but regained its poise, and for a moment, it became tranquil. The cloud of leaves next play'd in circling revolutions around the place, and then descended with the velocity of a swooping hawk, and sailed away into the Prairie in long straight lines, like a flight of swallows resting on their expanded wings. They were followed, for some distance by the snow-white tent, which, however, soon fell behind the rock, leaving its highest peak as naked, as when it lay in the entire solitude of the desert.

"The murderers have been here!" moaned Esther. "My babes, my babes!"

For a moment even Ishmael faltered before the weight of so unexpected a blow. But shaking himself, like an awakened lion, he sprang forward and pushing aside the impediments of the barrier, as if they had been feathers, he rushed up the ascent with an impetuosity, which proved how formidable a sluggish nature may become when thoroughly aroused.

CHAPTER XIV.

"Whose party do the townsmen yet admit?"

King John, II.i. 361

IN order to preserve an even pace between the incidents of the tale, it becomes necessary to revert to such events as occurred during the ward of Ellen Wade.

For the few first hours, the cares of the honest and warm hearted girl were confined to the simpler offices of satisfying the often repeated demands which her younger associates made on her time and patience, under the pretences of hunger, thirst, and all the other, ceaseless wants of captious and inconsiderate childhood. She had seized a moment, from their importunities, to steal into the tent, where she was administering to the comforts of one far more deserving of her tenderness, when an outcry, among the children, recalled her to the duties she had momentarily forgotten.

"See, Nelly, see," exclaimed half a dozen eager voices, "yonder ar' men, and Phoebe says that they ar' Sioux Indians!"

Ellen turned her eyes in the direction in which so many arms were already extended, and to her consternation, beheld several men, advancing manifestly and swiftly in a straight line towards the rock. She counted four, but was unable to make out any thing concerning their characters except, that they were not any of those, who of right, were entitled to admission into the fortress. It was a fearful moment for Ellen. Looking around at the juvenile and frightened flock that press'd upon the skirts of her garments, she endeavored to recall to her confused faculties some one of the many tales of female heroism, with which the history of the western frontier abounded. In one a stockade had been successfully defended by a single man supported by three or four women, for days against the assaults of a hundred enemies. In another, the women alone had been able to protect the children and the less valuable effects of their absent husbands; and a third was not wanting, in which a solitary female, had destroyed her sleeping captors and given liberty not only to herself, but to a brood of helpless young. This was the case most nearly assimilated to the situation in which Ellen now found herself, and with flushing cheeks and kindling eyes, the girl began to consider, and to prepare her slender means of defence.

She posted the larger girls, at the little levers that were to cast the rocks on the assailants, the smaller were to be used more for show than any positive service they could perform, while, like any other leader, she reserved her own person, as a superintendant, and encourager of the whole. When these dispositions were made, she endeavored to await the issue, with an air of composure that she intended should inspire her assistants with the confidence necessary to insure success.

Although Ellen was vastly their superior in that spirit which emanates from moral qualities, she was by no means the equal of the two eldest daughters of Esther in the important military property, of insensibility to danger. Reared in the hardihood of a migrating life, on the skirts of society, where they had become familiarised to the sights and dangers of the wilderness, these girls, promised fairly, to become at some future day no less distinguished than their mother, for daring and for that singular mixture of good and evil, which in a wider sphere of action, would probably have enabled the wife of the squatter to enroll her name, among the remarkable females of her time. Esther had already, on one occasion, made good the log tenement of Ishmael, against an inroad of savages, and on another, she had been left for dead, by her enemies, after a defence that with a more civilized foe, would have entitled her to the honours of a liberal capitulation. These facts, and sundry others, of a similar nature, had often been recapitulated with suitable exaltation, in the presence of her daughters, and the bosoms of the young Amazons, were now strangely fluctuating between natural terror, and the ambitious wish to do something that might render them worthy of being the children of such a mother. It appeared that the opportunity for distinction of this wild character, was no longer to be denied them.

The party of strangers was, already within a hundred rods of the rock. Either consulting their usual wary method of advancing, or admonished by the threatening attitudes of two figures, who had thrust forth the barrels of as many old muskets, from behind the stone entrenchment, the new comers halted, under favor of an inequality in the ground, where a growth of grass thicker than common, offered the advantage of concealment. From this spot, they reconnoitred the fortress, for several anxious, and to Ellen, interminable minutes. Then, one advanced singly, and apparently more in the character of a herald than of an assailant.

"Phoebe, *do you* fire," and "no, Hetty, *you,*" were beginning to be heard between the half frightened and yet eager daughters of the squatter, when Ellen probably saved the advancing stranger from some imminent alarm, if from no greater danger, by exclaiming—

"Lay down the muskets! 'tis Dr. Battius!"

Her subordinates so far complied, as to withdraw their hands from the locks, though the threatening barrels still maintained the portentous levels. The Naturalist who had advanced with sufficient deliberation to note the smallest hostile demonstration of the garrison, now raised a white handkerchief on the end of his fusee, and came within speaking distance of the fortress. Then, assuming what he intended should be an imposing and dignified semblance of authority, he blustered forth in a voice that might have been heard at a much greater distance—

"What, ho! I summon ye all, in the name of the Confederacy of the United, Sovereign States of North America, to submit yourselves to the laws."

"Doctor or no Doctor; he is an enemy, Nelly; hear him! hear him! he talks of the law!"

"Stop! stay, till I hear his answer!" said the nearly breathless Ellen, pushing aside the dangerous weapons which were again pointed in the direction of the shrinking person of the herald.

"I admonish and forewarn ye all," continued the startled Doctor, "that I am a peaceful Citizen of the before named Confederacy, or, to speak with greater accuracy, Union, a supporter of the Social Compact, and a lover of good order and amity." Then perceiving that the danger, was at least, temporarily, removed, he once more raised his voice to the hostile pitch. "I charge ye all, therefore, to submit to the laws."

"I thought you were a friend," Ellen replied, "and that you travelled with my uncle in virtue of an agreement—"

"It is void! I have been deceived in the very premises; and I, hereby, pronounce a certain compactum, entered into and concluded between Ishmael Bush, squatter, and Obed Battius M. D. to be incontinently null and of non-effect. Nay; children, to be null is merely a negative property, and is fraught with no evil to thy worthy parent, so lay aside the fire arms and listen to the admonitions of reason. I declare it vicious—null—abrogated. As for thee, Nelly, my feelings towards thee are not at all given to hostility; therefore listen to that which I have to utter, nor turn away thine ears in the wantonness of security. Thou knowest the character of the man with whom thou dwellest, young woman, and thou also knowest the danger of being found in evil company. Abandon then the trifling advantages of thy situation, and yield the rock peacably to the will of those who accompany me—a legion, young woman, I do assure you, an invincible and powerful legion. Render therefore the effects of this lawless, and wicked squatter— nay, children, such disregard of human life, is frightful in those who have so recently received the gift, in their own persons, point those dangerous weapons aside, I entreat of you, more for your own sakes than for mine. Hetty, hast thou forgotten who appeased thine anguish when thy auricular nerves were tortured by the colds and damps, of the naked earth! and thou, Phoebe, ungrateful, and forgetful Phoebe! but for this very arm, which you would prostrate with an endless paralysis, thine incisores would still be giving thee pain and sorrow! Lay, then, aside thy weapons, and hearken to the advice of one who has always been thy friend. And, now, young woman," still keeping a jealous eye on the muskets, which the girl had suffered to be diverted a little from their aim, "And now, young woman, for the last, and therefore the most solemn, asking, I demand of thee, the surrender of this rock, without delay or resistance, in the joint names of Power, of justice and of the—" Law, he would have added; but recollecting that this ominous word would again provoke the hostility of the squatter's children, he succeeded in swallowing it, in good season and concluded with the less dangerous and more convertible term of Reason.

This extraordinary summons, failed however, of producing the desired effect. It proved utterly unintelligible to his younger listeners, with the exception of the few offensive terms, already sufficiently distinguished, and though Ellen better comprehended the meaning of the herald, she appeared as little moved by his rhetoric as her companions. At those passages, which he intended should be tender and affecting, the intelligent girl, though tortured by painful feelings, had even manifested a disposition to laugh, while to the threats she turned an utterly insensible ear.

"I know not the meaning of all you wish to say, Dr. Battius," she quietly replied, when he had ended, "but I am sure if it would teach me to betray my trust, it is what I ought not to hear. I caution you to attempt no violence, for let my wishes be what they may, you see I am surrounded by a force that can easily put me down, and you know, or ought to know, too well the temper of this family, to trifle in such a matter, with any of its members, let them be of what sex or age they may."

"I am not entirely ignorant of human character," returned the Naturalist, prudently receding a little from the position, which he had, until now, stoutly maintained at the very base of the hill. "But here comes one, who may know its secret windings still better than I."

"Ellen! Ellen Wade," cried Paul Hover, who had advanced to his elbow, without betraying any of that sensitiveness which had so manifestly discomposed the Doctor, "I didn't expect to find an enemy in you!"

"Nor shall you, when you ask that, which I can grant, without treachery. You know that my uncle has trusted his family to my care, and shall I so far betray the trust, as to let in his bitterest enemies, to murder his children, perhaps, and to rob him of the little which the Indians have left!"

"Am I a murderer! is this old man, this Officer of the States," pointing to the trapper and his newly discovered friend, both of whom by this time, stood at his side, "is either of them likely to do the things you name."

"What is it then, you ask of me?" said Ellen, wringing her hands in excessive doubt.

"The beast — nothing more nor less than the squatter's hidden, ravenous, dangerous beast!"

"Excellent young woman," commenced the young stranger, who had so lately joined himself to the party on the Prairie — but his mouth was immediately stopped by a significant sign from the trapper, who whispered in his ear —

"Let the lad be our spokesman. Natur *will* work in the bosom of the child, and we shall gain our object, in good time."

"The whole truth is out, Ellen," Paul continued, "and we have lined the squatter into his most secret misdoings. We have come, to right the wronged, and to free the imprisoned, now if you are the girl of a true heart, as I have always believed, so far from throwing straws in our way, you will join in the general swarming, and leave old Ishmael and his hive to the bees of his own breed."

"I have sworn a solemn oath —"

"A compactum which is entered into, through ignorance or in duresse, is null in the sight of all good moralists," cried the Doctor.

"Hush, hush," again the trapper whispered; "leave it all to natur and the lad!"

"I have sworn, in the sight and by the name of him, who is the founder and ruler of all that is good, whether it be in morals or in religion," Ellen continued, "neither to reveal the contents of that tent, nor to help its prisoner to escape. We are both solemnly, terribly sworn; our lives perhaps have been the gift we received for the promises. It is true you are masters of the secret, but not through any means of ours; nor do I know that I can justify myself for even being neutral, while you attempt to invade the dwelling of my uncle, in this hostile manner."

"I can prove beyond the power of refutation," the Naturalist eagerly exclaimed, "by Payley, Berkeley, ay even by the immortal Binkerschoef,* that a compactum concluded, while one of the parties, be it a state or be it an individual, is in durence—"

"You will ruffle the temper of the child with your abusive language," said the cautious trapper, "while the lad, if left to human feelings, will bring her down to the meekness of a fawn—Ah! you are, like myself, little knowing in the natur' of hidden kindnesses!"

"Is this the only vow you have taken, Ellen!" Paul continued, in a tone which for the gay light-hearted bee-hunter, sounded dolorous and reproachful. "Have you sworn only to this! are the words which the squatter says to be as honey in your mouth and all other promises like so much useless comb?"

The paleness which had taken possession of the usually cheerful countenance of Ellen was hid in a bright glow, that was plainly visible even, at the distance at which she stood. She hesitated a moment, as if struggling to repress something very like resentment, before she answered, with all her native spirit—

"I know not what right any one has to question me, about oaths and promises, which can only concern her who has made them, if, indeed any of the sort, you mention, have ever been made at all. I shall hold no further discourse with one, who thinks so much of himself and takes advice merely of his own feelings."

"Now, old trapper! do you hear that;" said the unsophisticated bee-hunter, turning abruptly to his aged friend. "The meanest insect that skims the heavens, when it has got its load, flies, straight and honestly to its nest or hive, according to its kind; but the ways of a woman's mind, are as knotty as a gnarled oak, and more crooked than the windings of the Mississippi!"

"Nay, nay, child," said the trapper good naturedly interfering in behalf of the offending Paul, "you are to consider that youth is hasty and not overgiven to thought. But then a promise is a promise, and not to be thrown aside and forgotten, like the hoofs and horns of a buffaloe."

"I thank you for reminding me of my oath," said the still resentful

Ellen, biting her pretty nether lip with vexation; "I might else have proved forgetful!"

"Ah! female natur is awakened in her," said the old man, shaking his head in a manner to show how much he was disappointed in the result; "but it manifests itself against the true spirit!"

"Ellen!" cried the young stranger, who until now, had been an attentive listener to the parly — "since Ellen is the name by which you are known — "

"They often add to it another. I am sometimes called by the name of my father."

"Call her Nelly Wade, at once," muttered Paul. "It is her rightful name, and I care not if she keeps it forever!"

"Wade, I should have added," continued the youth, "you will acknowledge that, though bound by no oath myself, I at least, have known how to respect those of others. You are a witness, yourself, that I have foreborn to utter a single call, while I am certain it could reach those ears, it would gladden so much. Permit me then to ascend the rock, singly; I promise a perfect indemnity to your kinsman against any injury his effects may sustain."

Ellen seem'd to hesitate, but catching a glimpse of Paul, who stood, leaning proudly on his rifle, whistling with an appearance of the utmost indifference the air of a boating song, she recovered her recollection in time to answer —

"I have been left the Captain of the rock, while my uncle, and his sons hunt, and Captain will I remain, 'till he returns to receive back the charge."

"This is wasting moments that will not soon return, and neglecting an opportunity that may never occur again;" the young soldier, gravely, remarked. "The sun is beginning to fall, already, and many minutes cannot elapse, before the squatter and his savage brood, will be returning to their huts."

Doctor Battius, cast a glance behind him, and took up the discourse, by saying —

"Perfection is always found in maturity, whether it be in the Animal or in the Intellectual world. Reflection is the mother of wisdom, and wisdom the Parent of success. I propose that we retire to a discreet distance from this impregnable position, and there hold a convocation, or council, to deliberate in what manner we may sit down regularly before the place, or perhaps, by postponing the siege to another season, gain the aid of auxiliaries from the inhabited countries, and thus secure the dignity of the laws, from any danger of a repulse."

"A storm would be better," the soldier smilingly answered, measuring the height, and scanning all its difficulties with a deliberate eye—"twould be but a broken arm, or a bruised head at the worst."

"Then have at it!" shouted the impetuous bee-hunter, making a spring that at once put him out of danger from shot, by carrying him beneath the projecting ledge on which the garrison was posted. "Now do your worst, young devils of a wicked breed; you have but a moment to work your mischief in!"

"Paul! rash Paul!" shrieked Ellen; "another step, and these rocks will crush you! they hang but by a thread, and the girls are ready and willing to let them fall!"

"Then drive the accursed swarm from the hive; for scale the rock I will, though I find it covered with hornets!"

"Let her if she dare!" tauntingly cried the eldest of the girls, brandishing a musket with a mien and resolution, that would have done credit to her Amazonian dam. "I know you, Nelly Wade; you are with the lawyers in your heart, and if you come a foot nigher, you shall have frontier punishment. Put in another pry girls, in with it! I should like to see the man, of them all, that dare come up into the camp of Ishmael Bush, without asking leave of his children!"

"Stir not, Paul! for your life keep beneath the rock!—"

Ellen was interrupted by the same bright vision which on the preceeding day, had stay'd another scarcely less portentous tumult, by exhibiting itself on the same giddy height, where it was now seen.

"In the name of him, who commandeth all, I implore you to pause—both you who so madly incur the risk and you, who so rashly offer to take that, which you never can return!" said a voice, in a slightly foreign accent, that instantly drew all eyes, upward.

"Inez!" cried the Officer. "Do I again see you! mine shall you, now, be, though a million devils, were posted on this rock. Push up, brave woodsman, and give room for another!"

The sudden appearance of the figure from the tent, had created a momentary stupor, among the defendants of the rock, which might, with suitable forbearance, have been happily improved; but startled by the voice of Middleton, the surprised Phoebe, discharged her musket at the female, scarcely knowing whether she aimed at the life of a mortal, or at some being which belonged to another world. Ellen uttered a cry of horror, and darted after her alarmed or wounded friend, she knew not which, into the tent.

During this moment of dangerous bye-play the sounds of a serious attack, were very distinctly audible, beneath. Paul had profited by the commotion over his head, to change his place so far, as to make room for Middleton. The latter was followed by the naturalist, who in a state of mental aberration produced by the report of the musket, had instinctively rushed towards the rocks, for cover. The trapper remained, where he was last seen, an unmoved but close observer of the several proceedings. Though averse to enter into actual hostilities, the old man was, however, far from being useless. Favored by his position, he was enabled to apprise his friends of the movements of those who plotted their destruction above, and to advise and control their advance, accordingly.

In the mean time the children of Esther were true to the spirit they had inherited from their redoubtable mother. The instant they found themselves relieved from the presence of Ellen and her unknown companion, they bestowed an undivided attention on their more masculine, and certainly more dangerous assailants, who by this time had made a complete lodgement among the crags of their citadel. The repeated summons to surrender, which Paul uttered in a voice that he intended should strike terror in their young bosoms, were as little heeded as were the calls of the trapper, to abandon a resistance which might prove fatal to some among them, without offering the smallest probability of eventual success. Encouraging each other to persevere, they poised the fragments of rocks, prepared the lighter missiles for immediate service, and thrust forward the barrels of the muskets, with a business like air, and a coolness, that would have done credit to men long practised in warfare.

"Keep under the ledge," said the trapper pointing out to Paul the manner in which he should proceed, "keep in your foot, more, lad—ah! you see the warning was not amiss! had the stone struck it, the bees would have had the Prairies to themselves. Now—namesake of my Friend! Uncas, in name and spirit! now if you have the activity of le Cerf Agile, you may make a far leap to the right, and gain a good twenty feet, without danger. Beware the bush. Beware the bush! 'twill prove a treacherous hold! Ah! he has done it, safely and bravely has he done it! Your turn comes next, friend that follows the fruits of natur. Push you to the left, and divide the attention of the children. Nay, girls, fire. My old ears are used to the whistling of lead, and little reason have I to prove a doe-heart, with fourscore years on my back." He shook his head with a melancholy smile, but without flinching in a muscle, as the bullet which the exasperated Hetty fired, passed innocently, at no great distance from the spot where he stood. "It is safer keeping in your track than dodging when a weak finger pulls the trigger," he continued, "but it is a solemn sight to witness how much human natur' is inclined to evil, in one so young! Well done, my man of beasts and plants! Another such leap, and you may laugh at all the squatter's bars and walls. The Doctor has got his temper up! I see it in his eye, and something good will come of him! keep closer, man, keep, closer."

The trapper though he was not deceived as to the state of Doctor Battius' mind, was, however, greatly in error as to the exciting cause. While imitating the movements of his companions, and toiling his way upward, with the utmost caution, and not without great inward tribulation, the eye of the Naturalist had caught a glimpse of an unknown plant, a few yards above his head, and in a situation more than commonly exposed to the missiles which the girls were unceasingly hurling in the direction of the assailants. Forgetting, in an instant, every thing but the glory of being the first to give this jewel to the catalogues of science, he sprang upward at the prize, with the avidity with which the sparrow darts upon the butterfly. The rock which instantly came thundering down, announced that he was seen, and for a moment, while his form was concealed, in the cloud of dust and fragments, which followed the furious descent, the trapper gave him up for lost. At the next instant, he was seen, safely seated in a cavity formed by some of the projecting stones, which had yielded to the shock, holding, triumphantly, in his hand, the captured stem, which he was already devouring with delighted and, certainly, not unskillful, eyes. Paul profited by the opportunity. Turning his course, with the quickness of thought, he sprang to the post, which Obed thus securely occupied, and unceremoniously making a footstool of his shoulder, as the latter stooped over his treasure he bounded through the breach left by the fallen rock, and gained the level. He was followed by Middleton who joined him in seizing and disarming the girls. In this manner a bloodless and complete victory, was obtained over that citadel which Ishmael had vainly flattered himself, might prove impregnable.

CHAPTER XV.

"So smile the heavens upon this holy act,
That after-hours with sorrow chide us not!"

Romeo and Juliet, II.vi.1-2.

IT is proper that the course of the narrative should be staied, while we revert to those causes, which have brought in their train of consequences, the singular contest, just related. The interruption must, necessarily, be as brief, as we hope it may prove satisfactory to that class of readers who require, that no gap should be left, by those who assume the office of historians, for their own fertile imaginations to fill.

Among the troops sent, by the Government of the United States, to take possession of its newly acquired territory in the west, was a detachment led by the young soldier, who has become so busy an actor in the scenes of our Legend. The mild and indolent descendants of the Ancient Colonists received their new compatriots without distrust, well knowing that the transfer, raised them from the condition of subjects, to the more enviable distinction of citizens in a Government of Laws. The new rulers exercised their functions with discretion, and wielded their delegated authority without offence. In such a novel intermixture, however, of men born and nurtured in freedom and the compliant minions of absolute power, the catholic and the protestant, the active and the indolent, some little time was necessary to blend the discrepant elements of society. In attaining so desirable an end, woman was made to perform her accustomed and grateful office. The barriers of Prejudice and religion were broken through by the irresistible power of the Master Passion, and family unions, ere long, began to cement the political tie which had made a forced conjunction, between people so opposite in their habits, their educations, and their opinions.

Middleton was among the first of the new possessors of the soil, who became captive to the charms of a Louisianian Lady. In the immediate vicinity of the post he had been directed to occupy, dwelt the chief of one of those ancient colonial families, which had been content to slumber for ages amid the ease, indolence, and wealth of the spanish provinces. He was an officer of the crown, and had been induced to remove from the Floridas, among the French of the adjoining province, by a rich succession of which he had become the inheritor. The name of Don Augustin de Certavallos was scarcely known beyond the limits of the little town in which he resided, though he found a secret pleasure, himself, in pointing it out, in large scrolls of musty documents, to an only child, as enrolled among the former heroes and grandees of old and of New Spain. This fact, so important to himself and of so little moment to any body else, was the principal reason, that while his more vivacious Gallic neighbors were not slow to open a frank communion with their visiters, he chose to keep aloof, seemingly content with the society of his daughter, who was a girl just emerging from the condition of childhood into that of a woman.

The curiosity of the youthful Inez, however, was not so inactive. She had not heard the martial music of the garrison, melting on the evening air, nor seen the strange banner which fluttered over the height, that rose at no great distance from her Father's extensive grounds, without experiencing some of those secret impulses which are thought to distinguish the sex. Natural timidity, and that retiring and perhaps peculiar lassitude which forms the very ground work of female fascination, in the tropical Provinces of Spain, held her, in their, seemingly, indissoluble bonds, and it is more than probable that had not an accident occurred, in which Middleton was of some personal service to her father, so long a time would have elapsed before they met, that another direction might have been given to the wishes of one, who was just of an age to be alive to all the power of youth and beauty.

Providence, or if that imposing word is too just to be classical, Fate had otherwise decreed. The haughty and reserved Don Augustin was by far, too observant of the forms of that station, on which he so much valued himself to forget the duties of a gentleman. Gratitude for the kindness of Middleton, induced him to open his doors to the Officers of the Garrison, and to admit of a guarded but polite intercourse. Reserve gradually gave way before the propriety and candor of their spirited young leader, and it was not long ere, the affluent Planter rejoiced as much as his daughter, whenever the well known signal, at the gate, announced one of these agreeable visits from the commander of the post.

It is unnecessary to dwell on the impression which the charms of Inez produced on the soldier, or to delay the tale in order to write a wire-drawn account of the progressive influence, that elegance of deportment, manly beauty, and undivided assiduity, and intelligence were likely to produce on the sensitive mind of a romantic, warm-hearted and secluded girl of sixteen. It is sufficient for our purpose to say, that they lov'd—that the youth was not backward to declare his feelings, that he prevailed with some facility over the scruples of the maiden, and with no little difficulty over the objections of her father, and that, before the Province of Louisiana had been six months in the possession of the States, the officer of the latter, was the affianced husband of the richest heiress on the banks of the Mississippi.

Although we have presumed the reader to be acquainted with the manner in which such results are, commonly, attained, it is not to be supposed that the triumph of Middleton, either over the prejudices of the father or over those of the daughter, was achieved without difficulty. Religion formed a stubborn and, nearly, irremovable obstacle with both. The devoted young man patiently submitted to a formidable essay, which Father Ignatius was deputed to make, in order to convert him to the true faith. The effort on the part of the worthy priest was systematic, vigorous, and long sustained. A dozen times (it was at those moments when glimpses of the light, sylph like form of Inez flitted, like some fairy being past the scene of their conferences) the good Father fancied he was on the eve of a glorious triumph over infidelity; but all his hopes were frustrated by some unlook'd for opposition, on the part of the subject of his pious labors. So long as the assault on his faith was distant and feeble, Middleton, who was no great proficient in Polemics, submitted to its effects with the patience and humility of a martyr; but the moment the good father who felt such concern in his future happiness, was tempted to improve his vantage ground, by calling in the aid of some of the peculiar subtilities of his own creed, the young man was too good a soldier not to make head against the hot attack. He came to the contest, it is true, with no weapons more formidable than common sense, and some little knowledge of the habits of his country as contrasted with that of his adversary; but with these homebred implements he never failed to repulse the father with something of the power with which a nervous cudgel player would deal with a skilful master of the rapier, setting at naught his passados, by the direct and unanswerable arguments of a broken head and a shivered weapon.

Before the controversy was terminated, an inroad of Protestants had come to aid the soldier. The reckless freedom of such among them, as thought only of this life, and the consistent and tempered piety of others, caused the honest priest to look about him, in concern. The influence of example on one hand and the contamination of too free an intercourse on the other began to manifest themselves, even, in that portion of his own flock, which he had supposed to be too thoroughly folded in spiritual government ever to stray. It was time to turn his thoughts from the offensive, and to prepare his followers to resist the lawless deluge of opinion, which threatened to break down the barriers of their faith. Like a wise commander who finds he has occupied too much ground for the amount of his force, he began to curtail his out-works. The relics were concealed from profane eyes; his people were admonished not to speak of miracles before a race that not only denied their existence but who had even the desperate hardihood to challenge their proofs, and even the bible itself, was prohibited with terrible denunciations, for the triumphant reason that it was liable to be misinterpreted.

In the mean time, it became necessary to report to Don Augustin, the effects his arguments and prayers had produced on the heretical disposition of the young soldier. No man is prone to confess his weakness, at the very moment, when circumstances demand the utmost efforts of his strength. By a species of pious fraud, for which no doubt the worthy Priest found his absolution in the purity of his motives, he declared that, while no positive change was actually wrought in the mind of Middleton, there was every reason to hope, the entering wedge of argument had been driven to its head, and that in consequence an opening was left, through which, it might rationally be hoped, the blessed seeds of a religious fructification would find their way, especially if the subject was left uninterruptedly to enjoy the advantage of catholic communion.

Don Augustin, himself, was now seized with the desire of proselyting. Even, the soft and amiable Inez thought it would be a glorious consummation of her wishes, to be a humble instrument of bringing her lover into the bosom of the true church. The offers of Middleton were promptly accepted, and, while the father looked forward, impatiently, to the day assigned for the nuptials, as to the pledge of his own success, the daughter thought of it with feelings in which the holy emotions of her faith, were blended with the softer sensations of her years and situation.

The sun rose, the morning of her nuptials, on a day so bright and cloudless that Inez hailed it as a harbinger of future happiness. Father Ignatius performed the offices of the church, in a little chapel attached to the estate of Don Augustin, and long ere the sun had begun to fall, Middleton pressed the blushing and timid young creole to his bosom, his acknowledged and unalienable wife. It had pleased the parties to pass the day of the wedding in retirement dedicating it solely to the best and purest affections, aloof from the noisy and heartless rejoicings of a compelled festivity.

Middleton was returning through the grounds of Don Augustin, from a visit of duty, to his encampment, at that hour, in which the light of the sun begins to melt into the shadows of evening, when a glimpse of a robe similar to that, in which Inez had accompanied him to the altar, caught his eye, through the foliage of a retired arbour. He approached the spot, with a delicacy that was rather increased than diminished, by the claim she had perhaps given him to intrude on her private moments, but the sounds of her soft voice, which was offering up prayers, in which he heard himself named by the dearest of all appellations, overcame his scruples, and induced him to take a position where he might listen without the fear of detection. It was certainly grateful to the feelings of a husband to be able, in this manner, to lay bare the spotless soul of his wife, and to find that his own image lay enshrined amid its purest and holiest aspirations. His self esteem was too much flattered, not to induce him to overlook, the immediate object of the petitioner. While she prayed that she might become the humble instrument of bringing him into the flock of the faithful, she petitioned for forgiveness, on her own behalf, if presumption, or indifference to the counsel of the church, had caused her to set too high a value on her influence, and led her into the dangerous error of hazarding her own soul, by espousing a heretic. There was so much of fervent piety, mingled with so strong a burst of natural feeling, so much of the woman blended with the angel, in her prayers, that Middleton could have forgiven her, had she termed him a pagan, for the sweetness and interest with which she petitioned in his favor.

The young man waited until his bride arose from her knees, and then he joined her, as if entirely ignorant of what had occurred.

"It is getting late, my Inez," he said, "and Don Augustin would be apt to reproach you with inattention to your health, in being abroad at such an hour. What then am I to do, who am charged with all his authority and twice his love."

"Be like him, in *every* thing," she answered, looking up in his face, with tears in her eyes, and speaking with emphasis; "in *every* thing. Imitate my father, Middleton, and I can ask no more of you."

"Nor *for* me, Inez? I doubt not that I should be all you can wish, were I to become as good, as the worthy and respectable Don Augustin. But you are to make some allowances for the infirmities and habits of a soldier. Now, let us go, and join this excellent father."

"Not yet," said his bride, gently extricating herself from the arm that he had thrown around her slight form, while he urged her from the place; "I have still another duty to perform, before I can submit, so implicitly to your orders, soldier though you are. I promised the worthy Inesella, my faithful nurse, she who, as you heard, has so long been a mother to me, Middleton—I promised her a visit at this hour. It is the last, as she thinks, that she can receive from her own child, and I cannot disappoint her. Go you then to Don Augustin; in one short hour, I will rejoin you."

"Remember, it is but an hour!"

"One hour," repeated Inez, as she kissed her hand to him; and then blushing ashamed at her own boldness, she darted from the arbor, and was seen for an instant gliding toward the cottage of her nurse, in which, at the next moment, she disappeared.

Middleton returned, slowly and thoughtfully, to the house, often bending his eyes in the direction in which he had last seen his wife, as if he would fain trace her lovely form, in the gloom of the evening, still floating through the vacant space. Don Augustin received him with warmth and for many minutes his mind was amused by relating to his new kinsman, plans for the future. The exclusive old Spaniard, listened to his glowing but true account of the prosperity and happiness of those States, of which he had been an ignorant neighbor half his life, partly in wonder, and partly with that sort of incredulity, with which one attends to what he fancies are the exaggerated descriptions of a too partial friendship.

In this manner the hour for which Inez had conditioned pass'd away much sooner than her husband could have thought possible, in her absence. At length his looks began to wander to the clock, and then the minutes were counted, as one roll'd by after another, and Inez did not appear. The hand had already made half of another circuit, around the face of the dial, when Middleton arose, and announced his determination to go, and offer himself, as an escort to the absentee. He found the night dark, and the heavens charged with threatening vapor, which in that climate, was the infallible forerunner of a gust. Stimulated no less, by the unpropitious aspect of the skies, than by his secret uneasiness, he quickened his pace, making long and rapid strides in the direction of the cottage of Inesella. Twenty times he stopp'd, fancying that he caught glimpses of the fairy form of Inez, tripping across the grounds, on her return to the mansion-house, and as often he was obliged to resume his course, in disappointment. He reached the gate of the cottage, knocked, opened the door, entered, and even, stood in the presence of the aged nurse, without meeting the person of her he sought. She had, already, left the place, and had returned to her father's house! Believing that he must have passed her in the darkness, Middleton retraced his steps, to meet with another disappointment. Inez had not been seen. Without communicating his intention to any one, the bridegroom proceeded with a palpitating heart to the little sequestered arbor, where he had overheard his bride offering up those petitions for his happiness and conversion. Here too, he was disappointed, and then all was afloat, in the painful incertitude of doubt and conjecture.

For many hours, a secret distrust of the motives of his wife, caused Middleton to proceed in the search with delicacy and caution. But as day dawned, without restoring her to the arms of her father or her husband, reserve was thrown aside, and her unaccountable absence was loudly proclaimed. The inquiries after the lost Inez were now direct and open; but they prov'd equally fruitless. No one had seen her, or heard of her, from the moment that she left the cottage, of her nurse.

Day succeeded day, and still no tidings rewarded the search that was immediately instituted, until she was finally given over by most of her relatives and friends as irretrievably lost.

An event of so extraordinary a character was not likely to be soon forgotten. It excited speculation, gave rise to an infinity of rumours, and not a few inventions. The prevalent opinion, among such of those emigrants who were overrunning the country as had time, in the multitude of their employments, to think of any foreign concerns, was the simple and direct conclusion, that the absent bride, was no more nor less than a felo de se.* Father Ignatius had many doubts and much secret compunction of conscience, but like a wise chief, he endeavored to turn the sad event to some account, in the impending warfare of faith. Changing his battery, he whispered in the ears of a few of his oldest parishioners, that he had been deceived in the state of Middleton's mind, which he was now compelled to believe was completely stranded on the quicksands of heresy. He began to show his relicks again, and was even heard to allude once more, to the delicate and nearly forgotten subject of modern miracles. In consequence of these demonstrations, on the part, of the venerable priest, it came to be whispered among the faithful, and finally it was adopted as part of the parish creed, that Inez had been translated to heaven.

Don Augustin had all the feelings of a Father, but they were smothered in the lassitude of a Creole. Like his spiritual governor, he began to think that they had been wrong in consigning one so pure, so young, so lovely, and above all so pious to the arms of a heretic, and he was fain to believe that the calamity which had befallen his age, was a judgment on his presumption and want of adherence to established forms. It is true, that as the whispers of the congregation came to his ears, he found present consolation in their belief, but then nature was too powerful and had too strong a hold of the old man's heart, not to give rise to the rebellious thought, that the succession of his daughter to the heavenly inheritance was a little premature.

But Middleton, the lover, the husband, the bridegroom — Middleton was nearly crushed by the weight of the unexpected and terrible blow. Educated himself, under the dominion of a simple and rational faith, in which nothing is attempted to be concealed from the believers, he could have no other apprehensions for the fate of Inez, than such as grew out of his knowledge of the superstitious opinions, she entertained of his own church. It is needless to dwell on the mental tortures that he endured, or all the various surmises, hopes, and disappointments that he was fated to experience in the first few weeks of his misery. A jealous distrust of the motives of Inez, and a secret, lingering, hope that he should yet find her, had tempered his enquiries, without, however, causing him to abandon them entirely. But time was beginning to deprive him, even, of the mortifying reflection that he was intentionally, though perhaps temporarily, deserted, and he was gradually yielding to the more painful conviction that she was dead, when his hopes were suddenly revived, in a new and singular manner.

The young commander, was slowly and sorrowfully returning from an evening parade of his troops, to his own quarters, which stood at some little distance from the place of the encampment and on the same high bluff of land, when his vacant eyes fell on the figure of a man, who by the regulations of the place, was not entitled to be there, at that forbidden hour. The stranger was meanly dress'd, with every appearance, about his person and countenance, of squalid poverty and of the most dissolute habits. Sorrow had softened the military pride of Middleton, and as he passed the crouching form of the intruder, he said in tones of great mildness or rather of kindness—

"You will be given a night in the guard house, friend, should the patrole find you here. Here is a dollar—go: and get a better place to sleep in, and something to eat."

"I swallow all my food, Captain, without chewing;" returned the vagabond, with the low exultation of an accomplished villain, as he eagerly seized the silver. "Make this Mexican, twenty, and I will sell you a secret."

"Go, go," said the other, with a little of a soldier's severity, returning to his manner. "Go, before I order the guard to seize you."

"Well, go I will. But if I do go, captain, I shall take my knowledge with me, and then you may live a widower bewitched, 'till the tatoo of life is beat off."

"What mean, you, fellow!" exclaimed Middleton, turning quickly toward the wretch who was already dragging his diseased limbs from the place.

"I mean to have the value of this dollar in Spanish Brandy, and then come back and sell you my secret for enough to buy a barrel."

"If you have any thing to say, speak now," continued Middleton, restraining with difficulty the impatience that urged him to betray his feeling.

"I am a dry, and I can never talk with elegance, when my throat is husky, captain. How much will you give, to know what I can tell you, let it be something, handsome; such as one gentleman can offer to another."

"I believe it would be better justice, to order the drummer to pay you a visit, fellow. To what does your boasted secret relate?"

"Matrimony. A wife and no wife, a pretty face, and a rich bride; do I speak plain, now, captain?"

"If you know any thing relating to my wife, say it at once, you need not fear for your reward."

"Ay, Captain, I have drove many a bargain in my time, and sometimes I have been paid in money, and sometimes I have been paid in promises. Now, the last are what I call pinching food."

"Name your price."

"Twenty—no damnit, it's worth thirty dollars if it's worth a cent!"

"Here, then, is your money, but remember, if you tell me nothing worth knowing, I have a force that can easily deprive you of it, again, and punish your insolence, in the bargain."

The fellow examined the bank-bills he received, with a jealous eye, and then pocketted them, apparently well satisfied of their being genuine.

"I like a northern note," he said, very coolly, "they have a charcatur to lose, like myself. No fear of me, captain; I am a man of honour and I shall not tell you a word more, nor a word less, than I know of my own knowledge to be true."

"Proceed then, without further delay, or I may repent, and order you to be deprived of all your gains, the silver as well as the notes."

"Honor if you die for it!" returned the miscreant, holding up a hand in affected horror at so treacherous a threat. "Well, Captain, you must know, that gentlemen don't all live by the same calling, some keep what they've got, and some get what they can."

"You have been a thief."

"I scorn the word. I have been a humanity-hunter. Do you know what that means? ay, it has many interpretations! Some people think the woolly-heads are miserable, working on hot plantations under a broiling sun — and all such sorts of inconveniences. Well, captain, I have been, in my time, a man who has been willing to give them the pleasures of variety, at least, by changing the scene for them. You understand me?"

"You are, in plain language a kidnapper."

"Have been — my worthy Captain — have been; but just now a little reduced, like a merchant who leaves off selling tobacco by the hogshead to deal in it, by the yard. I have been a soldier, too, in my day. What is said to be the great secret of our trade; can you tell me that?"

"I know not," said Middleton beginning to tire of the fellow's trifling, "courage."

"No, legs — legs, to fight with and legs to run away with. And therein you see my two callings agreed. My legs are none of the best, just now, and without legs a kidnapper would carry on a losing trade. But then there are men enough left, better provided than I am."

"Stolen!" groaned the horror struck husband.

"On her travels, as sure as you are standing still!"

"Villain, what reason have you, for believing a thing so shocking!"

"Hands off — hands off — do you think my tongue can do its work the better, for a little squeezing of the throat! Have patience and you shall know it all; but if you treat me so ungenteelly again, I shall be obliged to call in the assistance of the Lawyers."

"Say on; but if you utter a single word more or less than the truth, expect instant vengeance."

"Are you fool enough to believe what such a scoundrel as I am, tells you, captain, unless it has probability to back it. I know you are not: therefore, I will give my facts and my opinions, and then leave you to chew on them, while I go and drink of your generosity. I know a man, who is called Abiram White. I believe the knave took that name to show his enmity to the race of blacks! But this gentleman is now, and has been, for years, to my certain knowledge a regular translator of the human body from one State to another. I have dealt with him, in my time, and a cheating dog he is! No more honor, in him, than meat in my stomach. I saw him, here, in this very town, the day of your wedding. He was in company with his wife's brother, and pretended to be a settler on the hunt for new land. A noble set they were, to carry on business—seven sons, each of them as tall as your sergeant with his cap on. Well, the moment I heard that your wife was lost, I saw at once that Abiram had laid his hands on her."

"Do you know this—can this be true! What reason have you to fancy a thing so wild!"

"Reason enough; I know Abiram White. Now, will you add a trifle just to keep my throat from parching?"

"Go, go, you are stupified with drink, already, miserable man, and know not what you say. Go, go, and beware the drummer."

"Experience is a good guide," the fellow call'd after the retiring Middleton, and then turning with a chuckling laugh, like one well satisfied with himself, he made the best of his way towards the shop of the suttler.

A hundred times in the course of that night did Middleton fancy that the communication of the miscreant was entitled to some attention, and as often did he reject the idea, as too wild and visionary for another thought. He was awakened early on the following morning, after passing a restless and, nearly, sleepless night, by his orderly who came, to report that a man was found dead on the parade, at no great distance from his quarters. Throwing on his clothes, he proceeded to the spot, and beheld the individual, with whom he had held the preceding conference in the precise situation in which he had first been found.

The miserable wretch had fallen a victim to his intemperance. This revolting fact was sufficiently proclaimed by his obtruding eye-balls, his bloated countenance, and the nearly insufferable odours that were even, then exhaling from his carcass. Disgusted with the odious spectacle, the youth was turning from the sight, after ordering the corpse to be removed, when the position of one of the dead man's hands struck him. On examination he found the fore finger extended, as if in the act of writing in the sand, with the following incomplete sentence, nearly illegible, but yet in a state to be deciphered. "Capt. it is true, as I am a gentle— " He had either died or fallen into a sleep, the forerunner of his death, before the latter word was finished.

Concealing this fact from the others, Middleton, repeated his orders and departed. The pertinacity of the deceased, and all the circumstances united, induced, him to set on foot some secret inquiries. He found that a family answering the description which had been given him, had, in fact passed the place the day of his nuptials. They were traced along the margin of the Mississippi, for some distance, until they took boat, and ascended the river to its confluence with the Missouri. Here they had disappeared, like hundreds of others, in pursuit of the hidden wealth of the interior.

Furnished with these facts, Middleton, detailed a small guard of his most trusty men, took leave of Don Augustin without declaring his hopes or his fears, and having arrived at the indicated point, he pushed into the wilderness, in pursuit. It was not difficult to trace a train like that of Ishmael, until he was well assured, its object lay far beyond the usual limits of the settlements. This circumstance, in itself, quickened his suspicions, and gave additional force to his hopes of final success.

After getting beyond the assistance of verbal directions, the anxious husband had recourse to the usual signs of a trail, in order to follow the fugitives. This he also found a task of no difficulty, until he reached the hard and unyielding soil of the rolling Prairies. Here, indeed, he was completely at fault. He found himself, at length, compelled to divide his followers, appointing a place of rendezvous at a distant day, and to endeavor to find the lost trail, by multiplying, as much as possible, the number of his eyes. He had been alone a week, when accident brought him in contact with the trapper and the bee-hunter. Part of their interview has been related, and the reader can readily imagine the explanations that succeeded the tale he recounted, and which led as has already been seen to the recovery of his bride.

CHAPTER XVI.

"These likelihoods confirm her flight from hence.
Therefore, I pray you, stay not to discourse,
But mount you presently;—"

Two Gentlemen of Verona, V.ii. 43-45.

An hour had slid by, in hasty and nearly incoherent questions and answers, before Middleton, hanging over his recovered treasure with that sort of jealous watchfullness, with which a miser would regard his hoards, closed the disjointed narrative of his own proceedings by demanding—

"And you, my Inez: in what manner were you treated?"

"In every thing, but the great injustice they did in separating me so forcibly from my friends, as well, perhaps, as the circumstances of my captors would allow. I think the man, who is certainly the master here, is but a new beginner in wickedness. He quarrelled, frightfully, in my presence, with the wretch who seized me, and then they made an impious bargain, to which I was compelled to acquiesce, and to which they bound me as well as themselves by oaths. Ah! Middleton, I fear the heretics are not so heedful of their vows as we who are nurtured in the bosom of the true church!"

"Believe it not. These villains are of no religion—did they foreswear themselves?"

"No; but perjured. But was it not awful to call upon the good God, to witness so sinful a compact!"

"And so we think, Inez, as truly as the most virtuous Cardinal of Rome. But how did they observe their oath, and what was its purport?"

"They conditioned to leave me unmolested and free from their odious presence, provided I would give a pledge to make no effort to escape, and that I would not, even, show myself, until a time that my masters saw fit to name."

"And that time!—" demanded the impatient Middleton, who so well knew the religious scruples of his wife—"That time—"

"It is already passed. I was sworn by my Patron Saint, and faithfully did I keep the vow, until the man they call Ishmael forgot the terms by offering violence. I then made one appearance on the rock; for the time, too, was passed—though I even, think that Father Ignatius would have absolved me from the vow, on account of the treachery of my keepers."

"If he had not," muttered the youth between his compressed teeth; "I would have absolved him forever from his spiritual care of your conscience."

"You, Middleton!" returned his wife looking up into his flush'd face while a bright blush suffused her own sweet countenance; "you may *receive* my vows; but, surely, you can have no power to *absolve* me from their observance!"

"No, no, no, Inez, you are right. I know but little of these conscientious subtilties, and I am any thing but a priest. Yet tell me, what has induced these monsters to play this desperate game—to trifle thus with my happiness?"

"You know my ignorance of the world, and how ill I am qualified to furnish reasons for the conduct of beings so different from any I have ever seen, before. But does not love of money drive men to acts, even, worse than this! I believe they thought that an aged and wealthy father could be tempted to pay them a rich ransom for his child; and perhaps," she added, stealing an enquiring glance through her tears, at the attentive Middleton, "they counted something on the fresh affections of a bridegroom."

"They might have extracted the blood from my heart, drop by drop!"

"Yes," resumed his young and timid wife, instantly withdrawing the stolen look she had hazarded, and, hurriedly, pursuing the train of the discourse as if glad to make him forget the liberty she had just taken, "I have been told there are men so base, as to perjure themselves at the altar, in order to command the gold of ignorant and confiding girls, and if love of money will lead to such baseness, we may surely expect it will hurry those who devote themselves to gain, into acts of lesser fraud!"

"It must be so, and, now Inez, though I am here to guard you, with my life, and we are in possession of this rock, our difficulties, perhaps our dangers, are not ended. You will summon all your courage to meet the trial, and prove yourself a soldier's wife, my Inez?"

"I am ready to depart this instant. The letter you sent by the physician, had prepared me to hope for the best, and I have every thing arranged for flight, at the shortest warning."

"Let us then leave this place, and join our friends."

"Friends!" interrupted Inez, glancing her eyes around the little tent in quest of the form of Ellen. "I too have a friend who must not be forgotten, but who is pledged to pass the remainder of her life with us. She is gone!"

Middleton gently led her from the spot, as he smilingly answered —

"She may have had like myself her own private communications for some favored ear."

The young man had not, however, done justice to the motives of Ellen Wade. The sensitive and intelligent girl, had readily perceived how little her presence was necessary in the interview, that has just been related, and had retired with that intuitive delicacy of feeling which seems to belong more properly to her sex. She was now to be seen seated on a point of the rock, with her person so entirely enveloped in her dress, as to conceal her features. Here she had remained for near an hour, no one approaching to address her, and as it appeared to her own quick and jealous eyes totally unobserved. In the latter particular, however, even, the vigilance of the quicksighted Ellen was deceived.

The first act of Paul Hover, on finding himself the master of Ishmael's citadel, had been to sound the note of victory, after the quaint and ludicrous manner, that is so often practised among the borderers of the west. Flapping his sides, with his hands, as the conquering game cock is wont to do with his wings, he raised a loud and laughable imitation of the exultation of this bird,* a cry which might have proved a dangerous challenge, had any one of the athletic sons of the squatter been within hearing.

"This has been a regular knock-down and drag-out," he cried, "and no bones broke! How now, old trapper, you have been one of your training, platoon, rank-and-file soldiers in your day, and have seen forts taken and batteries stormed, before this: am I right?"

"Ay, ay, that have I," answered the old man, who still maintained his post at the foot of the rock, so little disturbed by what he had just witnessed, as to return the grin of Paul, with a hearty indulgence in his own silent and peculiar laughter. "You have gone through the exploit like men!"

"Now tell me, is it not in rule, to call over the names of the living and to bury the dead, after every bloody battle."

"Some did and other some didn't. When Sir William push'd the German, Dieskau,* thro' the defiles at the foot of the Hori—"

"Your Sir William was a drone to Sir Paul, and knew nothing of regularity. So here begins the roll call—by-the-bye, old man, what between bee-hunting and buffaloe humps, and certain other matters, I have been too busy to ask your name; for I intend to begin with my rear guard, well knowing that my man in front is too busy to answer."

"Lord, lad, I've been called in my time, by as many names, as there are people among whom I've dwelt. Now, the Delawares nam'd me for my eyes, and I was called after the far-sighted hawk. Then ag'in the settlers in the Otsego hills christened me anew, from the fashion of my leggings,* and various have been the names by which I have gone through life: But little will it matter when the time shall come that all are to be muster'd, face to face, by what titles a mortal has play'd his part; I humbly trust I shall be able to answer to any of mine, in a loud and manly voice."

Paul paid little or no attention to this reply, more than half of which was lost in the distance, but pursuing the humour of the moment, he called out, in a stentorian voice to the naturalist to answer to his name. Doctor Battius had not thought it necessary to push his success beyond the comfortable niche, which accident had so opportunely formed for his protection and in which he now reposed from his labors, with a pleasing consciousness of security, added to great exultation at the possession of the botanical treasure already mentioned.

"Mount. Mount, my worthy mole-catcher! come and behold the prospect of skirting Ishmael! Come and look nature boldly in the face, and not go sneaking, any longer, among the Prairie grass and mullen tops, like a gobbler nibbling for grass hoppers."

The mouth of the light-hearted and reckless bee hunter was instantly closed, and he was rendered as mute, as he had just been boisterous and talkative, by the appearance of Ellen Wade. When the melancholy maiden took her seat on the point of the rock, as mentioned, Paul affected to employ himself in conducting a close inspection of the household effects of the squatter. He rummaged the drawers of Esther with no delicate hands, scattered the rustic finery of her girls on the ground without the least deference to its quality or elegance, and toss'd her pots and kettles here, and there, as though they had been vessels of wood instead of iron. All this industry, was, however, manifestly without an object. He reserved nothing for himself, not even, appearing conscious of the nature of the articles which suffered by his familiarity. When he had examined the inside of every cabin, taken a fresh survey of the spot where he had confined the children and where he had thoroughly secured them with cord, and kick'd one of the pails of the woman, like a foot-ball, fifty feet into the air, in sheer wantonness, he returned to the edge of the rock, and thrusting both his hands through his wampum belt, he began to whistle the Kentucky hunters,* as diligently as if he had been hired to supply his auditors with music, by the hour. In this manner pass'd the remainder of the time, until Middleton, as has been related, led Inez forth from the tent, and gave a new direction to the thoughts of the whole party. He summoned Paul from his flourish of music, tore the Doctor from the study of his plant, and as acknowledged leader, gave the necessary orders for immediate departure.

In the bustle and confusion that were likely to succeed such a mandate, there was little opportunity to indulge in complaints or reflections. As the adventurers had not come unprepared for victory, each individual employed himself in such offices, as were best adapted to his strength and situation. The trapper had already made himself master of the patient Asinus, who was quietly feeding at no great distance from the rock, and he was now busy in fitting his back with the complicated machinery, that Doctor Battius, saw fit to term a saddle of his own invention. The naturalist himself, seized upon his port-folios, herbals, and collection of insects, which he quickly transferred from the encampment of the squatter to certain pockets in the aforesaid ingenious invention, and which the trapper as uniformly cast away, the moment his back was turned. Paul showed his dexterity in removing such light articles as Inez and Ellen had prepared for their flight to the foot of the citadel, while Middleton, after mingling threats and promises, in order to induce the children to remain quietly in their bondage, assisted the females to descend. As time began to press upon them, and there was great danger of Ishmael's returning, these several movements were made with singular industry and despatch.

The trapper bestowed such articles as he conceived, were necessary to the comfort of the weaker and more delicate members of the party in those pockets, from which he had so unceremoniously expelled the treasures of the unconscious naturalist, and then gave way for Middleton to place Inez in one of those seats, which he had prepared on the back of the animal for her and her companion.

"Go, child," the old man said, motioning to Ellen to follow the example of the lady, and turning his head a little anxiously to examine the waste behind him, "It cannot be long afore the owner of this place will be coming to look after his house hold, and he is not a man to give up his property, however obtained, without complaint."

"It is true," cried Middleton, "we have wasted moments that are precious, and have the utmost need of industry."

"Ay, ay, I thought it; and would have said it, Captain; but I remembered how your grand'ther used to love to look upon the face of her he led away for a wife, in the days of his youth and his happiness! 'Tis natur', 'tis natur, and 'tis wiser to give way a little before its feelings than to try to stop a current that will have its course."

Ellen advanced to the side of the beast, and seizing Inez by the hand, she said with heart-felt warmth, after struggling to suppress an emotion that nearly choked her—

"God bless you, sweet lady. I hope you will forget and forgive the wrongs you have received from my uncle—"

The humbled and sorrowful girl could say no more; her voice becoming entirely inaudible in an ungovernable burst of grief.

"How is this!" cried Middleton, "did you not say, Inez, that this excellent young woman was to accompany us, and to live with us, for the remainder of her life, or, at least, until she found some more agreeable residence for herself."

"I did; and I still hope it. She has always given me reason to believe, that, after having shown so much commiseration and friendship in my misery, she would not desert me, should happier times return."

"I cannot, I ought not," continued Ellen, getting the better of her momentary weakness. "It has pleased God to cast my lot among these people, and I ought not to quit them. It would be adding the appearance of treachery to what will already seem bad enough, with one of his opinions. He has been kind to me, an orphan, after his rough customs, and I cannot steal from him at such a moment!"

"She is just as much a relation of skirting Ishmael, as I am a Bishop!" said Paul, with a loud hem, as if his throat wanted clearing. "If the old fellow has done the honest thing by her, in giving her a morsel of venison, now and then, or a spoon around his homminy dish, hasn't she pay'd him, in teaching the young devils to read their bible, or in helping old Esther to put her finery in shape and fashion. Tell me that a drone has a sting, and I'll believe you, as easily as I will that this young woman is a debtor to any of the tribe of Bush!"

"It is but little matter, who owns me, or where I'm in debt. There are none to care for a girl, who is fatherless and motherless and whose nearest kin are the offcasts of all honest people—no, no, go, lady, and heaven forever bless you. I am better here, in this desert, where there are none to know my shame."

"Now old trapper," retorted Paul, "this is what I call knowing which way the wind blows! You ar' a man that has seen life and you know something of fashions; I put it to your judgement, plainly, isn't it in the nature of things for the hive to swarm when the young get their growth, and if children will quit their parents, ought one who is of no kith nor kin—"

"Hist!" interrupted the man he addressed. "Hector is discontented. Say it out, plainly, pup. What is it, dog, what is it!"

The venerable hound had risen, and was scenting the fresh breeze which continued to sweep heavily over the Prairies. At the words of his master, he growled, and contracted the muscles of his lips, as if half disposed to threaten with the remnants of his teeth. The younger dog, who was resting after the chace of the morning, also made some signs that his nose detected a taint in the air, and then the two resumed their slumbers as if they had done enough.

The trapper seized the bridle of the Ass, and cried urging the beast onward—

"There is no time for words. The squatter and his brood are within a mile or two of this blessed spot!"

Middleton lost all recollection of Ellen, in the danger which now so imminently beset his recovered bride, nor is it necessary to add that Doctor Battius did not wait for a second admonition to commence his retreat. Following the route indicated by the old man, they turned the rock in a body, and pursued their way, as fast as possible across the Prairie, under the favor of the cover it afforded.

Paul Hover, however, remained in his tracks sullenly leaning on his rifle. Near a minute had elapsed, before he was observed by Ellen, who had buried her face in her hands, to conceal her fancied desolation from herself.

"Why do you not fly!" the weeping girl, exclaimed the instant she perceived she was not alone.

"I'm not used to it."

"My uncle will soon be here! you have nothing to hope from his pity."

"Nor from that of his niece, I reckon. Let him come; he can only knock me on the head!"

"Paul, Paul, if you love me, fly—"

"Alone! if I do, may I be—"

"If you value, your life, fly!"

"I value it not, compared to you."

"Paul!"

"Ellen!"

She extended both her hands, and burst into another and a still more violent flood of tears. The bee-hunter put one of his sturdy arms around her waist, and in another moment he was urging her over the plain, in rapid pursuit of their flying friends.

CHAPTER XVII.

"Approach the chamber, and destroy your sight
With a new Gorgon:–Do not bid me speak:
See, and then speak yourselves."

Macbeth, II.iii. 76-78.

THE little run which supplied the family of the squatter with water, and nourished the trees and bushes that grew near the base of the rocky eminence, took its rise at no great distance from the latter, in a small thicket of cotton-wood, and vines. Hither, then the trapper directed the flight, as to the place affording the only available cover, in so pressing an emergency. It will be remembered that the sagacity of the old man, which from long practice in similar scenes amounted nearly to an instinct in all cases of sudden danger, had first induced him to take this course, as it plac'd the hill between them and the approaching party. Favored by this circumstance he succeeded in reaching the bushes in sufficient time, and Paul Hover had just hurried the breathless Ellen into the tangled brush as Ishmael gained the summit of the rock, in the manner already described, where he stood like a man momentarily bereft of senses, gazing at the confusion which had been created among his chattels, or at his gagged and bound children, who had been safely bestowed, by the forethought of the bee-hunter, under the cover of a bark roof in a sort of irregular pile. A long rifle would have thrown a bullet from the height on which the squatter now stood, into the very cover, where the fugitives who had wrought all this mischief were clustered.

The trapper, was the first to speak, as the man on whose intelligence and experience they all depended for counsel, after running his eye over the different individuals, who gathered about him, in order to see that none were missing.

"Ah! natur' is natur' and has done its work!" he said, nodding to the exulting Paul with a smile of approbation, "I thought it would be hard for them who had so often met in fair and foul, by star-light and under the clouded moon, to part at last, in anger! Now, is there little time to lose, in talk, and every thing to gain, by industry! It cannot be long afore some of yonder brood will be nosing along the 'arth for our trail, and, should they find it, as find it they surely will, and should they push us to stand on our courage, the dispute must be settled with the rifle; which may He in Heaven forbid! Captain, can you lead us to the place where any of your warriors lie?—for the stout sons of the squatter will make a manly brush of it, or I am but little of a judge in warlike dispositions!"

"The place of rendezvous is many leagues from this, on the banks of La Platte."

"It is bad! it is bad—If fighting is to be done, it is always wise to enter on it, on equal terms. But what has one so near his time, to do with ill-blood and hot-blood, at his heart! Listen to what a gray head and some experience have to offer, and then if any among you can point out a wiser fashion for a retreat, we can just follow his design and forget that I have spoken. This thicket stretches for near a mile, as it may be slanting from the rock, and leads towards the sun-set instead of the settlements."

"Enough. Enough," cried Middleton too impatient to wait until the deliberative and perhaps loquacious old man could end his minute explanation. "Time is too precious, for words: Let us fly."

The trapper made a gesture of compliance, and turning in his tracks he lead Asinus across the trembling earth of the swale, and quickly emerged on the hard ground, on the side opposite to the encampment of the squatter.

"If old Ishmael gets a squint at that highway through the brush," cried Paul casting, as he left the place, a hasty glance, at the broad trail the party had made through the thicket, "he'll need no finger board to tell him which way his road lies. But let him follow! I know the vagabond would gladly cross his breed with a little honest blood, but if any son of his ever gets to be the husband of—"

"Hush, Paul, hush," said the terrified young woman who leaned on his arm for support, "your voice might be heard."

The bee-hunter was silent, though he did not cease to cast ominous looks behind him, as they flew along the edge of the run, which sufficiently betrayed the belligerent condition of his mind. As each one was busy for himself, but a few minutes elapsed before the party rose a swell of the Prairie, and descending, without a moment's delay on the opposite side, they were at once removed from every danger of being seen, by the sons of Ishmael, unless the pursuers should happen to fall upon their trail. The old man, now profited by the formation of the land, to take another direction, with a view to elude pursuit, as a vessel changes her course in fogs and darkness, to escape from the vigilance of her enemies.

Two hours passed in the utmost diligence, enabled them to make a half-circuit around the rock, and to reach a point that was exactly opposite to the original direction of their flight. To most of the fugitives their situation was as entirely unknown, as is that of a ship in the middle of the ocean to the uninstructed voyager, but the old man proceeded at every turn, and through every bottom with a decision that inspired his followers with confidence, as it spoke favorably of his own knowledge of the localities. His hound, stopping now and then to catch the expression of his eye, had preceded the trapper, throughout the whole distance, with as much certainty as though a previous and intelligible communion between them had established the route by which they were to proceed. But, at the expiration of the time, just named, the dog suddenly came to a stand; and then seating himself on the Prairie, he snuffed the air, a moment, and began a low and piteous whining.

"Ay, pup—ay. I know the spot. I know the spot, and reason there is to remember it well!" said the old man, stopping by the side of his uneasy associate, until those who followed had time to come up. "Now yonder is a thicket before us," he continued pointing forward, "where we may lie till tall trees grow on these naked fields, afore any of the squatter's kin, will venture to molest us."

"This is the spot where the body of the dead man lay!" cried Middleton examining the place with an eye that revolted at the recollection.

"The very same. But whether his friends have put him in the bosom of the ground or not remains to be seen. The hound knows the scent, but seems to be a little at a loss, too. It is therefore necessary that you advance, friend bee-hunter to examine, while I tarry to keep the dogs from complaining in too loud a voice."

"I!" exclaimed Paul thrusting his hand into his shaggy locks, like one who thought it prudent to hesitate before he undertook so formidable an adventure: "now, heark'ee, old trapper; I've stood in my thinnest cottons, in the midst of many a swarm that has lost its queen bee, without winking, and let me tell you, the man who can do that is not likely to fear any living son of skirting Ishmael; but as to meddling with dead men's bones, why it is neither my calling nor my inclination, so after thanking you for the favor of your choice, as they say when they make a man a corporal in Kentucky, I decline serving."

The old man turned a disappointed look towards Middleton who was too much occupied in solacing Inez to observe his embarrassment, which was, however, suddenly relieved from a quarter, whence, from previous circumstances, there was little reason to expect such a demonstration of fortitude.

Doctor Battius, had rendered himself a little remarkable throughout the whole of the preceding retreat, for the exceeding diligence with which he had labored to effect that desirable object. So very conspicuous was his zeal, indeed, as to have entirely gotten the better of all his ordinary predilections. The worthy naturalist belong'd to that species of discoverers who make the worst possible travelling-companions to a man who has reason to be in a hurry. No stone, no bush, no plant is ever suffered to escape the examination of their vigilant eyes, and thunder may mutter and rain fall, without disturbing the abstraction of their reveries. Not so, however, with the disciple of Linnæus,* during the momentous period, that it remained a mooted point at the tribunal of his better judgement, whether the stout descendants of the squatter were not likely to dispute his right to traverse the Prairie, in freedom. The highest blooded and best trained hound with his game in view, could not have run with an eye more rivetted than that with which the Doctor had pursued his curvilinear course. It was perhaps lucky for his fortitude that he was ignorant of the artifice of the trapper in leading them around the citadel of Ishmael, and that he had imbibed, the soothing impression, that every inch of Prairie he traversed was just so much added to the distance between his own person and the detested rock. Notwithstanding the momentary shock he certainly experienced when he discovered this error, he now boldly volunteered to enter the thicket in which there was some reason to believe the body of the murdered Asa still lay. Perhaps the naturalist was urged to show his spirit on this occasion, by some secret consciousness that his excessive industry in the retreat, might be liable to misconstruction, and it is certain, that whatever might be his peculiar notions of danger from the quick, his habits and his knowledge had plac'd him far above the apprehension of suffering harm from any communication with the dead.

"If there is any service to be performed, which requires the perfect command of the nervous system," said the man of science, with a look that was slightly blustering, "you have only to give a direction to his intellectual faculties, and here stands one, on whose physical powers you may depend."

"The man is given to speak in parables," muttered the single minded trapper, "but I conclude there is always some meaning hidden in his words, though it is as hard to find sense in his speeches, as to discover three eagles on the same tree. It will be wise, friend, to make a cover, lest the sons of the squatter should be out skirting on our trail, and as you well know, there is some reason to fear yonder thicket contains a sight that may horrify a woman's mind. Are you man enough to look death in the face, or shall I run the risk of the hounds raising an outcry and go in myself. You see the pup is willing to run with an open mouth, already."

"Am I man enough! venerable trapper, our communications have a recent origin, or thy interrogatory might have a tendency to embroil us in angry disputation. Am I man enough! I claim to be of the *class*, mammalia; *order*, Primates; *genus*, homo! Such are my physical attributes; of my moral properties, let posterity speak; it becomes me to be mute."

"Physick may do for such as relish it; to my taste and judgment, it is neither palatable nor healthy, but morals never did harm to any living mortal, be it that he was a sojourner in the forest, or a dweller in the midst of glazed windows, and smoking chimnies. It is only a few hard words that divide us, friend; for I'm of an opinion that, with use and freedom, we should come to understand one another, and mainly settle down into the same judgments of mankind and of the ways of the world. Quiet, Hector, quiet, what ruffles your temper, pup; is it not used to the scent of human blood!"

The Doctor bestowed a gracious but commiserating smile on the Philosopher of nature, as he retrograded a step or two from the place whither he had been impelled by his excess of spirit, in order to reply with less expenditure of breath and with a greater freedom of action and attitude. "A homo, is certainly a homo," he said, stretching forth an arm in an argumentative manner, "so far as the animal functions extend there are the connecting links of harmony, order, conformity, and design, between the whole genus; but there the resemblance ends. Man may be degraded to the very margin of the line which separates him from the brute, by ignorance; or he may be elevated to a communion with the Great Master Spirit of All by knowledge—nay, I know not, if time and opportunity were given him, but he might become the Master of all learning, and consequently equal to the great moving principle."

The old man, who stood leaning on his rifle, in a thoughtful attitude, shook his head, as he answered with a native steadiness that entirely eclipsed the imposing air which his antagonist had seen fit to assume—

"This is neither more nor less than mortal wickedness! Here have I been a dweller on the 'arth for fourscore and six changes of the seasons, and all that time have I look'd at the growing and the dying trees, and yet do I not know the reasons why the bud starts under the summer sun, or the leaf falls when it is pinch'd by the frosts. Your l'arning, though it is man's boast, is folly in the eyes of him, who sits in the clouds and looks down in sorrow at the pride and vanity of his creatur's. Many is the hour, that I've pass'd, lying in the shades of the woods, or stretch'd upon the hills of these open fields, looking up into the blue skies, where I could fancy, the Great One had taken his stand, and was solemnizing on the waywardness of man and brute, below, as I myself had often look'd at the ants tumbling over each other in their eagerness, though in a way and a fashion more suited to his mightiness and Power. Knowledge! it is his plaything—say, you who think it so easy to climb into the judgment seat above, can you tell me any thing of the beginning and the end? Nay, you're a dealer in ailings and cures—what is life, and what is death? Why does the eagle live, so long, and why is the time of the butterfly so short? Tell me a simpler thing: why is this hound so uneasy, while you, who have passed your days in looking into books can see no reason to be disturbed?"

The Doctor who had been a little astounded by the dignity and energy of the old man, drew a long breath, like a fallen wrestler who is just released from the throttling grasp of his antagonist, and seized on the opportunity of the pause, to reply—

"It is his instinct."

"And what is the gift of instinct?"

"An inferior gradation of reason—a sort of mysterious combination of thought and matter."

"And what is that which you call thought?"

"Venerable venator, this is a method of reasoning which sets at naught the uses of definitions, and such as I do assure you is not at all tolerated in the schools."

"Then is there more cunning in your schools than I had thought, for it is a certain method of showing them their vanity," returned the trapper, suddenly abandoning a discussion from which the naturalist was just beginning to anticipate great delight, by turning to his dog, whose restlessness he attempted to appease by playing with his ears. "This is foolish, Hector; more like an untrained pup, than a sensible hound—one who has got his education by hard experience, and not by nosing over the trails of other dogs, as a boy, in the settlements, follows on the track of his masters, be it right or be it wrong. Well, friend; you who can do so much, are you equal to looking into the thicket, or must I go in myself?"

The Doctor again assumed his air of resolution and without further parlance proceeded to do as desired. The dogs were so far restrained by the remonstrances of the old man, as to confine their complaints to low, but often repeated whinings. When they saw the naturalist advance, the pup, however, broke through all restraint and made a swift circuit around his person, scenting the earth as he proceeded, and then returning to his companion, he howled aloud.

"The squatter and his brood have left a strong taint upon the 'arth!" said the old man, watching as he spoke for some signal from his learned Pioneer, to follow; "I hope yonder school-bred man knows enough, to remember the errand on which I have sent him."

Doctor Battius had already disappeared in the bushes, and the trapper was beginning to betray additional evidences of impatience, when the person of the former was seen retiring from the thicket backwards with his face fastened on the place he had just left, as if his look was bound in the thraldom of some charm.

"Here is something skeary, by the wildness of the man's countenance!" exclaimed the old man, relinquishing his hold of Hector, and moving stoutly to the side of the totally unconscious naturalist. "How is it, friend, have you found a new leaf in your book of wisdom."

"It is a basilisk!" muttered the Doctor, whose altered visage betrayed the utter confusion which beset his faculties. "An animal of the *order* serpens. I had thought its attributes were fabulous, but mighty nature is equal to all that man can imagine!"

"What is't?—what is't? The snakes of the Prairies are harmless, unless it be, now and then, an angered rattler, and he always gives you notice with his tail, afore he works his mischief with his fangs. Lord, Lord, what a humbling thing is fear! Here is one who in common delivers words too big for a humble mouth to hold, so much beside himself that his voice is as fine as the whistle of the whip-poor-will!— Courage!—what is it, man?—what is't?"

"A Prodigy! a lusus naturæ! a monster that nature has delighted to form, in order to exhibit her power. Never before have I witnessed such an utter confusion in her Laws, or a specimen that so completely bids defiance to the distinctions of *Class* and *Genera.* Let me record its appearance," fumbling for his tabletts with hands that trembled too much to perform their office, "while time and opportunity are allowed—*eyes,* enthralling. *Colour,* various, complex, and profound—"

"One would think the man was craz'd, with his enthralling looks and pieball'd colours!" interrupted the discontented trapper, who began to grow a little uneasy that his party was, all this time, neglecting to seek the protection of some cover. "If there is a reptile in the brush, show me the creatur' and should it refuse to depart peaceably, why there must be a quarrel for the possession of the place."

"There!" said the Doctor pointing into a dense mass of the thicket, to a spot within fifty feet of that where they both stood. The trapper turned his look with perfect composure in the required direction, but the instant his practised glance met the object which had so utterly upset the philosophy of the naturalist, he gave a start, himself, threw his rifle rapidly forward and as instantly recovered it, as if a second flash of thought convinced him he was wrong. Neither the instinctive movement, nor the sudden recollection, was without a sufficient object. At the very margin of the thicket, and in absolute contact with the earth, lay an animate ball that might easily, by the singularity and fierceness of its aspect, have justified the disturbed condition of the naturalist's mind. It were difficult to describe the shape or colours of this extraordinary substance, except to say in general terms that it was nearly spherical and exhibited all the hues of the rainbow intermingled, without reference to harmony and without any very ostensible design. The predominant hues were a black and a bright vermillion. With these, however, the several tints of white, yellow, and crimson, were strangely and wildly blended. Had this been all, it would have been difficult to have pronounced that the object was possessed of life, for it lay motionless as any stone: but a pair of dark, glaring, and moving eye-balls, which watch'd with jealousy the smallest movement of the trapper and his companion, sufficiently established the important fact of its possessing vitality.

"Your reptile is a scouter, or I'm no judge of Indian paints and Indian deviltries," muttered the old man, dropping the butt of his weapon to the ground, and gazing with a steady eye at the frightful object, as he leaned on its barrel, in an attitude of great composure. "He wants to face us out of sight and reason, and make us think the head of a red-skin is a stone covered with the autumn leaf, or he has some other devilish artifice in his mind!"

"Is the animal human!" demanded the Doctor, "of the *genus* homo! I had fancied it a non-descript."

"It's as human, and as mortal too, as a warrior of these Prairies is ever known to be. I have seen the time when a red-skin would have shown a foolish daring to peep out of his ambushment in that fashion on a hunter I could name, but who is too old now, and too near his time, to be any thing better than a miserable trapper. It will be well to speak to the imp, and to let him know he deals with men whose beards are grown. Come, forth from your cover, friend," he continued in the language of the extensive tribes of the Dahcotahs; "there is room on the Prairie for another warrior."

The eyes appeared to glare more fiercely than before, but the mass which according to the trapper's opinion was neither more nor less than a human head, shorn, as usual among the warriors of the west, of its hair, still continued without motion, or any other sign of life.

"It is a mistake!" exclaimed the Doctor. "The animal is not even of the *class* Mammalia, much less a man."

"So much for your knowledge!" returned the trapper laughing with great exultation. "So much for the l'arning of one who has look'd into so many books that his eyes are not able to tell a moose from a wild-cat! Now, my Hector, here, is a dog of education after his fashion, and though the meanest primmer in the settlements would puzzle his schooling, you could'nt cheat the hound in a matter like this. As you think the object no man, you shall see his whole formation, and then let an ignorant old trapper who never passed a day within reach of a spelling book in his life, know by what name to call it. Mind, I mean no violence, but just to brush the devil from his ambushment."

The trapper very deliberately examined the priming of his rifle, taking care to make as great a parade as possible of his hostile intentions, in going through the necessary evolutions with the weapon. When he thought the stranger began seriously to apprehend some danger, he very deliberately presented the piece, and called aloud—

"Now, friend, am I all for peace, or all for war, as you may say. No! well it *is* no man, as the wise one, here, says, and there can be no harm in just firing into a bunch of leaves."

The muzzle of the rifle fell as he concluded, and the weapon was gradually settling into a steady, and what would easily have proved a fatal aim, when a tall Indian sprang from beneath that bed of leaves, and brush, which he had collected about his person at the approach of the party, and stood upright uttering the exclamation,

"Wagh!"*

CHAPTER XVIII.

"My visor is Philemon's roof; within the house
is Jove's."

Much Ado about Nothing, II.i. 99-100

THE trapper, who had meditated no violence, dropped his rifle again, and laughing at the success of his experiment, with great seeming self complacency, he drew the astounded gaze of the naturalist from the person of the savage to himself by saying—

"The imps will lie for hours like sleeping alligators, brooding their deviltries in dreams and other craftiness, till such time as they see some real danger is at hand and then they look to themselves the same as other mortals. But this is a scouter in his war-paint! There should be more of his tribe at no great distance. Let us draw the truth out of him, for an unlucky war-party may prove more dangerous to us, than a visit from the whole family of the squatter."

"It is truly a desperate and a dangerous species!" said the Doctor, relieving his amazement by a breath that seem'd to exhaust his lungs of air; "a violent race; and one that it is difficult to define or class within the usual boundaries of definitions. Speak to him, therefore, but let thy words be strong in amity."

The old man cast a keen eye, on every side of him, to ascertain the important particular whether the stranger was supported by any associates, and then making the usual signs of peace by exhibiting the palm of his naked hand he boldly advanced. In the mean time, the Indian betrayed no evidences, of uneasiness. He suffered the trapper to draw nigh, maintaining by his own mien and attitude a striking air of dignity and fearlessness. Perhaps the wary warrior also knew that owing to the difference in their weapons, he should be plac'd more on an equality, by being brought nearer to the stranger.

As a description of this individual may furnish some idea of the personal appearance of a whole race, it may be well to detain the narrative in order to present it to the reader in our hasty and imperfect manner. Would the truant eyes of Alston or Greenough*turn, but for a time, from their gaze at the models of antiquity to contemplate this wronged and humbled people, little would be left for such inferior artists as ourselves to delineate.

The Indian in question was in every particular a warrior of fine stature and admirable proportions. As he cast aside his masque composed of such party-coloured leaves, as he had hurriedly collected, his countenance appeared in all the gravity, the dignity and it may be added in the terror, of his profession. The outlines of his lineaments were strikingly noble, and nearly approaching to Roman, though the secondary features of his face were slightly marked with the well known traces of his Asiatic origin. The peculiar tint of the skin, which in itself is so well designed to aid the effect of a martial expression, had received an additional aspect of wild ferocity from the colours of the war-paint. But as if he disdained the usual artifices of his people, he bore none of those strange and horrid devices with which the children of the forest are accustomed, like the more civilized heroes of the moustache, to back their reputation for courage, contenting himself with a broad and deep shadowing of black that served as a sufficient and an admirable foil to the brighter gleamings of his native swarthiness. His head was as usual shaved to the crown where a large and gallant scalplock seem'd to challenge the grasp of his enemies. The ornaments that in peace were pendant from the cartilages of his ear had been removed on account of his present pursuit. His body, notwithstanding the lateness of the season, was nearly naked, and the portion that was clad, bore a vestment no warmer than a light robe of the finest dress'd deer skin, beautifully stained with the rude design of some daring exploit, and which was carelessly worn, as if more in pride than from any unmanly regard to comfort. His leggins were of bright scarlet cloth, the only evidence about his person that he had held communion with the traders of Pale faces. But as if to furnish some offset to this solitary submission to a womanish vanity, they were fearfully fringed, from the gartered knee to the bottom of the mockasin, with the hair of human scalps. He leaned lightly with one hand on a short hickory bow, while the other rather touched than sought support, from the long, delicate handle of an ashen lance. A quiver, made of the cougar skin, from which the tail of the animal depended,* as a characteristic ornament, was slung at his back, and a shield of hides, quaintly emblazoned with another of his warlike deeds, was suspended from his neck by a thong of sinews.

As the trapper approached, this warrior maintained his calm, upright attitude, discovering neither an eagerness to ascertain the character of those who advanced upon him, nor the smallest wish to avoid a scrutiny in his own person. An Eye, that was darker and more shining than that of the stag, was incessantly glancing, however, from one to another of the strange party, seemingly never knowing rest for an instant.

"Is my brother far from his village;" demanded the old man, in the Pawnee language, after examining the paint and those other little signs by which a practised eye, knows the tribe of the warrior he encounters in the American desert, with the same readiness and by the same sort of mysterious observation as that by which the seaman knows the distant sail.

"It is farther to the towns of the Big-knives," was the laconick reply.

"Why is a Pawnee-Loup so far from the Fork of his own river, without a horse to journey on, and in a spot empty as this?"

"Can the women and children of a Pale-face live without the meat of the bison! There was hunger in my lodge!"

"My brother is very young to be already the master of a lodge," returned the trapper looking steadily into the unmoved countenance of the youthful warrior; "but I dare say he is brave and that many a chief has offered him his daughters for wives. But he has been mistaken," pointing to the arrow which was dangling from the hand that held the bow, "in bringing a loose and barbed arrow head to kill the buffaloe. Do the Pawnees wish the wounds they give their game to rankle?"

"It is good to be ready for the Sioux; though he is not in sight, a bush may hide him."

"The man is a living proof of the truth of his words," muttered the trapper in English, "and a close-jointed and gallant looking lad he is, but far too young for a chief of any importance. It is wise, however to speak him fair, for a single arm thrown into either party if we come to blows with the squatter and his brood may turn the day. You see my children are weary," he continued in the dialect of the Prairie, pointing as he spoke to the rest of the party, who by this time were also approaching. "We wish to camp and eat. Does my brother own this spot?"

"The runners from the people on the Big-river tell us, that your nation have traded with the Tawney-faces who live beyond the salt lake, and that the Prairies are now the hunting grounds of the Big-knives."

"It is true as I hear, also from the hunters and trappers on La Platte. Though it is with the Frenchers and not with the men who claim to own the Mexicos, that my people have bargained."

"And warriors are wading up the Long River, to see that they have not been cheated, in what they have bought?"

"Ay, that is partly true, too, I fear; and it will not be long afore an accursed band of choppers and loggers will be following on their heels to humble the wilderness which lies so broad and rich on the western banks of the Mississippi, and then the land will be a peopled desert from the shores of the Maine sea to the foot of the Rocky Mountains, fill'd with all the abominations and craft of man and stript of the comfort and loveliness it received from the hand of the Lord!"

"And where were the chiefs of the Pawnee Loups, when this bargain was made!" suddenly demanded the youthful warrior, a look of startling fierceness gleaming at the same instant, athwart his dark visage. "Is a nation to be sold like the skin of a beaver!"

"Right enough, right enough; and where were truth and honesty also. But might is right according to the fashions of the 'arth and what the strong choose to do, the weak must call justice. If the Law of the Wahcondah was as much hearkened to, Pawnee, as the laws of the Long knives, your right to the Prairies would be as good as that of the greatest chief in the settlements, to the house which covers his head."

"The skin of the traveller is white," said the young native laying a finger impressively on the hard and wrinkled hand of the trapper, "does his heart say one thing and his tongue another?"

"The Wahcondah of a white-man has ears, and he shuts them to a lie. Look at my head; it is like a frosted pine, and must soon be laid in the ground. Why then should I wish to meet the Great Spirit, face to face, while his countenance is dark upon me."

The Pawnee gracefully threw his shield over one shoulder, and placing a hand on his chest he bent his head in deference to the gray locks exhibited by the trapper, after which his eye became more steady and his countenance less fierce. Still he maintained every appearance of a distrust and watchfulness that were rather tempered and subdued than forgotten. When this equivocal species of amity was established between the warrior of the Prairies and the experienced old trapper, the latter proceeded to give his directions to Paul, concerning the arrangements of the contemplated halt. While Inez and Ellen were dismounting and Middleton and the bee-hunter were attending to their comforts, the discourse was continued, sometimes in the language of the natives, but often as Paul and the Doctor mingled their opinions with the two principal speakers, in the English tongue. There was a keen and subtle trial of skill between the Pawnee and the trapper, in which each endeavored to discover the objects of the other, without betraying his own interest in the investigation. As might be expected when the struggle was between adversaries so equal, the result of the encounter answered the expectations of neither. The latter had put all the interrogatories his ingenuity and practice could suggest concerning the state of the tribe of the Loups, their crops, their store of provisions for the coming winter and their relations with their different warlike neighbors, without extorting any answer, that, in the slightest degree, elucidated the reason why he found a solitary warrior so far from his people. On the other hand, while the questions of the Indian were far more dignified and delicate, they were equally ingenious. He commented on the state of the trade in peltries; spoke of the good or ill success of many white hunters whom he had either encountered or heard named, and even alluded to the steady march, which the nation of his 'Great Father' as he courteously termed the government of the States, was making towards the hunting-grounds of his tribe. It was apparent, however, by this singular mixture of interest, contempt and indignation that were occasionally gleaming through the reserved manner of this warrior, that he knew the strange people, who were thus trespassing on his native rights, much more by report than by any actual intercourse. This personal ignorance of the whites, was as much betrayed by the manner in which he regarded the females, as by the brief, but energetick, expressions which, occasionally escaped him.

While speaking to the trapper he suffered his wandering glances, to stray towards the intellectual and nearly infantile beauty of Inez, as one might be supposed to gaze upon the loveliness of an ethereal being. It was very evident that he now saw, for the first time, one of those females, of whom the fathers of his tribe so often spoke, and who were considered of such rare excellence as to equal all that savage ingenuity could imagine in the way of loveliness. His observation of Ellen was less marked, but, notwithstanding the warlike and chastened expression of his eye, there was much of the homage which man is wont to pay to woman, even in the more cursory look he sometimes turned on her maturer and perhaps more animated beauty. This admiration, however, was so tempered by his habits and so smothered in the pride of a warrior, as completely to elude every eye but that of the trapper, who was too well skilled in Indian customs and was too well instructed in the importance of rightly conceiving the character of the stranger to let the smallest trait, or the most trifling of his movements escape him. In the mean time, the unconscious Ellen, herself, mov'd about the feeble, and less resolute Inez, with her accustomed assiduity and tenderness, exhibiting in her frank features those changing emotions of joy and regret, which occasionally beset her, as her active mind dwelt on the decided step she had just taken, with the contending doubts and hopes, and possibly with some of the mental vacillation, that was natural to her situation and sex.

Not so Paul; conceiving himself to have attained the two things dearest to his heart, the possession of Ellen and a triumph over the sons of Ishmael, he, now, enacted his part in the business of the moment, with as much coolness as though he were already leading his willing bride from solemnizing their nuptials before a border magistrate to the security of his own dwelling. He had hovered around the moving family during the tedious period of their weary march, concealing himself by day, and seeking interviews with his betrothed, as opportunities offered, in the manner already described, until fortune and his own intrepidity had united to render him successful, at the very moment when he was beginning to despair. He now cared neither for distance, nor violence, nor hardships. To his sanguine fancy and determined resolution, all the rest was easily to be achieved. Such were his feelings and such in truth they seem'd to be. With his cap cast on one side, and whistling a low air, he thrashed among the bushes, in order to make a place suitable for the females to repose on, while from time to time, he cast an approving glance at the agile form of Ellen as she tripp'd past him engaged in her own share of the duty.

"And so the wolf-tribe of the Pawnees have buried the hatchet with their neighbors, the Konzas," said the trapper pursuing a discourse which he had scarcely permitted to flag, though it had been, occasionally, interrupted by the different directions with which he saw fit to interlard it—the reader will remember that while he spoke to the native warrior in his own tongue, he necessarily addressed his white companions in English—"The Loups and the light-fac'd red-skins are again friends. Doctor, that is a tribe of which I'll engage you've often read, and of which many a round lie has been whispered in the ears of the ignorant people who live in the settlements. There was a story of a nation of Welshers, that liv'd, hereaway, in the Prairies, and how they came into the land, afore the uneasy-minded man who first let in the Christians to rob the heathens of their inheritance, had even dreamt that the sun set on a country as big as that it rose from. And how they knew the white ways and spoke with white tongues, and a thousand other follies and idle conceits."

"Have I not heard of them!" exclaimed the Naturalist, dropping a piece of jerked bison's meat which he was rather roughly discussing, at the moment. "I should be greatly ignorant not to have often dwelt with delight on so beautiful a theory, and one which so triumphantly establishes two positions which I have often maintained are unanswerable even without such living testimony in their favor, viz, that this continent can claim a more remote affinity with civilization than the time of Columbus, and that colour is the fruit of climate and condition and not a regulation of nature. Propound the latter question to this Indian gentleman, venerable hunter, he is of a reddish tint, himself, and his opinion may be said to make us masters of the two sides of the disputed point."

"Do you think a Pawnee is a reader of books, and a believer of printed lies, like the idlers in the towns!" contemptuously retorted the old man. "But it may be as well to humour the likings of the man, which after all, it is quite probable, are neither more nor less than his natural gifts, and therefore to be followed although they may be pitied. What does my brother think? all whom he sees here have white skins, but the Pawnee warriors are red, does he believe that man changes with the season, and that the son is not like his fathers?"

The young warrior regarded his interrogator for a moment with a steady and deliberating eye; then raising his finger upward he answered, with dignity—

"The Wahcondah pours the rain from his clouds; when he speaks he shakes the hills, and the fire which scorches the trees is the anger of his eye; but he fashioned his children with care and thought. What he has thus made never alters!"

"Ay, 'tis in the reason of natur' that it should be so, Doctor," continued the trapper when he had interpreted this answer to the disappointed naturalist. "The Pawnees are a wise and a great people, and I'll engage they abound in many a wholesome and honest tradition. The hunters and trappers I sometimes see speak of a great warrior of your race."

"My tribe are not women. A brave is no stranger in my village."

"Ay, but he he they speak of most, is a chief far beyond the renown of common warriors, and one that might have done credit to that once mighty but now fallen people the Delawares of the Hills."

"Such a warrior should have a name."

"They call him Hard-Heart*from the stoutness of his resolution; and well is he named if all I have heard of his deeds be true."

The stranger cast a glance which seem'd to read the guileless soul of the old man, as he demanded.—

"Has the pale face seen the Partizan of my tribe?"

"Never. It is not with me, now, as it used to be some forty years agone, when warfare and bloodshed were my calling and my gifts."

A loud shout from the reckless Paul interrupted his speech, and at the next moment the bee-hunter appeared leading an Indian war-horse from the side of the thicket opposite to the one occupied by the party.

"Here is a beast for a red-skin to straddle!" He cried, as he made the animal go through some of its wild paces. "There's not a brigadier in all Kentuck that can call himself master of so sleek and well jointed a nag! A Spanish saddle too, like a Grandee of the Mexico's, and look at the mane and tail! braided and platted down with little silver balls, as if it were Ellen, herself, getting her shining hair ready for a dance, or a husking frolick! Isn't this a real trotter, old trapper, to eat out of the manger of a savage!"

"Softly, lad, softly. The Loups are famous for their horses, and it's often that you see a warrior on the Prairies far better mounted, than a Congress-man in the settlements. But this, indeed, is a beast that none but a powerful chief should ride! The saddle, as you rightly think, has been sat upon in its day by a great Spanish Captain, who has lost it and his life together, in some of the battles, which this people often fight against the Southern Provinces. I warrant me, I warrant me, this youngster is the son of a great Chief, maybe of the mighty Hard-Heart himself."

During this rude interruption to the discourse the young Pawnee manifested neither impatience nor displeasure, but when he thought his beast had been the subject of sufficient comment, he very coolly, and with the air of one accustomed to have his will respected, relieved Paul of the bridle, and throwing the reins on the neck of the animal, he sprang upon his back with the activity of a professor of the equestrian art. Nothing could be finer or firmer than the seat of the savage. The highly wrought and cumbrous saddle was evidently more for show than use. Indeed it impeded rather than aided the action of limbs, which disdained to seek assistance, or admit of restraint from so womanish inventions as stirrups. The horse, which immediately began to prance, was like its rider, wild and untutored in all his motions, but while there was so little of art, there was all the freedom and grace of nature in the movements of both. The animal was probably indebted to the blood of Araby for its excellence, through a long Pedigree that embraced the steed of Mexico, the spanish barb, and the Moorish charger. The rider, in obtaining his steed from the Provinces of

Central-America, had also obtained that spirit and grace in controlling him, which unite to form the most intrepid and perhaps the most skilful horsemen in the world.

Notwithstanding this sudden occupation of his animal the Pawnee discovered no hasty wish to depart. More at his ease, and possibly more independant now he found himself secure of the means of retreat, he rode back and forth, eyeing the different individuals of the party with far greater freedom than before. But, at each extremity of his ride, just as the sagacious trapper, expected to see him profit by his advantage and fly, he would turn his horse and pass over the same ground, sometimes with the rapidity of the flying antelope, and at others more slowly, and with greater dignity of mien and movement. Anxious to ascertain such facts as might have an influence on his future proceedings the old man, determined to invite him to a renewal of their conference. He therefore made a gesture expressive at the same time of his wish to resume the interrupted discourse and of his own pacific intentions. The quick eye of the stranger was not slow to note the action, but it was not until a sufficient time had passed to allow him to debate the prudence of the measure in his own mind, that he seem'd willing to trust himself, again, so near a party that was so much superior to himself in physical power, and consequently one that was able, at any instant, to command his life, or controul his personal liberty. When he did approach nigh enough to converse with facility it was with a singular mixture of haughtiness and of distrust.

"It is far to the village of the Loups," he said, stretching his arm in a direction contrary to that in which the trapper well knew that the tribe dwelt, "and the road is very crooked — what has the Big-Knife to say?"

"Ay crooked enough!" muttered the old man in English, "if you are to set out on your journey by that path, but not half so winding as the cunning of an Indian's mind. Say, my Brother; do the chiefs of the Pawnees love to see strange faces in their lodges?"

The young warrior bent his body gracefully, though but slightly, over the saddle bow, as he replied —

"When have my people forgotten to give food to the stranger!"

"If I lead my daughters to the doors of the Loups, will the women take them by the hand and will the warriors smoke with my young men?"

"The country of the Pale faces is behind them. Why do they journey so far towards the setting sun! Have they lost the path or are these the women of the white-warriors, that I hear are wading up the river of 'the troubled water'?"

"Neither. They who wade the Missouri are the warriors of my Great Father, who has sent them on his message. But we are peace-runners. The White-men and the Red are neighbors, and they wish to be friends. Do not the Omahaws visit the Loups, when the tomahawk is buried in the path between the two nations?"

"The Omahaws are welcome."

"And the Yanktons, and the Burnt-wood Tetons who live in the elbow of the river with muddy water, do they not come into the lodges of the Loups, and smoke?"

"The Tetons are liars!" exclaimed the other. "They dare not shut their eyes in the night. No; they sleep in the sun. See," he added pointing with fierce triumph to the frightful ornaments of his leggings, "their scalps are so plenty, that the Pawnees tread on them! Go: let a Sioux live in banks of snow; the plains and buffaloes are for men!"

"Ah! The secret is out," said the trapper to Middleton who was an attentive, because a deeply interested, observer of what was passing. "This good-looking young Indian is scouting on the track of the Siouxes. You may see it by his arrow-heads, and his paint, ay, by his eye, too: for a red-skin lets his natur' follow the business he is on, be it for peace, or be it for war. Quiet, Hector, quiet. Have you never scented a Pawnee afore, pup; keep down, dog, keep down. My brother is right. The Siouxes are thieves. Men of all colours and nations say it of them, and say it truly. But the people from the rising-sun are not Siouxes, and they wish to visit the lodges of the Loups."

"The head of my brother is white," returned the Pawnee throwing one of those glances at the trapper which were so remarkably expressive of distrust, intelligence and pride, and then pointing as he continued, towards the eastern horizon, "and his eyes have look'd on many things. Can he tell me the name of what he sees yonder. Is it a buffaloe?"

"It looks more like a cloud, peeping above the skirt of the plain, with the sunshine lighting its edges. It is the smoke of the heavens!"

"It is a hill of the earth. And on its top, are the lodges of Pale-faces. Let the women of my brother wash their feet with the people of their own colour."

"The eyes of a Pawnee are good if he can see a white skin so far."

The Indian turned slowly towards the speaker, and after a pause of a moment, he sternly demanded—

"Can my brother hunt?"

"Alas! I claim to be no better than a miserable trapper!"

"When the plain is covered with the buffaloes, can he see them?"

"No doubt, no doubt, it is far easier to see than to take a scampering bull."

"And when the birds are flying from the cold, and the clouds are black with their feathers, can he see *them* too?"

"Ay—ay—it is not hard to find a duck, or a goose, when millions are darkening the heavens."

"When the snow falls, and covers the lodges of the Long-knives, can the stranger see flakes in the air?"

"My eyes are none of the best, now," returned the old man a little resentfully, "but the time has been, Pawnee, when I had a name for my sight."

"The Red-skins find the Big-knives as easily as the stranger sees the buffaloe, or the travelling birds, or the falling snow. Your warriors think the Master of Life has made the whole earth white; they are mistaken. They are pale, and it is their own faces that they see. Go, a Pawnee is not blind, that he need look long for your people!—"

The warrior suddenly paused, and bent his face aside like one who listened with all his faculties absorbed in the act. Then turning the head of his horse he rode to the nearest angle of the thicket and look'd intently across the bleak Prairie, in a direction opposite to the side on which the party stood. Returning slowly from this unaccountable, and to his observers startling, procedure, he rivetted his eyes on Inez, and pac'd back and forth several times, with the air of one who maintained a warm struggle on some difficult point, in the recesses of his own thought. He had drawn the reins of his impatient steed, and was seemingly about to speak, when his head again sunk on his chest, and he resumed his former attitude of attention. Galloping like a deer to the place of his former observations, he rode for a moment swiftly in short and rapid circles, as if still uncertain of his course, and then darted away like a bird that had been fluttering around its nest before it takes a distant flight. After scouring the plain for a minute, he was lost to the eye behind a swell of the land.

The hounds, who had also manifested great uneasiness for some time, followed him for a little distance and then terminated their chase, by seating themselves on the ground, and raising their usual, low, whining and warning howls.

CHAPTER XIX.

"How if he will not stand?"
  Much Ado about Nothing, III.iii. 28.

THE several movements, related in the close of the preceding chapter had passed in so short a space of time, that the old man, while he neglected not to note the smallest incident, had no opportunity of expressing his opinion concerning the stranger's motives. After the Pawnee had disappeared, however, he shook his head, and muttered while he walked slowly to the angle of the thicket that the Pawnee had just quitted.

"There are both scents and sounds in the air, though my miserable senses are not good enough to hear the one or to catch the taint of the other."

"There is nothing to be seen," cried Middleton who kept close at his side. "My eyes and my ears are good, and yet I can assure you that I neither hear nor see any thing."

"Your eyes are good! and you are not deaf!" returned the other with a slight air of contempt, "no, lad, no—they may be good to see across a church or to hear a town bell, but afore you had passed a year on these Prairies you would find yourself mistaking a turkey for a horse,* or conceiting fifty times that the roar of a buffaloe bull was the thunder of the Lord. There is a deception of natur' in these naked plains, in which the air throws up the image like water, and then is it hard to tell the Prairies from a sea. But yonder is a sign that a hunter never fails to know!"

The trapper pointed to a flight of vultures that were sailing over the plain at no great distance, and apparently in the direction in which the Pawnee had rivetted his eye. At first Middleton could not distinguish the small dark objects that were dotting the dusky clouds, but as they came swiftly onward, first their forms and then their heavy waving wings became distinctly visible.

"Listen;" said the trapper, when he had succeeded in making Middleton see the moving column of birds; "now you hear the buffaloes, or bisons as your knowing Doctor sees fit to call them, though buffaloes is their name among all the hunters of these regions. Now, I conclude that a hunter is a better judge of a beast and of its name," he added winking to the young soldier, "than any man who has turn'd over the leaves of a book, instead of travelling over the face of the 'arth, in order to find out the natur's of its inhabitants."

"Of their habits, I will grant you," cried the Naturalist, who rarely miss'd an opportunity to agitate any point which touched his favorite studies, "that is provided, always, that deference is had to the proper use of definitions, and that they are contemplated with scientific eyes."

"Eyes of a mole! as if man's eyes were not as good for names as the eyes of any other creatur'! who named the works of His hand, can you tell me that, with your books and college wisdom? Was it not the first man in the Garden, and is it not a plain consequence that his children inherit his gifts!"

"That is certainly the Mosaic account of the event," said the Doctor, "though your reading is by far too literal."

"My reading—nay, if you suppose that I have wasted my time in schools you do such a wrong to my knowledge, as one mortal should never lay to the door of another without sufficient reason. If I have ever craved the art of reading, it has been that I might better know the sayings of the book you name for it is a book, which speaks in every line according to human feelings and therein according to reason."

"And do you then believe," said the Doctor a little provoked by the dogmatism of his stubborn adversary, and perhaps secretly triumphing in his own more liberal, though scarcely as profitable, attainments. "Do you then believe that all these beasts were literally collected in a garden to be enrolled in the nomenclature of the first man?"

"Why not. I understand your meaning, for it is not needful to live in towns to hear all the devilish devices that the conceit of man can invent to upset his own happiness. What does it prove, except, indeed that it may be said to prove that the garden He made was not after the miserable fashions of our times, thereby directly giving the lie to what the world calls its civilizing. No, no, the Garden of the Lord, was the forest then and is the forest now, where the fruits do grow and the birds do sing according to his own wise ordering—Now, lads, you may see through the mystery of the vultures. There come the buffaloes themselves, and a noble herd it is! I warrant me, that Pawnee has a troop of his people in some of the hollows nigh by, and as he has gone scampering after them, you are about to see a glorious chase. It will serve to keep the squatter and his brood under cover, and for ourselves there is little reason to fear. A Pawnee is not apt to be a malicious savage."

Every eye was now drawn to the striking spectacle that succeeded. Even the timid Inez hastened to the side of Middleton to gaze at the sight, and Paul summoned Ellen from her culinary labors, to become a witness of the lively scene.

Throughout the whole of those moving events which it has been our duty to record, the Prairies had lain in the majesty of perfect solitude. The heavens had been blackened with the passage of the migratory birds, it is true, but the dogs of the party, and the ass of the Doctor, were the only quadrupeds that had enlivened the broad surface of the waste beneath. There was now a sudden exhibition of animal life which changed the scene, as it were by magic, to the very opposite extreme.

A few enormous Bison bulls were first observed scouring along the most distant roll of the Prairie, and then succeeded long files of single beasts, which in their turns were followed by a dark mass of bodies, until the dun-coloured herbage of the plain was entirely lost, in the deeper hue of their shaggy coats. The herd, as the column spread and thickened, was like the endless flocks of the smaller birds, whose extended flanks are so often seen to heave up out the abyss of the heavens, until they appear as countless and as interminable, as the leaves in those forests over which they wing their endless flight. Clouds of dust shot up in little columns from the centre of the mass, as some animal more furious than the rest ploughed the plain with his horns, and from time to time a deep hollow bellowing was borne along on the wind, as if a thousand throats vented their plaints in a discordant murmuring.

A long and musing silence reigned in the party as they gazed on this spectacle of wild and peculiar grandeur. It was at length broken by the trapper, who having been long accustomed to similar sights felt less of its influence, or rather felt it in a less thrilling and absorbing manner, than those to whom the scene was more novel.

"There go ten thousand oxen in one drove without keeper or master, except him, who made them and gave them these open plains for their pasture! Ay it is here that man may see the proofs of his wantonness and folly! Can the proudest Governor in all the States go into his fields and slaughter a nobler bullock than is here offered to the meanest hand, and when he has gotten his surloin, or his steak can he eat it with as good a relish as he who has sweetened his food with wholesome toil, and earned it according to the law of natur' by honestly mastering that which the Lord hath put before him?"

"If the Prairie platter is smoking with a buffaloe's hump, I answer, no;" interrupted the luxurious bee-hunter.

"Ay, boy; you have tasted and you feel the genuine reasoning of the thing! But the herd is heading a little, this-a-way, and it behoves us to make ready for their visit. If we hide ourselves, altogether, the horned brutes will break through the place, and trample us beneath their feet like so many creeping worms; so we will just put the weak ones apart, and take post as becomes men and hunters in the van."

As there was but little time to make the necessary arrangements the whole party set about them in good earnest. Inez and Ellen were placed in the edge of the thicket on the side farthest from the approaching herd, Asinus was posted in the centre, in consideration of his nerves, and then the old man with his three male companions divided themselves in such a manner as they thought would enable them to turn the head of the rushing column, should it chance to approach too nigh their position. By the vacillating movements of some fifty or a hundred bulls that led the advance it remained questionable for many moments what course they intended to pursue. But a tremendous and painful roar which came from behind the cloud of dust that rose in the centre of the horde, and which was horridly answered by the screams of the carrion birds that were greedily sailing directly above the flying drove, appeared to give a new impulse to their flight, and at once, to remove every symptom of indecision. As if glad to seek the smallest signs of the forest the whole of the affrighted herd became steady in its direction rushing in a straight line toward the little cover of bushes which has already been so often named.

The appearance of danger was now, in reality, of a character to try the stoutest nerves. The flanks of the dark, moving mass were advanced in such a manner as to make a concave line of the front, and every fierce eye that was glaring from the shaggy wilderness of hair in which the entire heads of the males were enveloped, was rivetted with mad anxiety on the thicket. It seem'd as if each beast strove to outstrip his neighbor, in gaining this desired cover, and as thousands in the rear press'd blindly on those in front, there was the appearance of an imminent risk that the leaders of the herd would be precipitated on the crouching party, in which case the destruction of every one of them was certain. Each of our adventurers felt the danger of his situation in a manner peculiar to his individual character and circumstances.

Middleton wavered. At times, he felt inclined to rush through the bushes and seizing Inez attempt to fly, then recollecting the impossibility of outstripping the furious speed of an alarmed bison, he felt for his arms, determined to make head against the countless drove. The faculties of Doctor Battius were quickly wrought up to the very summit of mental delusion. The dark forms of the herd lost their distinctness and then the Naturalist began to fancy he beheld a wild collection of all the creatures of the world rushing upon him in a body as if to revenge the various injuries, which in the course of a life of indefatigable labour in behalf of the natural sciences, he had inflicted on their several genera. The paralysis it occasioned in his system was like the effect of the Incubus. Equally unable to fly or to advance he stood rivetted to the spot, until the infatuation became so complete, that the worthy naturalist was beginning, by a desperate effort of scientific resolution, even to class the different specimens. On the other hand, Paul shouted and call'd on Ellen to come and assist him in shouting, but his voice was lost in the bellowings and trampling of the herd. Furious, and yet strangely excited by the obstinacy of the brutes and the wildness of the sight, and nearly maddened by sympathy and a species of unconscious apprehension, in which the claims of nature were singularly mingled with concern for his mistress, he nearly split his throat in exhorting his aged friend to interfere.

"Come forth, old trapper," he shouted, "with your Prairie inventions or we shall be all smothered under a mountain of buffaloe humps."

The old man, who had stood all this while leaning on his rifle and regarding the movements of the herd with a steady eye, now deem'd it time to strike his blow. Levelling his piece at the foremost bull, with an agility that would have done credit to his youth, he fired. The animal received the bullet on the matted hair between his horns, and fell to his knees: but shaking his head he instantly arose, the very shock seeming to increase his exertions. There was now, no longer time to hesitate. Throwing down his rifle, the trapper stretched forth his arms and advanced from the cover with naked hands, directly towards the rushing column of the beasts.

The figure of a man, when sustained by the firmness and steadiness that intellect can only impart rarely fails of commanding respect from all the inferior animals of the creation. The leading bulls recoiled and for a single instant there was a sudden stop to their speed, a dense mass of bodies rolling up in front, until hundreds were seen floundering and tumbling on the plain. Then came another of those hollow bellowings from the rear, and set the herd again, in motion. The head of the column, however, divided, the immovable form of the trapper cutting it, as it were, into two gliding streams of life. Middleton and Paul instantly profited by his example, and extended the feeble barrier by a similar exhibition of their own persons.

For a few moments the new impulse given to the animals in front served to protect the thicket, but as the body of the herd press'd more and more upon the open line of its defenders, and the dust thickened, so as to obscure their persons, there was, at each instant, a renewed danger of the brutes breaking through. It became necessary for the trapper and his companions to become still more and more alert, and they were gradually yielding before the headlong multitude, when a furious bull darted by Middleton, so near as to brush his person, and at the next instant swept through the thicket with the velocity of the wind.

"Close, and die for the ground," shouted the old man, "or a thousand of the devils will be at his heels."

All their efforts would have prov'd fruitless however, against the living torrent, had not Asinus, whose domains had just been so rudely entered lifted his voice, in the midst of the uproar. The most sturdy and furious of the bulls trembled at the alarming and unknown cry, and then each individual brute was seen madly pressing from that very thicket, which, the moment before, he had endeavored to reach, with the eagerness with which the murderer seeks the sanctuary.

As the stream divided, the place became clear, the two dark columns moving obliquely from the copse, to unite, again, at the distance of a mile on its opposite side. The instant the old man saw the sudden effect which the voice of Asinus had produced, he coolly commenced reloading his rifle, indulging at the same time in a heartfelt fit of his silent and peculiar merriment.

"There they go like dogs with so many half-filled shot pouches dangling at their tails, and no fear of their breaking their order, for what the brutes in the rear didn't hear with their own ears they'll conceit they did: besides, if they change their minds it may be no hard matter to get the Jack to sing the rest of his tune."

"The ass has spoken, but Balaam is silent!"*cried the Bee-hunter, catching his breath after a repeated burst of noisy mirth that might possibly have added to the panic of the buffaloes by its vociferation — "The man is as completely dumb-founded as if a swarm of young bees had settled on the end of his tongue, and he not willing to speak for fear of their answer."

"How now, friend;" continued the trapper, addressing the still motionless and entranced naturalist. "How now, friend; are you, who make your livelihood by booking the names and natur's of the beasts of the fields and the fowls of the air, frightened at a herd of scampering buffaloes. Though perhaps you are ready to dispute my right to call them by a word, that is in the mouth of every hunter and trader on the frontier!"

The old man was, however, mistaken in supposing he could excite the benumbed faculties of the Doctor, by provoking a discussion. From that time henceforth, he was never known except on one occasion to utter a word that indicated either the species, or the genus, of the animal. He obstinately refused the nutritious food of the whole ox family, and even to the present hour, now that he is established in all the scientific dignity and security of a *savan* in one of the maritime towns, he turns his back, with a shudder, on those delicious and unrivalled viands that are so often seen at the suppers of the craft, and which are unequalled by any thing that is served under the same name at the boasted chop-houses of London, or at the most renowned of the Parisian restaurans. In short the distaste of the worthy naturalist for beef was not unlike that which the shepherd sometimes produces by first muzzling and fettering his delinquent dog, and then leaving him as a stepping stone for the whole flock to use in its transit over a wall, or through the opening of a sheep-fold, a process which is said to produce in the culprit a species of surfeit on the subject of mutton, forever after. By the time Paul and the trapper saw fit to terminate the fresh bursts of merriment, which the continued abstraction of their learned companion did not fail to excite, he commenced breathing again as if the suspended action of his lungs had been renewed by the application of a pair of artificial bellows, and was heard to make use of the ever afterwards proscribed term on that solitary occasion to which we have just alluded.

"Boves Americani Horridi!" exclaimed the Doctor, laying great stress on the latter word after which he continued mute, like one who pondered on strange and unaccountable events.

"Ay, horrid eyes enough I will willingly allow," returned the trapper, "and altogether the creatur' has a frightful look, to one unused to the sights and bustle of a natural life. But then the courage of the beast is in no way equal to its countenance. Lord, man, if you should once get fairly beset by a brood of grizzly bears, as happened to Hector and I, at the great falls of the Miss—ah! here comes the tail of the herd, and yonder goes a pack of hungry wolves, ready to pick up the sick, or such as get a disjointed neck by a tumble—ha! there are mounted men on their trail, or I'm no sinner! here, lad; you may see them, hereaway, just where the dust is scattering afore the wind. They are hovering around a wounded buffaloe, making an end of the surly devil with their arrows!"

Middleton and Paul soon caught a glimpse of the dark groupe, that the quick eye of the old man had so readily detected. Some fifteen or twenty horsemen were, in truth, to be seen riding in quick circuits about a noble bull, which stood at bay, too grievously hurt to fly, and yet seeming to disdain to fall notwithstanding his hardy body had already been the target for a hundred arrows. A thrust from the lance of a powerful Indian, however, completed his conquest, and the brute gave up his obstinate hold of life with a roar, that past bellowing over the place where our adventurers stood, and reaching the ears of the affrighted herd, added a new impulse to their flight.

"How well that Pawnee knew the philosophy, of a buffaloe hunt!" said the old man, after he had stood regarding the animated scene for a few moments with evident satisfaction. "You saw how he went off like the wind before the drove. It was in order that he might not taint the air, and that he might turn the flank and join—Ha! how is this! yonder red-skins are not Pawnees. The feathers in their heads are from the wings and tails of owls. Ah, as I am but a miserable, half sighted, trapper it is a band of the accursed Siouxes! To cover, lads, to cover. A single cast of an eye this-a-way, would strip us of every rag of clothes as surely as the lightning scorches the bush, and it might be that our very lives would be far from safe."

Middleton had already turned from the spectacle to seek that which pleased him better; the sight of his young and beautiful bride. Paul seized the Doctor by the arm, and as the trapper followed with the smallest possible delay, the whole party was quickly collected within the cover of the thicket. After a few short explanations concerning the character of this new danger, the old man, on whom the whole duty of directing their movements was devolved in deference to his great experience, continued his discourse, as follows—

"This is a region, as you must all know, where a strong arm is far better than the right, and where the white law is as little known as heeded, therefore, does every thing, now, depend on judgment and power. If," he continued, laying his finger on his cheek, like one who considered deeply all sides of the embarrassing situation in which he found himself, "if, an invention could be framed which would set these Siouxes and the brood of the squatter by the ears, then might we come in like the buzzards after a fight atween the beasts and pick up the gleanings of the ground. There are Pawnees nigh us too! It is a certain matter; for yonder lad is not so far from his village without an errand. Here are therefore four parties within sound of a cannon, not one of whom can trust the other. All which makes movement a little difficult in a district where covers are far from plenty. But we are three well armed, and I think I may say three stout-hearted men—"

"Four;" interrupted Paul.

"Anan!" said the old man, looking up simply at his companion.

"Four," repeated the bee-hunter pointing to the Naturalist.

"Every army has its hangers-on and idlers," rejoined the blunt border man. "Friend, it will be necessary to slaughter this ass."*

"To slay Asinus! such a deed would be an act of supererogatory cruelty!"

"I know nothing of your words, which hide their meaning in sound; but that is cruel which sacrifices a christian to a brute. This is what I call the reason of marcy. It would be just as safe to blow a trumpet as to let the animal raise his voice ag'in; inasmuch as it would prove a manifest challenge to the Siouxes."

"I will answer for the discretion of Asinus, who seldom speaks without a reason."

"They say a man can be known by the company he keeps," retorted the old man, "and why not a brute! I once made a forced march and went through a great deal of jeopardy with a companion who never opened his mouth but to sing;*and trouble enough and great concern of mind did the fellow give me. It was in that very business with your grand'ther, Captain, but, then, he had a human throat, and well did he know how to use it, on occasion, though he didn't always stop to regard the time and seasons fit for such outcries. Ah's! me: if I was now, as I was then, it wouldn't be a band of thieving Siouxes that should easily drive me from such a lodgment as this! But what signifies boasting, when sight and strength are both failing. The warrior that the Delawares once saw fit to call after the Hawk for the goodness of his eyes, would now be better termed the Mole! In my judgement, therefore, it will be well to slay the brute."

"There's argument and good logic in it," said Paul, "Music is music, and it's always noisy whether it comes from a fiddle or a Jack-Ass. Therefore I agree with the old man, and say, kill the beast."

"Friends," said the naturalist looking with a sorrowful eye from one to another of his bloodily disposed companions, "slay not Asinus. He is a specimen of his kind of whom much good and little evil can be said. Hardy and docile for his *genus,* abstemious and patient even for his humble *species.* We have journeyed much together and his death would grieve me. How would it trouble thy spirit, venerable venator, to separate in such an untimely manner from your faithful hound?"

"The animal shall not die," said the old man, suddenly clearing his throat, in a manner that proved he felt the force of the appeal, "but his voice must be smothered. Bind his jaws with the halter, and then I think we may trust the rest to providence."

With this double security for the discretion of Asinus, for Paul instantly bound the muzzle of the ass in the manner required, the trapper seem'd content. After which he proceeded to the margin of the thicket to reconnoitre.

The uproar which attended the passage of the herd was now gone, or rather it was heard rolling along the Prairie, at the distance of a mile. The clouds of dust were already blown away by the wind, and a clear range was left to the eye, in that place, where ten minutes before there existed a scene of so much wildness and confusion.

The Siouxes had completed their conquest, and, apparently satisfied with this addition to the numerous previous captives they had made, they now seemed content to let the remainder of the herd escape. A dozen remained around the carcass, over which a few buzzards were balancing themselves with steady wings and greedy eyes, while the rest were riding about in quest of such further booty as might come in their way, on the trail of so vast a drove. The trapper measured the proportions and scanned the equipments of such individuals as drew nearer to the side of the thicket, with careful eyes. At length he pointed out one among them to Middleton as Weucha.

"Now, know we not only who they are, but their errand;" the old man continued deliberately shaking his head. "They have lost the trail of the squatter, and are on its hunt. These buffaloes have cross'd their path, and in chasing the animals bad luck has led them, in open sight of the hill on which the brood of Ishmael have harbored. Do you see, yon birds watching for the offals of the beast they have killed? Therein is a moral which teaches the manner of a Prairie life. A band of Pawnees are outlying for these very Siouxes as you see the buzzards looking down for their food, and it behooves us as Christian men who have so much at stake to look down upon them both. Ha! what brings yonder two skirting reptiles to a stand! As you live, they have found the place where the miserable son of the squatter met his death!"

The old man was not mistaken. Weucha and a savage who accompanied him, had reached that spot which has already been mentioned as furnishing the frightful evidences of violence and bloodshed. There they sat on their horses, examining the well known signs, with the intelligence that distinguishes the habits of Indians. Their scrutiny was long, and apparently not without distrust. At length they raised a cry, that was scarcely less hideous and startling than that which the hounds had before made over the same fatal signs, and which did not fail to draw the whole band immediately around them, as the fell bark of the jackall is said to gather his comrades to the chase.

CHAPTER XX.

"Welcome, ancient Pistol."

II Henry IV, II.iv. 120.

IT was not long, before the trapper pointed out the commanding person of Mahtoree as the leader of the Siouxes. This chief who had been among the last to obey the vociferous summons of Weucha, no sooner reach'd the spot where his whole party was now gathered than he threw himself from his horse and proceeded to examine the marks of the extraordinary trail, with that degree of dignity and attention which became his high and responsible station. The warriors, for it was but too evident that they were to a man of that fearless and ruthless class, awaited the result of his investigation with patient reserve; none, but a few of the principal braves, presuming even to speak while their leader was thus gravely occupied. It was several minutes before Mahtoree seem'd satisfied. He, then, directed his eyes along the ground to those several places where Ishmael had found the same revolting evidences of the passage of some bloody struggle, and motioned to his people to follow.

The whole band advanced in a body towards the thicket until they came to a halt, within a few yards of the precise spot, where Esther had stimulated her sluggish sons to break into the cover. The reader will readily imagine that the trapper and his companions were not indifferent observers of so threatening a movement. The old man summoned all who were capable of bearing arms to his side, and demanded in very unequivocal terms, though in a voice that was suitably lowered in order to escape the ears of their dangerous neighbors, whether they were disposed to make battle for their liberty or whether they should try the milder expedient of conciliation. As it was a subject in which all had an equal interest he put the question as to a Council of war, and not without some slight exhibition of the lingering vestiges of a nearly extinct military pride. Paul and the Doctor were diametrically opposed to each other in opinion; the former declaring for an immediate appeal to arms, and the latter as warmly espousing the policy of pacific measures. Middleton, who saw that there was great danger of a hot verbal dispute between two men who were governed by feelings so diametrically opposed, saw fit to assume the office of arbiter, or rather to decide the question, his situation making him a sort of umpire. He also leaned to the side of peace, for he evidently saw that in consequence of the vast superiority of their enemies violence would irretrievably lead to their destruction.

The trapper listened to the reasons of the young soldier with great attention, and as they were given with the steadiness of one who did not suffer apprehension to blind his judgement, they did not fail to produce a suitable impression.

"It is rational," rejoined the trapper, when the other had delivered his reasons; "It is very rational, for what man cannot move with his strength he must circumvent with his wits. It is reason that makes him stronger than the buffaloe, and swifter than the moose. Now stay you, here, and keep yourselves close. My life, and my traps are but of little value, when the welfare of so many human souls is concerned, and, moreover, I may say that I know the windings of Indian cunning. Therefore will I go alone upon the Prairie. It may so happen that I can yet draw the eyes of a Sioux from this spot, and give you time and room to fly."

As if resolved to listen to no remonstrance the old man quietly shouldered his rifle, and moving leisurely through the thicket, he issued on the plain at a point whence he might first appear before the eyes of the Siouxes without exciting their suspicions that he came from its cover.

The instant that the figure of a man, dressed in the garb of a hunter and bearing the well known and much dreaded rifle, appeared before the eyes of the Siouxes, there was a sensible, though a suppressed sensation in the band. The artifice of the trapper had so far succeeded, as to render it extremely doubtful whether he came from some point on the open Prairie, or from the thicket; though the Indians still continued to cast frequent and suspicious glances at the cover. They had made their halt at the distance of an arrow-flight from the bushes, but when the stranger came sufficiently nigh to show that the deep coating of red and brown, which time and exposure had given to his features, was laid upon the original colour of a Pale Face, they slowly receded from the spot until they reached a distance that might defeat the aim of fire-arms.

In the mean time the old man continued to advance until he had got nigh enough to make himself heard without difficulty. Here, he stopped and dropping his rifle to the earth, he raised his hand with the palm outward, in token of peace. After uttering a few words of reproach to his hound, who watch'd the savage groupe with eyes that seem'd to recognize them he spoke in the Sioux tongue—

"My brothers are welcome;" he said, cunningly constituting himself the master of the region in which they had met, and assuming the offices of hospitality. "They are far from their villages, and are hungry. Will they follow to my lodge, to eat and sleep."

No sooner was his voice heard, than the yell of pleasure, which burst from a dozen mouths, convinced the sagacious trapper that he also was recognized. Feeling that it was too late to retreat, he profited by the confusion which prevailed among them, while Weucha was explaining his character, to advance, until he was again face to face with the redoubtable Mahtoree. The second interview between these two men, each of whom was extraordinary in his way, was marked by the usual caution of the frontiers. They stood for nearly a minute examining each other without speaking.

"Where are your young men?" sternly demanded the Teton chieftain, after he found that the immoveable features of the trapper refused to betray any of their master's secrets, under his intimidating look.

"The Long-knives do not come in bands to trap the beaver. I am alone."

"Your head is white, but you have a forked tongue. Mahtoree has been in your camp. He knows that you are not alone. Where is your young wife, and the warrior that I found upon the Prairie?"

"I have no wife. I have told my brother, that the woman and her friend were strangers. The words of a gray head, should be heard, and not forgotten. The Dahcotahs found travellers asleep and they thought they had no need of horses. The women and children of a Pale-face are not used to go far on foot. Let them be sought, where you left them."

The eyes of the Teton flash'd fire, as he answered—

"They are gone; but Mahtoree is a wise chief and his eyes can see a great distance."

"Does the Partizan of the Tetons see men on these naked fields?" retorted the trapper with great steadiness of mien, "I am very old and my eyes grow dim: where do they stand?"

The chief remained silent a moment as if he disdained to contest any further, the truth of a fact concerning which he was already satisfied, then pointing to the traces on the earth, he said, with a sudden transition to mildness in his eye and manner—

"My father has learnt wisdom in many winters; can he tell me whose moccasin has left this trail?"

"There have been wolves and buffaloes on the Prairies, and there may have been cougars too."

Mahtoree glanced his eye at the thicket as if he thought the latter suggestion not impossible. Pointing to the place he ordered his young men reconnoitre it more closely, cautioning them at the same time with a stern look at the trapper to beware of treachery from the Big-knives. Three or four half-naked, eager-looking youths lash'd their horses, at the word, and darted away to obey the mandate. The old man trembled a little for the discretion of Paul when he saw this demonstration. The Tetons encircled the place, two or three times, approaching nigher and nigher, at each circuit, and then galloped back to their leader to report that the copse seem'd empty. Notwithstanding the trapper watch'd the eye of Mahtoree, in order to detect the inward movements of his mind and, if possible to anticipate in order to direct his suspicions, the utmost sagacity of one so long accustomed to study the cold habits of the Indian race could however detect no symptom, or expression, that denoted how far he credited or distrusted this intelligence. Instead of replying to the information of his scouts, he spoke kindly to his horse, and motioning to a youth to receive the bridle, or rather halter, by which he governed the animal, he took the trapper by the arm and led him a little apart from the rest of the band.

"Has my father been a warrior?" said the wily Teton, in a tone that he intended should be conciliating.

"Do the leaves cover the trees, in the season of fruits! Go. The Dahcotahs have not seen as many warriors living as I have look'd on in their blood! But what signifies idle remembrancing," he added in English, "when limbs grow stiff, and sight is failing!"

The chief regarded him a moment with a severe look as if he would lay bare the falsehood he had heard, but meeting in the calm eye and steady mien of the trapper a confirmation of the truth of what he said, he took the hand of the old man and laid it gently on his head, in token of the respect that was due to the other's years and experience.

"Why then do the Big-knives tell their red brethren to bury the tomahawk," he said, "when their own young men never forget that they are braves, and meet each other so often with bloody hands."

"My nation is more numerous than the buffaloes on the Prairies or the pigeons in the air. Their quarrels are frequent, yet their warriors are few. None go out on the war path, but they who are gifted with the qualities of a brave, and therefore such see many battles."

"It is not so—my Father is mistaken;" returned Mahtoree, indulging in a smile of exulting penetration, at the very instant he corrected the force of his denial, in deference to the years and services of one so aged. "The Big-knives are very wise; and they are men; all of them would be warriors. They would leave the red skins to dig roots and hoe the corn. But a Dahcotah is not born to live like a woman; he must strike the Pawnee and the Omawhaw, or he will lose the name of his Fathers."

"The Master of Life looks with an open eye on his children who die in a battle that is fought for the right; but he is blind, and his ears are shut to the cries of an Indian who is killed when plundering, or doing evil to his neighbor."

"My father is old," said Mahtoree looking at his aged companion, with an expression of irony that sufficiently denoted he was one of those who overstep the trammels of education, and who are perhaps a little given to abuse the mental liberty they thus obtain, "He is *very* old: Has he made a journey to the far country, and has he been at the trouble to come back to tell the young men what he has seen?"

"Teton," returned the trapper, throwing the breech of his rifle to the earth with startling vehemence, and regarding his companion with steady severity, "I have heard that there are men among my people who study their great medecines until they believe themselves to be Gods, and who laugh at all faith except in their own vanities. It may be true. It *is* true; for I have seen them. When man is shut up in towns and schools with his own follies, it may be easy to believe himself greater than the Master of Life; but a warrior who lives in a house with the clouds for its roof, where he can at any moment look both at the heavens and at the earth, and who daily sees the power of the Great Spirit, should be more humble. A Dahcotah chieftain ought to be too wise to laugh at justice."

The crafty Mahtoree, who saw that his free-thinking was not likely to produce a favorable impression on the old man, instantly changed his ground, by alluding to the more immediate subject of their interview. Laying his hand gently on the shoulder of the trapper, he led him forward until they both stood within fifty feet of the margin of the thicket. Here he fastened his penetrating eyes on the other's honest countenance, and continued the discourse—

"If my father has hid his young men in the bush, let him tell them to come forth. You see that a Dahcotah is not afraid. Mahtoree is a great Chief! A warrior whose head is white and who is about to go to the Land of Spirits cannot have a tongue with two ends, like a serpent."

"Dahcotah, I have told no lie. Since the Great Spirit made me a man, I have liv'd in the wilderness, or on these naked plains, without lodge or family. I am a hunter, and go on my path alone."

"My father has a good carabyne. Let him point it in the bush and fire."

The old man hestitated a moment, and then slowly prepared himself to give this delicate assurance of the truth of what he said, without which he plainly perceived the suspicions of his crafty companion could not be lulled. As he lowered his rifle, his eye, although greatly dimmed and weakened by age, ran over the confused collection of objects that lay embedded amid the party coloured foliage of the thicket until it succeeded in catching a glimpse of the brown covering of the stem of a small tree. With this object in view he raised the piece to a level and fired. The bullet had no sooner glided from the barrel, than a tremor seized the hands of the trapper which, had it occurred a moment sooner would have utterly disqualified him for so hazardous an experiment. A frightful silence succeeded the report, during which he expected to hear the shrieks of the females, and then as the smoke whirled away in the wind, he caught a view of the fluttering bark, and felt assured that all his former skill was not entirely departed from him. Dropping the piece to the earth, he turned again to his companion with an air of the utmost composure and demanded—

"Is my brother satisfied?"

"Mahtoree is a chief of the Dahcotahs," returned the cunning Teton laying his hand on his chest, in acknowledgement of the other's sincerity. "He knows that a warrior who has smoked at so many Council fires, until his head has grown white, would not be found in wicked company. But did not my father once ride on a horse, like a rich chief of the Pale-faces, instead of travelling on foot like a hungry Konza?"

"Never. The Wahcondah has given me legs, and he has given me resolution to use them. For sixty summers and winters did I journey in the woods of America, and ten tiresome years have I dwelt on these open fields, without finding need to call often upon the gifts of the other cre'turs of the Lord, to carry me from place to place."

"If my Father has so long liv'd in the shade, why has he come upon the Prairies. The sun will scorch him?"

The old man look'd sorrowfully about for a moment, and then turning with a confidential air to the other he replied—

"I passed the spring, summer, and autumn of life among the trees. The winter of my days had come, and found me where I lov'd to be, in the quiet, ay and in the honesty of the woods! Teton; then I slept, happily, where my eyes could look up through the branches of the pines and the beeches, to the very dwelling of the Good Spirit of my people. If I had need to open my heart to him, while his fires were burning above my head, the door was open and before my eyes. But the axes of the choppers awoke me. For a long time my ears heard nothing but the uproar of clearings. I bore it, like a warrior and a man; there was a reason that I should bear it.* But when that reason was ended, I bethought me to get beyond the accursed sounds. It was trying to the courage and to the habits, but I had heard of these vast and naked fields, and I came hither to escape the wasteful temper of my people. Tell me, Dahcotah, have I not done well?"

The trapper laid his long, lean finger on the naked shoulder of the Indian as he ended, and seem'd to demand his felicitations on his ingenuity and success, with a ghastly smile in which triumph was singularly blended with regret. His companion listened intently, and replied to the question, by saying in the sententious manner of his race—

"The head of my Father is very gray; he has always liv'd with men, and he has seen every thing. What he does is good; what he speaks is wise. Now let him say, is he sure that he is a stranger to the Big-knives who are looking for their beasts on every side of the Prairies and cannot find them."

"Dahcotah, what I have said is true. I live alone, and never do I mingle with men whose skins are white, if—"

His mouth was suddenly closed by an interruption that was as mortifying as it was unexpected. The words were still on his tongue when the bushes on the side of the thicket where they stood opened, and the whole of the party whom he had just left, and in whose behalf he was endeavoring to reconcile his love of truth, to the necessity of prevaricating, came openly into view. A pause of mute astonishment succeeded this unlooked-for spectacle. Then, Mahtoree, who did not suffer a muscle or a joint to betray the wonder and surprise he actually experienced motioned towards the advancing friends of the trapper, with an air of assumed civility, and a smile, that lighted his fierce, dark, visage, as the glare of the setting sun reveals the volume and load of the cloud, that is surcharged to bursting with the electric fluid. He, however, disdained to speak, or to give any other evidence of his intentions, than by calling to his side the distant band, who sprang forward at his beck, with the alacrity of willing subordinates.

In the mean time, the friends of the old man continued to advance. Middleton himself was foremost, supporting the light and aerial looking figure of Inez, on whose anxious and shaking countenance, he cast such occasional glances of tender interest, as, in similar circumstances, a father would have given to his child. Paul led Ellen, close in their rear. But while the eye of the bee-hunter did not neglect his blooming companion, it scowled angrily, resembling more the aspect of the sullen and retreating bear, than the soft intelligence of a favored suitor. Obed and Asinus came last, the former leading his companion with a degree of fondness that could hardly be said to be exceeded by any other of the Party. The approach of the naturalist was far less rapid than that of those who preceded him. His feet seem'd equally reluctant to advance, or to remain stationary; his position bearing a great analogy to that of Mahomet's coffin, with the exception that the quality of repulsion rather than that of attraction held him in a state of rest. The repulsive power in his rear, however, appeared to predominate, and by a singular exception, as he would have said himself, to all philosophical principles, it rather increased than diminished by distance. As the eyes of the naturalist steadily maintained a position that was the opposite of his route they served to give a direction to those of the observers of all these movements, and at once, furnished a sufficient clue by which to unravel the mystery of so sudden a debouchement from the cover.

Another cluster of stout, and armed men, was seen at no great distance, just rounding a point of the thicket, and moving directly though cautiously towards the place where the band of the Siouxes was posted, as a squadron of cruisers is often seen to steer across the waste of waters towards the rich but well-protected convoy. In short, the family of the squatter, or at least such among them as were capable of bearing arms, appeared in view, on the broad Prairie, evidently bent on revenging their wrongs.

Mahtoree and his party slowly retired from the thicket, the moment they caught a view of the strangers, until they halted on a swell that commanded a wide and unobstructed view of the naked fields on which they stood. Here the Dahcotah appeared disposed to make his stand, and to bring matters to an issue. Notwithstanding this retreat, in which he compelled the trapper to accompany him, Middleton still advanced until he too, halted on the same elevation, and within speaking distance of the warlike Siouxes. The borderers in their turn took a favourable position, though at a much greater distance. The three groupes now resembled so many fleets at sea, lying with their top-sails to the masts, with the commendable precaution of recon-noitring, before each could ascertain who among the strangers might be considered as friends, and who as foes.

During this moment of suspense the dark, threatening, eye of Mahtoree rolled from one of the strange parties to the other, in keen and hasty examination, and then it turned its withering look on the old man, as the chief said, in a tone of high and bitter scorn—

"The Big-knives are fools. It is easier to catch the Cougar asleep, than to find a blind Dahcotah. Did the 'white-head' think to ride on the horse of a Sioux?"

The trapper, who had found time to collect his perplexed faculties, saw at once that Middleton, having perceived Ishmael on the trail by which they had fled, preferred trusting to the hospitality of the savages than to the treatment he would be likely to receive from the hands of the squatter. He therefore disposed himself to clear the way for the favorable reception of his friends, since he found that the unnatural coalition became necessary to secure the liberty, if not, the lives of the party.

"Did my brother ever go on a war path to strike my people?" he calmly demanded of the indignant chief, who still awaited his reply.

The lowering aspect of the Teton warrior so far lost its severity, as to suffer a gleam of pleasure and triumph to lighten its ferocity as, sweeping his arm in an entire circle around his person, he answered.

"What tribe or nation has not felt the blows of the Dahcotahs? Mahtoree is their Partizan."

"And has he found the Big-knives women, or has he found them men?"

A multitude of fierce passions were struggling in the tawny coun-tenance of the Indian. For a moment inextinguishable hatred seem'd to hold the mastery, and then a nobler expression, and one that better became the character of a brave got possession of his features and maintained itself, until, first throwing aside his light robe of pictured deer-skin, and pointing to the scar of a bayonet on his breast, he replied—

"It was given, as it was taken; face to face."

"It is enough. My brother is a brave chief, and he should be wise. Let him look; is that a warrior of the Pale-faces? Was it one such as that, who gave the Great Dahcotah his hurt?"

The eyes of Mahtoree followed the direction of the old man's extended arm, until they rested on the drooping form of Inez. The look of the Teton was long, rivetted, and admiring. Like that of the young Pawnee, it resembled more the gaze of a mortal on some heavenly image, than the admiration with which man is wont to contemplate even the loveliness of woman. Starting, as if suddenly self-convicted of forgetfulness, the chief next turned his eyes on Ellen, where they lingered an instant with a much more intelligible expression of admiration, and then pursued their course until they had taken another glance at each individual of the party.

"My brother sees that my tongue is not forked," continued the trapper watching the emotions the other betrayed, with a readiness of comprehension little inferior to that of the Teton himself. "The Big-knives do not send their women to war. I know that the Dahcotahs will smoke with the strangers."

"Mahtoree is a great chief! The Big-knives are welcome," said the Teton, laying his hand on his breast with an air of lofty politeness that would have done credit to any state of society. "The arrows of my young men are in their quivers."

The trapper motioned to Middleton to approach, and in a few moments the two parties were blended, in one, each of the males having exchanged friendly greetings, after the fashions of the Prairie warriors. But even while engaged in this hospitable manner, the Dahcotah did not fail to keep a strict watch on the more distant party of white men, as if he still distrusted an artifice, or sought further explanation. The old man, in his turn, perceived the necessity of being more explicit, and of securing the slight and equivocal advantage he had, already obtained. While affecting to examine the groupe, which still lingered at the spot where it had first halted, as if to discover the characters of those who composed it, he plainly saw that Ishmael contemplated immediate hostilities. The result of a conflict, on the open Prairies, between a dozen resolute border men, and the half armed natives, even though seconded by their white allies, was in his experienced judgement a point of great uncertainty, and, though far from reluctant to engage in the struggle on account of himself, the aged trapper thought it far more worthy of his years, and his character, to avoid than to court the contest. His feelings were, for obvious reasons, in accordance with those of Paul and Middleton, who had lives still more precious than their own to watch over and protect. In this dilemma, the three consulted on the means of escaping the frightful consequences which might immediately follow a single act of hostility on the part of the borderers, the old man taking care that their communication should, in the eyes of those who noted the expression of their countenances with jealous watchfulness, bear the appearance of explanations, as to the reason why such a party of travellers was met so far in the deserts.

"I know that the Dahcotahs are a wise and great people," at length the trapper commenced, again addressing himself to the chief—"but does not their partizan know a single brother who is base?"

The eye of Mahtoree wandered proudly around his band, but rested a moment reluctantly, on Weucha as he answered—

"The Master of Life has made chiefs, and warriors, and women," conceiving that he thus embraced all the gradations of human excellence from the highest to the lowest.

"And he has also made pale faces who are wicked. Such are they, whom my brother sees yonder."

"Do they go on foot, to do wrong," demanded the Teton, with a wild gleam from his eyes, that sufficiently betrayed how well he knew the reason why they were reduced to so humble an expedient.

"Their beasts are gone. But their powder and their lead and their blankets remain."

"Do they carry their riches in their hands, like miserable Konzas, or are they brave, and leave them with the women, as men should do, who know where to find what they lose?"

"My brother sees the spot of blue, across the Prairie, look, the sun has touch'd it for the last time, to-day."

"Mahtoree is not a mole."

"It is a rock, and on it are the goods of the Big-knives."

An expression of savage joy shot into the dark countenance of the Teton as he listened. Turning to the old man, he seem'd to read his soul, as if to assure himself he was not deceived. Then he bent his look on the party of Ishmael, and counted its numbers.

"One warrior is wanting;" he said.

"Does my brother see the buzzards. There is his grave. Did he find blood, on the Prairie. It was his."

"Enough; Mahtoree is a wise chief. Put your women on the horses of the Dahcotahs—we shall see, for our eyes are open very wide."

The trapper wasted no unnecessary words in explanation. Familiar with the brevity and promptitude of the Natives he immediately communicated the result to his companions. Paul was mounted in an instant, with Ellen at his back. A few more moments were necessary to assure Middleton of the security and ease of Inez. While he was thus engaged, Mahtoree advanced to the side of the beast he had allotted to this service, which was his own, and manifested an intention to occupy his customary place on its back. The young soldier seized the reins of the animal, and glances of sudden anger and lofty pride were exchanged between them.

"No man takes this seat but myself!" said Middleton, sternly, in English.

"Mahtoree is a great chief!" retorted the savage, neither comprehending the meaning of the other's words.

"The Dahcotah will be too late," whispered the old man at his elbow; "see, the Big-knives are afraid, and they will soon run."

The Teton chief instantly abandoned his claim, and threw himself on another horse, directing one of his young men to furnish a similar accommodation for the trapper. The warriors who were dismounted, got up behind as many of their companions; Doctor Battius, bestrode Asinus, and, notwithstanding the brief interruption, in half the time we have taken to relate it, the whole party was prepared to move.

When he saw that all were ready, Mahtoree, gave the signal to advance. A few of the best mounted of the warriors, the chief himself included, moved a little in front, and made a threatening demonstration, as if they intended to attack the strangers. The squatter who was in truth slowly retiring, instantly halted his party, and showed a willing front. Instead, however, of coming within reach of the dangerous aim of the western rifle, the subtle savages, kept wheeling about the strangers, until they had made a half circuit, keeping the latter in constant expectation of an assault. Then perfectly secure of their object, the Tetons raised a loud shout, and darted across the Prairie in a line for the distant rock, as directly and nearly with the velocity of the arrow, that has just been shot from its bow.

CHAPTER XXI.

"Dally not with the gods, but get thee gone."

The Taming of the Shrew, IV.iv. 68.

MAHTOREE had scarcely given the first intimation of his real design, before a general discharge from the borderers proved how well they understood it. The distance and the rapidity of the flight, however, rendered the fire harmless. As a proof of how little he regarded the hostility of their Party, the Dahcotah chieftain answered the report with a yell, and flourishing his carabyne above his head, he made a circuit on the plain, followed by his chosen warriors, in scorn of the impotent attempt of his enemies. As the main body continued the direct course, this little band of the *elite,* in returning from its wild exhibition of savage contempt, took its place in the rear, with a dexterity, and a concert of action, that showed the manoeuvre had been contemplated.

Volley swiftly succeeded volley, until the enraged squatter was reluctantly compelled to abandon the idea of injuring his enemies, by means so feeble. Relinquishing his fruitless attempt, he commenced a rapid pursuit, occasionally discharging a rifle in order to give the alarm to the garrison, which he had prudently left, under the command of the redoubtable Esther, herself. In this manner the chase was continued for many minutes, the horsemen gradually gaining on their pursuers, who maintained the race, however, with an incredible power of foot.

As the little speck of blue rose against the heavens, like an island issuing from the deep, the savages occasionally raised a yell of triumph. But the mists of evening were already gathering along the whole of the eastern margin of the Prairie, and before the band had made half of the necessary distance, the dim outline of the rock had melted into the haze of the background. Indifferent to this circumstance, which rather favored than disconcerted his plans, Mahtoree, who had again ridden in front, held on his course, with the accuracy of a hound of the truest scent, merely slackening his speed a little, as the horses of his party were, by this time, thoroughly blown. It was at this stage of the enterprise, that the old man rode up to the side of Middleton, and addressed him, as follows, in English—

"Here is likely to be a thieving business, and one in which I must say, I have but little wish to be a partner."

"What would you do. It would be fatal to trust ourselves in the hands of the miscreants in our rear."

"Tut for miscreants, be they red or be they white. Look ahead, lad, as if ye were talking of our medecines, or perhaps, praising the Teton beasts. For the knaves love to hear their horses commended, the same as a foolish mother, in the settlements, is fond of hearing the praises of her wilful child. So pat the animal and lay your hand on the gew-gaws with which the red-skins have ornamented his mane, giving your eye, as it were, to one thing, and your mind to another. Listen, if matters are managed with judgement we may leave these Tetons as the night sets in."

"A blessed thought!" exclaimed Middleton, who retained a painful remembrance of the look of admiration with which Mahtoree had contemplated the loveliness of Inez, as well as of his subsequent presumption in daring to wish to take the office of her protecter on himself.

"Lord, Lord! what a weak creatur' is man, when the gifts of natur' are smothered in bookish knowledge, and womanly manners! Such another start would tell these imps at our elbows that we were plotting against them, just as plainly as if it were whispered in their ears by a Sioux tongue. Ay, Ay, I know the devils: they look as innocent as so many frisky fawns, but there is not one among them all that has not an eye on our smallest motions. Therefore what is to be done is to be done, in wisdom, in order to circumvent their cunning. That is right, pat his neck, and smile as if you praised the horse, and keep the ear on my side open to my words. Be careful not to worry your beast, for though but little skilled in horses, reason teaches that breath is needful in a hard push, and that a weary leg makes a dull race. Be ready to mind the signal when you hear a whine from old Hector. The first will be to make ready, the second to edge out of the crowd, and the third to go. Am I understood?"

"Perfectly, perfectly;" said Middleton, trembling in his excessive eagerness to put the plan in instant execution, and pressing the little arm which encircled his body, to his heart. "Perfectly. Hasten. Hasten."

"Ay, the beast is no sloth," continued the trapper in the Teton language, as if he continued the discourse, edging cautiously through the dusky throng at the same time, until he found himself riding at the side of Paul. He communicated his intentions in the same guarded manner as before. The high-spirited and fearless bee-hunter received the intelligence with delight declaring his readiness to engage the whole of the savage band should it become necessary to effect their object. When the old man drew off from the side of this pair also, he cast his eyes about him to discover the situation occupied by the naturalist.

The Doctor with infinite labor to himself and Asinus had maintained a position in the very centre of the Siouxes, so long as there existed the smallest reason for believing that any of the missiles of Ishmael might arrive in contact with his person. After this danger had diminished or rather disappeared, entirely, his own courage revived while that of his steed began to droop. To this mutual but very material change was owing the fact that the rider and the ass were now to be sought among that portion of the band who formed a sort of rear guard. Hither then the trapper contrived to turn his steed without exciting the suspicions of any of his subtle companions.

"Friend," commenced the old man when he found himself in a situation favorable to discourse, "should you like to pass a dozen years among the savages, with a shaved head, and a painted countenance, with perhaps a couple of wives and five or six children, of the half-breed to call you father?"

"Impossible!" exclaimed the startled naturalist, "I am indisposed to matrimony, in general, and more especially to all admixture of the varieties of *species,* which only tend to tarnish the beauty and to interrupt the harmony of nature. Moreover, it is a painful innovation on the order of all nomenclatures!"

"Ay, ay, you have reason, enough for your distaste to such a life, but should these Siouxes get you fairly into their village such would be your luck, as certain as that the sun rises and sets at the pleasure of the Lord."

"Marry me to a woman who is not adorned with the comeliness of the *species!*" responded the Doctor. "Of what crime have I been guilty that so grievous a punishment should await the offense. To marry a man against the movements of his will is to do a violence to human nature!"

"Now that you speak of natur' I have hopes that the gift of reason has not altogether deserted your brain," returned the old man, with a covert expression playing about the angles of his deep set eyes, which betrayed he was not entirely destitute of humour. "Nay, they may conceive you a remarkable subject for their kindness, and, for that matter, marry you to five or six. I have known, in my day, favored chiefs who had numberless wives."

"But why should they meditate this vengeance?" demanded the Doctor, whose hair began to rise as if each fibre was possessed of sensibility; "what evil have I done?"

"It is the fashion of their kindness. When they come to learn that you are a great medecine, they will adopt you in the tribe, and some mighty chief will give you his name, and perhaps his daughter, or it may be a wife or two of his own, who have dwelt long in his lodge and of whose value he is a judge, by experience."

"The Governor and Founder of Natural Harmony Protect me!" ejaculated the Doctor. "I have no affinity to a single consort, much less to duplicates and triplicates of the *class!* I shall certainly essay a flight from their abodes, before I mingle in so violent a conjunction."

"There is reason in your words: but why not attempt the race you speak of, now?"

The naturalist look'd fearfully around, as if he had an inclination to make an instant exhibition of his desperate intention, but the dusky figures who were riding on every side of him, seem'd suddenly tripled in number and the darkness that was already thickening on the Prairie appeared, in his eyes, to possess the glare of high noon.

"It would be premature, and reason forbids it;" he answered: "Leave me, venerable venator, to the council of my own thoughts, and when my plans are properly classed, I will advise you of my resolutions."

"Resolutions!" repeated the old man, shaking his head a little contemptuously, as he gave the rein to his horse and allowed him to mingle with the steeds of the savages, "Resolution is a word that is talk'd of in the settlements, and felt on the borders! Does my brother know the beast on which the Pale face rides?" he continued, addressing a gloomy looking warrior, in his own tongue, and making a motion with his arm that at the same time directed his attention to the Naturalist and the meek Asinus.

The Teton turned his eyes for a minute, on the animal, but disdained to manifest the smallest portion of that wonder he had felt, in common with all his companions, on first viewing so rare a quadruped. The trapper was not ignorant that, while asses and mules were beginning to be known to those tribes who dwelt nearest the Mexicos they were not usually encountered so far north as the waters of La Platte. He, therefore, managed to read the mute astonishment, that lay so deeply concealed in the tawny visage of the savage, and took his measures accordingly.

"Does my brother think that the rider is a warrior of the Pale-faces?" he demanded, when he believed that sufficient time had elapsed, for a full examination of the pacific mien of the naturalist.

The flash of scorn, which shot across the features of the Teton, was visible, even by the dim light of the stars.

"Is a Dahcotah a fool," was the answer.

"They are a wise nation whose eyes are never shut; much do I wonder, that they have not seen the Great Medecine of the Big knives!"

"Wah!" exclaimed his companion, suffering the whole of his amazement to burst out of his dark rigid countenance, at the surprise, like a flash of lightning illuminating the gloom of midnight.

"The Dahcotah knows that my tongue is not forked. Let him open his eyes wider. Does he not see a very great Medicine!"

The light was not necessary to recall to the savage, each feature in the really remarkable costume and equipage of Doctor Battius. In common with the rest of the band, and in conformity with the universal practice of the Indians, this warrior, while he had suffered no gaze of idle curiosity to disgrace his manhood, had not permitted a single distinctive mark which might characterize any one of the strangers to escape his vigilance. He knew the air, the stature, the dress, and the features, even to the colour of the eyes and of the hair, of every one of the Big-knives whom he had thus strangely encountered, and deeply had he ruminated on the causes which could have led a party so singularly constituted into the haunts of the rude inhabitants of his native wastes. He had, already considered the several physical powers of the whole party; and had duly compared their abilities with what he supposed might have been their intentions. Warriors they were not, for the Big knives, like the Siouxes, left their women in their villages when they went out on the bloody path. The same objections applied to them as hunters, and even as traders, the two characters under which the white men, commonly appeared in their villages. He had heard of a Great Council, at which the Menahashah,* or Long knives and the Washsheomantiqua,* or Spaniards, had smoked together, when the latter had sold to the former their incomprehensible rights over those vast regions, through which his nation had roam'd, in freedom, for so many ages. His simple mind had not been able to embrace the reasons why one people should thus assume a superiority over the possessions of another, and it will readily be perceived, that, at the hint just received from the trapper, he was not indisposed to fancy that some of the hidden subtilty of that magical influence of which he was so firm a believer, was about to be practised by the unsuspecting subject of their conversation in furtherance of these mysterious claims. Abandoning, therefore, all the reserve and dignity of his manner, under the conscious helplessness of ignorance, he turned to the old man, and stretching forth his arms, as if to denote how much he lay at his mercy, he said:

"Let my father look at me. I am a wild man of the Prairies. My body is naked; my hands, empty; my skin, red. I have struck the Pawnees, the Konzas, the Omawhaws, the Osages, and even the Long knives. I am a man amid warriors, but a woman among the conjurors. Let my Father speak; the ears of the Teton are open. He listens like a deer to the step of the cougar."

"Such are the wise and uns'archable ways of one, who alone knows, good from evil!" exclaimed the trapper in English. "To some he grants cunning and on others he bestows the gift of manhood! It is humbling, and it is afflicting to see so noble a creatur' as this, who has fou't in many a bloody fray, truckling before his superstition, like a beggar asking for the bones you would throw to the dogs. The Lord will forgive me, for playing with the ignorance of the savage, for he knows I do it, in no mockery of his state or in idle vaunting of my own, but in order to save mortal life, and to give justice to the wronged, while I defeat the deviltries of the wicked! Teton," speaking again in the language of the listener, "I ask you, is not that a wonderful medicine? If the Dahcotahs are wise they will not breathe the air he breathes, nor touch his robes. They know that the Wahconshecheh (bad spirit) loves his own children, and will not turn his back on him that does them harm."

The old man delivered this opinion in an ominous and sententious manner, and then rode apart, as if he had said enough. The result justified his expectations. The warrior to whom he had addressed himself was not slow to communicate his important knowledge to the rest of the rear guard, and in a very few moments the naturalist was the object of general observation and reverence. The trapper, who understood that the natives often worshipped, with a view to propitiate, the evil spirit, awaited the workings of his artifice, with the coolness of one who had not the smallest interest in its effects. It was not long before he saw one dark figure after another, lashing his horse and galloping ahead into the centre of the band, until Weucha, alone, remained nigh the persons of himself and Obed. The very dullness of this grovelling-minded savage, who continued gazing at the supposed conjuror with a sort of stupid admiration, opposed, now, the only obstacle to the complete success of his artifice.

Thoroughly understanding the character of this Indian, the old man lost no time in getting rid of him also. Riding to his side, he said in an affected whisper—

"Has Weucha drunk of the milk of the Big knives, to day?"

"Hugh!" exclaimed the savage, every dull thought instantly recalled from heaven to earth by the question.

"Because the Great Captain of my people, who rides in front, has a cow that is never empty. I know it will not be long before he will say, 'are any of my red brethren dry?'"

The words were scarcely uttered, before Weucha in his turn, quickened the gait of his beast, and was soon blended with the rest of the dark groupe who were riding at a more moderate pace a few rods in advance. The trapper, who knew how fickle and sudden were the changes of a savage mind, did not lose a moment, in profiting by this advantage. He loosened the reins of his own impatient steed and in an instant, he was again at the side of Obed.

"Do you see the twinkling star, that is, maybe, the length of four rifles above the Prairie, hereaway to the North I mean."

"Ay, it is of the Constellation—"

"A tut for your Constellation man; do you see the star I mean?— tell me in the English of the Land, yes or no."

"Yes."

"The moment my back is turned, pull upon the rein of your ass, until you lose sight of the savages. Then take the Lord for your dependance and yonder star for your guide. Turn neither to the right hand, nor to the left, but make diligent use of your time, for your beast is not quick of foot, and every inch of Prairie you gain is a day added to your liberty, or to your life!" Without waiting to listen to the queries which the Naturalist was about to put, the old man, again loosened the reins of his horse and presently he too, was blended with the groupe in front.

Obed was now, alone. Asinus willingly obeyed the hint which his master soon, gave rather in desperation, than with any very collected understanding of the orders he had received, and checked his pace, accordingly. As the Tetons, however, rode at a hard gallop, but a moment of time was necessary, after the ass began to walk, to remove them effectually from before the vision of his rider. Without plan, expectation or hope of any sort, except that of escaping from his dangerous neighbors, the Doctor, first feeling to assure himself that the package which contained the miserable remnants of his specimens, and notes was safe at his crupper, turned the head of the beast in the required direction, and kicking him with a species of fury, he soon succeeded in exciting the speed of the patient animal into a smart run. He had barely time to descend into a hollow and ascend the adjoining swell of the Prairie, before he heard, or fancied he heard, his name shouted, in good English, from the throats of twenty Tetons. The delusion gave a new impulse to his ardor, and no professor of the saltant art ever applied himself with greater industry, than the naturalist now used his heels on the ribs of Asinus. The conflict endured for several minutes without interruption, and to all appearances it might have continued to the present moment, had not the meek temper of the beast become unduly excited. Borrowing an idea from the manner in which his master exhibited his agitation, Asinus so far changed the application of his own heels as to raise them simultaneously with a certain indignant flourish into the air; a measure that instantly decided the controversy in his favor. Obed took leave of his seat, as of a position no longer tenable, continuing however the direction of his flight, while the Ass like a conqueror took possession of the field of battle, beginning to crop the dry herbage, as the fruits of victory.

When Doctor Battius had recovered his feet, and rallied his faculties, which were in a good deal of disorder from the hurried manner in which he had abandoned his former situation, he returned in quest of his specimens and of his Ass. Asinus displayed enough of magnanimity to render the interview amicable, and thenceforth the Naturalist continued the required route with very commendable industry but with a much more tempered discretion.

In the mean time, the old trapper had not lost sight of the important movements that he had undertaken to control. Obed had not been mistaken in supposing that he was already missed and sought, though his imagination had corrupted certain savage cries into the well known sounds that composed his own latinized name. The truth was simply this. The warriors of the rear guard had not failed to apprise those in front of the mysterious character, with which it had pleased the trapper, to invest the unsuspecting naturalist. The same untutored admiration which on the receipt of this intelligence had driven those in the rear to the front, now drove many of the front to the rear. The Doctor was of course absent, and the outcry was no more than the wild yells which were raised in the first burst of savage disappointment.

But the authority of Mahtoree was prompt to aid the ingenuity of the trapper, in suppressing these dangerous sounds. When order was restored, and the former was made acquainted with the reason why his young men had betrayed so strong a mark of indiscretion, the old man, who had taken a post at his elbow, saw, with alarm, the gleam of keen distrust that flashed in his swarthy visage.

"Where is your conjuror?" demanded the chief, turning suddenly to the trapper, as if he meant to make him responsible for the reappearance of Obed.

"Can I tell, my brother the number of the stars! the ways of a great medicine, are not like the ways of other men."

"Listen to me, gray-head; and count my words;" continued the other bending on his rude saddle bow, like some Chevalier of a more civilized race, and speaking in the haughty tones of absolute power; "the Dahcotahs have not chosen a woman for their Chief. When Mahtoree feels the power of a great medicine, he will tremble. Until then, he will look with his own eyes, without borrowing sight from a Pale face. If your conjuror is not with his friends, in the morning, my young men shall look for him. Your ears are open. Enough."

The trapper was not sorry to find that so long a respite was granted. He had before found reason to believe, that the Teton Partizan was one of those bold spirits, who overstep the limits, which use and education fix to the opinions of man, in every state of society, and he now saw, plainly, that he must adopt some artifice to deceive him, different from that which had succeeded so well with his followers. The sudden appearance of the rock, however, which hove up, a black and ragged mass, out of the darkness ahead, put an end, for the present, to their discourse, Mahtoree giving all his thoughts to the execution of his designs on the rest of the squatter's moveables. A murmur ran through the band, as each dark warrior caught a glimpse of the desired haven, after which the nicest ear might have listened in vain, to catch a sound louder than the rustling of feet among the tall grass of the Prairie.

But the vigilance of Esther was not easily deceived. She had long listened anxiously to the suspicious sounds which approached the rock across the naked waste, nor had the sudden outcry been unheard by the unwearied sentinels of the rock. The savages, who had dismounted at some little distance, had not time to draw around the base of the hill, in their customary silent and insidious manner, before the voice of the Amazon was raised, demanding—

"Who is beneath? answer: for your lives? Siouxes or devils I fear ye not!"

No answer was given to this challenge, every warrior halting where he stood, confident that his dusky form was blended with the shadows of the plain. It was at this moment that the trapper determined to escape. He had been left, with the rest of his friends, under the surveillance of those who were assigned to the duty of watching the horses, as they all continued mounted, the moment appeared favorable to his project. The attention of the guards was drawn to the rock, and a heavy cloud driving above them, at that instant, obscured even the feeble light which fell from the stars. Leaning on the neck of his horse the old man muttered—

"Where's my pup? where is it, Hector, where is it, dog?"

The hound caught the well known sounds and answered by a whine of friendship, which threatened to break out into one of his piercing howls. The trapper was in the act of raising himself, from this successful exploit, when he felt the hand of Weucha grasping his throat, as if determined to suppress his voice, by the very unequivocal process of strangulation. Profiting by the circumstance, he raised another low sound as if in the natural effort of breathing, which drew a second responsive cry from the faithful hound. Weucha, instantly abandoned his hold of the master in order to wreak his vengeance on the dog. But the voice of Esther was again heard, and every other design was abandoned in order to listen.

"Ay, whine, and deform your throats as you may, ye imps of darkness," she said, with a cracked but scornful laugh, "I know ye! Tarry and ye shall have light for your misdeeds. Put in the coals, Phoebe; put in the coal, your Father and the boys shall see that they are wanted at home, to welcome their guests!"

As she spoke, a strong light, like that of a brilliant star was seen on the very pinnacle of the rock; then followed a forked flame which curled for a moment, amid the windings of an enormous pile of brush, and flashing upward in an united sheet, it wavered to and fro, in the passing air, shedding a bright glare on every object within its influence. A taunting laugh, was heard from the height, in which the voices

of all ages mingled, as though they triumphed in having so successfully exposed the treacherous intentions of the Tetons.

The trapper look'd about him to ascertain in what situations he
might find his friends. True to the signals, Middleton and Paul had
drawn a little apart, and now stood ready, by every appearance, to
commence their flight at the third repetition of the cry. Hector had
escaped his savage pursuer, and was again crouching at the heels
of his master's horse. But the broad circle of light was gradually
increasing in extent and power, and the old man, whose eye and
judgment so rarely failed him, patiently awaited a more propitious
moment for his enterprise.

"Now Ishmael, my man, if sight and hand ar' true as ever, now is
the time, to work upon these red-skins, who claim to own all your
property, even to wife and children! Now, my good man, prove both
breed and character!"

A distant shout was heard, in the direction of the approaching party
of the squatter, assuring the female garrison that succour was not far
distant. Esther answered to the grateful sounds, by a crack'd cry of
her own, lifting her form in the first burst of her exultation above the
rock, in a manner to be visible to all below. Not content with this
dangerous exposure of her person, she was in the act of tossing her
arms in triumph, when the dark figure of Mahtoree, shot into the
light, and pinioned them to her side. The forms of three other warriors
glided across the top of the rock, looking like naked demons, flitting
among the clouds. The air was filled with the brands of the beacon,
and a heavy darkness succeeded, not unlike that of the appalling
instant when the last rays of the sun are excluded by the intervening
mass of the moon. A yell of triumph burst from the savages in their
turn, and was rather accompanied than followed by a long, loud whine
from Hector.

In an instant the old man was between the horses of Middleton and
Paul, extending a hand to the bridle of each, in order to check the
impatience of their riders.

"Softly. Softly," he whispered, "their eyes are as marvellously shut,
for the minute, as if the Lord had stricken them blind: but their ears
are open. Softly, softly, for fifty rods at least we must move no faster
than a walk."

The five minutes of doubt that succeeded seemed like an age to all
but the trapper. As their sight was gradually restored, it appeared to

each that the momentary gloom which followed the extinction of the beacon, was to be replaced by as broad a light as that of noon day. Gradually the old man, however, suffered the animals to quicken their steps until they had gained the centre of one of the Prairie bottoms, then laughing in his quiet manner, he released the reins and said—

"Now, let them give play to their legs, but keep on the old fog, to deaden the sounds."

It is needless to say how cheerfully he was obeyed. In a few more minutes they ascended and cross'd a swell of the land, after which the flight was continued at the top of their horses' speed, keeping the indicated star in view, as the laboring bark steers for the light which points the way to a haven and security.

CHAPTER XXII.

"The clouds and sunbeams o'er his eye,
That once their shades and glories threw,
Have left in yonder silent sky,
No vestige where they flew."

Montgomery, "The Common Lot," ll. 33-36.

Astillness as deep as that which marked the gloomy waste in their front, was observed by the fugitives to distinguish the spot they had just abandoned. Even the trapper lent his practised faculties, in vain, to detect any of the well known signs which might establish the important fact, that hostilities had actually commenced between the parties of Mahtoree and Ishmael, but their horses carried them out of the reach of sounds, without the occurrence of the smallest evidence of that sort. The old man, from time to time, muttered his discontent, but manifested the uneasiness he actually entertained in no other manner, unless it might be in exhibiting a growing anxiety to urge the animals to increase their speed. He pointed out in passing, the deserted swale, where the family of the squatter had encamped the night they were introduced to the reader, and afterwards he maintained an ominous silence; ominous, because his companions had already seen enough of his character, to be convinced that the circumstances must be critical, indeed, which possessed the power to disturb the well regulated tranquility of the old man's mind.

"Have we not done, enough," Middleton demanded, in tenderness to the inability of Inez and Ellen to endure so much fatigue, at the end of some hours; "we have ridden hard, and have cross'd a wide tract of Plain. It is time to seek a place of rest."

"You must seek it then, in heaven, if you find yourselves unequal to a longer march;" murmured the old trapper. "Had the Tetons and the squatters come to blows, as any one might see in the natur' of things they were bound to do, there would be time to look about us, and to calculate, not only the chances but the comforts of the journey; but as the case actually is, I should consider it certain death, or endless captivity to trust our eyes with sleep until our heads are fairly hid in some uncommon cover."

"I know not;" returned the youth who reflected more on the sufferings of the fragile being he supported than on the experience of his companion. "I know not. We have ridden leagues, and I can see no extraordinary signs of danger. If you fear for yourself, my good friend, believe me, you are wrong, for—"

"Your grand'ther were he living and here," interrupted the old man, stretching forth a hand and laying a finger impressively on the arm of Middleton, "would have spared those words. He had some reason to think, that in the prime of my days, when my eye was quicker than the hawk's and my limbs were as active as the legs of the fallow deer, I never clung too eagerly and fondly to life: then, why should I, now, feel such childish affection for a thing that I know to be vain and the companion of pain and sorrow. Let the Tetons do their worst; they will not find a miserable and worn out trapper the loudest in his complaints, or his prayers!"

"Pardon me, my worthy, my inestimable friend," exclaimed the repentant young man, warmly grasping the hand which the other was in the act of withdrawing; "I knew not what I said—or rather I thought, only, of those whose tenderness we are most bound to consider."

"Enough. It is natur', and it is right. Therein your grand'ther would have done the very same. Ah's me! what a number of seasons, hot and cold, wet and dry, have rolled over my poor head since the time we worried it out together, among the red Hurons of the Lakes, back in those rugged mountains of old York! and many a noble buck, has since that day fallen by my hand; ay! and many a thieving Mingo, too! Tell me, lad, did the General, for General I know he got to be, did he ever tell you of the deer we took, that night the outlyers of the accursed tribe drove us to the caves, on the island, and how we feasted and drunk in security?"

"I have often heard him mention the smallest circumstance of the night you mean; but—"

"And the singer; and his open throat, and his shoutings in the fights?" continued the old man, laughing joyously at the strength of his own recollections.

"All—All—he forgot nothing, even to the most trifling incident. Do you not—"

"What did he tell you of the imp behind the log—and of the miserable devil who went over the fall—or of the wretch in the tree?"

"Of each and all, with every thing that concerned them.[1] I should think—"

"Ay," continued the old man, in a voice which betrayed how powerfully his own faculties retained the impression of the spectacle. "I have been a dweller in forests, and in the wilderness for threescore and ten years, and if any man can pretend to know the world or to have seen scary sights, it is myself! But never before nor since have I seen human man in such a state of mortal despair as that very savage, and yet he scorned to speak or to cry out, or to own his forlorn condition! It is their gift, and nobly did he maintain it!"

"Harkee, old trapper," interrupted Paul, who, content with the knowledge that his waist was grasped by one of the arms of Ellen, had hitherto ridden in unusual silence, "my eyes are as true and as delicate as a humming bird's in the day, but they are nothing worth boasting of by star-light. Is that a sick buffaloe, crawling along, in the bottom, there, or is it one of the stray cattle of the savages?"

The whole party drew up, in order to examine the object which Paul had pointed out. During most of the time they had ridden in the little vales in order to seek the protection of the shadows, but just at that moment, they had ascended a roll of the Prairie, in order to cross into the very bottom where this unknown animal was now seen.

"Let us descend," said Middleton. "Be it beast or man, we are too strong to have any cause of fear."

"Now if the thing was not morally impossible," cried the trapper, who, the reader must have already discovered, was not always exact in the use of qualifying words, "if the thing was not morally impossible, I should say that was the man who journeys in search of reptiles and insects: our fellow traveller the Doctor."

"Why, impossible? did you not direct him to pursue this course, in order to rejoin us."

"Ay, but I did not tell him to make an Ass outdo the speed of a horse—you are right, you are right," said the trapper, interrupting himself, as by gradually lessening the distance between them, his eyes assured him it was Obed and Asinus whom he saw, "you are right, as certainly as the thing is a miracle. Lord, what a thing is fear! How now, friend; you have been industrious to have got so far ahead in so short a time. I marvel at the speed of the ass!"

"Asinus, is overcome," returned the Naturalist, mournfully. "The

---

[1] They who have read the preceding books, in which the trapper appears as a hunter and a scout, will readily understand the allusions. [1832]

animal has certainly not been idle since we separated, but he declines all my admonitions and invitations to proceed. I hope there is no instant fear from the savages?"

"I cannot say that; I cannot say that; matters are not as they should be, atween the squatter and the Tetons, nor will I answer, as yet, for the safety of any scalp among us. The beast is broken down! you have urged him beyond his natural gifts, and he is like a worried hound. There is pity and discretion in all things, even, though a man be a-riding for his life."

"You indicated the star," returned the Doctor, "and I deem'd it expedient to use great diligence in pursuing the direction."

"Did you expect to reach it, by such haste! Go, go; you talk boldly of the creatur's of the Lord, though I plainly see that you are but a child in matters that concern their gifts and instincts. What plight would you now be in, if there was need for a long and a quick push, with our heels!"

"The fault exists in the formation of the quadruped," said Obed, whose placid temper began to revolt under so many scandalous imputations. "Had there been rotary levers for two of the members, a moiety of the fatigue would have been saved, for one item—"

"That, for your moiety's and rotary's, and items, man; a jaded ass is a jaded ass, and he who denies it is but a brother of the beast itself! Now, Captain are we driven to choose one of two evils. We must either abandon this man, who has been too much with us, through good and bad to be easily cast away, or we must seek a cover to let the animal rest."

"Venerable venator!" exclaimed the alarmed Obed. "I conjure you by all the secret sympathies of our common nature, by all the hidden—"

"Ah, fear has brought him to talk a little rational sense! It is not natur' truly to abandon a brother in distress, and the Lord he knows, that I have never yet done the shameful deed. You are right, friend, you are right, we must all be hidden, and that speedily. But what to do with the Ass! Friend, Doctor, do you truly value the life of the creatur'?"

"He is an ancient and faithful servant," returned the disconsolate Obed, "and with pain should I see him come to any harm. Fetter his lower limbs, and leave him to repose in this bed of herbage. I will engage he shall be found where he is left, in the morning."

"And, the Siouxes? What would become of the beast, should any of the red imps catch a peep at his ears, growing up out of the grass, like two mullein tops!" cried the bee-hunter. "They would stick him as full of arrows, as a woman's cushion, is full of pins, and then believe that they had done the job for the Father of all rabbits! My word for it, but they would find out their blunder, at the first mouthful!"

Middleton who began to grow impatient under the protracted discussion, interposed, and as a good deal of deference was paid to his rank, he quickly prevailed in his efforts to effect a sort of compromise. The humble Asinus, too meek and too weary to make any resistance was soon tethered and deposited in his bed of dying grass, where he was left, with a perfect confidence on the part of his master, of finding him again at the expiration of a few hours. The old man strongly remonstrated against this arrangement and more than once hinted that the knife was much more certain than the tether, but the petitions of Obed, aided perhaps by the secret reluctance of the trapper to destroy the beast, were the means of saving its life. When Asinus was thus secured, and as his master believed secreted, the whole party proceeded to find some place, where they might rest, themselves, during the time required for the repose of the animal.

According to the calculations of the trapper, they had ridden twenty miles since the commencement of their flight. The delicate frame of Inez began to droop under the excessive fatigue, nor was the more robust, but still feminine person of Ellen insensible to the extraordinary effort she had made. Middleton himself, was not sorry to repose, nor did the vigorous and high spirited Paul hesitate to confess that he should be all the better for a little rest. The old man, alone, seem'd indifferent to the usual claims of nature. Although but little accustomed to the unusual description of exercise he had just been taking, he appeared to bid defiance to all the usual attacks of human infirmities. Though evidently so near its dissolution, his attenuated frame still stood like the shaft of seasoned oak, dry, naked, and tempest-riven, but unbending, and apparently indurated to the consistency of stone. On the present occasion he conducted the search for a resting place, which was immediately commenced, with all the energy of youth tempered by the discretion and experience of his great age.

The bed of grass in which the Doctor had been met, and in which his ass had just been left, was followed, a little distance, until it was found that the rolling swells of the Prairie were melting away into one vast, level plain, that was covered for miles on miles, with the same species of herbage.

"Ah! this may do, this may do," said the old man, when they arrived on the borders of this sea of withered grass: "I know the spot, and often have I lain in its secret holes, for days at a time, while the savages have been hunting the buffaloes on the open ground. We must enter it with great care, for a broad trail might be seen, and Indian curiosity is a dangerous neighbor."

Leading the way, himself, he selected a spot where the tall coarse herbage stood most erect, growing not unlike a bed of reeds, both in height and density. Here he entered, singly, directing the others to follow as nearly as possible in his own footsteps. When they had passed for some hundred or two feet into the wilderness of weeds, he gave his directions to Paul and Middleton, who continued a direct route deeper into the place, while he dismounted and returned on his tracks to the margin of the meadow. Here he passed many minutes in replacing the trodden grass, and in effacing, as far as possible every evidence of their passage.

In the mean time, the rest of the party continued their progress, not without toil and consequently at a very moderate gait, until they had penetrated a mile into the place. Here they found a spot suited to their circumstances, and dismounting they began to make their dispositions to pass the remainder of the night. By this time the trapper had rejoined the party, and again resumed the direction of their proceedings.

The weeds and grass were soon plucked and cut from an area of sufficient extent, and a bed for Inez and Ellen was speedily made, a little apart, which for sweetness and ease might have rivalled one of down. The exhausted females, after receiving some light refreshments from the provident stores of Paul and the old man soon sought their repose, leaving their more stout companions at liberty to provide for their own necessities. Middleton and Paul were not long in following the examples of their betrothed, leaving the trapper and the Naturalist still seated around a savory dish of bison's meat, which had been cooked at a previous halt, and which was, as usual, eaten cold.

A certain lingering sensation which had so long been uppermost in the mind of Obed temporarily banished sleep, and as for the old man, his wants were rendered by habit and necessity, as seemingly subject to his will, as if they altogether depended on the pleasures of the moment. Like his companion he chose, therefore, to watch instead of sleeping.

"If the children of ease and security knew the hardships and dangers, the students of nature encounter in their behalf," said Obed, after a moment of silence when Middleton took his leave for the night, "pillars of silver and statues of brass would be reared as the ever-lasting monuments of their glory!"

"I know not, I know not," returned his companion. "Silver is far from plenty, at least in the wilderness, and your brazen idols are forbidden in the Commandments of the Lord."

"Such indeed was the opinion of the Great Law Giver of the Jews, but the Egyptians, and the Chaldeans, the Greeks, and the Romans were wont to manifest their gratitude, in these types of the human form. Indeed, many of the illustrious masters of Antiquity have by the aid of science and skill, even outdone the works of nature, and exhibited a beauty and perfection in the human form, that are difficult to be found in the rarest living specimens of any of the species, *genus,* homo."

"Can your idols, walk, or speak, or have they the glorious gift of reason!" demanded the trapper, with some indignation in his voice; "though but little given to run into the noise and chatter of the settlements, yet have I been into the towns, in my day, to barter the Peltry for lead and powder, and often have I seen your waxen dolls, with their tawdry clothes and glass eyes— "

"Waxen dolls!" interrupted Obed, "it is profanation in the view of the arts to liken the miserable handy work of the dealers in wax to the pure models of antiquity."

"It is profanation in the eyes of the Lord," retorted the old man, "to liken the works of his creatur's, to the power of his own hand!"

"Venerable venator," resumed the naturalist clearing his throat, like one who was much in earnest, "let us discuss understandingly, and in amity. You speak of the dross of ignorance, whereas my memory dwells on those precious jewels which it was my happy fortune, formerly, to witness, among the treasured glories of the old world."

"*Old* World!" retorted the trapper, "that is the miserable cry of all the half-starved miscreants that have come into this blessed land, since the days of my boyhood! They tell you of the *old* world, as if the Lord had not the power and the will to create the universe in a day! or, as if he had not bestowed his gifts with an equal hand, though, not with an equal mind, or equal wisdom, have they been received and used! were they to say a *worn* out, and an *abused,* and a *sacrilegious* world, they might not be so far from the truth!"

Doctor Battius, who found it quite as arduous a task to maintain any of his favorite positions with so irregular an antagonist, as he would have found it difficult to keep his feet within the hug of a western wrestler, hemmed aloud, and profited, by the new opening the trapper had made, to shift the grounds of the discussion —

"By old and new world, my excellent associate," he said; "it is not to be understood, that the hills, and the vallies, the rocks and the rivers of our own moiety of the earth, do not, physically speaking, bear a date as ancient, as the spot on which the bricks of Babylon are found. It merely signifies that its moral existence is not co-equal with its physical, or geological formation."

"Anan!" said the old man looking up inquiringly into the face of the Philosopher.

"Merely, that it has not been so long known in morals, as the other countries of Christendom."

"So much the better, so much the better. I am no great admirator of your old morals, as you call them, for I have ever found, and I have liv'd long, as it were, in the very heart of natur', that your old morals are never of the best. Mankind twist and turn the rules of the Lord, to suit their own wickedness when their devilish cunning has had too much time to trifle with his commands."

"Nay, venerable hunter, still am I not comprehended. By morals, I do not mean the limited and literal signification of the term, such as is convey'd in its synonyme, morality, but the practices of men, as connected with their daily intercourse, their institutions, and their laws."

"And such I call, barefaced and downright wantonness and waste," interrupted his sturdy disputant.

"Well be it so," returned the Doctor, abandoning the explanation in despair. "Perhaps I have conceded too much," he, then, instantly added, fancying that he still saw the glimmerings of an argument through another chink in the discourse, "Perhaps I have conceded too much, in saying that this hemisphere is literally as old in its formation, as that which embraces the venerable quarters of Europe, Asia and Africa."

"It is easy to say that a pine is not so tall as an alder, but it would be hard to prove. Can you give a reason for such a belief?"

"The reasons are numerous and powerful," returned the Doctor delighted by this encouraging opening. "Look into the plains of Egypt and Araby, their sandy deserts teem with the monuments of their antiquity; and then we have also recorded documents of their glory, doubling the proofs of their former greatness, now that they lie stripped of their fertility, while we look in vain for similar evidences that man has ever reach'd the summit of civilization on this Continent, or search

without our reward for the path, by which he has made the downward journey to his present condition of second child-hood."

"And what see you in all this?" demanded the trapper, who, though
a little confused by the terms of his companion, seized the thread of
his ideas.

"A demonstration of my Problem, that nature did not make so vast
a region to lie so many ages an uninhabited waste. This is merely the
moral view of the subject; as to the more exact and geological—"

"Your morals are exact enough for me," returned the old man, "for
I think I see in them the very *pride* of *folly.* I am but little gifted in the
fables of what you call the *old* world, seeing that my time has been
mainly passed looking natur' steadily in the face, and in reasoning on
what I've seen rather than on what I've heard in traditions. But I have
never shut my ears to the words of the good book, and many is the
long winter evening that I have passed, in the wigwams of the Delawares, listening to the good Moravians as they dealt forth the history
and doctrines of the elder times to the people of the Lenape. It was
pleasant to hearken to such wisdom after a weary hunt! Right pleasant
did I find it, and often have I talked the matter over with the Great
Serpent of the Delawares, in the more peaceful hours of our outly-
ings, whether it might be on the trail of a war-party of the Mingoes,
or on the watch for a York deer. I remember to have heard it, then
and there said that the blessed Land was once fertile as the bottoms of
the Mississippi, and groaning with its stores of grain and fruits; but
that the judgement has since fallen upon it, and that it is now more
remarkable for its barrenness than any qualities to boast of."

"It is true; but Egypt, nay much of Africa furnishes still more
striking proofs of this exhaustion of nature."

"Tell me," interrupted the old man, "is it a certain truth that
buildings are still standing in that land of Pharoah, which may be
likened in their stature to the hills of the 'arth?"

"It is as true, as that nature never refuses to bestow her incisores on
the *animals,* mamalia; *genus,* Homo;—"

"It is very marvellous! and it proves how great He must be, when
his miserable creatur's can accomplish such wonders! Many men, must
have been needed to finish such an edifice; ay! and men gifted with
strength and skill, too! Does the land abound with such a race, to this
hour."

"Far from it. Most of the Country is a desert, and but for a mighty
river all would be so."

"Yes; rivers are rare gifts to such as till the ground, as any one may see, who journeys far atween the Rocky Mountains and the Mississippi. But how do you account for these changes on the face of the 'arth itself, and for this downfall of nations; you men of the schools?"

"It is to be ascribed to moral cau—"

"You're right! it is their morals! their wickedness and their pride, and chiefly their waste that has done it all! now listen to what the experience of an old man teaches him. I have lived long, as these gray hairs and wrinkled hands will show, even though my tongue should fail in the wisdom of my years. And I have seen much of the folly of man; for his natur' is the same, be he born in the wilderness or be he born in the towns. To my weak judgement it hath ever seem'd that his gifts are not equal to his wishes. That he would mount into the Heavens with all his deformities about him, if he only knew the road, no one will gainsay that witnesses his bitter strivings upon 'arth. If his power is not equal to his will, it is because the wisdom of the Lord hath set bounds to his evil workings."

"It is much too certain that certain facts will warrant a theory which teaches the natural depravity of the *genus;* but if science could be fairly brought to bear on a whole species, at once, for instance, education might eradicate the evil principle."

"That, for your education! the time has been when I have thought it possible to make a companion of a beast. Many are the cubs, and many are the speckled fawns that I have reared with these old hands, until I have even fancied them rational and altered beings, but what did it amount to! the bear would bite, and the deer would run, notwithstanding my wicked conceit, in fancying I could change a temper that the Lord himself had seen fit to bestow! Now if man is so blinded in his folly, as to go on, ages on ages, doing harm chiefly to himself, there is the same reason to think that he has wrought his evil here, as in the Countries you call so old. Look about you, man; where are the multitudes that once peopled these Prairies; the Kings, and the Palaces; the riches and the riotousnesses, of this desert?"

"Where are the monuments, that would prove the truth of so vague a theory?"

"I know not what you call a monument."

"The works of man! the glories of Thebes and Balbec. Columns, catacombs and Pyramids, standing amid the sands of the East, like wrecks on a rocky shore, to testify to the storms of ages!"

"They are gone. Time has lasted too long for them; for why? time was made by the Lord, and they were made by man. This very spot of reeds and grass on which you now sit, may, once have been the garden of some mighty King. It is the fate of all things, to ripen, and then to decay. The tree blossoms, and bears its fruit, which falls, rots, withers, and even the seed is lost. Go count the rings of the oak and of the sycamore; they lie in circles, one about another, until the eye is blinded in striving to make out their numbers, and yet a full change of the seasons comes round while the stem is winding one of those little lines about itself, like the buffaloe changing his coat, or the buck his horns, and what does it all amount to! there does the noble tree fill its place in the forest, loftier, and grander, and richer, and more difficult to imitate, than any of your pitiful pillars, for a thousand years, until the time which the Lord hath given it, is full. Then come the winds, that you cannot see, to rive its bark, and the waters from the heavens to soften its pores, and the rot, which all can feel and none can understand, to humble its pride and bring it to the ground. From that moment its beauty begins to perish. It lies another hundred years, a mouldering log, and then a mound of moss and 'arth, a sad effigy of a human grave. This is one of your genuine monuments, though made by a very different power than such as belongs to your chiselling masons; and after all the cunningest scout of the whole Dahcotah nation might pass his life in searching for the spot where it fell, and be no wiser when his eyes grew dim, than when they were first opened. As if that was not enough to convince man of his ignorance, and as though it were put there in mockery of his conceit, a pine shoots up from the roots of the oak, just as barrenness comes after fertility, or as these wastes have been spread, where a garden may have been created. Tell me not of your worlds that are old, it is blasphemous to set bounds and seasons in this manner, to the works of the Almighty, like a woman counting the ages of her young."

"Friend hunter, or trapper," returned the naturalist clearing his throat in some intellectual confusion at the vigorous attack of his companion, "your deductions, if admitted by the world, would sadly circumscribe the efforts of reason, and much abridge the boundaries of knowledge."

"So much the better, so much the better; for I have always found that a conceited man never knows content. All things prove it. Why have we not the wings of the pigeon, the eyes of the eagle and the legs of the moose, if it had been intended that man should be equal to all his wishes?"

"These are mere physical defects, venerable trapper, in which I am always ready to admit great and happy alterations might be suggested. For example, in my own order of Phalangacru—"

"Cruel enough would be the order that should come from miserable hands like thine! A touch from such a finger would destroy the mocking deformity of a monkey! Go, go, human folly is not needed to fill up the great design of God. There is no stature, no beauty, no proportions nor any colours, in which man himself can well be fashioned that is not already done to his hand."

"That is touching another great and much disputed question!" exclaimed the Doctor, who seized upon every distinct idea that the ardent and somewhat dogmatic old man left exposed to his mental grasp, with the vain hope of inducing a logical discussion in which he might bring his battery of syllogisms to annihilate the unscientific defences of his antagonist.

It is however unnecessary to our narrative to relate the erratic discourse that ensued. The old man eluded the annihilating blows of his adversary, as the light armed soldier is wont to escape the efforts of the more regular warrior even while he annoys him most, and an hour passed away without bringing any of the numerous subjects on which they touch'd to a satisfactory conclusion. The arguments acted however, on the nervous system of the Doctor like so many soothing soporifics, and by the time his aged companion was disposed to lay his head on his pack, Obed, refreshed by his recent mental joust, was in a condition to seek his natural rest, without enduring the torments of the Incubus in the shapes of Teton warriors and bloody tomahawks.

CHAPTER XXIII.

"—Save you, sir."

Coriolanus, IV.iv.6

THE sleep of the fugitives lasted for several hours. The trapper was the first to shake off its influence as he had been the last to court its refreshment. Rising, just as the gray light of day began to brighten that portion of the studded vault which rested on the eastern margin of the plain, he summoned his companions from their warm lairs, and pointed out the necessity of their being, once more, on the alert. While Middleton attended to the arrangements necessary to the comforts of Inez and Ellen in the long and painful journey which lay before them, the old man and Paul prepared the meal, which the former had advised them to take before they proceeded to horse. These several dispositions were not long in making, and the little groupe was soon seated about a repast, which though it might want the elegancies to which the bride of Middleton had been accustomed, was not deficient in the more important requisites of savour and nutriment.

"When we get lower into the hunting grounds of the Pawnees," said the trapper, laying a morsel of delicate venison before Inez on a little trencher neatly made of horn, and expressly for his own use, "we shall find the buffaloe fatter and sweeter, the deer in more abundance, and all the gifts of the Lord abounding to satisfy our wants. Perhaps we may even strike a beaver, and get a morsel from his tail,[1] by way of a rare mouthful."

"What course do you mean to pursue when you have once thrown these blood-hounds from the chace?" demanded Middleton.

"If I might advise," said Paul, "it would be to strike a water-course, and get upon its downward current, as soon as may be. Give me a cotton-wood, and I will turn you out a canoe that shall carry us all, the jackass excepted, in perhaps the work of a day and a night. Ellen, here, is a lively girl enough, but then she is no great race-rider, and it would be far more comfortable to boat six or eight hundred miles,

---

[1] The American hunters consider the tail of the beaver the most nourishing of all food. [1832]

than to go loping along like so many elks measuring the Prairies: besides, water leaves no trail."

"I will not swear to that," returned the trapper; "I have often thought the eyes of a red skin would find a trail in the air."

"See, Middleton!" exclaimed Inez in a sudden burst of youthful pleasure, that caus'd her for a moment to forget her situation. "How lovely is that sky! surely it contains a promise of happier times!"

"It is glorious!" returned her husband. "Glorious and heavenly is that streak of vivid red—and here is a still brighter crimson—rarely have I seen a richer rising of the sun."

"Rising of the sun!" slowly repeated the old man, lifting his tall person from its seat, with a deliberate and abstracted air, while he kept his eye rivetted on the changing and certainly beautiful tints that were garnishing the vault of heaven. "Rising of the sun! I like not such risings of the sun! Ah's me; the imps have circumvented us with a vengeance. The Prairie is on fire!"

"God in Heaven protect us!" cried Middleton catching Inez to his bosom, under the instant impression of the imminence of their danger. "There is no time to lose, old man; each instant is a day; let us fly!"

"Whither?" demanded the trapper motioning him with calmness and dignity to arrest his steps. "In this wilderness of grass and reeds, you are like a vessel on the broad lakes without a compass. A single step on the wrong course might prove the destruction of us all. It is seldom that danger is so pressing, that there is not time enough for reason to do its work, young officer; therefore let us await its biddings."

"For my own part," said Paul Hover, looking about him with no equivocal expression of concern, "I acknowledge that should this dry bed of weeds get fairly in a flame a bee would have to make a flight higher than common to prevent his wings from scorching. Therefore, old trapper, I agree with the Captain, and say mount and run."

"Ye are wrong, ye are wrong, man is not a beast to follow the gift of instinct, and to snuff up his knowledge by a taint in the air or a rumbling in the sound, but he must see, and reason, and then conclude. So follow me a little to the left, where there is a rise in the ground, whence we may make our reconnoitrings."

The old man waved his hand with authority, and led the way without further parlance to the spot he had indicated, followed by the whole of his alarmed companions. An eye less practised than that of the trapper might have failed in discovering the gentle elevation, to which he alluded, and which look'd on the surface of the meadow like a growth a little taller than common. When they reach'd the place, however, the stunted grass, itself, announced the absence of that moisture which had fed the rank weeds of most of the plain, and furnished a clue to the evidence by which he had judged of the formation of the ground hidden beneath. Here a few minutes were lost in breaking down the tops of the surrounding herbage, which, notwithstanding the advantage of their position, rose even above the heads of Middleton and Paul, and in obtaining a look-out, that might command a view of the surrounding sea of fire.

The frightful prospect added nothing to the hopes of those who had so fearful a stake in the result. Although the day was beginning to dawn, the vivid colours of the sky continued to deepen, as if the fierce element were bent on an impious rivalry of the light of the sun. Bright flashes of flame shot up, here and there, along the margin of the waste, like the nimble corruscations of the North, but far more angry and threatening in their colour and changes. The anxiety on the rigid features of the trapper sensibly deepened as he leisurely traced these evidences of a conflagration, which spread in a broad belt about their place of refuge, until he had encircled the whole horizon.

Shaking his head, as he again turned his face to the point where the danger seem'd nighest and most rapidly approaching, the old man said—

"Now have we been cheating ourselves with the belief, that we had thrown those Tetons from our trail, while here is proof enough that they not only know where we lie, but that they intend to smoke us out, like so many skulking beasts of prey. See; they have lighted the fire, around the whole bottom at the same moment, and we are as completely hemm'd in by the Devils, as an island by its waters."

"Let us mount and ride;" cried Middleton. "Is life not worth a struggle!"

"Whither would ye go! Is a Teton horse a salamander that can walk amid fiery flames, unhurt; or do ye think the Lord will show his might in your behalf as in the days of old, and carry you harmless through such a furnace*as you may see glowing beneath yonder red sky! There are Siouxes too, hemming the fire with their arrows and knives on every side of us, or I am no judge of their murderous deviltries."

"We will ride into the centre of the whole tribe," retorted the youth, fiercely, "and put their manhood to the test."

"Ay, it's well in words, but what would it prove in deeds! Here is a dealer in bees, who can teach you wisdom in a matter like this."

"Now, for that matter, old trapper," said Paul, stretching his athletic form like a mastiff conscious of his strength, "I am on the side of the

Captain, and am clearly for a race, against the fire, though it line me into a Teton wigwam. Here is Ellen, who will—"

"Of what use, of what use, are your stout hearts when the element of the Lord is to be conquered as well as human men. Look about you, friends; the wreath of smoke that is rising from the bottoms, plainly says that there is no outlet from the spot, without crossing a belt of fire. Look for yourselves, my men; look for yourselves; if you can find a single opening, I will engage to follow."

The examination which his companions so instantly and so intently made, rather served to assure them of their desperate situation, than to appease their fears. Huge columns of smoke were rolling up from the plain, and thickening in gloomy masses, around the horizon. The red glow which gleamed upon their enormous folds, now lighting their volumes with the glare of the conflagration and now flashing to another point, as the flame beneath glided ahead, leaving all behind enveloped in awful darkness, and proclaiming, louder than words, the character of the imminent and approaching danger.

"This is terrible!" exclaimed Middleton, folding the trembling Inez to his heart. "At such a time as this, and in such a manner!"

"The gates of Heaven are open to all who truly believe," murmured the pious devotee in his bosom.

"This resignation is maddening! But we are men and will make a struggle for our lives! How now, my brave and spirited friend; shall we yet mount and push across the flames, or shall we stand here, and see these we most love perish, in this frightful manner, without an effort!"

"I am for a swarming time and a flight, before the hive is too hot to hold us;" said the bee-hunter, to whom it will be at once seen that Middleton addressed himself. "Come, old trapper, you must acknowledge this is but a slow way of getting out of danger: if we tarry here much longer, it will be in the fashion that the bees lie around the straw after the hive has been smoked for its honey. You may hear the fire begin to roar, already, and I know by experience that when the flame once gets fairly into the Prairie grass, it is no sloth that can outrun it."

"Think you," returned the old man pointing scornfully at the mazes of the dry and matted grass which environed them, "that mortal feet can outstrip the speed of fire, on such a path. If I only knew now on which side them miscreants lay."

"What say you, friend, Doctor," cried the bewildered Paul, turning to the naturalist, with that sort of helplessness with which the strong are often apt to seek aid of the weak when human power is baffled by the hand of a mightier being. "What say you, have you no advice to give away in a case of life and death?"

The naturalist stood, tabletts in hand, looking at the awful spectacle with as much composure as if the conflagration had been lighted in order to solve the difficulties of some scientific problem. Aroused by the question of his companion, he turned to his equally calm, though differently occupied associate the trapper, demanding with the most provoking insensibility to the urgent nature of their situation—

"Venerable hunter, you have often witnessd similar prismatick experiments—"

He was rudely interrupted by Paul, who struck the tabletts from his hands, with a violence that betrayed the utter intellectual confusion which had overset the equanimity of his mind. Before time was allowed for remonstrance, the old man, who had continued during the whole scene like one much at a loss how to proceed though also like one who was rather perplexed than alarmed, suddenly assumed a decided air, as if he no longer doubted on the course it was most adviseable to pursue.

"It is time to be doing," he said interrupting the controversy that was about to ensue between the Naturalist and the bee-hunter. "It is time to leave off books and moanings and to be doing."

"You have come to your recollections too late, miserable old man;" cried Middleton. "The flames are within a quarter of a mile of us, and the wind is bringing them down upon us, in this quarter, with dreadful rapidity."

"Anan! the flames! I care but little for the flames. If I only knew how to circumvent the cunning of the Tetons as I know how to cheat the fire of its prey, there would be nothing needed but thanks to the Lord for our deliverance. Do you call this a fire! If you had seen what I have witnessed in the Eastern hills,* when mighty mountains were like the furnace of a smith, you would have known what it was to fear the flames and to be thankful that you were spared. Come, lads, come; 'tis time to be doing, now, and to cease talking; for yonder curling flame is truly coming on like a trotting moose. Put hands upon this short and withered grass where we stand and lay bare the 'arth."

"Would you think to deprive the fire of its victims in this childish manner!" exclaimed Middleton.

A faint but solemn smile passed over the features of the old man as he answered—

"Your gran'ther would have said, that when the enemy was nigh a soldier could do no better than to obey."

The Captain felt the reproof and instantly began to imitate the industry of Paul, who was tearing the decayed herbage from the ground in a sort of desperate compliance with the trapper's directions. Even Ellen lent her hands to the labor, nor was it long before Inez was seen similarly employed, though none amongst them, knew why or wherefore. When life is thought to be the reward of labor, men are wont to be industrious. A very few minutes sufficed to lay nearly bare a spot of some thirty feet in diameter. Into one edge of this little area the trapper brought the females, directing Middleton and Paul to cover their light and inflammable dresses with the blankets of the party. So soon as this precaution was observed the old man approached the opposite margin of the grass which still environed them in a tall and dangerous circle, and selecting a handful of the driest of the herbage he placed it over the pan of his rifle. The light combustible kindled at the flash. Then he placed the little flame in a bed of the standing fog, and withdrawing from the spot, to the centre of the ring, he patiently awaited the result.

The subtle element seized with avidity upon its new fuel, and, in a moment, forked flames were gliding among the grass, as the tongues of ruminating animals are seen rolling among their food, apparently in quest of its sweetest portions.

"Now," said the old man, holding up a finger and laughing in his peculiarly silent manner, "you shall see fire fight fire! Ah's me; many is the time I have burnt a smooty path from wanton laziness to pick my way across a tangled bottom!"

"But is this not fatal," cried the amazed Middleton; "are you not bringing the enemy nigher to us instead of avoiding it?"

"Do ye scorch so easily! Your Gran'ther had a tougher skin. But we shall live to see, we shall all live to see."

The experience of the trapper was in the right. As the fire gained strength and heat, it began to spread on three sides, dying of itself on the fourth for want of aliment. As it increased, and the sullen roaring announced its power, it cleared every thing before it, leaving the black and smoking soil far more naked than if the scythe had swept the place. The situation of the fugitives would have still been hazardous had not the area enlarged as the flame encircled them. But by advancing, to the spot where the trapper had kindled the grass, they avoided the heat, and in a very few moments the flames began to recede in every quarter, leaving them enveloped in a cloud of smoke, but perfectly safe from the torrent of fire that was still furiously rolling onward.

The spectators regarded the simple expedient of the trapper with that species of wonder, with which the courtiers of Ferdinand are said to have viewed the manner in which Columbus made his egg stand on its end,* though with feelings that were filled with gratitude instead of envy.

"Most wonderful!" said Middleton, when he saw the complete success of the means by which they had been rescued from a danger that he had conceived to be unavoidable. "The thought was a gift from heaven, and the hand that executed it should be immortal!"

"Old trapper," cried Paul, thrusting his fingers through his shaggy locks, "I have lined many a loaded bee into his hole, and know something of the nature of the woods, but this is robbing a hornet of his sting without touching the insect!"

"It will do, it will do," returned the old man, who after the first moment of his success, seem'd to think no more of the exploit; "now get the horses in readiness. Let the flames do their work for a short half hour, and then we will mount. That time is needed to cool the meadow for these unshod Teton beasts are as tender on the hoof, as a bare-footed girl."

Middleton and Paul who considered their unlooked-for escape as a species of resurrection, patiently awaited the time the trapper mentioned with renewed confidence in the infallibility of his judgement. The Doctor regained his tablets, a little the worse from having fallen among the grass which had been subject to the dominion of the flames, and was consoling himself for this slight misfortune, by recording, uninterruptedly, such different vacillations in light and shadow as he chose to consider phenomena.

In the mean time, the veteran, on whose experience they all so implicitly relied for protection, employed himself in reconnoitring objects in the distance, through the openings which the air occasionally made in the immense bodies of smoke that, by this time, lay in enormous piles on every part of the plain.

"Look you here, lads," the trapper said, after a long and anxious examination; "your eyes are young and may prove better than my worthless sight—though the time has been when a wise and brave people saw reason to think me quick on a look-out, but those times are gone, and many a true and tried friend has passed away with them. Ah's me! If I could choose a change in the orderings of providence—which I cannot, and which it would be blasphemy to attempt, seeing that all things are governed by a wiser mind than belongs to mortal weakness—but if I were to choose a change it would be to say, that such as they who have liv'd long together in friendship and kindness, and who have prov'd their fitness to go in company by many acts of suffering and daring in each other's behalf, should be permitted to give up life at such times, as when the death of one, leaves the other but little reason to wish to live."

"Is it an Indian that you see?" demanded the impatient Middleton.

"Red-skin or white-skin it is much the same. Friendship and use can tie men as strongly together in the woods as in the towns—ay, or for that matter, stronger. Here are the young warriors of the Prairies—Often do they sort themselves in pairs, and set apart their lives for deeds of friendship, and well and truly do they act up to their promises. The death blow to one is commonly mortal to the other! I have been a solitary man much of my time, if he can be called solitary who has lived for seventy years in the very bosom of natur' and where he could at any instant open his heart to God, without having to strip it of the cares and wickednesses of the settlements, but making that allowance, have I been a solitary man, and yet have I always found that intercourse with my kind was pleasant, and painful to break off, provided that the companion was brave and honest. Brave because a skeary comrade in the woods" suffering his eyes inadvertently to rest a moment on the person of the abstracted naturalist, "is apt to make a short path, long, and honest, inasmuch, as craftiness is rather an instinct of the brutes than a gift becoming the reason of a human man."

"But the object that you saw—was it a Sioux?"

"What this world of America is coming to, and where the machinations and inventions of its people are to have an end, the Lord, he only knows. I have seen in my day, the chief, who in his time, had beheld the first christian that plac'd his wicked foot in the regions of York! How much has the beauty of the wilderness been deformed in two short lives! My own eyes were first opened on the shores of the Eastern sea, and well do I remember that I tried the virtues of the first rifle I ever bore, after such a march, from the door of my father to the forest, as a stripling could make between sun and sun, and that without offence to the rights, or prejudices, of any man who set himself up to be the owner of the beasts of the fields. Natur' then lay in its glory along the whole coast, giving a narrow stripe between the woods and the ocean to the greediness of the settlers. And where am I now! Had I the wings of an eagle, they would tire before a tenth of the distance, which separates me from that sea, could be passed; and towns, and villages, farms and high ways, churches, and schools, in short all the inventions and deviltries of man are spread across the region! I have known the time when a few red-skins shouting along the borders, could set the Provinces in a fever, and men were to be armed, and troops were to be called to aid from a distant land, and prayers were said, and the women frighted, and few slept in quiet, because the Iroquois was on the war path, the accursed Mingo had the tomahawk in hand. How is it now. The country sends out her ships to foreign lands to wage their battles, cannon are plentier than the rifle used to be, and trained soldiers are never wanting in tens of thousands, when need calls for their services. Such is the difference atween a Province and a State, my men; and I, miserable and worn out as I seem, have liv'd to see it all!"

"That you must have seen many a chopper skimming the cream from the face of the earth, and many a settler gathering the very honey of nature, old trapper," said Paul, "no reasonable man can, or for that matter, shall doubt. But here is Ellen growing uneasy about the Siouxes, and now you have opened your mind, so freely, concerning these matters, if you will just put us on the line of our flight, the swarm will make another move."

"Anan!"

"I say that Ellen is getting uneasy, and as the smoke is lifting from the plain, it may be prudent to take another flight."

"The boy is reasonable. I had forgotten we were in the midst of a raging fire and that Siouxes were round about us, like hungry wolves watching a drove of buffaloes. But when memory is at work in my old brain, on times long past, it is apt to overlook the matters of the day. You say right, my children; it is time to be moving, and now comes the real nicety of our case. It is easy to outwit a furnace for it is nothing but a raging element, and it is not always difficult to throw a grizzly bear from his scent, for the creatur' is both enlightened and blinded by his instinct, but to shut the eyes of a waking Teton is a matter of greater judgement, inasmuch, as his deviltry is backed by reason."

Notwithstanding the old man appeared so conscious of the difficulty of the undertaking, he set about its achievement with great steadiness and alacrity. After completing the examination which had been interrupted by the melancholy wanderings of his mind, he gave the signal to his companions to mount. The horses, which had continued passive and trembling amid the raging of the fire, received their burthens with a satisfaction so very evident as to furnish a favorable augury of their future industry. The trapper invited the Doctor to take his own steed, declaring his intention to proceed on foot.

"I am but little used to journeying with the feet of others," he added as a reason for the measure, "and my legs are weary of doing nothing. Besides, should we light, suddenly, on an ambushment, which is a thing far from impossible, the horse will be in a better condition for a hard run, with one man on his back, than with two. As for me, what matters it whether my time is to be a day shorter, or longer! Let the Tetons take my scalp, if it be God's pleasure; they will find it covered with gray hairs, and it is beyond the craft of man to cheat me of the knowledge and experience by which they have been whitened."

As no one, among the impatient listeners seemed disposed to dispute the arrangement it was acceded to in silence. The Doctor though he muttered a few mourning exclamations on behalf of the lost Asinus, was by far too well pleased in finding that his speed was likely to be sustained by four legs instead of two, to be long in complying, and consequently, in a very few moments, the bee-hunter, who was never last to speak on such occasions, vociferously announced that they were ready to proceed.

"Now look off, yonder, to the east," said the old man, as he began to lead the way across the murky and still smoking plain; "little fear of cold feet in journeying such a path as this—but look you off to the east, and if you see a sheet of shining white, glistening like a plate of beaten silver through the openings of the smoke, why that is water. A noble stream is running, thereaway, and I thought I got a glimpse of it a while since, but other thoughts came, and I lost it. It is a broad and swift river, such as the Lord has made many of its fellows in this desert. For here may natur' be seen in all its richness, trees alone excepted. Trees, which are to the 'arth as fruits are to a garden; without them nothing can be pleasant, or thoroughly useful. Now watch all of you, with open eyes, for that stripe of glittering water; we shall not be safe until it is flowing between our trail and these sharp sighted Tetons."

The latter declaration was enough to insure a vigilant look-out for the desired stream, on the part of all the trapper's followers. With this object in view the party proceeded, in profound silence, the old man having admonished them of the necessity of caution, as they entered the clouds of smoke which were rolling like masses of fog along the plain, more particularly over those spots where the fire had encountered occasional pools of stagnant water.

They travelled near a league, in this manner, without obtaining the desired glimpse of the river. The fire was still raging in the distance and as the air swept away the first vapor of the conflagration fresh volumes rolled along the place, limiting the view. At length the old man, who had begun to betray some little uneasiness which caused his followers to apprehend that even his acute faculties were beginning to be confused, in the mazes of the smoke, made a sudden pause, and dropping his rifle to the ground, he stood apparently musing over some object at his feet. Middleton and the rest, rode up to his side and demanded the reason of the halt.

"Look ye here," returned the trapper, pointing to the mutilated carcass of a horse that lay more than half consumed in a little hollow of the ground, "here may you see the power of a Prairie conflagration. The 'arth is moist, hereaway, and the grass has been taller than usual. This miserable beast has been caught in his bed. You see the bones—the crackling and scorched hide, and the grinning teeth. A thousand winters could not wither an animal so thoroughly, as the element has done it, in a minute."

"And this might have been our fate!" said Middleton, "had the flames come upon us, in our sleep!"

"Nay, I do not say that. I do not say that. Not but what man will burn as well as tinder, but that being more reasoning than a horse, he would better know how to avoid the danger."

"Perhaps this then has been but the carcass of an animal; or he too would have fled?"

"See you these marks in the damp soil? Here have been his hoofs, and there is a moccasin print, as I'm a sinner! The owner of the beast has tried hard to move him from the place, but it is in the instinct of the creatur' to be faint-hearted and obstinate in a fire!"

"It is a well known fact. But if the animal has had a rider, where is he?"

"Ay, therein lies the mystery;" returned the trapper stooping to examine the signs in the ground, with a closer eye. "Yes, yes, it is plain there has been a long struggle atween the two. The master has tried hard to save his beast, and the flames must have been very greedy, or he would have had better success."

"Harkee, old trapper," interrupted Paul, pointing to a little distance where the ground was drier, and the herbage had, in consequence, been less luxuriant, "just call them two horses. Yonder lies another."

"The boy is right! can it be that the Tetons have been caught in their own snares! Such things do happen; and here is an example to all evil-doers. Ay, look you, here; this is iron; there have been some white inventions about the trappings of this beast, it must be so, it must be so. A party of the knaves have been skirting in the grass after us, while their friends have fired the Prairie, and look you at the consequences; they have lost their beasts and happy have they been if their own souls are not now skirting along the path, which leads to the Indian heaven."

"They had the same expedient at command as yourself," rejoined Middleton as the party slowly proceeded, approaching the other carcass which lay directly on their route.

"I know not that. It is not every savage that carries his steel and flint, or a good rifle pan, like this old friend of mine. It is slow making a fire with two sticks, and a little time was given to consider, or invent, just at this spot, as you may see by yon streak of flame, which is flashing along afore the wind, as if it were on a trail of powder. It is not many minutes since the fire has passed, hereaway, and it may be well to look at our primings, not that I would willingly combat the Tetons, God forbid, but if a fight needs be, it is always wise to get the first shot."

"This has been a strange beast, old man," said Paul, who had pulled the bridle, or rather halter, of his steed, over the second carcass, which the rest of the party were already, passing, in their eagerness to proceed. "A strange horse do I call it: it has neither head nor hoofs!"

"The fire has not been idle," returned the trapper, keeping his eye vigilantly employed in profiting by those glimpses of the horizon which the whirling smoke offered to his examination. "It would soon bake you a buffaloe whole, or for that matter powder his hoofs and horns into white ashes. Shame, shame, old Hector; as for the captain's pup, it is to be expected that he would show his want of years and I may say I hope without offence, his want of education too; but for a hound like you, who have liv'd so long in the forest afore you came into these plains, it is very disgraceful, Hector, to be showing your teeth and growling at the carcass of a roasted horse, the same as if you were telling your master that you found the trail of a grizzly bear."

"I tell you, old trapper, this is no horse, neither in hoofs, head, nor hide."

"Anan. Not a horse! your eyes are good for the bees, and for the hollow trees, my lad, but—bless me, the boy is right! That I should mistake the hide of a buffaloe, scorched and crimpled as it is, for the carcass of a horse! Ah's, me! The time has been, my men, when I would tell you the name of a beast as far as eye could reach, and that too with most of the particulars of colour, age, and sex."

"An inestimable advantage have you, then, enjoyed in your day, venerable venator," observed the attentive naturalist. "The man who can make these distinctions in a desert is saved the pain of many a weary walk, and, often, of an inquiry that in its result proves useless. Pray tell now did your exceeding excellence of vision extend so far as to enable you to decide on their *Order,* or *Genus?*"

"I know not what you mean by your orders of genius."

"No!" interrupted the bee-hunter a little disdainfully for him when speaking to his aged friend. "Now, old trapper, that is admitting your ignorance of the English language, in a way I should not expect from a man of your experience and understanding. By order, our comrade, means, whether they go in promiscuous droves like a swarm that is following its Queen-bee, or, in single file, as you often see the Buffaloe trailing each other through a Prairie. And as for genius, I'm sure *that* is a word well understood, and in every body's mouth. There is the congress-man, in our district, and that tonguey little fellow who puts out the paper in our County, they are both so called, for their smartness, which is what the Doctor means, as I take it, seeing that he seldom speaks without a particular meaning."

When Paul finished this very clever explanation, he look'd behind him with an expression which rightly interpreted would have said, "You see, though I don't often trouble myself in these matters; I am no fool."

Ellen admired Paul for any thing but his learning. There was enough in his frank, fearless, and manly character, backed as it was by great personal attraction, to awaken her sympathies, without the necessity of prying into his mental attainments. The poor girl reddened like a rose, her pretty fingers played with the belt by which she sustained herself on the horse, and she hurriedly observed, as if anxious to divert the attentions of the other listeners from a weakness on which her own thoughts could not bear to dwell—

"And this is not a horse after all?"

"It is nothing more, nor less, than the hide of a buffaloe," continued the trapper, who had been no less puzzled by the explanation of Paul than by the language of the Doctor. "The hair is beneath, and the fire has run over it, as you see, for being fresh, the flames could take no hold. The beast has not been long killed, and it may be that some of the beef is, still, here away."

"Lift the corner of the skin, old trapper," said Paul, with the tone of one who felt, as if he had now proved his right to mingle his voice in any council. "If there is a morsel of the hump, left, it must be well cooked, and it shall be welcome."

The old man laughed, heartily, at the conceit of his companion. Thrusting his foot beneath the skin, it moved. Then it was suddenly cast aside, and an Indian warrior sprang from its cover, to his feet, with an agility that bespoke how urgent he deemed the occasion.

CHAPTER XXIV.

"But tell me, Hal; art thou not horribly
afeard?"—

I Henry IV, II.iv. 365-66.

A second glance sufficed to convince the whole of the startled party that the young Pawnee, whom they had already encountered, again stood before them. Surprise kept both sides mute, and more than a minute was passed in surveying each other, with eyes of astonishment, if not of distrust. The wonder of the young warrior was, however, much more tempered and dignified than that of his christian acquaintances. While Middleton and Paul felt the tremors which shook the persons of their dependant companions, thrilling through their own quickened blood, the glowing eye of the Indian rolled from one to another as if it could never quail, before the rudest assaults. His gaze after making the circuit of every wondering countenance finally settled in a steady look on the equally immoveable features of the trapper. The silence was first broken by Doctor Battius, in the ejaculation of,

"*Order,* primates; *genus,* homo; *species,* Prairie!"

"Ay, ay, the secret is out!" said the old trapper, shaking his head like one who congratulated himself on having mastered the mystery of some knotty difficulty. "The lad has been in the grass for a cover; the fire has come upon him, in his sleep, and having lost his horse, he has been driven to save himself under that fresh hide of buffaloe.*No bad invention when powder and flint were wanting to kindle a ring! I warrant me, now, this is a clever youth, and one that it would be safe to journey with! I will speak to him kindly, for anger can at least serve no turn of ours. My brother is welcome, again," using the language which the other understood; "the Tetons have been smoking him, as they would a raccoon."

The young Pawnee roll'd his eye over the place, as if he were examining the terrific danger from which he had just escaped, but he disdained to betray the smallest emotion, at its imminency. His brow contracted as he answered to the remark of the trapper, by saying—

"A Teton is a dog. When the Pawnee war-whoop is in their ears, the whole nation howls."

"It is true. The imps are on our trail, and I am glad to meet a warrior with the tomahawk in his hand, who does not love them. Will my brother lead my children to his village? If the Siouxes follow on our path, my young men shall help him to strike them."

The young Pawnee turned his eyes from one to another of the strangers, in a keen scrutiny, before he saw fit to answer so important an interrogatory. His examination of the males was short and apparently satisfactory. But his gaze was fastened long and admiringly, as in their former interview, on the surpassing and unwonted beauty of a being so fair and so unknown as Inez. Though his glance wandered, for moments, from her countenance to the more intelligible and yet extraordinary charms of Ellen, it did not fail to return promptly, to the study of a creature, who, in the view of his unpractised eye and untutored imagination, was formed with all that perfection, with which the youthful poet is apt to endow the glowing images of his brain. Nothing so fair, so ideal, so every way worthy to reward the courage and self devotion of a warrior had ever before been encountered on the Prairies, and the young brave appeared to be deeply and intuitively sensible to the influence of so rare a model of the loveliness of the sex. Perceiving, however, that his gaze gave uneasiness to the subject of his admiration, he withdrew his eyes, and laying his hand, impressively, on his chest, he, modestly, answered—

"My father shall be welcome. The young men of my nation shall hunt with his sons; Chiefs shall smoke with the grey head. The Pawnee girls will sing in the ears of his daughters."

"And if we meet the Tetons?"—demanded the trapper, who wished to understand, thoroughly, the more important conditions of this new alliance.

"The enemy of the Big-knives shall feel the blow of the Pawnee."

"It is well. Now let my brother and I meet in Council, that we may not go on a crooked path, but that our road to his village may be like the flight of the pigeons."

The young Pawnee made a significant gesture of assent, and followed the other a little apart, in order to be removed from all danger of interruption from the reckless Paul, or the abstracted naturalist. Their conference was short, but, as it was conducted in the sententious manner of the natives, it served to make each of the parties acquainted with all the necessary information of the other. When they rejoined their associates the old man saw fit to explain a portion of what had passed between them, as follows—

"Ay, I was not mistaken," he said, "this good looking young warrior,

for good looking and noble looking he is, though a little horrified
perhaps with paint,—this good looking youth, then, tells me he is out
on the scout for these very Tetons. His party was not strong enough to
strike the devils, who are down from their towns in great numbers to
hunt the buffaloe, and runners have gone to the Pawnee villages for
aid. It would seem that this lad is a fearless boy, for he has been
hanging on their skirts alone, until like ourselves he was driven to the
grass for a cover. But he tells me more, my men, and what I am
mainly sorry to hear, which is, that the cunning Mahtoree, instead of
going to blows with the squatter has become his friend, and that both
broods, red and white, are on our heels, and outlying around this
very burning plain to circumvent us to our destruction."

"How knows he all this to be true?" demanded Middleton.

"Anan!"

"In what manner does he know that these things are so?"

"In what manner! Do you think news-papers and town criers are
needed to tell a scout what is doing on the Prairies, as they are in the
bosom of the States. No gossiping woman, who hurries from house to
house to spread evil of her neighbor, can carry tidings with her tongue,
so fast as these people will spread their meaning, by signs and warnings that they alone understand. 'Tis their l'arning, and what is better,
it is got in the open air, and not within the walls of a school. I tell you,
Captain, that what he says is true."

"For that matter," said Paul, "I'm ready to swear to it. It is reasonable,
and therefore it must be true."

"And well you might, lad; well you might. He furthermore declares
that my old eyes, for once, were true to me, and that the river lies,
hereaway, at about the distance of half a league. You see the fire has
done most of its work in that quarter, and our path is clouded in
smoke. He also agrees that it is needful to wash our trail in water. Yes,
we must put that river atween us and the Sioux eyes, and then by the
favor of the Lord, not forgetting our own industry, we may gain the
village of the Loups."

"Words will not forward us a foot," said Middleton; "let us move."

The old man assented, and the party once more prepared to renew
its route. The Pawnee threw the skin of the buffaloe over his shoulder,
and led the advance, casting many a stolen glance behind him, as he
proceeded, in order to fix his gaze on the extraordinary, and, to him,
unaccountable loveliness of the unconscious Inez.

An hour sufficed to bring the fugitives to the bank of the stream,
which was one of the hundred rivers that serve to conduct, through

the mighty arteries of the Missouri and Mississippi, the waters of that vast and still uninhabited region to the ocean. The river was not deep, but its current was troubled and rapid. The flames had scorched the earth to its very margin, and as the warm steams of the fluid mingled, in the cooler air of the morning, with the smoke of the raging conflagration, most of its surface was wrapped in a mantle of moving vapour. The trapper pointed out the circumstance with pleasure, saying as he assisted Inez to dismount on the margin of the water course—

"The knaves have outwitted themselves! I am far from certain that I should not have fired the Prairie to have got the benefit of this very smoke to hide our movements, had not the heartless imps saved us the trouble. I've known such things done in my day, and done with success. Come, lady; put your tender foot upon the ground, for a fearful time has it been to one of your breeding and skeary qualities. Ahs! me: what have I not known the young, and the delicate, and the virtuous and the modest to undergo, in my time, among the horrifications and circumventions of Indian warfare!—Come, it is a short quarter of a mile to the other bank, and then our trail, at least, will be broken."

Paul had by this time assisted Ellen to dismount, and he now stood looking with rueful eyes at the naked banks of the river. Neither tree nor shrub grew along its borders, with the exception, of here and there, a solitary thicket of low bushes, from among which it would not have been an easy matter to have found a dozen stems of a size sufficient to make an ordinary walking-stick.

"Harkee, old trapper," the moody looking bee-hunter exclaimed; "it is very well to talk of the other side of this ripple of a river or brook or whatever you may call it, but in my judgement it would be a smart rifle that would throw its lead across it, that is to any detriment to Indian, or deer."

"That it would, that it would; though I carry a piece here, that has done its work, in time of need, at as great a distance."

"And do you mean to shoot Ellen, and the Captain's lady, across or do you intend them to go trout fashion with their mouths under water?"

"Is this river too deep to be forded?" asked Middleton, who like Paul began to consider the impossibility of transporting her whose safety he valued more than his own to the opposite shore.

"When the mountains above, feed it with their torrents, it is as you see a swift and powerful stream. Yet have I crossed its sandy bed, in my time, without wetting a knee. But we have the Sioux horses, I warrant me, that the kicking imps will swim like so many deer."

"Old trapper," said Paul, thrusting his fingers into his mop of a head, as was usual with him, when any difficulty confounded his philosophy, "I have swam like a fish, in my day and I can do it again, when there is need; nor do I much regard the weather. But I question if you get Nelly to sit a horse, with this water whirling like a mill-race before her eyes—besides it is manifest the thing is not to be done dry shod."

"Ah! the lad is right! We must to our inventions, therefore, or the river cannot be crossed." Cutting the discourse short, he turned to the Pawnee, and explained to him the difficulty which existed in relation to the women. The young warrior listened gravely, and throwing the buffaloe skin from his shoulder he immediately commenced, assisted by the occasional aid of the understanding old man, the preparations necessary to effect this desirable object.

The hide was soon drawn into the shape of an umbrella top or an inverted parachute, by thongs of deer-skin, with which both the laborers were well provided. A few light sticks served to keep the parts from collapsing or falling in.* When this simple and natural expedient was arranged, it was placed on the water, the Indian making a sign that it was ready to receive its freight. Both Inez and Ellen hesitated to trust themselves in a bark of so frail a construction, nor would Middleton or Paul consent that they should do so, until each had assured himself by actual experiment that the vessel was capable of sustaining a load much heavier than it was destined to receive. Then, indeed, their scruples were reluctantly overcome, and the skin was made to receive its precious burthen.

"Now, leave the Pawnee to be the pilot," said the trapper, "my hand is not so steady as it used to be, but he has limbs like toughened hickory. Leave all to the wisdom of the Pawnee."

The husband and lover could not well do otherwise, and they were fain to become, deeply interested it is true, but passive spectators of this primitive species of ferrying. The Pawnee selected the beast of Mahtoree, from among the three horses, with a readiness that proved he was far from being ignorant of the properties of that noble animal, and throwing himself upon its back, he rode into the margin of the river. Thrusting an end of his lance into the hide, he bore the light vessel up against the stream, and giving his steed the rein, they push'd boldly into the current. Middleton and Paul followed, pressing as nigh the bark, as prudence would at all warrant. In this manner, the young warrior bore his precious cargo to the opposite bank, in perfect safety, without the slightest inconvenience to the passengers, and with a steadiness and celerity which proved that both horse and rider were not unused to the operation. When the shore was gained, the young Indian undid his work, threw the skin over his shoulder, plac'd the sticks under his arm, and returned without speaking, to transfer the remainder of the party, in a similar manner, to what was very justly considered the safer side of the river.

"Now, friend Doctor," said the old man, when he saw the Indian plunging into the river a second time, "do I know there is faith in yonder red-skin. He is a good-looking, ay, and an honest looking youth, but the winds of heaven are not more deceitful than these savages when the devil has fairly beset them. Had the Pawnee been a Teton, or one of them heartless Mingos that used to be prowling through the woods of York, a time back, that is, some sixty years agone, we should have seen his back and not his face turned towards us. My heart had its misgivings when I saw the lad choose the better horse, for it would be as easy to leave us, with that beast, as it would for a nimble pigeon to part company from a flock of noisy and heavy winged crows. But you see, the truth is in the boy, and make a red-skin once your friend he is yours so long as you deal honestly by him."

"What may be the distance to the sources of this stream?" demanded Doctor Battius, whose eyes were rolling over the whirling eddies of the current, with a very portentous expression of doubt. "At what distance may its secret springs be found?"

"That may be as the weather proves. I warrant me your legs would be a-weary before you had followed its bed into the Rocky Mountains, but then there are seasons when it might be done without wetting a foot."

"And in what particular divisions of the year do these periodical seasons occur?"

"He that passes this spot a few months from this time, will find that foaming watercourse a desert of drifting sand."

The naturalist pondered deeply. Like most others who are not endowed with a superfluity of physical fortitude, the worthy man had found the danger of passing the river, in so simple a manner, magnifying itself, in his eyes, so rapidly as the moment of adventure approached, that he actually contemplated the desperate effort of going round the river in order to escape the hazard of crossing it. It may not be necessary to dwell on the incredible ingenuity with which terror will at any time, prop a tottering argument. The worthy Obed had gone over the whole subject with commendable diligence, and had just arrived at the consoling conclusion that there was nearly as much glory in discerning the hidden sources of so considerable a stream, as in adding a plant, or an insect, to the lists of the learned, when the Pawnee reach'd the shore for the second time. The old man took his seat with the utmost deliberation in the vessel of skin (so soon as it had been duly arranged for his reception) and having carefully disposed of Hector, between his legs he beckoned to his companion to occupy the third place.

The naturalist plac'd a foot in the frail vessel, as an elephant will try a bridge, or a horse is often seen to make a similar experiment before he will trust the whole of his corporeal treasure on the dreaded flat, and then withdrew, just as the old man believed he was about to seat himself.

"Venerable venator," he said, mournfully, "this is a most unscientific bark! there is an inward monitor which bids me distrust its security!"

"Anan!" said the old man, who was pinching the ears of the hound, as a father would play with the same members in a favorite child.

"I incline not to this irregular mode of experimenting on fluids. The vessel has neither form, nor proportions."

"It is not as handsomely turned as I have seen a canoe in birchen bark, but comfort may be taken in a wigwam as well as in a Palace."

"It is impossible that any vessel constructed on principles so repugnant to science can be safe. This tub, venerable hunter, will never reach the opposite shore in safety!"

"You are a witness of what it has done."

"Ay; but it was an anomaly in prosperity. If exceptions were to be taken as rules, in the government of things, the human race would speedily be plunged in the abysses of ignorance. Venerable trapper, this expedient in which you would repose your safety is, in the annals of regular inventions, what a lusus naturæ may be termed in the lists of Natural History—a monster."

How much longer Doctor Battius might have felt disposed to prolong the discourse it is difficult to say, for in addition to the powerful personal considerations which induced him to procrastinate an experiment which was certainly not without its dangers, the pride of reason was beginning to sustain him in the discussion. But fortunately for the credit of the old man's forbearance, when the naturalist reach'd the word with which he terminated his last speech, a sound arose on the air, that seem'd a sort of supernatural echo to the idea itself. The young Pawnee, who had awaited the termination of the incomprehensible discussion with grave and characteristic patience, raised his head, and listened to the unknown cry, like a stag whose mysterious faculties had detected the footsteps of the distant hounds in the gale. The trapper and the Doctor were not, however, entirely so uninstructed as to the nature of the extraordinary sounds. The latter recognized in them, the well known voice of his own beast, and he was about to rush up the little bank which confined the current, with all the longings of strong affection, when Asinus himself, galloped into view, at no great distance, urged to the unnatural gait, by the impatient and brutal Weucha, who bestrode him.

The eyes of the Teton and those of the fugitives met. The former raised a long, loud and piercing yell in which the notes of exultation were fearfully blended with those of warning. The signal served for a finishing blow to the discussion on the merits of the bark, the Doctor stepping as promptly to the side of the old man, as if a mental mist had been miraculously removed from his eyes. In another instant the steed of the young Pawnee was struggling with the torrent.

The utmost strength of the horse was needed to urge the fugitives, beyond the flight of arrows that came sailing through the air at the next moment. The cry of Weucha had brought fifty of his comrades to the shore, but fortunately among them all, there was not one of a rank sufficient to entitle him to the privilege of bearing a fusee. One half the stream, however, was not passed, before the form of Mahtoree, himself, was seen on its bank and an ineffectual discharge of fire arms announced the rage and disappointment of the chief. More than once, the trapper had raised his rifle, as if about to try its power, on his enemies, but he as often, lowered it, without firing. The eyes of the Pawnee warrior glared like those of the cougar, at the sight of so many of the hostile tribe, and he answered the impotent effort of their chief, by tossing a hand into the air in contempt, and raising the war-cry of his nation. The challenge was too taunting to be endured. The Tetons dashed into the stream, in a body, and the river became dotted with the dark forms of beasts and riders.

There was now a fearful struggle for the friendly bank. As the Dahcotahs advanced with beasts which had not, like that of the Pawnee, expended their strength in former efforts, and as they moved unincumbered by any thing but their riders, the speed of the pursuers greatly outstripped that of the fugitives. The trapper who clearly comprehended the whole danger of their situation, calmly turned his eyes from the Tetons to his young Indian associate, in order to examine whether the resolution of the latter began to falter as the former lessened the distance between them. Instead of betraying fear, however, or any of that concern which might so readily have been excited by the peculiarity of his risque, the brow of the young warrior contracted to a look which indicated high and deadly hostility.

"Do you greatly value life, friend Doctor?" demanded the old man, with a sort of philosophical calmness which made the question doubly appalling to his companion.

"Not for itself," returned the naturalist sipping some of the water of the river from the hollow of his hand, in order to clear his husky throat. "Not for itself. But exceedingly, inasmuch as Natural History has so deep a stake in my existence. Therefore—"

"Ay," resumed the other who mused too deeply to dissect the ideas of the Doctor with his usual sagacity, "tis in truth the history of natur', and a base and craven feeling it is! Now is life as precious to this young Pawnee as to any Governor in the States, and he might save it, or at least stand some chance of saving it, by letting us go down the stream, and yet you see he keeps his faith, manfully and like an Indian warrior. For myself, I am old, and willing to take the fortune that the Lord may see fit to give, nor do I conceit that you are of much benefit to mankind, and it is a crying shame if not a sin, that so fine a youth as this should lose his scalp for two beings so worthless as ourselves. I am therefore disposed, provided that it shall prove agreeable to you, to tell the lad to make the best of his way, and to leave us to the mercy of the Tetons."

"I repel the proposition, as repugnant to nature, and as treason to science!" exclaimed the alarmed naturalist. "Our progress is miraculous and as this admirable invention moves with so wonderful a facility a few more minutes will serve to bring us to land."

The old man regarded him, intently, for an instant and shaking his head, he said—

"Lord, what a thing is fear! it transforms the creatur's of the world and the craft of man, making that which is ugly, seemly in our eyes, and that which is beautiful, unsightly! Lord, Lord, what a thing is fear!"

A termination was, however, put to the discussion by the increasing interest of the chace. The horses of the Dahcotahs had, by this time, gained the middle of the current, and their riders, were already filling the air with yells of triumph. At this moment, Middleton and Paul, who had led the females to a little thicket, appeared again on the margin of the stream, menacing their enemies with the rifle.

"Mount, mount," shouted the trapper, the instant he beheld them. "Mount and fly, if you value those who lean on you for help. Mount, and leave us in the hands of the Lord."

"Stoop your head, old trapper," returned the voice of Paul. "Down with ye both into your nest. The Teton Devil is in your line—down with your heads, and make way for a Kentucky bullet."

The old man turned his head, and saw that the eager Mahtoree, who preceded his party some distance, had brought himself nearly in a line with the bark and the bee-hunter, who stood perfectly ready to execute his hostile threat. Bending his body low, the rifle was discharged and the swift lead whizzed harmlessly past him, on its more distant errand. But the eye of the Teton chief was not less quick and certain than that of his enemy. He threw himself from his horse, the moment preceding the report, and sunk into the water. The beast snorted with terror and anguish, throwing half his form out of the river in a desperate plunge. Then he was seen drifting away in the torrent, and dying the turbid waters with his blood.

The Teton chief soon reappeared on the surface, and understanding the nature of his loss, he swam with vigorous strokes to the nearest of the young men, who relinquished his steed, as a matter of course, to so renowned a warrior. The incident, however, created a confusion in the whole of the Dahcotah band, who appeared to await the intention of their leader, before they renewed their efforts to reach the shore. In the mean time, the vessel of skin had reach'd the land, and the fugitives were once more united on the margin of the river.

The savages were now swimming about in indecision, as a flock of pigeons is often seen to hover, in confusion, after receiving a heavy discharge into its leading column, apparently hesitating on the risk of storming a bank so formidably defended. The well known precaution of Indian warfare prevailed, and Mahtoree, admonished by his recent adventure, led his warriors back to the shore from which they had come, in order to relieve their beasts, which were already becoming unruly.

"Now, mount you, with the tender ones, and ride for yonder hillock," said the trapper, "beyond it, you will find another stream, into which you must enter, and turning to the sun follow its bed for a mile, until you reach a high and sandy plain. There will I meet you. Go. Mount. This Pawnee youth and I, and my stout friend the Physicianer, who is a desperate warrior are men enough to keep the bank, seeing that show and not use is all that is needed."

Middleton and Paul saw no use in wasting their breath in remonstrances against this proposal. Glad to know that their rear was to be covered even in this imperfect manner, they hastily got their horses in motion and soon disappeared on the required route. Some twenty or thirty minutes succeeded this movement, before the Tetons on the opposite shore seem'd inclined to enter on any new enterprise. Mahtoree was distinctly visible in the midst of his warriors, issuing his mandates, and betraying his desire for vengeance, by occasionally shaking an arm in the direction of the fugitives, but no step was taken which appeared to threaten any further act of immediate hostility. At length a yell arose among the savages which announced the occurrence of some fresh event. Then Ishmael and his sluggish sons were seen in the distance, and soon the whole of the united force mov'd down to the very limits of the stream. The squatter proceeded to examine the position of his enemies, with his usual coolness, and, as if to try the power of his rifle, he sent a bullet among them with a force sufficient to do execution even at the distance at which he stood.

"Now let us depart!" exclaimed Obed, endeavoring to catch a furtive glimpse of the lead, which he fancied was whizzing at his very ear, "we have maintained the bank, in a gallant manner, for a sufficient length of time, quite as much military skill is to be displayed in a retreat as in an advance."

The old man cast a look behind him, and seeing that the equestrians had reached the cover of the hill, he made no objections to the proposal. The remaining horse was given to the Doctor with instructions to pursue the course just taken by Middleton and Paul. When the naturalist was mounted and in full retreat, the trapper and the young Pawnee stole from the spot, in such a manner as to leave their enemies some time in doubt as to their movements. Instead, however, of proceeding across the plain towards the hill, a route on which they must have been in open view, they took a shorter path, covered by the formation of the ground, and intersected the little water course at the point where Middleton had been directed to leave it, and just in season to join his party. The Doctor had used so much diligence in the retreat as to have already overtaken his friends, and of course all the fugitives were again assembled.

The trapper, now look'd about him for some convenient spot, where the whole party might halt, as he expressed it for some five or six hours.

"Halt!" exclaimed the Doctor, when the alarming proposal reached his ears, "venerable hunter, it would seem that on the contrary, many days should be passed in industrious flight!"

Middleton and Paul were both of his opinion, and each in his particular manner expressed as much.

The old man heard them with patience, but shook his head like one who was unconvinced, and then answered all their arguments, in one general and positive reply.

"Why should we fly?" he asked. "Can the legs of mortal men out strip the speed of horses! Do you think the Tetons will lie down and sleep, or will cross the water and nose for our trail. Thanks be to the Lord we have washed it well in this stream, and if we leave the place with discretion and wisdom we may yet throw them off its track. But a Prairie is not a wood. *There* a man may journey long, caring for nothing but the prints his moccasin leaves, whereas in these open plains, a runner, plac'd on yonder hill for instance, could see far on every side of him like a hovering hawk, looking down on his prey. No, no, night must come, and darkness be upon us afore we leave this spot. But listen to the words of the Pawnee, he is a lad of spirit, and I warrant me, many is the hard race that he has run with the Sioux bands! Does my brother think our trail is long enough?" he demanded in the Indian tongue.

"Is a Teton a fish, that he can see it in the river?"

"But my young men think we should stretch it, until it reaches across the Prairie."

"Mahtoree has eyes—he will see it."

"What does my brother counsel?"

The young warrior studied the heavens a moment and appeared to hesitate. He mused some time with himself, and then he replied like one whose opinion was fixed.

"The Dahcotahs are not asleep," he said, "we must lie in the grass."

"Ah! the lad is of my mind," said the old man, briefly explaining the opinion of his companion to his white friends. Middleton was obliged to acquiesce, and, as it was confessedly dangerous to remain upon their feet, each one set about assisting in the means to be adopted for their security. Inez and Ellen were quickly bestowed, beneath the warm and not uncomfortable shelter of the buffaloe skins, which formed a thick covering, and tall grass was drawn over the place, in such a manner as to evade any examination from a common eye. Paul and the Pawnee fettered the beasts and cast them to the earth, where after supplying them with food, they were also left concealed in the fog of the Prairie. No time was lost when these several arrangements were completed, before each of the others sought a place of rest and concealment, and then the plain appeared again deserted to its solitude.

The old man had advised his companions of the absolute necessity of their continuing for hours in this concealment. All their hopes of escape depended on the success of the artifice. If they might elude the cunning of their pursuers, by this simple and therefore less suspected expedient, they could renew their flight as the evening approached, and by changing their course, the chance of final success would be greatly increased. Influenced by these momentous considerations, the whole party lay, musing on their situation, until thoughts grew weary, and sleep finally settled on them all, one after another.

The deepest silence had prevailed for hours, when the quick ears of the trapper and the Pawnee were startled, by a faint cry of surprise from Inez. Springing to their feet like men who were about to struggle for their lives, they found the vast plain, the rolling swells, the little hillock, and the scattered thickets covered in one white dazzling sheet of snow.

"The Lord have mercy on ye all!" exclaimed the old man, regarding the prospect with a rueful eye, "now, Pawnee, do I know the reason why you studied the clouds so closely; but it is too late, it is too late. A squirrel would leave his trail on this light coating of the 'arth! Ha! there come the imps to a certainty. Down with ye all, down with ye, your chance is but small, and yet it must not be wilfully cast away."

The whole party was instantly concealed, again, though many an anxious and stolen glance was directed through the tops of the grass on the movements of their enemies. At the distance of half a mile, the Teton band was seen riding in a circuit which was gradually contracting itself, and evidently closing upon the very spot where the fugitives lay. There was but little difficulty in solving the mystery of this movement. The snow had fallen in time to assure them, that those they sought were in their rear, and they were now employed with the unwearied perseverance and patience of Indian warriors in circling the certain boundaries of their place of concealment.

Each minute added to the jeopardy of the fugitives. Paul and

Middleton deliberately prepared their rifles, and as the occupied Mahtoree came, at length, within fifty feet of them, keeping his eyes riveted on the grass through which he rode, they levelled them together and pulled the triggers. The effort was answered by the mere snapping of the locks.

"Enough," said the old man, rising with dignity, "I have cast away the priming, for certain death would follow your rashness. Now, let us meet our fates like men. Cringing and complaining find no favor in Indian eyes."

His appearance was greeted by a yell, that spread far and wide over the plain, and in a moment a hundred savages were seen riding madly to the spot. Mahtoree received his prisoners with great self-restraint, though gleams of fierce joy broke through his clouded brow, and the heart of Middleton grew cold as he caught the expression of that eye, which the chief turned on the nearly insensible but still lovely Inez.

The exultation of receiving the white captives was so great, as, for a time to throw the dark and immovable form of their young Indian companion entirely out of view. He stood apart, disdaining to turn an eye on his enemies, as motionless, as if he were frozen in that attitude of dignity and composure. But when a little time had passed, even this secondary object attracted the attention of the Tetons. Then it was that the trapper first learned by the shout of triumph and the long drawn yell of delight, which burst at once from a hundred throats, as well as by the terrible name which fill'd the air, that his youthful friend was no other than that redoubtable and hitherto invincible warrior, Hard-Heart.

CHAPTER XXV.

"What, are ancient pistol and
You friends, yet?"

Henry V, II.i.3-4.

THE curtain of our imperfect drama must fall to rise upon another scene. The time is advanced several days; during which very material changes had occurred in the situation of the actors. The hour is noon, and the place an elevated plain, that rose, at no great distance from the water, somewhat abruptly from a fertile bottom which stretched along the margin of one of the numberless water-courses of that region. The river took its rise near the base of the Rocky Mountains, and after washing a vast extent of plain, it mingled its waters with a still larger stream, to become finally lost in the turbid current of the Missouri.

The landscape was changed materially for the better, though the hand which had impressed so much of the desert on the surrounding region, had laid a portion of its power on this spot. The appearance of vegetation was, however, less discouraging than in the more sterile wastes of the rolling Prairies. Clusters of trees were scattered in greater profusion, and a long outline of ragged forest marked the northern boundary of the view. Here and there on the bottom, were to be seen the evidences of a hasty and imperfect culture of such indigenous vegetables as were of a quick growth, and which were known to flourish, without the aid of art, in deep and alluvial soils. On the very edge of what might be called the table-land, were pitch'd the hundred lodges of a horde of wandering Siouxes.*These light tenements were arranged without the least attention to order. Proximity to the water seemed to be the only consideration which had been consulted in their disposition, nor had even this important convenience been always regarded. While most of the lodges stood along the brow of the plain, many were to be seen at greater distances, occupying such places, as had first pleased the capricious eyes of their untutored owners. The encampment was not military or in the slightest degree protected from surprise by its position or defences. It was open on every side, and on every side as accessible as any other point in those wastes, if the imperfect and natural obstruction offered by the river, be excepted. In short, the place bore the appearance of having been tenanted longer than its occupants had originally intended, while it was not wanting in the signs of readiness for a hasty or even a compelled departure.

This was the temporary encampment of that portion of his people who had long been hunting under the direction of Mahtoree, on those grounds which separated the stationary abodes of his nation from those of the warlike tribes of the Pawnees. The lodges were tents of skin, high, conical and of the most simple and primitive construction. The shield, the quiver, the lance and the bow of its master were to be seen suspended from a light post before the opening, or door of each habitation; the different domestic implements of his one, two or three wives, as the brave was of greater or lesser renown, were carelessly thrown at its side, and, here and there, the round, full, patient countenance of an infant might be found, peeping from its comfortless wrappers of bark, as, suspended by a deer skin thong, from the same post, it rocked in the passing air. Children of a larger growth were tumbling over each other in piles, the males, even at that early age, making themselves distinguished for that species of domination, which, in after life, was to mark the vast distinction between the sexes. Youths were on the bottom, essaying their juvenile powers in curbing the wild steeds of their fathers, while here and there a truant girl was to be seen, stealing from her labors, to admire their fierce and impatient daring.

Thus far the picture was the daily exhibition of an encampment confident in its security. But immediately in front of the lodges was a gathering that seemed to forbode some movements of more than usual interest. A few of the withered and remorseless crones of the band were clustering together, in readiness to lend their fell voices if needed, to aid in exciting their descendants to an exhibition, which their depraved tastes covetted, as the luxurious Roman dame witnessed the struggles and the agony of the gladiator. The men were subdivided into groupes, assorted according to the deeds and reputations of the several individuals of whom they were composed.

They, who were of that equivocal age which admitted them to the hunts while their discretion was still too doubtful to permit them to be trusted on the war-path, hung around the skirts of the whole, catching, from the fierce models before them, that gravity of demeanour and restraint of manner, which in time, was to become so deeply engrafted in their own characters. A few of a still older class, and who had heard the whoop in anger, were a little more presuming, pressing nigher to the chiefs, though far from presuming to mingle in their Councils, sufficiently distinguished by being permitted to catch the wisdom which fell from lips so venerated. The ordinary warriors of the band were still less diffident, not hesitating to mingle among the chiefs of lesser note, though far from assuming the right to dispute the sentiments of any established brave, or to call in question the prudence of measures that were recommended by the more gifted counsellors of the nation.

Among the chiefs themselves there was a singular compound of exterior. They were divided into two classes; those who were mainly indebted for their influence to physical causes and to deeds in arms, and those who had become more distinguished rather for their wisdom than for their services in the field. The former was by far the most numerous and the most important class. These were men of stature and mien, whose stern countenances were often rendered doubly imposing by those evidences of their valour which had been roughly traced on their lineaments by the hands of their enemies. That class which had gained its influence by a moral ascendancy was extremely limited. They were uniformly to be distinguished by the quick and lively expression of their eyes, by the air of distrust that marked their movements, and occasionally by the vehemence of their utterance in those sudden outbreakings of the mind, by which their present consultations were from time to time, distinguished.

In the very centre of a ring formed by these chosen counsellors, was to be seen the person of the disquieted, but seemingly calm, Mahtoree. There was a conjunction of all the several qualities of the others in his person and character. Mind as well as matter had contributed to establish his authority. His scars were as numerous and deep, as those of the whitest head in his nation; his limbs were in their greatest vigor; his courage at its fullest height. Endowed with this rare combination of moral and physical influence, the keenest eye in all that assembly was wont to lower before his threatening glance. Courage and cunning had established his ascendancy, and it had been rendered, in some degree sacred by time. He knew so well how to unite the powers of reason and force, that in a state of society which admitted of a greater display of his energies, the Teton would in all probability have been both a conqueror and a despot.

A little apart from the gathering of the band, was to be seen a set of beings of an entirely different origin. Taller and far more muscular in their persons, the lingering vestiges of their Saxon and Norman ancestry were yet to be found beneath the swarthy complexions, which had been bestowed by an American sun. It would have been a curious investigation, for one skilled in such an inquiry, to have traced those points of difference by which the offspring of the most western European was still to be distinguished from the descendant of the most remote Asiatic, now that the two, in the revolutions of the world, were approximating in their habits, their residence and not a little in their characters. The groupe of whom we write was composed of the family of the squatter. They stood, indolent, lounging and inert, as usual when no immediate demand was made on their dormant energies, clustered in front of some four or five habitations of skin, for which they were indebted to the hospitality of their Teton allies. The terms of their unexpected confederation were sufficiently explained, by the presence of the horses and domestic cattle, that were quietly grazing on the bottom beneath, under the jealous eyes of the spirited Hetty. The wagons were drawn about the lodges in a sort of irregular barrier, which at once manifested, that their confidence was not entirely restored, while, on the other hand, their policy or indolence prevented any very positive exhibition of distrust. There was a singular union of passive enjoyment and of dull curiosity slumbering in every dull countenance, as each of the party stood leaning on his rifle, regarding the movements of the Sioux conference. Still no sign of expectation or interest escaped from the youngest among them, the whole appearing to emulate the most phlegmatic of their savage allies, in an exhibition of patience. They rarely spoke; and when they did, it was in some short and contemptuous remark, which served to put the physical superiority of a white man, and that of an Indian, in a sufficiently striking point of view. In short, the family of Ishmael appeared now, to be in the plenitude of an enjoyment which depended on inactivity, but which was not entirely free from certain confused glimmerings of a perspective, in which their security stood in some little danger of a rude interruption from Teton treachery. Abiram alone, formed a solitary exception to this state of equivocal repose.

After a life passed in the commission of a thousand mean and insignificant villainies, the mind of the kidnapper had become hardy enough to attempt the desperate adventure which has been laid before the reader, in the course of the narrative. His influence over the bolder, but less active spirit of Ishmael was far from great, and had not the latter been suddenly expelled from a fertile bottom of which he had taken possession with intent to keep it, without much deference to the forms of law, he would never have succeeded in enlisting the husband of his sister, in an enterprise that required so much decision and forethought. Their original success and subsequent disappointment have been seen, and Abiram now sat apart, plotting the means by which he might secure to himself the advantages of his undertaking, which he perceived were each moment becoming more uncertain, through the open admiration of Mahtoree, for the innocent subject of his villainy. We shall leave him to his vacillating and confused expedients in order to pass to the description of certain other personages in the drama.

There was still another corner of the picture that was occupied. On a little bank, at the extreme right of the encampment, lay the forms of Middleton and Paul. Their limbs were painfully bound with thongs, cut from the skin of a bison, while by a sort of refinement in cruelty, they were so placed that each could see a reflection of his own misery in that of his neighbor. Within a dozen yards of them, a post was set firmly in the ground, and against it was bound the light and Apollo-like person of Hard-Heart. Between the two stood the trapper, deprived of his rifle, his pouch and his horn, but otherwise left in a sort of contemptuous liberty. Some five or six young warriors however with quivers at their backs and long tough bows dangling from their shoulders, who stood with grave watchfullness at no great distance from the spot, sufficiently proclaimed how fruitless any attempt to escape on the part of one so aged and so feeble might prove. Unlike the other spectators of the important conference, these individuals were engaged in a discourse, that for them contained an interest of its own.

"Captain," said the bee-hunter, with an expression of comical concern that no misfortune could repress in one of his buoyant feelings, "do you really find that accursed strap of untanned leather cutting into your shoulder, or is it only the tickling in my own arm, that I feel?"

"When the spirit suffers so deeply, the body is insensible to pain," returned the more refined, though scarcely so spirited Middleton, "would to Heaven that some of my trusty artillerists might fall upon this accursed encampment!"

"You might as well wish that these Teton lodges were so many hives of hornets, and that the insects would come forth and battle with yonder tribe of half-naked savages." Then chuckling with his own conceit, the bee-hunter turned away from his companion, and sought a momentary relief from his misery, by imagining that so wild an idea might be realized, and fancying the manner in which the attack would upset even the well established patience of an Indian.

Middleton was glad to be silent, but the old man who had listened to their words drew a little nigher, and continued the discourse.

"Here is likely to be a marciless and a hellish business!" he said shaking his head in a manner to prove that even his experience was at a loss for a remedy in so trying a dilemma. "Our Pawnee friend is already staked for the torture, and I well know by the eye and the countenance of the Great Sioux, that he is leading on the temper of his people to further enormities."

"Harkee, old trapper," said Paul, writhing in his bonds, to catch a glimpse of the other's melancholy face—"you ar' skilled in Indian tongues, and know somewhat of Indian deviltries. Go you to the council, and tell their chiefs in my name, that is to say in the name of Paul Hover of the State of Kentucky, that provided they will guarantee the safe return of one Ellen Wade into the States, they are welcome to take his scalp, when and in such manner as best suits their amusements; or, if-so-be, they will not trade on these conditions, you may throw in an hour or two of torture, beforehand, in order to sweeten the bargain to their damnable appetites."

"Ah! Lad, it is little that they would hearken to such an offer, knowing as they do, that you are already like a bear in a trap, as little able to fight as to fly. But be not downhearted; for the colour of a white man is sometimes his death warrant, among these far tribes of savages, and sometimes his shield. Though they love us not, cunning often ties their hands. Could the red nations work their will, trees would shortly be growing, again, on the plough'd fields of America, and woods would be whitened with christian bones. No one can doubt that, who knows the quality of the love which a red-skin bears a Pale face; but they have counted our numbers until their memories fail them, and they are not without their policy. Therefore, is our fate unsettled; but I fear me there is small hope left for the Pawnee!"

As the old man concluded, he walk'd slowly towards the subject of his latter observation, taking his post at no great distance from his side. Here he stood, observing such a silence and mien as became him to manifest to a chief so renowned and so situated as his captive associate. But the eye of Hard-Heart was fastened on the distance, and his whole air was that of one whose thoughts were entirely removed from the present scene.

"The Siouxes are in Council on my brother," the trapper at length observed, when he found that he could only attract the other's attention by speaking.

The young partizan turned his head, with a calm smile, as he answered—

"They are counting the scalps over the lodge of Hard-Heart!"

"No doubt, no doubt their tempers begin to mount as they remember the number of Tetons you have struck, and better would it be for you, now, had more of your days been spent in chasing the deer, and fewer on the war-path. Then some childless mother of this tribe, might take you in the place of her lost son, and your time would be fill'd in Peace."

"Does my father think that a warrior can ever die! The Master of Life does not open his hand to take away his gifts, again. When he wants his young men he calls them, and they go. But the red-skin he has once breathed on, lives forever."

"Ay, this is a more comfortable and a more humble faith than that which yonder heartless Teton harbors! There is something in these Loups, which opens my inmost heart to them. They seem to have the courage, ay, and the honesty, too, of the Delawares of the Hills. And this lad,—it is wonderful, it is very wonderful—but the age, and the eye, and the limbs are as if they might have been brothers! Tell me, Pawnee, have you ever, in your traditions heard of a Mighty People, who once lived on the shores of the Salt Lake, hard by the rising sun,—"

"The earth is white, by people of the colour of my father."

"Nay, nay, I speak not, now, of any strollers who have crept into the land to rob the lawful owners of their birth-right, but of a people who are, or rather were, what with natur' and what with paint, red as the berry on the bush."

"I have heard the old men say, that there were bands who hid themselves in the woods, under the rising sun, because they dared not come upon the open Prairies, to fight with men."

"Do not your traditions tell you of the greatest, the bravest, and the wisest nation of red-skins that the Wahcondah has ever breathed upon!"

Hard-Heart, raised his head with a loftiness and dignity that even his bonds could not repress, as he answered—

"Has age blinded my father, or does he see so many Siouxes, that he believes there are no longer any Pawnees!"

"Ah! such is mortal vanity and pride!" exclaimed the disappointed old man, in English. "Natur' is as strong in a red-skin, as in the bosom of a man of white gifts. Now would a Delaware conceit himself far mightier, than a Pawnee, just as a Pawnee boasts himself to be of the Princes of the 'arth. And so it was atween the Frenchers of the Canadas, and the red coated English that the King did use to send into the States, when States they were not, but outcrying and petitioning Provinces. They fout, and they fout, and what marvellous boastings did they give forth to the world of their own valor and victories, while both parties forgot to name the humble soldier of the land, who did the real service, but who as he was not privileged then to smoke at the Great Council Fire of his Nation, seldom heard of his deeds, after they were once bravely done."

When the old man had thus given vent to the nearly dormant but far from extinct Military Pride, that had so unconsciously led him into the very error he deprecated, his eye which had begun to quicken and glimmer with some of the ardor of his youth softened, and turned its anxious look on the devoted captive, whose countenance was also restored to its former cold look of abstraction and thought.

"Young warrior," he continued, in a voice that was growing tremulous, "I have never been father, or brother. The Wahcondah made me to live alone. He never tied my heart, to house or field, by the cords with which the men of my race are bound to their lodges; if he had I should not have journeyed so far and seen so much. But I have tarried long among a people, who liv'd in those woods you mention, and much reason did I find to imitate their courage and love their honesty. The Master of Life has made us all, Pawnee, with a feeling for our kind. I never was a father, but well do I know what is the love of one. You are like a lad, I valued,* and I had even begun to fancy that some of his blood might be in your veins. But, what matters that! You are a true man, as I know by the way in which you keep your faith, and honesty is a gift too rare to be forgotten. My heart yearns to you, boy, and gladly would I do you good."

The youthful warrior listened to the words which came from the lips of the other with a force and simplicity that established their truth, and he bow'd his head on his naked bosom in testimony of the respect with which he met the proffer. Then lifting his dark eye to the level of the view he seem'd to be, again, considering of things removed from every personal consideration. The trapper, who well knew how high the pride of a warrior would sustain him, in those moments he believed to be his last, awaited the pleasure of his young friend with a meekness and patience that he had acquired by his association with that remarkable race. At length the gaze of the Pawnee began to waver, and then quick, flashing glances were turned, from the countenance of the old man to the air, and from the air, to his deeply marked lineaments, again, as if the spirit which governed their movements was beginning to be troubled.

"Father," the young brave finally answered in a voice of confidence and kindness, "I have heard your words. They have gone in at my ears, and are now within me. The white headed Long-knife has no son, the Hard-Heart of the Pawnees is young, but he is already the oldest of his family. He found the bones of his father on the hunting grounds of the Osages, and he has sent them, to the Prairies of the Good Spirits. No doubt, the great Chief, his father, has seen them, and knows what is part of himself. But the Wahcondah will soon call to us both — you, because you have seen all that is to be seen in this country, and Hard-Heart, because he has need of a warrior who is young. There is not time for the Pawnee to show the Pale Face the duty that a son owes to his Father."

"Old as I am, and miserable and helpless as I now stand to what I once was, I may live to see the sun go down in the Prairie. Does my son expect to do as much?"

"The Tetons are counting the scalps on my lodge," returned the young chief with a smile whose melancholy was singularly illuminated by a gleam of triumph.

"And they find them many. Too many for the safety of its owner, while he is in their revengeful hands. My son is not a woman and he looks on the path he is about to travel with a steady eye. Has he nothing to whisper in the ears of his people, before he starts. These legs are old, but they may yet carry me to the forks of the Loup river."

"Tell them that Hard-Heart has tied a knot in his wampum for every Teton," burst from the lips of the captive, with that vehemence with which sudden passion is known to break through the barriers of artificial restraint. "If he meets one of them all, in the Prairie of the Master of Life, his heart will become Sioux!"

"Ah! that feeling would be a dangerous companion for a man with white gifts to start with on so solemn a journey!" muttered the old man in English. "This is not what the good Moravians said to the Councils of the Delawares, nor what is so often preach'd to the white-skins in the settlements though to the shame of the colour be it said, it is so little heeded. Pawnee, I love you, but being a Christian man, I cannot be the runner to bear such a message."

"If my father is afraid, that the Tetons will hear him, let him whisper it softly, to our old men."

"As for fear, young warrior, it is no more the shame of a Pale face than of a red-skin. The Wahcondah teaches us to love the life he gives; but it is, as men love their hunts, and their dogs and their carybines, and not with the doting that a mother looks upon her infant. The Master of Life will not have to speak aloud twice when he calls my name. I am as ready to answer to it, now, as I shall be to-morrow—or at any time, it may please his mighty will. But what is a warrior without his traditions! Mine forbid me to carry your words."

The chief made a dignified motion of assent, and here there was great danger that those feelings of confidence which had been so singularly awakened would as suddenly subside. But the heart of the old man had been too sensibly touched, through long dormant but still living recollections to break off the communication so rudely. He pondered for a minute, and then bending his look wistfully on his young associate, again, continued—

"Each warrior must be judged by his gifts. I have told my son what I cannot, but let him open his ears to what I can do. An elk shall not measure the Prairie much swifter than these old legs, if the Pawnee will give me a message that a white man may bear."

"Let the Pale face listen," returned the other, after hesitating a single instant longer, under a lingering sensation of his former disappointment. "He will stay here till the Siouxes have done counting the scalps of their dead warriors. He will wait until they have tried to cover the heads of eighteen Tetons with the skin of one Pawnee. Then he will open his eyes wide that he may see the place, where they bury the bones of a warrior."

"All this will I, and may I do, noble boy."

"He will mark the spot that he may know it."

"No fear, no fear that I shall forget the place;" interrupted the other, whose fortitude began to give way under so trying an exhibition of calmness and resignation.

"Then I know that my father, will go to my people. His head is gray, and his words will not be blown away with the smoke. Let him get on my lodge and call the name of Hard-Heart, aloud. No Pawnee will be deaf. Then let my father ask for the colt that has never been ridden, but which is sleeker than the buck and swifter than the elk."

"I understand you, boy, I understand you;" interrupted the attentive old man, "and what you say shall be done, ay, and well done too, or I'm but little skilled in the wishes of a dying Indian."

"And when my young men have given my father, the halter of that colt, he will lead him by a crooked path to the grave of Hard-Heart?"

"Will I! ay, that I will brave youth, though the winter covers these plains in banks of snow, and the sun is hidden as much by day as by night. To the head of the holy spot will I lead the beast, and place him with his eyes looking towards the setting sun."

"And my father will speak to him, and tell him that the master, who has fed him since he was foaled, has now need of him."

"That too will I do; though the Lord he knows that I shall hold discourse with a horse not with any vain conceit that my words will be understood but only to satisfy the cravings of Indian superstition. Hector, my pup, what think *you*, dog, of talking to a horse?"

"Let the gray-head speak to him with the tongue of a Pawnee," interrupted the young victim, perceiving that his companion had used an unknown language for the preceding speech.

"My son's will shall be done. And with these old hands, which I had hoped had nearly done with blood-shed, whether it be of man or beast will I slay the animal on your grave."

"It is good," returned the other, a gleam of satisfaction flitting across his features. "Hard-Heart will ride his horse to the blessed Prairies, and he will come before the Master of Life like a chief!"

The sudden and striking change which instantly occurred in the countenance of the Indian, caused the trapper to look aside, when he perceived, that the conference of the Siouxes had ended, and that Mahtoree, attended by one or two of the principal warriors, was deliberately approaching his intended victims.

CHAPTER XXVI.

"I am not prone to weeping as our sex
Commonly are. — "
— "But I have that honorable
Grief lodged here, which burns worse than
Tears drown."

The Winter's Tale, II.i. 108-09, 110-12.

WHEN within twenty feet of the prisoners the Tetons stopped, and their leader made a sign to the old man to draw nigh. The trapper obeyed, quitting the young Pawnee with a significant look, which was received as it was meant, for an additional pledge that he would never forget his promise. So soon as Mahtoree found that the other had stopped within reach of him, he stretch'd forth his arm, and laying a hand upon the shoulder of the attentive old man, he stood regarding him, a minute, with eyes that seem'd willing to penetrate the recesses of his most secret thoughts.

"Is a Pale face always made with two tongues?" he demanded, when he found, that, as usual with the subject of this examination, he was as little intimidated by his present frown, as mov'd by any apprehensions of the future.

"Honesty lies deeper than the skin."

"It is so. Now let my father hear me. Mahtoree has but one tongue, the gray-head, has many. They may be all straight and none of them forked. A Sioux is no more than a Sioux, but a Pale face is every thing! He can talk to the Pawnee, and the Konza and the Omahaw, and he can talk to his own people."

"Ay, there are linguisters in the settlements, that can do still more. But what profits it all. The Master of Life has an ear for every language!"

"The gray-head has done wrong. He has said one thing when he meant another. He has looked before him with his eyes, and behind him with his mind. He has ridden the horse of a Sioux too hard. He has been the friend of the Pawnee, and the enemy of my people."

"Teton, I am your prisoner. Though my words are white, they will not complain. Act your will."

"No; Mahtoree will not make a white hair, red. My father is free. The Prairie is open on every side of him. But before the gray-head turns his back on the Siouxes let him look well at them, that he may tell his own Chief how great is a Dahcotah."

"I am not in a hurry to go on my path. You see a man with a white head, and no woman, Teton; therefore shall I not run myself out of breath to tell the nations of the Prairie what the Siouxes are doing."

"It is good. My Father has smok'd with the chiefs at many Councils," returned Mahtoree, who now thought himself sufficiently sure of the other's favor to go more directly to his object. "Mahtoree will speak with the tongue, of his very dear friend and father. A young pale-face will listen when an old man of that nation opens his mouth. Go. My father will make what a poor Indian says, fit for a white ear."

"Speak aloud," said the trapper, who readily understood the metaphorical manner in which the Teton expressed a desire that he should become an interpreter of his words, into the English language; "speak, my young men, listen. Now Captain, and you, too, friend bee-hunter, prepare yourselves to meet the deviltries of this savage, with the stout hearts of white warriors. If you find yourselves giving way under his threats, just turn your eyes on that noble looking Pawnee, whose time is measured with a hand, as niggardly as that with which a trader in the towns gives forth the fruits of the Lord, inch by inch, in order to satisfy his covetousness. A single look at the boy, will set you both up, in resolution."

"My brother has turned his eyes on the wrong path," interrupted Mahtoree, with a complacency that betrayed how unwilling he was to offend his intended interpreter.

"The Dahcohtah will speak to my young men!"

"After he has sung in the ear of the 'flower of the pale faces.'"

"The Lord forgive the desperate villain!" exclaimed the old man in English. "There are none so tender, or so young, or so innocent as to escape his ravenous wishes. But hard words, and cold looks will profit nothing, therefore it will be wise to speak him fair. Let Mahtoree open his mouth."

"Would my father cry out, that the women and children should hear the wisdom of Chiefs! We will go into the lodge and whisper."

As the Teton ended he pointed significantly towards a tent, vividly emblazoned with the history of one of his own boldest and most commended exploits, and which stood a little apart from the rest, as if to denote it was the residence of some privileged individual of the band. The shield and quiver at its entrance were richer than common, and the high distinction of a fusee, attested the importance of its proprietor. In every other particular, it was rather distinguished by signs of poverty than of wealth. The domestic utensils were fewer in number and simpler in their forms, than those to be seen about the openings of the meanest lodges, nor was there a single one of those high prized articles of civilized life, which were occasionally bought of the traders, in bargains that bore so hard on the ignorant natives. All these had been bestowed, as they had been acquired, by the generous chief on his subordinates to purchase an influence, that might render him the master of their lives and persons, a species of wealth that was certainly more noble in itself, and far dearer to his ambition.

The old man well knew this to be the lodge of Mahtoree, and in obedience to the sign of the chief, he held his way towards it with slow and reluctant steps. But there were others present, who were equally interested in the approaching conference, whose apprehensions were not to be so easily suppressed. The watchful eyes and jealous ears of Middleton had taught him enough to fill his soul with horrible forebodings. With an incredible effort, he succeeded in gaining his feet, and called aloud to the retiring trapper —

"I conjure you, old man, if the love you bore my parents was more than words, or if the love you bear your God is that of a Christian man, utter not a syllable that may wound the ear of that innocent."

Exhausted in spirit and fettered in limbs, he then fell, like an inanimate log to the earth, where he lay like one dead.

Paul had however, caught the clue, and completed the exhortation, in his peculiar manner.

"Harkee, old trapper," he shouted vainly endeavoring at the same time to make a gesture of defiance with his hand, "if you ar' about to play the interpreter speak such words to the ears of that damnable savage, as becomes a white man to use, and a heathen to hear. Tell him from me, that if he does or says the thing that is uncivil, to the girl called Nelly Wade, that I'll curse him with my dying breath; that I'll pray for all good Christians in Kentucky to curse him; sitting and standing; eating and drinking; fighting, praying, or at horse-races; in-doors and out-doors; in summer or winter or in the month of March; in short I'll — ay, it ar' a fact morally true that I'll finally haunt him, if the ghost of a pale-face can contrive to lift itself from a grave made by the hands of a red-skin."

Having thus vented the most terrible denunciation he could devise, and the one, which in the eyes of the honest bee-hunter there seem'd the greatest likelihood of his being able to put in execution, he was obliged to await the fruits of his threat, with that resignation which would be apt to govern a western border man, who in additon to the prospects just named, had the advantage of contemplating them in fetters and bondage. We shall not detain the narrative, to relate the quaint morals with which he next endeavored to cheer the drooping spirits of his more sensitive companion, or the occasional pithy and peculiar benedictions that he pronounced on all the bands of the Dahcotahs, commencing with those whom he accused of stealing, or murdering on the banks of the distant Mississippi, and concluding, in terms of suitable energy, with the Teton tribe. The latter more than once received, from his lips curses as sententious and as complicated as that celebrated anathema of the church, for a knowledge of which most unlettered Protestants are indebted to the pious researches of the worthy Tristram Shandy.*But as Middleton recovered from his exhaustion he was fain to appease the boisterous temper of his associate, by admonishing him of the uselessness of such denunciations, and of the possiblility of their hastening the very evil he deprecated, by irritating the resentments of a race, who were sufficiently fierce and lawless even, in their most pacific moods.

In the mean time the trapper and the Sioux chief pursued their way to the lodge. The former had watched, with painful interest the expression of Mahtoree's eye, while the words of Middleton and Paul were pursuing their footsteps, but the mien of the Indian was far too much restrained and self-guarded to permit the smallest of his emotions to escape through any of those ordinary outlets, by which the condition of the human volcano is commonly betrayed. His look was fastened on the little habitation they approached, and, for the moment, his thoughts appeared to brood alone on the purposes of this extraordinary visit.

The appearance of the interior of the lodge corresponded with its exterior. It was larger than most of the others, more finished in its form and finer in its materials, but there its superiority ceased. Nothing could be more simple and republican than the form of living that the ambitious and powerful Teton chose to exhibit to the eyes of his people. A choice collection of weapons for the chace, some three or four medals bestowed by the traders and political agents of the Canadas as a homage to, or rather as an acknowledgement of his rank, with a few of the most indispensable articles of personal accommodation, composed its furniture. It abounded in neither venison, nor the wild beef of the Prairies, its crafty owner, having well understood that the liberality of a single individual, would be abundantly rewarded by the daily contributions of a band. Although as pre-eminent in the chase, as in war, a deer or a buffaloe was never seen to enter whole into his lodge. In return, an animal was rarely brought into the encampment, that did not contribute to support the family of Mahtoree. But the policy of the chief seldom permitted more to remain, than sufficed for the wants of the day, perfectly assured that all must suffer, before hunger, the bane of savage life, could lay its fell fangs on so important a victim.

Immediately beneath the favorite bow of the chief, and encircled in a sort of magical ring, of spears, shields, lances and arrows, all of which had in their time done good service, was suspended the mysterious and sacred medicine bag. It was highly wrought in wampum, and profusely ornamented, with beads, and porcupine's quills, after the most cunning devices of Indian ingenuity. The peculiar freedom of Mahtoree's religious creed, has been more than once intimated, and by a singular species of contradiction he appeared to have lavished his attentions on this emblem of a supernatural agency, in a degree that was precisely inverse to his faith. It was merely the manner in which the Sioux imitated the well known expedient of the Pharisees "in order that they might be seen of men."*

The tent had not, however, been entered by its owner since his return from the recent expedition. As the reader has already anticipated it had been made the prison of Inez and Ellen. The bride of Middleton was seated on a simple couch of sweet scented herbs, covered with skins. She had already suffered so much, and witnessed so many wild and unlooked for events, within the short space of her captivity, that every additional misfortune fell with a diminished force on her, seemingly, devoted head. Her cheeks were bloodless, her dark, and usually animated eye, was contracted in an expression of settled concern and her form appeared shrinking and sensitive, nearly to extinction. But in the midst of these evidences of natural weakness, there were at times such an air of pious resignation, such gleams of meek but holy hope, lighting her countenance, as might well have rendered it a question whether the hapless captive was most a subject of pity, or of admiration. All the precepts of Father Ignatius were riveted in her faithful memory, and not a few of his pious visions were floating before her imagination. Sustained by so sacred resolutions, the mild, the patient, and the confiding girl was bowing her head to this new stroke of Providence with the same sort of meekness as she would have submitted to any other prescribed penitence for her sins, though nature, at moments, warred powerfully, with so compelled a humility.

On the other hand, Ellen had exhibited far more of the woman, and consequently of the passions of the world. She had wept until her eyes were swollen and red. Her cheeks were flushed and angry, and her whole mien was distinguished by an air of spirit and resentment that was not a little, however, qualified by apprehensions for the future. In short there was that about the eye, and step of the betrothed of Paul, which gave a warranty, that should happier times arrive, and the constancy of the bee-hunter finally meet with its reward, he would possess a partner every way, worthy to cope with his own thoughtless and buoyant temperament.

There was still another, and a third figure in that little knot of females. It was the youngest, the most highly gifted, and, until now, the most favored of the wives of the Teton. Her charms had not been without the most powerful attraction in the eyes of her husband, until they had so unexpectedly opened on the surpassing loveliness of a woman of the Pale faces. From that hapless moment the graces, the attachment, the fidelity of the young Indian had lost their power to please. Still the complexion of Tachechana,* though less dazzling than that of her rival, was, for her race, clear and healthy, her hazel eye had the sweetness and playfulness of the antelope's, her voice was soft and joyous as the song of the wren, and her happy laugh was the very melody of the forest. Of all the Sioux girls, Tachechana (or the Fawn) was the lightest-hearted and the most envied. Her father had been a distinguished brave, and her brothers had already left their bones on a distant and dreary war-path. Numberless were the warriors who had sent presents to the lodge of her parents, but none of them were listened to, until a messenger from the great Mahtoree had come. She was his third wife it is true, but she was confessedly the most favored of them all. Their union had existed but two short seasons, and its fruits now lay sleeping at her feet, wrapped in the customary ligatures of skin and bark, which form the swaddlings of an Indian infant.

At the moment when Mahtoree and the trapper arrived at the opening of the lodge, the young Sioux wife, was seated on a simple stool, turning her soft eyes, with looks that varied, like her emotions, with love and wonder from the unconscious child, to those rare beings who had filled her youthful and uninstructed mind with so much

admiration and astonishment. Though Inez and Ellen had passed an
entire day in her sight, it seemed as if the longings of her curiosity
were increasing with each new gaze. She regarded them as beings of
an entirely different nature and condition from the females of the
Prairie. Even the mystery of their complicated attire had its secret
influence on her simple mind, though it was the grace and charm of
sex, to which nature has made every people so sensible, that most
attracted her admiration. But while her ingenuous disposition freely
admitted the superiority of the strangers, over the less brilliant attrac-
tions of the Dahcotah maidens, she had seen no reason, to deprecate
their advantages. The visit that she was now about to receive was the
first which her husband had made to the tent since his return from
the recent inroad, and he was ever present to her thoughts, as a
successful warrior, who was not ashamed, in the moments of inaction,
to admit the softer feelings of a father and a husband.

We have every where endeavored to show, that, while Mahtoree was
in all essentials a warrior of the Prairies, he was much in advance of
his people, in those acquirements which announce the dawnings of
civilization. He had held frequent communion with the traders and
troops of the Canadas, and the intercourse had unsettled many of
those wild opinions which were his birth-right, without perhaps sub-
stituting any others, of a nature sufficiently definite to be profitable.
His reasoning was rather subtle than true and his philosophy far
more audacious than profound. Like thousands of more enlightened
beings who fancy they are able to go through the trials of human
existence without any other support than their own resolutions, his
morals were accommodating, and his motive, selfish. These several
characteristics will be understood always with reference to the situation of the Indian, though little apology is needed for finding resem-
blances between men who essentially possess the same nature, however
it may be modified by circumstances.

Notwithstanding the presence of Inez and Ellen the entrance of the
Teton warrior into the lodge of his favorite wife was made with the
tread and mien of a master. The step of his moccasin was noiseless,
but the rattling of his bracelets and of the silver ornaments of his
leggings, sufficed to announce his approach, as he push'd aside the
skin covering of the opening of the tent, and stood in the presence of
its inmates. A faint cry of pleasure burst from the lips of Tachechana,
but the emotion was instantly suppressed in that subdued demeanor
which better became a matron of her tribe. Instead of returning the

stolen glance of his youthful, and secretly rejoicing wife, Mahtoree mov'd to the couch occupied by his prisoners, and placed himself at his ease, before them in the haughty upright attitude of an Indian chief. The old man had glided past him, and already taken a position suited to the office he had been commanded to fill.

Surprise kept the females silent and nearly breathless. Though accustomed to the sight of savage warriors, in the horrid panoply of their profession, there was something so startling in the entrance, and so audacious in the look of their conqueror, that the eyes of both sunk to the earth under a feeling of terror and embarrassment. Then Inez recovered herself, and addressing the trapper, she demanded with the dignity of an offended gentlewoman, though with her accustomed grace, to what circumstance they owed this extraordinary and unexpected visit. The old man hesitated, but clearing his throat, like one who was about to make an effort to which he was little used, he ventured on the following reply—

"Lady," he said, "a savage is a savage, and you are not to look for the uses and formalities of the settlements on a bleak and windy Prairie. As these Indians would say, fashions and courtesies are things so light, that they would blow away. As for myself, though a man of the forest, I have seen the ways of the great, in my time, and I am not to learn that they differ from the ways of the lowly. I was long a serving man in my youth, not one of your beck and nod runners about a household, but a man that went through the servitude of the forest with his officer, and well do I know, in what manner to approach the wife of a Captain. Now, had I the ordering of this visit, I would first have hemm'd aloud at the door, in order that you might hear that strangers were coming, and then I—"

"The manner is indifferent," interrupted Inez, too anxious to await the prolix explanations of the old man. "Why is the visit made."

"Therein shall the savage speak for himself. The daughters of the Pale faces, wish to know, why the Great Teton has entered his lodge?"

Mahtoree regarded his interrogator with a surprise which show'd how extraordinary he deemed the question; then placing himself in a posture of condescension, after a moment's delay, he answered—

"Sing in the ears of the dark-eye. Tell her that the lodge of Mahtoree is very large, and that it is not full. She shall find room in it; and none shall be greater than she. Tell the light hair, that she too may stay in the lodge of a brave, and eat of his venison. Mahtoree is a great chief. His hand is never shut."

"Teton," returned the trapper, shaking his head in evidence of the strong disapprobation with which he heard this language, "the tongue of a red-skin must be coloured white, before it can make music in the ears of a Pale-face. Should your words be spoken, my daughters would shut their ears, and Mahtoree would seem a trader, to their eyes. Now listen to what comes from a gray-head, and then speak accordingly. My people is a mighty people: The sun rises on their eastern, and sets on their western border. The land is filled with bright-eyed and laughing girls, like these you see, ay. Teton, I tell no lie," observing his auditor to start with an air of distrust; "bright-eyed and pleasant to behold, as these before you."

"Has my father a hundred wives!" interrupted the savage, laying a finger on the shoulder of the trapper, with a look of curious interest in the reply.

"No, Dahcotah; the Master of Life has said to me, 'live alone.' Your lodge shall be the forest, the roof of your wigwam the clouds. But though never bound in the secret faith which, in my nation, ties one man to one woman, often have I seen the workings of that kindness which brings the two together. Go, into the regions of my people. You will see the daughters of the land, fluttering through the Towns, like many coloured and joyful birds in the season of blossoms, you will meet them singing and rejoicing along the great paths of the country and you will hear the woods ringing with their laughter. They are very excellent to behold, and the young men find pleasure in looking at them."

"Hugh!" ejaculated the attentive Mahtoree.

"Ay, well may you put faith in what you hear, for it is no lie. But when a youth has found a maiden to please him, he speaks to her in a voice so soft that none else can hear. He does not say 'my lodge is empty, and there is room for another'; but, 'shall I build, and will the virgin show me near what spring she would dwell?' His voice is sweeter than honey from the locust, and goes into the ear thrilling like the song of a wren. Therefore if my brother wishes his words to be heard, he must speak with a white tongue."

Mahtoree pondered deeply and in a wonder that he did not attempt to conceal. It was reversing all the order of society, and, according to his established opinions, endangering the dignity of a chief for a warrior thus to humble himself before a woman. But, as Inez sat before him, reserved, and imposing in air, utterly unconscious of his object and least of all suspecting the true purport of so extraordinary a visit, the savage felt the influence of a manner, to which he was unaccustomed. Bowing his head, in acknowledgment of his error, he stepp'd a little back, and placing himself in an attitude of easy dignity he began to speak with the confidence of one who had been no less distinguished for eloquence, than for deeds in arms, keeping his eyes riveted on the unconscious bride of Middleton he proceeded in the following words.

"I am a man with a red-skin, but my eyes are dark. They have been open since many snows. They have seen many things. They know a brave from a coward. When a boy I saw nothing but the bison and the deer. I went to the hunts and I saw the cougar and the bear. This made Mahtoree a man. He talk'd with his mother no more, his ears were open to the wisdom of the old men. They told him every thing, they told him of the Big-knives. He went on the war-path. He was then the last; now, he is the first. What Dahcotah dare say he will go before Mahtoree into the hunting grounds of the Pawnees. The Chiefs met him at their doors and they said, my son is without a home. They gave him their lodges, they gave him their riches, and they gave him their daughters. Then Mahtoree became a chief, as his fathers had been. He struck the warriors of all the nations, and he could have chosen wives from the Pawnees, the Omahaws and the Konzas. But he looked at the hunting ground and not at his village. He thought a horse was pleasanter than a Dahcotah girl. But he found a flower on the Prairies, and he pluck'd it, and brought it into his lodge. He forgets that he is the master of a single horse. He gives them all to the stranger, for Mahtoree is not a thief; he will only keep the flower he found on the Prairie. Her feet are very tender. She cannot walk to the door of her father, she will stay in the lodge of a valiant warrior for ever."

When he had finished this extraordinary address, the Teton awaited to have it translated, with the air of a suitor who entertained no very disheartening doubts of his success. The trapper had not lost a syllable of the speech, and he now prepared himself to render it into English, in such a manner as should leave its principal idea even more obscure than in the original. But as his reluctant lips were in the act of parting, Ellen lifted a finger, and with a keen glance from her quick eye at the still attentive Inez, she interrupted him.

"Spare your breath," she said; "all that a savage says is not to be repeated before a Christian Lady."

Inez started, blushed, and bowed with an air of reserve, as she coldly thanked the old man for his intentions and observed that she could now wish to be alone.

"My daughters have no need of ears to understand what a great Dahcotah says," returned the trapper, addressing himself to the expectant Mahtoree. "The look he has given and the signs he has made, are enough. They understand him. They wish to think of his words; for the children of great braves, such as their fathers are, do nothing without much thought."

With this explanation, so flattering to the energy of his eloquence, and so promising to his future hopes, the Teton was every way content. He made the customary ejaculation of assent, and prepared to retire. Saluting the females in the cold, but dignified manner of his people, he drew his robe about him, and moved from the spot where he had stood, with an air of ill-concealed triumph.

But there had been a stricken, though a motionless and unobserved auditor of the foregoing scene. Not a syllable had fallen from the lips of the long and anxiously expected husband, that had not gone directly to the heart of his unoffending wife. In this manner had he wooed her from the lodge of her father, and it was to listen to similar pictures of the renown and deeds of the greatest brave in her tribe, that she had shut her ears to the tender tales of so many of the Sioux youths.

As the Teton turned to leave his lodge, in the manner just mentioned, he found this unexpected and half-forgotten object before him. She stood, in the humble guise and with the shrinking air of an Indian girl, holding the pledge of their former love in her arms, directly in his path. Starting, the chief regained the marble-like indifference of countenance which distinguished in so remarkable a degree the restrained or more artificial expression of his features, and signed to her, with an air of authority, to give place.

"Is not Tachechana the daughter of a chief!" demanded a subdued voice, in which pride struggled with anguish; "were not her brothers, braves!"

"Go. The men are calling their partisan. He has no ears for a woman."

"No," replied the supplicant; "it is not the voice of Tachechana that you hear, but this boy, speaking with the tongue of his mother. He is the son of a chief, and his words will go up to his father's ears. Listen to what he says. When was Mahtoree hungry, and Tachechana had not food for him. When did he go on the path of the Pawnees and find it empty, that my mother did not weep. When did he come back with the marks of their blows, that she did not sing. What Sioux girl has given a brave a son like me. Look at me, well, that you may know me. My eyes are the eagle's. I look at the sun and laugh. In a little time, the Dahcotahs will follow me to the hunts and on the war-path. Why does my father turn his eyes from the woman that gives me milk. Why has he so soon forgotten the daughter of a mighty Sioux."

There was a single instant, as the exulting father suffered his cold eye to wander to the face to his laughing boy, that the stern nature of the Teton seemed touched. But shaking off the grateful sentiment, like one who would gladly be rid of any painful because reproachful emotion, he laid his hand calmly on the arm of his wife, and led her directly in front of Inez. Pointing to the sweet countenance that was beaming on her own, with a look of tenderness and commiseration, he paused, to allow his wife to contemplate a loveliness, which was quite as excellent to her ingenuous mind, as it had proved dangerous to the character of her faithless husband. When he thought abundant time had passed to make the contrast sufficiently striking, he suddenly raised a small mirror that dangled at her breast, an ornament he had himself bestowed, in an hour of fondness, as a compliment to her beauty, and placed her own dark image in its place. Wrapping his robe, again, about him the Teton motioned to the trapper to follow, and stalked haughtily from the lodge, muttering as he went.

"Mahtoree is very wise! What nation has so great a chief as the Dahcotahs."

Tachechana stood frozen into a statue of humility. Her mild, and usually joyous countenance worked, as if the struggle within was about to dissolve the connexion between her soul and that more material part, whose deformity was becoming so loathsome. Inez and Ellen were utterly ignorant of the nature of her interview with her husband, though the quick and sharpened wits of the latter led her to suspect a truth to which the entire innocence of the former furnished no clue. They were both, however, about to tender those sympathies which are so natural to and so graceful in the sex, when their necessity seemed suddenly to cease. The convulsions in the features of the young Sioux disappeared, and her countenance became cold and rigid, like chiselled stone. A single expression of subdued anguish which had made its impression on a brow that had rarely before contracted with sorrow, alone remained. It was never removed, in all the changes of seasons, fortunes and years which in the vicissitudes of a suffering, female, savage life she was subsequently doomed to endure. As in the case of a premature blight, let the plant quicken and revive, as it may, the effects of that withering touch were always present.

Tachechana first stripped her person of every vestige of those rude, but highly prized ornaments, which the liberality of her husband, had been wont to lavish on her, and she tendered them, meekly and without a murmur, as an offering to the superiority of Inez. The bracelets were forced from her wrists, the complicated mazes of beads from her leggings and the broad silver band from her brow. Then she paused long and painfully. But it would seem that the resolution she had once adopted was not to be conquered by the lingering emotions of any affection, however natural. The boy, himself, was next laid at the feet of her supposed rival, and well might the self abased wife of the Teton believe that the burthen of her sacrifice was now full.

While Inez and Ellen stood regarding these several strange movements with eyes of wonder, a low, soft, musical voice was heard saying, in a language that to them was unintelligible—

"A strange tongue will tell my boy the manner to become a man. He will hear sounds that are new, but he will learn them and forget the voice of his mother. It is the will of the Wahcondah, and a Sioux girl should not complain. Speak to him softly, for his ears are very little. When he is big, your words may be louder. Let him not be a girl, for very sad is the life of a woman. Teach him to keep his eyes on the men. Show him how to strike them that do him wrong, and let him never forget to return blow for blow. When he goes to hunt, the 'flower of the Pale faces',," she concluded, using in bitterness the metaphor which had been supplied by the imagination of her truant husband, "will whisper softly in his ears, that the skin of his mother was red, and that she was once the Fawn of the Dahcotahs."

Tachechana pressed a kiss on the lips of her son, and withdrew to the farther side of the lodge. Here she drew her light calicoe robe over her head, and took her seat, in token of humility on the naked earth. All efforts to attract her attention were fruitless. She neither heard remonstrances nor felt the touch. Once or twice her voice rose, in a sort of wailing song, from beneath her quivering mantle, but it never mounted into the wildness of savage music. In this manner she remained unseen for hours, while events were occurring without the lodge which not only materially changed the complexion of her own fortunes, but left a lasting and deep impression on the future movements of the wandering Sioux.

CHAPTER XXVII.

"I'll no swaggerers: I am in good name and fame
with the very best:—Shut the door;—
There come no swaggerers here:
I have not lived all this while, to have swaggering now:
—shut the door I pray you."

II Henry IV, II.iv. 81-85.

Mahtoree encountered at the door of his lodge, Ishmael, Abiram and Esther. The first glance of his eye, at the countenance of the heavy-moulded squatter, served to tell the cunning Teton, that the treacherous truce he had made with these dupes of his superior sagacity was in some danger of a violent termination.

"Look you here, old gray-beard," said Ishmael, seizing the trapper, and whirling him round, as if he had been a top, "that I'm tired of carrying on a discourse, with fingers and thumbs, instead of a tongue, ar' a natural fact; so you'll play linguister, and put my words into Indian, without much caring whether they suit the stomach of a red-skin, or not."

"Say on, friend," calmly, returned the trapper. "They shall be given as plainly as you send them."

"Friend!" repeated the squatter, eyeing the other, for an instant with an expression of indefinable meaning. "But it is no more than a word, and sounds break no bones, and survey no farms. Tell this thieving Sioux, then, that I come to claim the conditions of our solemn bargain, made at the foot of the rock."

When the trapper had rendered his meaning into the Sioux language, Mahtoree demanded with an air of surprise—

"Is my brother cold? buffalo skins are plenty. Is he hungry? let my young men carry venison into his lodges."

The squatter elevated his clenched fist in a menacing manner, and struck it with violence on the palm of his open hand, by way of confirming his determination, as he answered.

"Tell the deceitful liar, I have not come like a beggar to pick his bones, but like a free man asking for his own, and have it I will— and moreover tell him I claim that you, too, miserable sinner as you ar', should be given up to justice. There's no mistake. My prisoner, my niece, and you. I demand the three at his hands, according to a sworn agreement."

The immovable old man smiled, with an expression of singular intelligence, as he answered—

"Friend squatter, you ask what few men would be willing to grant. You would first cut the tongue from the mouth of the Teton, and then the heart from his bosom!"

"It is little, that Ishmael Bush regards, who or what is damaged in claiming his own. Put you the questions, in straight-going Indian, and when you speak of yourself, make such a sign as a white man will understand, in order that I may know there is no foul-play."

The trapper laughed in his silent fashion, and muttered a few words to himself, before he addressed the chief.

"Let the Dahcotah open his ears very wide," he said, "that big words may have room to enter. His friend the Big-knife comes with an empty hand, and he says that the Teton must fill it."

"Wagh. Mahtoree is a rich chief. He is master of the Prairies."

"He must give the dark-hair!"

The brow of the chief contracted in an ominous frown, that threatened instant destruction to the audacious squatter, but as suddenly recollecting his policy, he craftily replied—

"A girl is too light for the hand of such a brave. I will fill it with buffaloes."

"He says, that he has need of the light-hair, too; who has his blood in her veins."

"She shall be the wife of Mahtoree; then the Long-knife will be the Father of a chief!"

"And, me," continued the trapper, making one of those expressive signs by which the natives communicate, with nearly the same facility as with their tongues, and turning to the squatter, at the same time, in order that the latter might see he dealt fairly by him, "he asks for a miserable and worn out trapper!"

The Dahcotah threw his arm over the shoulder of the old man, with an air of great affection, before he replied to this third and last demand.

"My friend is old," he said, "and cannot travel far. He will stay, with the Tetons, that they may learn wisdom from his words. What Sioux has a tongue, like my Father! No. Let his words be very soft, but let them be very clear. Mahtoree will give skins, and buffaloes. He will give the young men of the Pale-faces wives, but he cannot give away any who live in his own lodge."

Perfectly satisfied, himself, with this laconick reply, the chief was moving towards his expecting counsellors, when, suddenly returning, he interrupted the translation of the trapper, by adding—

"Tell the Great Buffaloe," (a name by which the Tetons had already christened Ishmael), "that Mahtoree has a hand which is always open. See," he added pointing to the hard and wrinkled visage of the attentive Esther, "his wife is too old for so great a chief. Let him put her out of his lodge. Mahtoree loves him as a brother. He *is* his brother. He shall have the youngest wife of the Teton. Tachechana, the pride of the Sioux girls, shall cook his venison, and many braves will look at him with longing minds. Go. A Dahcotah is always generous."

The singular coolness with which the Teton concluded this audacious proposal confounded even the practised trapper. He stared after the retiring form of the Indian with an astonishment he did not care to conceal, nor did he renew his attempt at interpretation, until the person of Mahtoree was blended with the cluster of warriors, who had so long and with so characteristic patience awaited his return.

"The Teton chief has spoken very plainly," the old man continued. "He will not give you the lady, to whom the Lord in Heaven, he knows you have no claim, unless it be such as the wolf has to the lamb. He will not give you, the child you call your niece; and therein, I acknowledge that I am far from certain he has the same justice on his side. Moreover, neighbour squatter, he flatly denies your demand for me, miserable and worthless as I am, nor do I think he has been unwise in so doing, seeing that I should have many reasons against journeying far in your company. But he makes you an offer which it is right and convenient you should know. The Teton says through me, who am no more than a mouth-piece and therein, not answerable for the sin of his words, but he says that as this good woman is getting past the comely age, it is reasonable for you to tire of such a wife. He therefore tells you to turn her out of your lodge, and when it is empty, he will send his own favorite, or rather she that was his favorite, the 'Skipping Fawn' as the Siouxes call her, to fill her place. You see, neighbor, though the red-skin is minded to keep your property, he is willing to give you wherewithal to make yourself some return."

Ishmael listened to these replies, to his several demands, with that species of gathering indignation, with which the dullest tempers mount into the most violent paroxysms of rage. He even affected to laugh at the conceit of exchanging his long tried partner for the more flexible support of the youthful Tachechana, though his voice was hollow and unnatural in the effort. But Esther was far from giving the proposal so facetious a reception. Lifting her voice to its most audible key, she broke forth, after catching her breath like one who had been in some imminent danger of strangulation, as follows—

"Hoity-toity! who set an Indian up for a maker and breaker of the rights of wedded wives! Does he think a woman is a beast of the Prairie that she is to be chased from a village, by dog and gun. Let the bravest squaw of them all come forth and boast of her doings, can she show such a brood as mine! A wicked tyrant is that thieving red-skin, and a bold rogue I warrant me. He would be captain in-doors, as well as out! A honest woman is no better, in his eyes, than one of your broom-stick jumpers.* And you, Ishmael Bush, the father of seven sons and so many comely daughters, to open *your* sinful mouth except to curse him! Would ye disgrace colour, and family, and nation, by mixing white blood with red, and would ye be the parent of a race of mules. The Devil has often tempted you, my man, but never before has he set so cunning a snare as this. Go, back among your children, friend, go, and remember that you are not a prowling bear but a Christian man, and thank God, that you ar' a lawful husband."

The clamor of Esther was anticipated by the judicious trapper. He had easily foreseen that her meek temper would overflow at so scandalous a proposal as repudiation, and he, now, profited by the tempest to retire to a place, where he was at least safe from any immediate violence on the part of her less excited, but certainly more dangerous husband. Ishmael, who had made his demands with a stout determination to enforce them, was diverted by the wordy torrent, like many a more obstinate husband, from his purpose, and in order to appease a jealousy, that resembled the fury with which the bear defends her cubs, was fain to retire to a distance from the lodge that was known to contain the unoffending object of the sudden uproar.

"Let your copper-coloured minx come forth, and show her tawney beauty before the face of a woman, who has heard more than one church bell, and seen a power of real quality," cried Esther, flourishing her hand in triumph, as she drove Ishmael and Abiram before her, like two truant boys towards their own encampment. "I warrant me, I warrant me, here is one who would shortly talk her down. Never think to tarry here, my men, never think to shut an eye in a camp, through which the devil walks as openly as if he were a gentleman, and was sure of his welcome. Here, you, Abner, Enoch, Jesse, where ar' ye gotten to. Put to, put to. If that weak-minded, soft-feeling man your father, eats or drinks again in this neighborhood, we shall see him poisoned with the craft of the red-skins. Not that I care, I, who comes into my place when it is once lawfully empty, but, Ishmael, I never thought that you, who have had one woman with a white skin, would find pleasure in looking on a brazen — ay, that she is copper, ar' a fact you cant deny, and I warrant me brazen enough is she too."

Against this ebullition of wounded female pride the experienced husband made no other head, than by an occasional exclamation which he intended to be the precursor of a simple asseveration of his own innocence. The fury of the woman would not be appeased. She listened to nothing but her own voice, and consequently nothing was heard, but her mandates to depart.

The squatter had collected his beasts and loaded his wagons as a measure of precaution, before proceeding to the extremity he contemplated. Esther, consequently found every thing favorable to her wishes. The young men stared at each other, as they witnessed the extraordinary excitement of their mother, but took little interest in an event, which in the course of their experience had found so many parallels. By command of their father, the tents were thrown into the vehicles, as a sort of reprisal for the want of faith in their late ally, and then the train left the spot, in its usual, listless and sluggish order.

As a formidable division of well-armed borderers protected the rear of the retiring party, the Siouxes saw it depart without manifesting the smallest evidence of surprise, or resentment. The savage, like the tiger, rarely makes his attack on an enemy who expects him, and if the warriors of the Tetons meditated any hostility, it was in the still and patient manner with which the feline beasts watch for the incautious moment, in order to ensure the blow. The Councils of Mahtoree, however, on whom so much of the policy of his people depended, lay deep in the depository of his own thoughts. Perhaps he rejoiced at so easy a manner of getting rid of claims so troublesome, perhaps he awaited a fitting time to exhibit his power, or it even might be that matters of so much greater importance were pressing on his mind, that it had not leisure to devote any of its faculties to an event of so much indifference.

But it would seem, that while Ishmael made such a concession to the awakened feelings of Esther, he was far from abandoning his original intentions. His train followed the course of the river for a mile, and then it came to a halt, on the brow of the elevated land, and in a place which afforded the necessary facilities. Here he, again, pitch'd his tents, unharnessed his teams, sent his cattle on the bottom, and in short made all the customary preparations to pass the night with the same coolness and deliberation, as if he had not hurled an irritating defiance into the teeth of his dangerous neighbors.

In the mean time the Tetons proceeded to the more regular business of the hour. A fierce and savage joy had existed in the camp from the instant when it had been announced that their own Chief was returning with the long dreaded and hated Partizan of their enemies. For many hours the crones of the tribe had been going from lodge to lodge, in order to stimulate the tempers of the warriors to such a pass, as might leave but little room for mercy. To one, they spoke of a son whose scalp was drying in the smoke of a Pawnee lodge. To another, they enumerated his own scars, his disgraces and defeats. With a third, they dwelt on his losses of skins and horses, and a fourth was reminded of vengeance, by a significant question concerning some flagrant adventure in which he was known to have been a sufferer.

By these means the men had been so far excited as to have assembled, in the manner already related, though it still remained a matter of doubt how far they intended to carry their revenge. A variety of opinions prevailed on the policy of executing their prisoners, and Mahtoree had suspended the discussions, in order to ascertain how far the measure might propitiate, or retard his own particular views. Hitherto, the consultations had merely been preliminary, with a design that each chief might discover the number of supporters his particular views would be likely to obtain when the important subject should come before a more solemn council of the tribe. The moment for the latter had now arrived, and the preparations were made with a dignity and solemnity suited to the momentous interests of the occasion.

With a refinement in cruelty that none but an Indian would have imagined, the place selected for this grave deliberation was immediately about the post, to which the most important of its subjects, was attached. Middleton and Paul were brought, in their bonds, and laid at the feet of the Pawnee, and then the men began to take their places according to their several claims to distinction. As warrior after warrior approached, he seated himself in the wide circle, with a mien as composed and thoughtful as if his mind were actually in a condition to deal out justice, tempered as it should be, with the heavenly quality of mercy. A place was reserved for three or four of the principal chiefs, and a few of the oldest of the women, as withered, as age, exposure, hardships and lives of savage passions could make them, thrust themselves into the foremost circle, with a temerity to which they were impelled by their insatiable desire for cruelty, and which nothing but their years and their long tried fidelity to the nation would have excused.

All but the chiefs already named were now in their places. These had delayed their appearance, in the vain hope that their own unanimity might smooth the way to that of their respective factions; for, notwithstanding the superior influence of Mahtoree, his power was to be maintained only by constant appeals to the opinions of his inferiors. As these important personages, at length entered the circle in a body, their sullen looks and clouded brows notwithstanding the time thus given to consultation, sufficiently proclaimed the discontent which reigned among them. The eye of Mahtoree was varying in its expression, from sudden gleams, that seemed to kindle with the burning impulses of his soul, to that cold and guarded steadiness which was thought more peculiarly to become a chief in Council. He took his seat, with the studied simplicity of a demagogue, though the keen and flashing glance that he immediately threw around the silent assembly, betrayed the more predominant temper of a tyrant.

When all were present an aged warrior lighted the great pipe of his people, and blew the smoke towards the four quarters of the heavens. So soon as this propitiatory offering was made, he tendered it, to Mahtoree, who in affected humility passed it to a gray-headed chief by his side. After the influence of the soothing weed had been courted by all, a grave silence succeeded, as if each was not only qualified to, but actually did, think more deeply on the matters before them. Then an old Indian arose, and spoke as follows—

"The eagle at the falls of the endless river was in its egg, many snows after my hand had struck a Pawnee. What my tongue says my eyes have seen. Bohrecheena is very old. The hills have stood longer in their places, than he has been in his tribe, and the rivers were full and empty before he was born; but where is the Sioux that knows it, besides himself. What he says they will hear. If any of his words fall to the ground, they will pick them up, and hold them to their ears. If any blow away in the wind, my young men, who are very nimble, will catch them. Now listen. Since water ran and trees grew, the Sioux has found the Pawnee on his war path. As the cougar loves the antelope, the Dahcotah loves his enemy. When the wolf finds the fawn, does he lie down and sleep? When the Panther sees the doe at the spring, does he shut his eyes? You know that he does not. He drinks too; but it is of blood. A Sioux is a leaping panther, a Pawnee a trembling deer. Let my children hear me. They will find my words good. I have spoken."

A deep, guttural exclamation of assent broke from the lips of all the partisans of Mahtoree, as they listened to this sanguinary advice from one, who was certainly among the most aged men of the nation. That deeply seated love of vengeance, which formed so prominent a feature in their character, was gratified by his metaphorical allusions, and the chief himself augured favorably of the success of his own schemes, by the number of supporters who manifested themselves to be in favor of the counsel of his friend. But still unanimity was far from prevailing. A long and decorous pause was suffered to succeed the words of the first speaker, in order that all might duly deliberate on their wisdom, before another chief took on himself the office of refutation. This second orator, though past the prime of his days was far less aged than the one who had preceded him. He felt the disadvantage of this circumstance, and endeavored to counteract it, as far as possible by the excess of his humility.

"I am but an infant," he commenced, looking furtively around him, in order to detect how far his well established character for prudence and courage contradicted his assertion. "I have lived with the women, since my father has been a man. If my head is getting gray, it is not because I am old. Some of the snow which fell on it, while I have been sleeping on the war-paths, has frozen there, and the hot sun near the Osage villages has not been strong enough, to melt it." A low murmur was heard, expressive of admiration of the services to which he thus artfully alluded. The orator modestly waited for the feeling to subside a little, and then he continued with increasing energy, encouraged by their commendations. "But the eyes of a young brave are good. He can see very far. He is a Lynx. Look at me, well. I will turn my back that you may see both sides of me. Now do you know I am your friend, for you look on a part that a Pawnee never yet saw. Now look at my face; not in this seam, for there your eyes can never see into my spirit. It is a hole cut by a Konza. But here is an opening made by the Wahcondah, through which you may look into the soul. What am I? a Dahcotah, within and without. You know it. Therefore hear me. The blood of every creature on the Prairies is red. Who can tell the spot where a Pawnee was struck, from the place where my young men took a bison? It is of the same colour. The Master of Life made them for each other. He made them alike. But will the grass grow green where a Pale-face is killed? My young men must not think *that* Nation so numerous that it will not miss a warrior. They call them over often, and say, 'where are my sons'? If they miss one, they will send into the Prairies to look for him. If they cannot find him, they will tell their runners to ask for him among the Siouxes. My Brethren, the Big-knives are not fools. There is a mighty medecine of their nation, now, among us. Who can tell how loud is his voice, or how long is his arm—"

The speech of the orator, who was beginning to enter into his subject with warmth, was cut short by the impatient Mahtoree, who suddenly arose, and exclaimed in a voice, in which authority was mingled with contempt, and, at the close with a keen tone of irony, also—

"Let my young men, lead the Evil Spirit of the Pale faces to the Council. My brother, shall see his Medecine, face to face."

A death-like and solemn stillness succeeded this extraordinary interruption. It not only involved a deep offence against the sacred courtesy of debate, but the mandate was likely to brave the unknown power of one of those incomprehensible beings, whom few Indians were enlightened enough, at that day, to regard without reverence, or few hardy enough to oppose. The subordinates, however, obeyed; and Obed was led forth from a lodge, mounted on Asinus, with a ceremony and state which was certainly intended for derision, but which, nevertheless, was greatly enhanced by fear. As they entered the ring, Mahtoree, who had foreseen and had endeavored to anticipate the influence of the Doctor by bringing him into contempt, cast an eye around the assembly, in order to gather his success in the various dark visages by which he was encircled.

Truly nature and art had combined to produce such an effect from the air and appointments of the naturalist as might have made him the subject of wonder in any place. His head had been industriously shaved, after the most approved fashion of Sioux taste. A gallant scalp-lock, which would probably not have been spared had the Doctor himself been consulted in the matter, was all that remained of an exuberant, and at that particular season of the year, far from uncomfortable head of hair. Thick coats of paint had been laid on the naked poll, and certain fanciful designs, in the same material, had even been extended into the neighborhood of the eyes and mouth, lending to the keen expression of the former, a look of twinkling cunning, and to the dogmatism of the latter not a little of the grimness of necromancy. He had been despoiled of his upper garments, and in their stead, his body was sufficiently protected from the cold, by a fantastickally painted robe of dressed deer skin. As if in mockery of his pursuit, sundry toads, frogs, lizards, butterflies, etc. all duly prepared to take their places, at some future day, in his own private cabinet were attached to the solitary lock on his head, to his ears, and to various other conspicuous parts of his person. If, in addition to the effect produced by these quaint auxiliaries to this costume, we add the portentous and troubled gleamings of doubt, which rendered his visage doubly austere and proclaimed the misgivings of the worthy Obed's mind, as he beheld his personal dignity thus prostrated, and, what was of far greater moment in his eyes, himself led forth, as he firmly believed, to be the victim of some heathenish sacrifice, the reader will find no difficulty in giving credit, to the sensation of awe, that was excited by his appearance, in a band already more than half prepared to worship him, as a powerful agent of the Evil Spirit.

Weucha led Asinus directly into the centre of the circle, and leaving them together, (for the legs of the Naturalist were attached to the beast in such a manner that the two animals might be said to be incorporated and to form a new order,) he withdrew to his proper place, gazing at the conjuror as he retired with a wonder and admiration that were natural to the grovelling dulness of his mind.

The astonishment seemed mutual, between the spectators and the subject of this strange exhibition. If the Tetons contemplated the mysterious attributes of the Medecine, with awe and fear, the Doctor gazed on every side of him, with a mixture of quite as many extraordinary emotions, in which the latter sensation, however, formed no inconsiderable ingredient. Every where his eyes, which just at that moment, possessed a secret magnifying quality, seemed to rest on several dark, savage, and obdurate countenances at once, from none of which could he extract a solitary gleam of sympathy or commiseration. At length his wandering gaze fell on the grave and decent features of the trapper, who with Hector at his feet, stood in the edge of the circle, leaning on that rifle, which he had been permitted, as an acknowledged friend to resume, and apparently musing, on the events that were likely to succeed a Council, marked by so many and such striking ceremonies.

"Venerable venator, or hunter, or trapper," said the disconsolate Obed, "I rejoice greatly in meeting thee, again. I fear that the precious time which had been allotted me, in order to complete a mighty labor, is drawing to a premature close, and I would gladly unburthen my mind to one, who if not a pupil of science, has at least some of the knowledge which civilization imparts to its meanest subjects. Doubtless many and earnest enquiries will be made after my fate, by the learned societies of the world, and perhaps expeditions will be sent into these regions to remove any doubts which may arise on so important a subject. I esteem myself happy, that a man who speaks the vernacular is present, to preserve the record of my end. You will say that after a well spent and glorious life, I died a martyr to science, and a victim to mental darkness. As I expect to be particularly calm and abstracted in my last moments, if you add a few details concerning the fortitude and scholastic dignity with which I met my death, it may serve to encourage future aspirants for similar honour, and assuredly give offence to no one. And now, friend trapper, as a duty I owe to human nature, I will conclude by demanding if all hope has deserted me, or if any means still exist, by which so much valuable information may be rescued from the grasp of ignorance, and preserved to the pages of Natural History."

The old man lent an attentive ear to this melancholy appeal, and, apparently, he reflected on every side of the important question, before he would presume to answer.

"I take it, friend physicianer," he, at length, gravely replied, "that the chances of life and death, in your particular case, depend altogether on the will of Providence, as it may be pleased to manifest it, through the accursed windings of Indian cunning. For my own part, I see no great difference in the main end to be gained, inasmuch, as it can matter no one greatly, yourself excepted, whether you live or die."

"Would you account the fall of a corner stone from the foundations of the edifice of learning, a matter of indifference, to contemporaries, or to posterity!" interrupted Obed. "Besides, my aged associate," he reproachfully added, "the interest that a man has in his own existence, is by no means trifling, however it may be eclipsed by his devotion to more general and philanthropic feelings."

"What I would say is this," resumed the trapper, who was far from understanding all the subtle distinctions, with which his more learned companion so often saw fit to embellish his discourse. "There is but one birth and one death to all things, be it hound, or be it deer— be it red-skin, or be it white. Both are in the hands of the Lord; it being as unlawful for man to strive to hasten the one, as impossible to prevent the other. But I will not say that something may not be done to put the last moment aside, for a while at least; and therefore it is a question that any one has a right to put to his own wisdom, how far he will go, and how much pain he will suffer, to lengthen out a time, that may have been too long already. Many a dreary winter and scorching summer has gone by, since I have turned, to the right hand or to the left, to add an hour to a life that has already stretched beyond four-score years. I keep myself as ready to answer to my name as a soldier, at evening roll-call. In my judgment, if your cases, are left to Indian tempers, the policy of the Great Sioux, will lead his people to sacrifice you all, nor do I put much dependance on his seeming love for me; therefore it becomes a question whether you are ready for such a journey, and if, being ready, whether this is not as good a time to start as another. Should my opinion be asked, thus far will I give it in your favor; that is to say, it is my belief your life has been innocent enough touching any great offences that you may have committed, though honesty compels me to add, that I think all you can lay claim to, on the score of activity in deeds, will not amount to any thing worth naming in the great account."

Obed turned a rueful eye on the calm, philosophic countenance of the other, as he answered with so discouraging a statement of his case, clearing his throat as he did so, in order to conceal the desperate concern which began to beset his faculties, with a vestige of that pride which rarely deserts poor human nature, even in the greatest emergencies.

"I believe, venerable hunter," he replied, "considering the question in all its bearings, and assuming that your theory is just, it will be the safest to conclude that I am not prepared to make so hasty a departure, and that measures of precaution should be, forthwith, resorted to."

"Being in that mind," returned the deliberate trapper, "I will act for you as I would for myself, though as time has begun to roll down the hill with you, I will just advise that you look to your case, speedily, for it may so happen that your name will be heard, when quite as little prepared to answer to it, as now."

With this amicable understanding, the old man drew back, again, into the ring, where he stood musing on the course he should now adopt, with the singular mixture of decision and resignation, that proceeded from his habits and his humility, and which united to form a character in which excessive energy and the most meek submission to the will of Providence were oddly enough combined.

CHAPTER XXVIII.

"The witch, in Smithfield, shall be burned to ashes,
And you three shall be strangled on the gallows."

II Henry VI, II. iii. 7-8.

THE Siouxes had awaited the issue of the foregoing dialogue with commendable patience. Most of the band were restrained by the secret awe, with which they regarded the mysterious character of Obed, while a few of the more intelligent chiefs gladly profited by the opportunity to arrange their thoughts for the struggle that was plainly foreseen. Mahtoree, influenced by neither of these feelings, was content to show the trapper how much he conceded to his pleasure, and when the old man discontinued the discourse, he received from the chief, a glance, that was intended to remind him of the patience with which he had awaited his movements. A profound and motionless silence succeeded the short interruption. Then Mahtoree arose, evidently prepared to speak. First placing himself in an attitude of dignity he turned a steady and severe look on the whole assembly. The expression of his eye, however, changed as it glanced across the different countenances of his supporters and of his opponents. To the former the look, though stern was not threatening, while it seemed to tell the latter all the hazards they incurred, in daring to brave the resentment of one so powerful.

Still, in the midst of so much hauteur and confidence, the sagacity and cunning of the Teton did not desert him. When he had thrown the gauntlett as it were, to the whole tribe, and sufficiently asserted his claim to superiority, his mien became more affable and his eye less angry. Then it was that he raised his voice, in the midst of a death-like stillness, varying its tones to suit the changing character of his images and of his eloquence.

"What is a Sioux?" the chief sagaciously began. "He is Ruler of the Prairies, and Master of its beasts. The fishes in the 'river of troubled waters,'*know him, and come at his call. He is a fox in Council; an eagle in sight; a grizzly bear in combat. A Dahcotah is a man." After waiting for the low murmur of approbation which followed this flattering portrait of his people to subside, the Teton continued. "What is a Pawnee? A thief, who only steals from women; a red-skin, who is not brave; a hunter, that begs for his venison. In Council, he is a squirrel, hopping from place to place; he is an owl, that only goes on the Prairies at night; in battle, he is an elk, whose legs are long. A Pawnee is a woman." Another pause succeeded, during which a yell of delight broke from several mouths, and a demand was made that the taunting words should be translated by the trapper to the unconscious subject of their biting contempt. The old man took his cue from the eye of Mahtoree, and complied. Hard-Heart listened gravely, and then as if apprised that his time to speak had not arrived, he once more bent his look on the vacant air. The orator watched his countenance with an expression that manifested how inextinguishable was the hatred he felt, for the only chief, far and near, whose fame might advantageously be compared with his own. Though disappointed in not having touched the pride of one, whom he regarded as a boy, he proceeded to what he considered as far more important, to quicken the tempers of the men of his own tribe in order that they might be prepared to work his savage purposes. "If the earth was covered with rats, which are good for nothing," he said, "there would be no room for buffaloes, which give food and clothes to an Indian. If the Prairies were covered with Pawnees, there would be no room for the foot of a Dahcotah. A Loup is a rat, a Sioux a heavy buffaloe. Let the buffaloes tread upon the rats, and make room for themselves.

"My Brothers; a little child has spoken to you. He tells you his hair is not gray, but frozen. That the grass will not grow where a pale face has died! Does he know the colour of the blood of a Big-knife? No; I know he does not; he has never seen it. What Dahcotah besides Mahtoree has ever struck a Pale face? Not one. But Mahtoree must be silent. Every Teton will shut his ears when he speaks. The scalps over his lodge were taken by the women. They were taken by Mahtoree and he is a woman. His mouth is shut, he waits for the feasts to sing among the girls."

Notwithstanding the exclamations of regret and resentment which followed so abasing a declaration, the chief took his seat, as if determined to speak no more. But the murmurs grew louder and more general, and there were threatening symptoms that the Council would dissolve itself, in confusion, and he arose and resumed his speech, by changing his manner to the fierce and hurried enunciation of a warrior bent on revenge.

"Let my young men go look for Tetao;" he cried, "they will find his scalp, drying in Pawnee smoke. Where is the son of Borecheena?

His bones are whiter than the faces of his murderers. Is Mahhah asleep in his lodge? You know it is many moons since he started for the blessed Prairies. Would he were here that he might say of what color was the hand that took his scalp!"

In this strain, the artful chief continued for many minutes, calling those warriors by name, who were known to have met their deaths, in battle with the Pawnees, or in some of those lawless frays which so often occurred between the Sioux bands, and a class of white men, who were but little removed from them, in the qualities of civilization. Time was not given to reflect on the merits or rather the demerits of most of the different individuals to whom he alluded, in consequence of the rapid manner in which he ran over their names, but so cunningly did he time his events, and so thrillingly did he make his appeals, aided as they were by the power of his deep-toned and stirring voice, that each of them struck an answering chord in the breast of some one of his auditors.

It was in the midst of one of his highest flights of eloquence, that a man so aged as to walk with the greatest difficulty entered the very centre of the circle, and took his stand directly in front of the speaker. An ear of great acuteness might possibly have detected that the tones of the orator faltered a little as his flashing look first fell on this unexpected object, though the change was so trifling that none but such as thoroughly knew the parties, would have suspected it. The stranger had once been as distinguished for his beauty and proportions, as had been his eagle eye for its irresistible and terrible glance. But his skin was now wrinkled and his features furrowed with so many scars, as to have obtained for him, half a century before, from the French of the Canadas a title which has been borne by so many of the heroes of France, and which had now been adopted into the language of the wild horde of whom we are writing, as the one most expressive of the deeds of their own brave. The murmur of Le Balafré, that ran through the assembly when he appeared, announced not only his name and the high estimation of his character but how extraordinary his visit was considered. As he neither spoke nor moved, however, the sensation created by his appearance soon subsided, and then every eye was again turned upon the speaker, and every ear once more drunk in the intoxication of his maddening appeals.

It would have been easy to have traced the triumph of Mahtoree, in the reflecting countenances of his auditors. It was not long before a look of ferocity and of revenge was to be seen seated on the grim visages of most of the warriors, and each new and crafty allusion to the policy of extinguishing their enemies, was followed by fresh and less restrained bursts of approbation. In the height of this success, the Teton closed his speech, by a rapid appeal to the pride and hardihood of his native band, and suddenly took his seat.

In the midst of the murmurs of applause which succeeded so remarkable an effort of eloquence, a low, feeble and hollow voice was heard rising in the tumult, as if it rolled from the inmost cavities of the human chest, and gathered strength and energy as it issued into the air. A solemn stillness followed the sounds, and then the lips of the aged man were first seen to move.

"The day of Le Balafré, is near its end," were the first words which were distinctly audible. "He is like a buffaloe on whom the hair will grow no longer. He will soon be ready to leave his lodge, to go in search of another, that is far from the villages of the Siouxes. Therefore what he has to say, concerns not him, but those he leaves behind him. His words are like the fruit on the tree, ripe and fit to be given to chiefs."

"Many snows have fallen since Le Balafré has been found on the war path. His blood has been very hot, but it has had time to cool. The Wahcondah gives him dreams of war, no longer; he sees that it is better to live in peace."

"My Brothers, one foot is turned to the Happy hunting grounds, the other will soon follow; and then an old chief will be seen looking for the prints of his Father's moccasins, that he may make no mistake, but be sure to come before the Master of Life by the same path, as so many good Indians have already travelled. But who will follow? Le Balafré has no son. His oldest has ridden too many Pawnee horses; the bones of the youngest, have been gnawed by Konza dogs! Le Balafré has come to look for a young arm on which he may lean, and to find a son, that when he is gone his lodge may not be empty. Tachechana, the skipping fawn of the Tetons, is too weak to prop a warrior who is old. She looks before her, and not backwards. Her mind is in the lodge of her husband."

The enunciation of the veteran warrior had been calm, but distinct, and decided. His declaration was received in silence, and though several of the chiefs who were in the councils of Mahtoree turned their eyes on their leader, none presumed to oppose so aged and so venerated a brave, in a resolution that was strictly in conformity to the usages of the Nation. The Teton, himself, was content to await the result, with seeming composure, though the gleams of ferocity that played about his eye, occasionally betrayed the nature of those feelings, with which he witnessed a procedure that was likely to rob him of that one of all his intended victims, whom he most hated.

In the mean time, Le Balafré moved with a slow and painful step towards the captives. He stopped before the person of Hard-Heart, whose faultless form, unchanging eye, and lofty mien, he contemplated long, with high and evident satisfaction. Then making a gesture of authority, he awaited until his order had been obeyed, and the youth was released from the post and his bonds, by the same blow of the knife. When the young warrior was led nearer to his dimmed and failing sight, the examination was renewed with strictness of scrutiny, and that admiration, which physical excellence is so apt to excite in the breast of a savage.

"It is good," the wary veteran murmured, when he found that all his skill in the requisites of a brave could detect no blemish, "this is a leaping panther! Does my son speak with the tongue of a Teton?"

The intelligence which lighted the eyes of the captive, betrayed how well he understood the question, but still he was far too haughty to communicate his ideas, through the medium of a language that belonged to a hostile people. Some of the surrounding warriors explained to the old chief, that the captive was a Pawnee-Loup.

"My son opened his eyes on the 'waters of the wolves',"*said Le Balafré in the language of that nation; "but he will shut them in the bend of the 'river with a troubled stream.' He was born a Pawnee, but he will die a Dahcotah. Look at me. I am a sycamore that once covered many with my shadow. The leaves are fallen and the branches begin to drop. But a single succor is springing from my roots. It is a little vine and it winds itself about a tree that is green. I have long look'd for one, fit to grow by my side. Now have I found him. Le Balafré is no longer without a son; his name will not be forgotten when he is gone! Men of the Tetons, I take this youth, into my lodge."

No one was bold enough to dispute a right, that had so often been exercised, by warriors far inferior to the present speaker, and the adoption was listened to, in grave and respectful silence. Le Balafré, took his intended son by the arm, and leading him into the very centre of the circle, he stepped aside, with an air of triumph, in order that the spectators might approve of his choice. Mahtoree betrayed no evidence of his intentions, but rather seemed to await a moment better suited to the crafty policy of his character. The more experienced and sagacious chiefs distinctly foresaw the utter impossibility of two partisans so renowned, so hostile, and who had so long been rivals in fame, as their prisoner and their native leader, existing amicably in the same tribe. Still the character of Le Balafré was so imposing, and the custom to which he had resorted so sacred, that none dared to lift a voice in opposition to the measure. They watched the result with increasing interest, but with a coldness of demeanor that concealed the nature of their inquietude. From this state of embarrassment, and, as it might readily have proved, of disorganisation, the tribe was unexpectedly relieved by the decision of the one most interested in the success of the aged chief's design.

During the whole of the foregoing scene, it would have been difficult to have traced a single distinct emotion in the lineaments of the captive. He had heard his release proclaimed with the same indifference as the order to bind him to the stake. But now that the moment had arrived when it became necessary to make his election, he spoke in a way to prove that the fortitude which had bought for him so distinguished a name, had, in no degree, deserted him.

"My father, is very old, but he has not yet look'd upon every thing;" said Hard-Heart, in a voice so clear as to be heard by all in presence. "He has never seen a buffaloe change to a bat. He will never see a Pawnee become a Sioux!"

There was a suddenness and yet a calmness, in the manner of delivering this decision which assured most of the auditors, that it was unalterable. The heart of Le Balafré, however, was yearning towards the youth, and the fondness of age was not so readily repulsed. Reproving the burst of admiration and triumph, to which the boldness of the declaration and the freshened hopes of revenge, had given rise, by turning his gleaming eye around the band, the veteran, again addressed his adopted child as if his purpose was not to be denied.

"It is well," he said. "Such are the words a brave should use, that the warriors may see his heart. The day has been when the voice of Le Balafré was loudest amongst the lodges of the Konzas. But the root of a white hair is wisdom. My child will show the Tetons that he is brave, by striking their enemies. Men of the Dahcotahs this is my son!"

The Pawnee hesitated a moment, and then stepping in front of the chief, he took his hard and wrinkled hand, and laid it, with reverence on his head, as if to acknowledge the extent of his obligation. Then recoiling a step, he raised his person to its greatest elevation, and looked upon the hostile band by whom he was environed, with an air of loftiness and disdain, as he spoke aloud in the language of the Siouxes.

"Hard-Heart has look'd at himself, within and without. He has thought of all that he has done, in the hunts and in the wars. Every where he is the same. There is no change. He is in all things a Pawnee. He has struck so many Tetons, that he could never eat in their lodges. His arrows would fly backwards; the point of his lance would be on the wrong end; their friends would weep at every whoop he gave; their enemies would laugh. Do the Tetons know a Loup? Let them look at him again. His head is painted; his arm is flesh; his heart is rock. When the Tetons see the sun come from the Rocky Mountains and move toward the land of the pale-faces, the mind of Hard-Heart will soften, and his spirit will become Sioux! Until that day, he will live and die a Pawnee."

A yell of delight, in which admiration and ferocity were strangely mingled, interrupted the speaker, and but too clearly announced the character of his fate. The captive awaited a moment, for the commotion to subside, and then turning again to Le Balafré he continued in tones conciliating and kind, as if he felt the propriety of softening his refusal, in a manner not to wound the pride of one who would so gladly be his benefactor.

"Let my father lean heavier on the 'fawn of the Dahcotahs'," he said. "She is weak now, but as her lodge fills with young, she will be stronger. See," he added directing the eyes of the other to the earnest countenance of the attentive trapper, "Hard-Heart is not without a gray-head to show him the path to the blessed Prairies. If he ever has another father, it shall be that just warrior."

Le Balafré turned away in disappointment from the youth, and approached the stranger who had thus anticipated his design. The examination between these two aged men was long, mutual, and curious. It was not easy to detect the real character of the trapper, through the mask which the hardships of so many years had laid upon his features, especially when aided, by his wild and peculiar attire. Some moments elapsed before the Teton spoke, and then it was in doubt whether he addressed one like himself, or some wanderer of that race who, he had heard, were spreading themselves like hungry locusts, throughout the land.

"The head of my brother is very white," he said, "but the eye of Le Balafré is no longer like the eagle's. Of what colour is his skin?"

"The Wahcondah made me like these you see waiting for a Dahcotah judgement; but fair and foul have coloured me darker than the skin of a fox. What of that! Though the bark is ragged and riven, the heart of the tree is sound."

"My brother is a Big-Knife! Let him turn his face toward the setting sun, and open his eyes. Does he see the salt Lake, beyond the mountains?"

"The time has been, Teton, when few could see the white on the eagle's head farther than I, but the glare of fourscore and seven winters has dimmed my eyes, and, but little can I boast of sight, in my latter days. Does the Sioux think a pale face is a God, that he can look through hills!"

"Then let my brother look at me. I am nigh him, and he can see that I am a foolish red-man. Why cannot his people see every thing, since they crave all."

"I understand you, chief; nor will I gainsay the justice of your words, seeing that they are too much founded in truth. But though born of the race you love so little, my worst enemy, not even a lying Mingo, would dare to say, that I ever laid hands on the goods of another, except such as were taken in manful warfare, or that I ever coveted more ground, than the Lord has intended each man to fill."

"And yet my brother has come among the red-skins to find a son?"

The trapper laid a finger on the naked shoulder of Le Balafré, and looked into his scarred countenance, with a wistful and confidential expression as he answered.

"Ay, but it was only that I might do good to the boy. If you think, Dahcotah, that I adopted the youth in order to prop my age, you do as much injustice to my good will, as you seem to know little of the merciless intentions of your own people. I have made him my son, that he may know that one is left behind him—Peace, Hector, peace: Is this decent, pup, when gray-heads are counselling together, to break in upon their discourse with the whinings of a hound! The dog is old, Teton, and though well taught in respect of behavior, he is getting like ourselves, I fancy, something forgetful of the fashions of his youth"—

Further discourse, between these veterans, was interrupted by a discordant yell, which burst, at that moment, from the lips of the dozen withered crones who have already been mentioned, as having forced themselves into a conspicuous part of the circle. The outcry was excited by a sudden change in the air of Hard-Heart. When the old men turned towards the youth, they saw him standing in the very centre of the ring, with his head erect, his eye fixed on vacancy, one leg advanced, and an arm a little raised, as if all his faculties were absorbed in the act of listening. A smile lighted his countenance, for a single moment, and then the whole man sunk, again, into his former look of dignity and coldness, suddenly recalled to self-possession. The movement had been construed into contempt, and even the tempers of the chiefs began to be excited. Unable to restrain their fury, the women broke into the circle in a body, and commenced their attack by loading the captive with the most bitter revilings. They boasted of the various exploits which their sons had achieved at the expense of the different tribes of the Pawnees. They undervalued his own reputation, and told him to look at Mahtoree, if he had never yet seen a warrior. They accused him of having been suckled by a doe, and of having drunk in cowardice with his mother's milk. In short they lavished upon their unmoved captive a torrent of that vindictive abuse, in which the women of the savages are so well known to excel, but which has been too often described to need a repetition here.

The effect of this outbreaking was inevitable. Le Balafré turned away disappointed, and hid himself in the crowd, while the trapper whose honest features were working with his emotions, pressed nigher to his young friend, as those who are linked to the criminal by ties so strong as to brave the opinions of men, are often seen to stand about the place of execution, to support his dying moments. The excitement soon spread among the inferior warriors, though the chiefs, still forbore to make the signal which committed the victim to their mercy. Mahtoree, who had awaited such a movement among his fellows, with the wary design of concealing his own jealous hatred, soon grew weary of delay, and by a glance of his eye encouraged the tormentors to proceed.

Weucha, who eager for this sanction had long stood watching the countenance of the chief, bounded forward, at the signal, like a blood hound loosened from the leash. Forcing his way into the centre of the hags, who were already proceeding from abuse to violence, he reproved their impatience, and bade them wait, until a warrior had begun to torment, and then they should see their victim shed tears like a woman.

The heartless savage commenced his efforts, by flourishing his tomahawk about the head of the captive, in such a manner as to give reason to suppose each blow would bury the weapon in the flesh, while, it was so governed as not to touch the skin. To this customary expedient Hard-Heart was perfectly insensible. His eye kept the same, steady, riveted look on air, though the glittering ax described, in its evolutions, a bright circle of light, before his countenance. Frustrated in this attempt, the callous Sioux, laid the cold edge on the naked head of his victim, and began to describe the different manners, in which a prisoner might be flayed. The women kept time to his cruelties with their taunts, and endeavored to force some expression of the longings of nature from the insensible features of the Pawnee. But he evidently reserved himself for the chiefs, and for those moments of extreme anguish, when the loftiness of his spirit might evince itself, in a manner better becoming his high and untarnished reputation.

The eyes of the trapper followed every movement of the tomahawk, with the interest of a real father, until, at length, unable to command his indignation, he exclaimed in the native language of his friend—

"My son has forgotten his cunning. This is a low-minded Indian and one, easily, hurried into folly. I cannot do the thing myself, for my traditions forbid a dying warrior to revile his persecutors, but the gifts of a red-skin are different. Let the Pawnee say the bitter words, and purchase an easy death. I will answer for his success provided he speaks before the grave men, set their wisdom to back the folly of this fool."

The savage Sioux, who heard his words without comprehending their meaning, turned to the speaker and menaced him with death, for his temerity.

"Ay, work your will," said the unflinching old man. "I am as ready now, as I shall be to-morrow. Though it would be a death that an honest man might not wish to die. Look at that noble Pawnee, Teton; and see what a red-skin may become, who fears the Master of Life, and follows his laws. How many of your people has he sent to the distant Prairies;" he continued, in a sort of pious fraud, thinking that while the danger menaced himself there could surely be no sin in extolling the merits of another, "how many howling Siouxes has he struck like a warrior in open combat, while arrows were sailing in the air plentier than flakes of falling snow. Go. Will Weucha, speak the name of one enemy he has ever struck?"

"Hard-Heart!" shouted the Sioux, turning in his fury, and aiming a deadly blow, at the head of his victim. His arm fell into the hollow of the captive's hand. For a single moment the two stood, as if entranced, in that attitude, the one paralyzed by so unexpected a resistance and the other, bending his head, not to meet his death, but in the act of the most intense attention. The women screamed with triumph, for they thought the nerves of the captive had at length failed him. The trapper trembled for the honor of his friend, and Hector, as if conscious of what was passing, raised his nose into the air, and uttered a piteous howl.

But the Pawnee hesitated, only for that moment. Raising the other hand, like lightning, the tomahawk flashed in the air, and Weucha sunk to his feet, brained to its eye. Then cutting a way with the bloody weapon, he darted through the opening left by the frightened women, and seemed to descend the declivity at a single bound.

Had a bolt from heaven fallen in the midst of the Teton band, it would not have occasioned greater consternation, than this act of desperate hardihood. A shrill, plaintive cry burst from the lips of all the women, and there was a moment that even the oldest warriors appeared to have lost their faculties. This stupor endured only for the instant. It was succeeded by a yell of revenge, that burst from a hundred throats, while as many warriors started forward at the cry, bent on the most bloody retribution. But a powerful and authoritative call from Mahtoree arrested every foot. The chief, in whose countenance disappointment and rage were struggling with the affected composure of his station extended an arm towards the river, and the whole mystery was explained.

Hard-Heart, had already cross'd half the bottom, which lay between the acclivity and the water. At this precise moment a band of armed and mounted Pawnees, turned a swell, and galloped to the margin of the stream, into which the plunge of the fugitive was distinctly heard. A few minutes sufficed for his vigorous arm, to conquer the passage, and then, the shout from the opposite shore, told the humbled Tetons the whole extent of the triumph of their adversaries.

CHAPTER XXIX.

"If that shepherd be not in hand-fast, let him fly;
The curses he shall have, the tortures he shall feel,
Will break the back of man, the heart of monster."

The Winter's Tale, IV.iv. 795-98.

IT will readily be seen that the event just related was attended by an extraordinary sensation among the Siouxes. In leading the hunters of the band, back to the encampment their chief had neglected none of the customary precautions of Indian prudence, in order that his trail might escape the eyes of his enemies. It would seem however that the Pawnees had not only made the dangerous discovery, but had managed, with great art, to draw nigh the place, by the only side on which it was thought unnecessary to guard the approaches with the usual line of sentinels. The latter, who were scattered along the different little eminences, which lay in the rear of the lodges, were among the last to be apprised of the danger.

In such a crisis, there was little time for deliberation. It was by exhibiting the force of his character in scenes of similar difficulty, that Mahtoree had obtained and strengthened his ascendancy among his people, nor did he seem likely to lose it, by the manifestation of any indecision on the present occasion. In the midst of the screams of the young, the shrieks of the women, and the wild howlings of the crones, which were sufficient of themselves to have created a chaos in the thoughts of one less accustomed to act in emergencies, he promptly asserted his authority, issuing his orders with the coolness of a veteran.

While the warriors were arming, the boys were dispatched to the bottom for the horses. The tents were hastily struck by the women, and disposed of on such of the beasts, as were not deemed fit to be trusted in combat. The infants were cast upon the backs of their mothers, and those children who were of a size to march, were driven to the rear, like a herd of less reasoning animals. Though these several movements were made amid outcries and a clamor that likened the place to another Babel,* they were executed with incredible alacrity and intelligence.

In the mean time, Mahtoree neglected no duty that belonged to his responsible station. From the elevation on which he stood, he could command a perfect view of the force and evolutions of the hostile party. A grim smile lighted his visage, when he found, that in point of numbers, his own band was greatly the superior. Notwithstanding this advantage, however, there were other points of inequality, which would probably have a tendency to render his success in the approaching conflict, exceedingly doubtful. His people were the inhabitants of a more northern and less hospitable region than their enemies, and were far from being rich in that species of property, horses and arms, which constitutes the most highly prized wealth of a western Indian. The band in view, was mounted to a man, and, as it had come so far to rescue or to revenge their greatest partisan, he had no reason to doubt its being composed entirely of braves. On the other hand, many of his followers were far better in a hunt than in a combat; men who might serve to divert the attention of his foes but from whom he could expect little desperate service. Still, his flashing eye glanced over a body of warriors, on whom he had often relied, and who had never deceived him, and, though, in the precise position in which he found himself, he felt no disposition to precipitate the conflict, he certainly would have had no intention to avoid it, had not the presence of his women and children placed the option altogether in the power of his adversaries.

On the other hand, the Pawnees, so unexpectedly successful in their first and greatest object, manifested no intention to drive matters to an issue. The river was a dangerous barrier to pass, in the face of a determined foe, and it would now have been in perfect accordance with their cautious policy to have retired for a season, in order that their onset might be made in the hours of darkness, and of seeming security. But there was a spirit in their chief, that elevated him, for the moment, above the ordinary expedients of savage warfare. His bosom burned with the desire to wipe out that disgrace of which he had been the subject, and it is possible, that he believed the retiring camp of the Siouxes contained a prize, that begun to have a value in his eyes, far exceeding any that could be found in fifty Teton scalps. Let that be as it might, Hard-Heart had no sooner received the brief congratulations of his band, and communicated to the chiefs such facts as were important to be known, than he prepared himself to act such a part, in the coming conflict, as would at once maintain his well earned reputation, and gratify his secret wishes. A led horse, one that had been long trained in the hunts, had been brought to receive his master, with but little hope however that his services would ever be needed again, in this life. With a delicacy and consideration that proved how much the generous qualities of the youth had touched the feelings of his people, a bow, a lance, and a quiver, were thrown across the animal, which it had been intended to immolate on the grave of the young brave, a species of care, that would have superseded the necessity for the pious duty that the trapper had pledged himself to perform.

Though Hard-Heart was sensible of the kindness of his warriors, and believed that a chief furnished with such appointments, might depart with credit, for the distant hunting grounds of the Master of Life, he seemed equally disposed to think that they might be rendered quite as useful, in the actual state of things. His countenance lighted with stern pleasure, as he tried the elasticity of the bow, and poised the well balanced spear. The glance he bestowed on the shield was more cursory and indifferent, but the exultation with which he threw himself on the back of his favored war-horse was so great, as to break through the forms of Indian reserve. He rode, to and fro, among his scarcely less delighted warriors, managing the animal with a grace and address that no artifical rules can ever supply, at times flourishing his lance, as if to assure himself of his seat, and at others examining critically into the condition of the fusee with which he had also been furnished, with the fondness of one, who was miraculously restored to the possession of treasures, that constituted his pride and his happiness.

At this particular moment, Mahtoree, having completed the necessary arrangements, prepared to make a more decisive movement. The Teton had found no little embarrassment in disposing of his captives. The tents of the squatter were still in sight, and his wary cunning did not fail to apprise him, that it was quite as necessary to guard against an attack from that quarter, as to watch the motions of his more open and more active foes. His first impulse had been to make the tomahawk suffice for the men, and to trust the females under the same protection as the women of his band, but the manner in which so many of his braves continued to regard the imaginary Medecine of the Long-knives, forewarned him of the danger of so hazardous an experiment on the eve of a battle. It might be deemed the omen of defeat. In this dilemma, he motioned to a superannuated warrior, to whom he had confided the charge of the noncombatants, and leading him apart he placed a finger significantly on his shoulder, as he said in a tone, in which authority was tempered by confidence—

"When my young men are striking the Pawnees, give the women knives. Enough; my father is very old; he does not want to hear wisdom from a boy."

The grim old savage, returned a look of ferocious assent, and then the mind of the chief, appeared to be at rest on this important subject. From that moment he bestowed all his care, on the achievement of his revenge and the maintenance of his martial character. Throwing himself on his horse, he made a sign with the air of a Prince, to his followers to imitate his example, interrupting without ceremony the war songs and solemn rites by which many among them were stimulating their spirits to deeds of daring. When all were in order, the whole moved with great steadiness and silence towards the margin of the river.

The hostile bands were, now, separated by the water. The width of the stream was too great to admit of the use of the ordinary Indian missiles, but a few useless shots were exchanged from the fusees of the chiefs, more in bravado, than with any expectation of doing execution. As some time was suffered to elapse, in demonstrations and abortive efforts, we shall leave them, for that period, to return to such of our characters as remained in the hands of the savages.

We have shed much ink in vain, and wasted quires that might possibly have been better employed, if it be necessary, now, to tell the reader that few of the foregoing movements escaped the observation of the experienced trapper. He had been, in common with rest, astonished at the sudden act of Hard-Heart, and there was a single moment when a feeling of regret and mortification got the better of his longings to save the life of the youth. The simple and well-intentioned old man would have felt, at witnessing any failure of firmness on the part of a warrior who had so strongly excited his sympathies, the same species of sorrow that a christian parent would suffer in hanging over the dying moments of an impious child. But, when instead of an impotent and unmanly struggle for existence, he found that his friend had forborne with the customary and dignified submission of an Indian warrior, until an opportunity had offered to escape, and that he had then manifested the spirit and decision of the most gifted brave, his gratification became nearly too powerful to be concealed. In the midst of the wailing and commotion which succeeded the death of Weucha and the escape of the captive, he placed himself nigh the persons of his white associates, with a determination of interfering at every hazard should the fury of the savages take that direction. The appearance of the hostile band spared him however so desperate and probably so fruitless an effort, and left him to pursue his observations, and to mature his plans more at leisure.

He particularly remarked that, while by far the greater part of the women and all the children, together with the effects of the party, were hurried to the rear, probably with an order to secrete themselves in some of the adjacent woods, the tent of Mahtoree himself was left standing, and its contents undisturbed. Two chosen horses, however, stood near by, held by a couple of youths, who were too young to go into the conflict, and yet of an age to understand the management of the beasts. The trapper perceived in this arrangement the reluctance of Mahtoree to trust his newly found 'flowers' beyond the reach of his eye, and at the same time his forethought in providing against a reverse of fortune. Neither had the manner of the Teton in giving his commission to the old savage, nor the fierce pleasure with which the latter had received the bloody charge, escaped his observation. From all these mysterious movements, the old man was aware that a crisis was at hand, and he summoned the utmost knowledge he had acquired, in so long a life, to aid him in the desperate conjecture. While musing on the means to be employed, the Doctor, again, attracted his attention to himself, by a piteous appeal for assistance.

"Venerable trapper, or as I may now say liberator," commenced the dolorous Obed, "It would seem that a fitting time has at length arrived to dissever the unnatural and altogether irregular connexion which exists between my inferior members and the body of Asinus. Perhaps if such a portion of my limbs were released as might leave me master of the remainder, and this favorable opportunity were suitably improved, by making a forced march towards the settlements, all hopes of preserving the treasures of knowledge of which I am the unworthy receptacle, would not be lost. The importance of the results, is surely worth the hazard of the experiment."

"I know not, I know not," returned the deliberate old man. "The vermin and reptiles which you bear about you, were intended by the Lord for the Prairies, and I see no good in sending them into regions that may not suit their natur's. And, moreover you may be of great and particular use as you now sit on the Ass; though it creates no wonder, in my mind, to perceive that you are ignorant of it, seeing that usefulness is altogether a new calling to so bookish a man."

"Of what service can I be, in this painful thraldom, in which the animal functions are in a manner suspended and the spiritual or intellectual, blinded by the secret sympathy that unites mind to matter. There is likely to be blood spilt between yonder adverse hosts of heathens, and, though but little desiring the office, it would be better that I should employ myself in surgical experiments, than in thus wasting the precious moments, mortifying both soul and body."

"It is little that a red-skin would care to have a physicianer at his hurts while the whoop is ringing in his ears. Patience is a virtue in an Indian, and can be no shame to a Christian white-man. Look at these hags of squaws, friend Doctor; I have no judgement in savage tempers if they are not bloody-minded, and ready to work their accursed pleasures on us all. Now, so long as you keep upon the ass and maintain the fierce look, which is far from being your natural gift, fear of so great a Medicine may serve to keep down their courage. I am placed, here, like a general at the opening of the battle, and it has become my duty, to make such use of all my forces, as in my judgement each is best fitted to perform. If I know these niceties, you will be more serviceable for your countenance, just now, than in any more stirring exploits."

"Harkee, old trapper," shouted Paul, whose patience could no longer maintain itself, under the calculating and prolix explanations of the other, "suppose you cut two things I can name, short off. That is to say, your conversation, which is agreeable enough over a well baked buffaloe hump, and these damnable thongs of hide, which, according to my experience, can be pleasant, no where. A single stroke of your knife would be of more service, just now, than the longest speech that was ever made in a Kentucky Court-House."

"Ay Court-Houses are the 'happy hunting grounds' as a red-skin would say, for them that are born with gifts no better than such as lie in the tongue! I was carried into one of the lawless holes myself, once, and it was all about a thing of no more value than the skin of a deer. The Lord forgive them, the Lord forgive them; they knew no better, and they did according to their weak judgements, and therefore the more are they to be pitied. And yet it was a solemn sight to see an aged man, who had always lived in the air, laid neck and heels, by the law, and held up as a spectacle for the women and boys of a wasteful settlement to point their fingers at!"

"If such be your opinions of confinement, honest friend, you had better manifest the same, by putting us at liberty, with as little delay as possible," said Middleton, who like his companion, began to find the tardiness of his often-tried companion, quite as extraordinary as it was disagreeable.

"I should greatly like to do the same; especially in your behalf, Captain, who being a soldier might find not only pleasure but profit, in examining, more at your ease, into the circumventions and cunning of an Indian fight. As to our friend, here, it is of but little matter how much of this affair he examines, or how little, seeing that a bee is not to be overcome, in the same manner as an Indian."

"Old man, this trifling with our misery is inconsiderate, to give it a name no harsher—"

"Ay; your gran'ther was of a hot and hurrying mind, and one must not expect that the young of a Panther will crawl the 'arth like the litter of a porcupine. Now, keep you both silent, and what I say shall have the appearance of being spoken concerning the movements that are going on in the bottom; all of which will serve to put jealousy to sleep, and to shut the eyes of such as rarely close them, on wickedness and cruelty. In the first place, then, you must know, that I have reason to think, yonder treacherous Teton has left an order to put us all to death, so soon as he thinks the deed may be done, secretly and without tumult."

"Great Heaven! will you suffer us to be butchered like unresisting sheep."

"Hist, Captain, hist—a hot temper is none of the best, when cunning is more needed than blows. Ah! the Pawnee is a noble boy! it would do your heart good to see how he draws off from the river in order to invite his enemies to cross, and yet according to my failing sight, they count two warriors to his one! But as I was saying, little good comes of haste and thoughtlessness. The facts are so plain, that any child may see into their wisdom. The savages are of many minds, as to the manner of our treatment. Some fear us for our colour, and would gladly let us go, and other some would show us the mercy that the doe receives from the hungry wolf. When opposition gets fairly into the Councils of a tribe, it is rare that humanity is the gainer. Now see you, these wrinkled and cruel minded squaws—no, you cannot see them as you lie, but nevertheless they are here, ready and willing, like so many raging she-bears to work their will upon us, so soon as the proper time shall come."

"Harkee, old gentlemen trapper," interrupted Paul, with a little bitterness in his manner: "Do you tell us these matters for our amusement, or for your own. If for ours, you may keep your breath for the next race you run, as I am tickled nearly to suffocation already with my part of the fun."

"Hist—" said the trapper, cutting with great dexterity and rapidity the thong, which bound one of the arms of Paul to his body and dropping his knife at the same time within reach of the liberated hand. "Hist, boy, hist. That was a lucky moment, the yell from the bottom drew the eyes of these blood-suckers in another quarter, and so far we are safe. Now make a proper use of your advantages, but be careful that what you do, is done without being seen."

"Thank you for this small favor, old deliberation," muttered the bee-hunter, "though it comes, like a snow in May, somewhat out of season."

"Foolish boy," reproachfully exclaimed the other, who had moved to a little distance from his friends, and appeared to be attentively regarding the movements of the hostile parties; "will you never learn to know the wisdom of patience! And, you too, Captain; though a man, myself, that seldom ruffles his temper by vain feelings, I see that you are silent, because you scorn to ask favors any longer from one you think too slow to grant them. No doubt, ye are both young, and filled with the pride of your strength and manhood, and I dare say you thought it only needful to cut the thongs, to leave you masters of the ground. But he that has seen much, is apt to think much. Had I run like a bustling woman to have given you freedom, these hags of the Siouxes would have seen the same, and then where would you both have found yourselves! Under the tomahawk and the knife, like helpless and outcrying children, though gifted with the size and beards of men. Ask our friend the bee-hunter in what condition he finds himself to struggle with a Teton boy, after so many hours of bondage, much less with a dozen marciless and blood-thirsty squaws!"

"Truly, old trapper," returned Paul, stretching his limbs which were by this time entirely released, and endeavoring to restore the suspended circulation, "you have some judgematical notions in these matters. Now, here am I, Paul Hover, a man who will give in to few, at wrestle or race, nearly as helpless as the day I paid my first visit to the house of old Paul, who is dead and gone, the Lord forgive him any little blunders he may have made, while he tarried in Kentucky. Now there is my foot on the ground, so far as eye-sight has any virtue, and yet it would take no great temptation to make me swear, it didn't touch the earth by six inches! I say, honest friend, since you have done so much have the goodness to keep these damnable squaws, of whom you say so many interesting things, at a little distance 'till I have got the blood of this arm in motion, and am ready to receive them."

The trapper made a sign that he perfectly understood the case, as he walked towards the superannuated savage, who began to manifest an intention of commencing his assigned task, leaving the bee-hunter to recover the use of his limbs as well as he could, and to put Middleton in a similar situation to defend himself.

Mahtoree had not mistaken his man, in selecting the one he did to execute his bloody purpose. He had chosen one of those ruthless savages, more or less of whom are to be found in every tribe, who had purchased a certain share of military reputation, by the exhibition of a hardihood that found its impulses in an innate love of cruelty. Contrary to the high and chivalrous sentiment, which, among the Indians of the Prairies, renders it a deed of even greater merit to bear off the trophy of victory from a fallen foe, than to slay him, he had been remarkable for preferring the pleasure of destroying life, to the glory of striking the dead. While the more self-devoted and ambitious braves were intent on personal honor, he had always been seen established behind some favorable cover, depriving the wounded of hope, by finishing that which a more gallant warrior had begun. In all the cruelties of the tribe he had ever been foremost, and no Sioux was so uniformly found on the side of merciless councils.

He had awaited, with an impatience which his long practised restraint could with difficulty subdue, for the moment to arrive, when he might proceed to execute the wishes of the Great Chief, without whose approbation and powerful protection, he would not have dared to undertake a step, that had so many opposers in the nation. But events had been hastening to an issue, between the hostile parties, and the time had, now, arrived, greatly to his secret and malignant joy, when he was free to act his will.

The trapper found him distributing knives to the ferocious hags, who received the presents, chanting a low monotonous song, that recalled the losses of their people, in various conflicts with the whites, and which extolled the pleasures and glory of revenge. The appearance of such a groupe, was enough of itself to have deterred one, less accustomed to such sights than the old man, from trusting himself within the circle of their wild and repulsive rites.

Each of the crones, as she received the weapon, commenced a slow, and measured, but ungainly, step, around the savage, until the whole were circling him in a sort of magic dance. Their movements were timed, in some degree, by the words of their songs, as were their gestures by the ideas. When they spoke of their own losses, they tossed their long straight locks of gray into the air, or suffered them to fall in confusion upon their withered necks, but as the sweetness of returning blow for blow, was touched upon by any among them, it was answered by a common howl as well as by gestures that were sufficiently expressive of the manner in which they were exciting themselves, to the necessary state of fury.

Into the very centre of this ring of seeming demons, the trapper, now, stalked, with the same calmness and observation, as he would have walked into a village church. No other change was made by his appearance, than a renewal of the threatening gestures, with, if possible, a still less equivocal display of their remorseless intentions. Making a sign for them to cease, the old man demanded—

"Why do the mothers of the Tetons sing with bitter tongues? The Pawnee prisoners are not yet in their village; their young men have not come back loaded with scalps!"

He was answered by a general howl, and a few of the boldest of the furies even ventured to approach him, flourishing their knives within a dangerous proximity of his own steady eye-balls.

"It is a warrior you see, and no runner of the Long-knives whose face grows paler at the sight of a tomahawk;" returned the trapper, without moving a muscle. "Let the Sioux women think. If one white-skin dies, a hundred spring up where he falls."

Still the hags made no other answer, than by increasing their speed in the circle, and, occasionally, raising the threatening expressions of their chaunt, into louder and more intelligible strains. Suddenly, one of the oldest, and the most ferocious of them all broke out of the ring, and skirred away in the direction of her victims, like a rapacious bird, that having wheeled on poised wings, for the time necessary to insure its object, makes the final dart upon its prey. The others followed, a disorderly and screaming flock, fearful of being too late, to reap their portion of the sanguinary pleasure.

"Mighty Medicine of my people!" shouted the old man, in the Teton tongue, "lift your voice, and speak that the Sioux nation may hear!"

Whether Asinus had acquired so much knowledge by his recent experience, as to know the value of his sonorous properties, or the strange spectacle of a dozen hags flitting past him, filling the air with such sounds as were even grating to the ears of an ass, most moved his temper, it is certain that the animal did that which Obed was requested to do, and probably with far greater effect, than if the naturalist, had strove with his mightiest effort to be heard. It was the first time, that the strange beast had spoken, since his arrival in the encampment. Admonished by so terrible a warning, the hags scattered themselves, like vultures frightened from their prey, still screaming, and but half-diverted from their purpose.

In the mean time the sudden appearance and the imminency of the danger, quickened the blood in the veins of Paul and Middleton, more than all their laborious frictions, and physical expedients. The former had actually risen to his feet, and assumed an attitude which perhaps threatened more than the worthy bee-hunter was able to perform, and even the latter had mounted to his knees, and showed a disposition to do good service for his life. The unaccountable release of the captives from their bonds was attributed, by the hags, to the incantations of the Medecine and the mistake was probably of as much service, as the miraculous and timely interposition of Asinus in their favor.

"Now, is the time to come out of our ambushment," exclaimed the old man, hastening to join his friends, "and to make open and manful war. It would have been policy to have kept back the struggle, until the Captain was in better condition to join, but as we have unmasked our battery why we must maintain the ground"—

He was interrupted by feeling a gigantic hand on his shoulder. Turning under a sort of confused impression that necromancy was actually abroad in the place, he found that he was in the hands of a sorcerer—no less dangerous and powerful than Ishmael Bush. The file of the squatter's well-armed sons, that was seen issuing from behind the still standing tent of Mahtoree, explained at once not only the manner in which their rear had been turned, while their attention had been so earnestly bestowed on matters in front, but the utter impossibility of resistance.

Neither Ishmael, nor his sons deemed it necessary to enter into prolix explanations. Middleton and Paul were bound, again, with extraordinary silence and dispatch, and this time not even the aged trapper was exempt from a similar fortune. The tent was struck, the females placed upon the horses, and the whole were on the way towards the squatter's encampment with a celerity that might well have served to keep alive the idea of magic.

During this summary and brief disposition of things, the disappointed Agent of Mahtoree and his callous associates were seen flying across the plain in the direction of the retiring families, and when Ishmael left the spot with his prisoners and his booty, the ground which had so lately been alive with the bustle and life of an extensive Indian encampment was as still and empty as any other spot in those extensive wastes.

CHAPTER XXX.

"Is this proceeding just and honorable?"

II Henry IV, IV. ii. 110.

DURING the occurrence of these events on the upland plain, the warriors on the bottom had not been idle. We left the adverse bands watching one another on the opposite banks of the stream, each endeavoring to excite its enemy to some act of indiscretion by the most reproachful taunts and revilings. But the Pawnee chief was not slow to discover that his crafty antagonist had no objection to waste the time in so idle, and as they mutually proved, so useless expedients. He changed his plans accordingly, and withdrew from the bank, as has been already explained through the mouth of the trapper, in order to invite the more numerous host of the Siouxes to cross. The challenge was not accepted, and the Loups, were compelled to frame some other method to attain their end.

Instead of any longer throwing away the precious moments, in fruitless endeavors to induce his foe to cross the stream, the young Partisan of the Pawnees led his troop, at a swift gallop, along its margin, in quest of some favorable spot where, by a sudden push, he might throw his own band, without loss, to the opposite shore. The instant, his object was discovered, each mounted Teton received a footman behind him, and Mahtoree was still enabled to concentrate his whole force against the effort. Perceiving that his design was anticipated, and unwilling to blow his horses by a race, that would disqualify them for service, even after they had succeeded in outstripping the more heavily burthened cattle of the Sioux, Hard-Heart drew up, and came to a dead halt on the very margin of the water-course.

As the country was too open for any of the usual devices of savage warfare, and time was so pressing, the chivalrous Pawnee resolved to bring on the result by one of those acts of personal daring for which the Indian braves are so remarkable, and by which they often purchase their highest and dearest renown. The spot he had selected was favorable to such a project. The river, which throughout most of its course was deep and rapid, had expanded there to more than twice its customary width, and the rippling of its waters, proved that it flowed over a shallow bottom. In the centre of the current there was an extensive and naked bed of sand, but a little raised above the level of the stream, and of a colour and consistency that told a practised eye, that it afforded a firm and safe foundation for the foot. To this spot the partisan now turned his wistful gaze, nor was he long in making his decision. First speaking to his warriors and apprising them of his intentions, he dashed into the current, and partly by swimming and more by the use of his horse's feet, he reached the island in safety.

The experience of Hard-Heart had not deceived him. When his snorting steed issued from the water, he found himself on a quivering but damp and compact bed of sand, that was admirably adapted to the exhibition of the finest powers of the animal. The horse seemed conscious of the advantage, and bore his warlike rider, with an elasticity of step and a loftiness of air, that would have done no discredit to the highest trained and most generous charger. The blood of the chief himself, quickened, with the excitement of his situation. He sat the beast, as if conscious that the eyes of two tribes were on his movements, and as nothing could be more acceptable and grateful to his own band than this display of native grace and courage, so nothing could be more taunting and humiliating to their enemies.

The sudden appearance of the Pawnee, on the sands, was announced among the Tetons, by a general yell of savage anger. A rush was made to the shore, followed by a discharge of fifty arrows and a few fusees, and, on the part of several braves, there was a plain manifestation of a desire to plunge into the water, in order to punish the temerity of their insolent foe. But a call and a mandate, from Mahtoree, checked the rising and nearly ungovernable temper of his band. So far from allowing a single foot to be wet, or a repetition of the fruitless efforts of his people to drive away their foe with missiles, the whole of the party was commanded to retire from the shore, while he himself communicated his intentions to one or two of his most favored followers.

When the Pawnees observed the rush of their enemies twenty warriors rode into the stream, but so soon as they perceived that the Tetons had withdrawn, they fell back to a man, leaving their young chief to the support of his own often-tried skill and well established courage. The instructions of Hard-Heart on quitting his band had been worthy of the self-devotion and daring of his character. So long as single warriors came against him, he was to be left to the keeping of the Wahcondah and his own arm, but should the Siouxes attack him in numbers, he was to be sustained, man for man, even to the extent of his whole force. These generous orders were strictly obeyed, and though so many hearts in the troop, panted to share in the glory and danger of their partisan, not a warrior was found among them all who did not know how to conceal his impatience, under the usual mask of Indian self-restraint. They watched the issue with quick and jealous eyes, nor did a single exclamation of surprise escape them, when they saw, as will soon be apparent, that the experiment of their chief was as likely to conduce to peace as to war.

Mahtoree was not long in communicating his plans to his confidants, whom he as quickly dismissed to join their fellows in the rear. The Teton entered a short distance into the stream and halted. Here he raised his hand several times, with the palm outwards, and made several of those other signs which are construed into a pledge of amicable intentions among the inhabitants of those regions. Then, as if to confirm the sincerity of his faith, he cast his fusee to the shore, and entered deeper into the water, where he again came to a stand in order to see in what manner, the Pawnee would receive his pledges of peace.

The crafty Sioux had not made his calculations on the noble and honest nature of his more youthful rival, in vain. Hard-Heart had continued galloping across the sands, during the discharge of missiles and the appearance of a general onset, with the same proud and confident mien, as that with which he had first braved the danger. When he saw the well known person of the Teton partisan enter the river, he waved his hand in triumph, and flourishing his lance, he raised the thrilling war-cry of his people, as a challenge for him to come on. But when he saw the signs of a truce, though deeply practised in the treachery of savage combats, he disdained to show a less manly reliance on himself, than that which his enemy had seen fit to exhibit. Riding to the farthest extremity of the sands he cast his own fusee, from him, and returned to the point whence he had started.

The two chiefs were now armed alike. Each had his spear, his bow, his quiver, his little battle axe, and his knife, and each had also a shield of hides, which might serve as a means of a defense against a surprise from any of these weapons. The Sioux no longer hesitated, but advanced deeper into the stream, and soon landed on a point of the island, which his courteous adversary had left free for that purpose. Had one been there to watch the countenance of Mahtoree, as he crossed the water that separated him from the most formidable and the most hated of all his rivals, he might have fancied that he could trace the gleamings of a secret joy, breaking through the cloud which deep cunning and heartless treachery had drawn before his swarthy visage, and yet, there would have been moments, when he might have believed, that the flashings of the Teton's eye, and the expansion of his nostrils, had their origin in a nobler sentiment and one more worthy of an Indian chief.

The Pawnee awaited the time of his enemy with calmness and dignity. The Teton made a short turn or two, to curb the impatience of his steed, and to recover his seat, after the effort of crossing, and then he rode into the centre of the place, and invited the other, by a courteous gesture to approach. Hard-Heart drew nigh, until he found himself at a distance equally suited to advance or to retreat, and, in his turn, he came to a stand, keeping his glowing eye riveted on that of his enemy. A long and grave pause succeeded this movement, during which these two distinguished braves, who were now for the first time, confronted with arms in their hands, sat regarding each other, like warriors who knew how to value the merits of a gallant foe, however hated. But the mien of Mahtoree was far less stern and warlike than that of the partisan of the Loups. Throwing his shield over his shoulder, as if to invite the confidence of the other, he made a gesture of salutation, and was the first to speak.

"Let the Pawnees go upon the hills," he said, "and look from the morning to the evening sun, from the country of snows to the land of many flowers, and they will see that the earth is very large. Why cannot the red men find room on it, for all their villages!"

"Has the Teton ever known a warrior of the Loups come to his towns to beg a place for his lodge?" returned the young brave, with a look in which pride and contempt were not attempted to be concealed. "When the Pawnees hunt, do they send runners to ask Mahtoree, if there are no Siouxes on the Prairies!"

"When there is hunger in the lodge of a warrior, he looks for the buffaloe, which is given him for food," the Teton continued, struggling to keep down the ire excited by the other's scorn. "The Wahcondah has made more of them, than he has made Indians. He has not said this buffaloe shall be for a Pawnee, and that for a Dahcotah, this beaver for a Konza and that for an Omawhaw. No; he said, there are enough. I love my red children, and I have given them great riches. The swiftest horse shall not go from the village of the Tetons to the village of the Loups in many suns. It is far from the towns of the Pawnees to the river of the Osages. There is room for all that I love. Why, then, should a red-man strike his brother?"

Hard-Heart dropped one end of his lance to the earth, and having also cast his shield across his shoulder, he sat leaning lightly on the weapon, as he answered with a smile of no doubtful expression.

"Are the Tetons weary of the hunts, and of the war-path! do they wish to cook the venison, and not to kill it! Do they intend to let the hair cover their heads, that their enemies shall not know where to find their scalps! Go; a Pawnee warrior will never come among such Sioux squaws for a wife!"

A frightful gleam of ferocity broke out of the restraint of the Dahcotah's countenance as he listened to this biting insult; but he was quick in subduing the tell-tale feeling, in an expression much better suited to his present purpose.

"This is the way a young chief should talk of war," he answered with singular composure. "But Mahtoree has seen the misery of more winters than his brother. When the nights have been long and darkness has been in his lodge, while the young men slept, he has thought of the hardships of his people. He has said to himself, Teton, count the scalps in your smoke. They are all red but two! Does the wolf destroy the wolf, or the rattler strike his brother? You know they do not; therefore Teton, are you wrong, to go on a war-path that leads to the village of a red-skin, with a tomahawk in your hand."

"The Sioux would rob the warrior of his fame! He would say to his young men go, dig roots in the Prairies and find holes to bury your tomahawks in; you are no longer braves!"

"If the tongue of Mahtoree ever says thus," returned the crafty chief, with an appearance of strong indignation, "let his women cut it out, and burn it with the offals of the buffaloe. No," he added, advancing a few feet nigher to the immovable Hard-Heart, as if in the sincerity of confidence, "the red-man can never want an enemy. They are plentier than the leaves on the trees, the birds in the heavens, or the buffaloes on the Prairies. Let my brother open his eyes wide; does he no where see an enemy he would strike?"

"How long is it since the Teton counted the scalps of his warriors that were drying in the smoke of a Pawnee lodge! The hand that took them is here, and ready to make eighteen, twenty."

"Now let not the mind of my brother go on a crooked path. If a red-skin strikes a red-skin, forever, who will be masters of the Prairies,*when no warriors are left to say they are mine. Hear the voices of the old men. They tell us, that, in their days, many Indians have come out of the woods, under the rising sun, and that they have filled the

Prairies with their complaints of the robberies of the Long-knives. Where a Pale-face comes, a red-man cannot stay. The land is too small. They are always hungry. See, they are here already."

As the Teton spoke he pointed towards the tents of Ishmael, which were in plain sight, and then, he paused to await the effect of his words on the mind of his ingenuous foe. Hard-Heart listened like one, in whom a train of novel ideas had been excited by the reasoning of the other. He mused, for a minute before he demanded—

"What do the wise chiefs of the Sioux say must be done?"

"They think that the moccasin of every pale face, should be followed like the track of the bear. That the Long-knife who comes upon the Prairie, should never go back. That the path shall be open to those who come, and shut to those who go. Yonder are many. They have horses and guns. They are rich, but we are poor. Will the Pawnees meet the Tetons in Council; and when the sun is gone behind the Rocky Mountains, they will say this is for a Loup and this for a Sioux."

"Teton. No. Hard-Heart has never struck the stranger. They come into his lodge and eat, and they go out in safety. A mighty chief is their friend! When my people call the young men to go on the war-path, the moccasin of Hard-Heart is the last. But his village is no sooner hid by the trees, than it is the first. No. Teton. His arm will never be lifted against the stranger."

"Fool; then die, with empty hands!" Mahtoree exclaimed, setting an arrow to his bow, and sending it with a sudden and deadly aim full at the naked bosom of his generous and confiding enemy.

The action of the treacherous Teton was too quick, and too well matured to admit of any of the ordinary means of defense on the part of the Pawnee. His shield was hanging at his shoulder, and even the arrow had been suffered to fall from its place, and lay in the hollow of that hand which grasped his bow. But the quick eye of the brave had time to see the movement, and his ready thoughts did not desert him. Pulling hard and with a jerk upon the rein, his steed reared his forward legs into the air, and as the rider bent his body low, the horse served for a shield against the danger. So true however, was the aim, and so powerful the force by which it was sent, that the arrow entered the neck of the animal, and broke the skin on the opposite side.

Quicker than thought, Hard-Heart sent back an answering arrow. The shield of the Teton was transfixed, but his person was untouched. For a few moments the twang of the bow and the glancing of arrows were incessant, notwithstanding, the combatants were compelled to give so large a portion of their care to the means of defense. The quivers were soon exhausted, and though blood had been drawn, it was not in sufficient quantities to impair the energy of the combat.

A series of masterly and rapid evolutions with the horses now commenced. The wheelings, the charges, the advances and the circuitous retreats, were like the flights of circling swallows. Blows were struck with the lance, the sand was scattered in the air, and the shocks often seemed to be unavoidably fatal, but still each party kept his seat, and still each rein was managed with a steady hand. At length the Teton was driven to the necessity of throwing himself from his horse, in order to escape a thrust that would otherwise have proved fatal. The Pawnee passed his lance through the beast, uttering a shout of triumph as he galloped by. Turning in his tracks, he was about to push the advantage, when his own mettled steed, staggered, and fell under a burthen, that he could no longer sustain. Mahtoree answered his premature cry of victory and rushed upon the entangled youth with knife and tomahawk. The utmost agility of Hard-Heart had not sufficed to extricate himself in season from the fallen beast. He saw that his case was desperate. Feeling for his knife, he took the blade between a finger and thumb, and cast it with admirable coolness at his advancing foe. The keen weapon whirled a few times in the air, and its point meeting the naked breast of the impetuous Sioux, the blade was buried to the buck-horn haft.

Mahtoree laid his hand on the weapon, and seemed to hesitate whether to withdraw it or not. For a moment his countenance darkened with the most inextinguishable hatred and ferocity, and then, as if inwardly admonished how little time he had to lose, he staggered to the edge of the sands, and halted with his feet in the water. The cunning and duplicity which had so long obscured the brighter and nobler traits of his character were lost, in the never dying sentiment of pride, which he had imbibed in the days of his youth and of his comparative innocence.

"Boy of the Loups!" he said, with a smile of grim satisfaction, "the scalp of a mighty Dahcotah shall never dry in Pawnee smoke!"

Drawing the knife from the wound, he hurled it towards his enemy, in disdain. Then, shaking his arm at his successful foe, his swarthy countenance appearing to struggle with volumes of scorn and hatred that he could not utter with the tongue, he cast himself headlong into one of the most rapid, veins of the current, his hand still waving, in triumph, above the fluid even after his body had sunk into the tide, forever. Hard-Heart was by this time free. The silence which had hitherto reigned in the bands, was broken by general and tumultuous shouts. Fifty of the adverse warriors were already in the river, hastening to destroy or to defend the conqueror, and the combat was rather on the eve of its commencement than near its termination. But to all these signs of danger and need, the young victor was insensible. He sprang for the knife, and bounded with the foot of an antelope, along the sands looking for the receding fluid which concealed his prize. A dark, bloody spot, indicated the place, and, armed with the knife, he plunged into the stream, resolute to die in the flood or to return with his trophy.

In the mean time the sands became a scene of bloodshed and violence. Better mounted, and perhaps more ardent the Pawnees had, however, reached the spot in sufficient numbers to force their enemies to retire. The victors pushed their success to the opposite shore, and gained solid ground in the mélée of the fight. Here they were met by all the unmounted Tetons, and in their turn, they were forced to give way.

The combat now became more characteristic and circumspect. As the hot impulses which had driven both parties to mingle in so deadly a struggle began to cool, the chiefs were enabled to exercise their influence, and to temper the assaults with prudence. In consequence of the admonitions of their leaders, the Siouxes sought such covers as the grass afforded, or here and there some bush or slight inequality of the ground, and the charges of the Pawnee warriors necessarily became more wary and of course less fatal.

In this manner the contest continued with a varied success, and without much loss. The Siouxes had succeeded in forcing themselves into a thick growth of rank grass, where the horses of their enemies could not enter, or where when entered they were worse than useless. It became necessary to dislodge the Tetons from this cover or the objects of the combat must be abandoned. Several desperate efforts had been repulsed, and the disheartened Pawnees were beginning to think of a retreat, when the well known war-cry of Hard-Heart was heard at hand, and at the next instant the chief appeared in their centre flourishing the scalp of the Great Sioux, as a banner that would lead to victory.

He was greeted by a shout of delight and followed into the cover with an impetuosity that for the moment drove all before it. But the bloody trophy, in the hand of the partisan served as an incentive to the attacked, as well as to the assailants. Mahtoree had left many a daring brave behind him in his band, and the orator, who in the debates of that day had manifested such pacific thoughts, now exhibited the most generous self-devotion, in order to wrest the memorial of a man he had never loved, from the hands of the avowed enemies of his people.

The result was in favor of numbers. After a severe struggle, in which the finest displays of personal intrepidity were exhibited by all the chiefs, the Pawnees were compelled to retire upon the open bottom, closely pressed by the Siouxes, who failed not to seize each foot of ground ceded by their enemies. Had the Tetons stayed their efforts on the margin of the grass, it is probable that the honor of the day would have been theirs, notwithstanding the irretrievable loss they had sustained in the death of Mahtoree. But the more reckless braves of the band were guilty of an indiscretion, that entirely changed the fortunes of the fight, and suddenly stripped them of their hard earned advantages.

A Pawnee chief had sunk under the numerous wounds he had received, and he fell, a target for a dozen arrows in the very last groupe of his retiring party. Regardless, alike, of inflicting further injury on their foes, and of the temerity of the act, the Sioux braves bounded forward with a whoop, each man burning with the wish to reap the high renown of striking the body of the dead. They were met by Hard-Heart and a chosen knot of warriors, all of whom were just as stoutly bent on saving the honor of their nation, from so foul a stain. The struggle was hand to hand, and blood began to flow more freely. As the Pawnees retired with the body, the Siouxes pressed upon their footsteps, and, at length the whole of the latter broke out of the cover with a common yell, and threatened to bear down all opposition, by sheer physical superiority.

The fate of Hard-Heart and his companions, all of whom would have died rather than relinquish their object, would have been quickly sealed, but for a powerful and unlooked for interposition in their favor. A shout was heard from a little brake on the left. A volley from the fatal western rifle immediately succeeded. Some five or six Siouxes, leaped forward in the death agony and every arm among them was as suddenly suspended as if the lightning had flashed from the clouds to aid the cause of the Loups. Then came Ishmael and his stout sons, in open view, bearing down upon their late treacherous allies, with looks and voices that proclaimed the character of the succour.

The shock was too much for the fortitude of the Tetons. Several of their bravest chiefs had already fallen, and those that remained were instantly abandoned by the whole of the inferior herd. A few of the most desperate braves still lingered nigh the fatal symbol of their honor, and there nobly met their deaths, under the blows of the re-encouraged Pawnees. A second discharge from the rifles of the squatter and his party, completed the victory.

The Siouxes were now to be seen flying to more distant covers, with the same eagerness and desperation as a few moments before, they had been plunging into the fight. The triumphant Pawnees bounded forward in chase, like so many high-blooded and well trained hounds. On every side were heard the cries of victory, or the yells of revenge. A few of the fugitives endeavored to bear away the bodies of their fallen warriors, but the hot pursuit quickly compelled them to abandon the slain in order to preserve the living. Among all the struggles which were made, on that occasion, to guard the honor of the Siouxes from the stain which their peculiar opinions attached to the possession of the scalp of a fallen brave, but one solitary instance of success occurred.

The opposition of a particular chief to the hostile proceedings in the Councils of that morning has been already seen. But after having raised his voice, in vain, in support of peace, his arm was not backward, in doing its duty in the war. His prowess has been mentioned, and it was chiefly by his courage and example that the Tetons sustained themselves in the heroic manner they did, when the death of Mahtoree was known. This warrior, who, in the figurative language of his people was called, 'the Swooping Eagle,' had been the last to abandon the hopes of victory. When he found that the support of the dreaded rifle had robbed his band of their hard earned advantages, he sullenly retired amid a shower of missiles, to the secret spot where he had hid his horse, in the mazes of the highest grass. Here he found a new and an entirely unexpected competitor ready to dispute with him for the possession of the beast. It was Borecheena, the aged friend of Mahtoree; he whose voice had been given in opposition to his own wiser opinions, transfixed with an arrow, and evidently suffering under the pangs of approaching death.

"I have been on my last war-path," said the grim old warrior, when he found that the real owner of the animal had come to claim his property, "shall a Pawnee carry the white hairs of a Sioux into his village, to be a scorn to his women and children."

The other grasped his hand, answering to the appeal with the stern look of inflexible resolution. With this silent pledge, he assisted the wounded man to mount. So soon as he had led the horse to the margin of the cover, he threw himself also on its back, and securing his companion to his belt, he issued on the open plain, trusting entirely to the well known speed of the beast, for their mutual safety. The Pawnees were not long in catching a view of these new objects, and several turned their steeds to pursue. The race continued for a mile, without a murmur from the sufferer, though in addition to the agony of his body he had the pain of seeing his enemies approach at every leap of their horses.

"Stop," he said, raising a feeble arm to check the speed of his companion. "The eagle of my tribe must spread his wings wider. Let him carry the white hairs of an old warrior into the burnt-wood village."

Few words were necessary, between men who were governed by the same feelings of glory, and who were so well trained in the principles of their romantic honor. The Swooping Eagle, threw himself, from the back of the horse, and assisted the other to alight. The old man raised his tottering frame to its knees and, first casting a glance upward at the countenance of his countryman, as if to bid him adieu, he stretched out his neck to the blow he himself invited. A few strokes of the tomahawk, with a circling gash from the knife, sufficed to severe the head from the less valued trunk. The Teton mounted, again, just in season to escape a flight of arrows, which came from his eager and disappointed pursuers. Flourishing the grim and bloody visage, he darted away from the spot, with a shout of triumph, and was seen scouring the plains as if he were actually borne along on the wings of the powerful bird, from whose qualities he had received his flattering name. The Swooping Eagle reached his village in safety. He was one of the few Siouxes who escaped from the massacre of that fatal day, and for a long time he alone of the saved was able to lift his voice, in the Councils of his nation, with undiminished confidence.

The knife and the lance cut short the retreat of the larger portion of the vanquished. Even the retiring party of the women and children were scattered by the conquerors, and the sun had long sunk behind the rolling outline of the western horizon, before the fell business of that disastrous defeat was entirely ended.

CHAPTER XXXI.

"Which is the merchant here, and which the Jew."

The Merchant of Venice, IV.i. 174.

THE day dawned, the following morning, on a more tranquil scene. The work of blood had entirely ceased, and as the sun arose its light was shed on a broad expanse of quiet and solitude. The tents of Ishmael were still standing, where they had been last seen; but not another vestige of human existence could be traced in any other part of the waste. Here and there, little flocks of ravenous birds were sailing and screaming above those spots where some heavy-footed Teton had met his death, but every other sign of the recent combat had passed away. The river was to be traced far through the endless meadows by its serpentine and smoking bed, and the little silvery clouds of vapor which hung above the pools and springs were beginning to melt in air, as they felt the quickening warmth, which, pouring from the glowing sky, shed its bland and subtle influence on every object of the vast and unshadowed region. The Prairie was, like the heavens after the passage of the gust, soft, calm and soothing.

It was in the midst of such a scene, that the family of the squatter assembled to make their final decision, concerning the several individuals, who had been thrown into their power, by the fluctuating chances of the incidents related. Every being possessing life and liberty had been afoot, since the first streak of gray had lighted the east, and even the youngest of the erratic brood seemed conscious that the moment had arrived when circumstances were about to transpire that might leave a lasting impression on the wild fortunes of their semi-barbarous condition.

Ishmael moved through his little encampment with the seriousness of one who had been unexpectedly charged with matters of a gravity, exceeding any of the ordinary occurrences of his irregular existence. His sons, however, who had so often found occasions to prove the inexorable severity of their father's character, saw, in his sullen mien and cold eye rather a determination to adhere to his resolutions, which usually were as obstinately enforced as they were harshly conceived, than any evidences of wavering or doubt. Even Esther was sensibly affected by the important matters that pressed so heavily on the interests of her family. While she neglected none of those domestic offices, which would probably have proceeded under any conceivable circumstances, just as the world turns round with earthquakes rending its crust, and volcanoes consuming its vitals, yet her voice was pitched to a lower and more foreboding key than common, and the still frequent chidings of her children were tempered by something like the milder dignity of parental authority.

Abiram, as usual, seemed the one most given to solicitude and doubt. There were certain misgivings in the frequent glances that he turned on the unyielding countenance of Ishmael, which might have betrayed how little of their former confidence and good-understanding existed between them. His looks appeared to be vacillatory between hope and fear. At times his countenance lighted with the gleamings of a sordid joy, as he bent his look on the tent which contained his recovered prisoner, and then, again, the impression seemed unaccountably chased away by the shadows of intense apprehension. When under the influence of the latter feeling, his eye never failed to seek the visage of his dull and impenetrable kinsman. But there he rather found reason for alarm than grounds of encouragement, for the whole character of the squatter's countenance expressed the fearful truth that he had redeemed his dull faculties from the influence of the kidnapper, and that his thoughts were now brooding only on the achievement of his own stubborn intentions.

It was in this state of things that the sons of Ishmael, in obedience to an order from their father, conducted the several subjects of his contemplated decisions from their places of confinement into the open air. No one was exempted from this arrangement. Middleton and Inez, Paul and Ellen, Obed and the trapper were all brought forth, and placed in situations that were deemed suitable to receive the sentence of their arbitrary judge. The younger children gathered around the spot, in momentary but engrossing curiosity, and even Esther quitted her culinary labors and drew nigh to listen.

Hard-Heart, alone, of all his band, was present to witness the novel and far from unimposing spectacle. He stood leaning gravely on his lance, while the smoking steed, that grazed nigh, showed that he had ridden far and hard to be a spectator, on the occasion.

Ishmael had received his new ally with a coldness that showed his entire insensibility to that delicacy, which had induced the young chief to come alone, in order that the presence of his warriors might not create uneasiness, or distrust. He neither courted their assistance, nor dreaded their enmity, and he now proceeded to the business of the hour, with as much composure as if the species of patriarchal power he wielded was universally recognized.

There is something elevating in the possession of authority, however it may be abused. The mind is apt to make some efforts to prove the fitness between its qualities and the condition of its owner, though it may often fail, and render that ridiculous which was only hated before. But the effect on Ishmael Bush was not so disheartening. Grave in exterior, saturnine by temperament, formidable by his physical means and dangerous from his lawless obstinacy, his self-constituted tribunal excited a degree of awe, to which even the intelligent Middleton could not bring himself to be entirely insensible. Little time, however, was given to arrange his thoughts; for the squatter though unaccustomed to haste, having previously made up his mind, was not disposed to waste the moments in delay. When he saw that all were in their places, he cast a dull look over his prisoners, and addressed himself to the Captain as the principal man among the imaginary delinquents.

"I am called upon, this day, to fill the office, which in the settlements you give unto judges who are set apart to decide on matters that arise between man and man. I have but little knowledge of the ways of the courts, though there is a rule that is known unto all, and which teaches that an 'eye must be returned for an eye' and 'a tooth for a tooth.' I am no troubler of County houses, and least of all do I like living on a plantation that the sheriff has surveyed, yet there is a reason in such a law that makes it a safe rule to journey by, and therefore it ar' a solemn fact, that this day shall I abide by it, and give unto all and each, that which is his due and no more."

When Ishmael had delivered his mind thus far, he paused and looked about him as if he would trace the effects in the countenances of his hearers. When his eye met that of Middleton he was answered by the latter—

"If the evil doer is to be punished, and he that has offended none to be left to go at large, you must change situations with me, and become a prisoner instead of a Judge."

"You mean to say that I have done you wrong in taking the lady from her father's house, and leading her so far against her will into these wild districts," returned the unmoved squatter, who manifested as little resentment as he betrayed compunction at the charge. "I shall not put the lie on the back of an evil deed, and deny your words.

Since things have come to this pass, between us, I have found time to think the matter over at my leisure, and though none of your swift thinkers, who can see or who pretend to see into the nature of all things, by a turn of the eye, yet am I a man open to reason, and give me my time, one who is not given to deny the truth. Therefore have I mainly concluded that it was a mistake to take a child from its parent, and the Lady shall be returned whence she has been brought, as tenderly and as safely as man can do it."

"Ay, ay," added Esther, "the man is right. Poverty and labor bore hard upon him especially as county officers were getting troublesome, and in a weak moment he did the wicked act; but he has listened to my words, and his mind has got round again into its honest corner. An awful and a dangerous thing it is, to be bringing the daughters of other people into a peaceable and well-governed family!"

"And who will thank you, for the same, after what has been already done!" muttered Abiram, with a grin of disappointed cupidity, in which malignity and terror were disgustingly united. "When the devil has once made out his account, you may look for your receipt in full, only, at his hands."

"Peace!" said Ishmael, stretching his heavy hand towards his kinsman, in a manner that instantly silenced the speaker. "Your voice is like a raven's in my ears. If *you* had never spoken, I should have been spared this shame."

"Since then you are beginning to lose sight of your errors and to see the truth," said Middleton, "do not things by halves, but, by the generosity of your conduct, purchase friends, who may be of use in warding off any future danger from the law—"

"Young man," interrupted the squatter, with a dark frown, "*you*, too, have said enough. If fear of the law had come over me, you would not be here to witness the manner in which Ishmael Bush deals out justice."

"Smother not your good intentions, and remember if you contemplate violence to any among us, that the arm of that law you affect to despise reaches far, and that though its movements are sometimes slow, they are not the less certain."

"Yes, there is too much truth in his words, squatter," said the trapper, whose attentive ears rarely suffered a syllable to be uttered unheeded in his presence. "A busy and a troublesome arm, it often proves to be, here, in this land of America, where as they say, man is left greatly to the following of his own wishes, compared to other countries, and happier, ay, and, more manly, and more honest too, is he for the privilege. Why, do you know, my men, that there are regions where the law is so busy as to say, in this fashion shall you live, in that fashion shall you die, and in such another fashion shall you take leave of the world to be sent before the judgement seat of the Lord! A wicked and a troublesome meddling is that with the business of one, who has not made his creatures to be herded, like oxen and driven from field to field, as their stupid and selfish keepers may judge of their need and wants. A miserable land must that be where they fetter the mind as well as the body, and where the creatures of God, being born children are kept so by the wicked inventions of men who would take upon themselves the office of the great Governor of all!"

During the delivery of this pertinent opinion Ishmael was content to be silent, though the look with which he regarded the speaker manifested any other feeling than that of amity. When the old man was done, he turned to Middleton, and continued the subject which the other had interrupted.

"As to ourselves, young Captain, there has been wrong on both sides. If I have borne hard upon your feelings, in taking away your wife, with an honest intention of giving her back to you when the plans of that devil incarnate were answered, so have you broken into my encampment, aiding and abetting, as they have called many an honester bargain, in destroying my property."

"But what I did, was to liberate—"

"The matter is settled between us," interrupted Ishmael, with the air of one, who, having made up his own opinion on the merits of the question, cared very little for those of other people. "You and your wife are free to go and come, when and how you please. Abner, set the Captain at liberty; and now if you will tarry until I am ready to draw nigher to the settlements you shall both have the benefit of carriage; if not, never say that you did not get a friendly offer."

"Now may the strong oppress me and my sins be visited harshly on my own head if I forget your honesty, however slow it has been in showing itself," cried Middleton, hastening to the side of the weeping Inez, the instant he was released; "and, Friend, I pledge you the honor of a soldier that your own part of this transaction shall be forgotten, whatever I may deem fit to have done, when I reach a place where the arm of Government can make itself felt."

The dull smile with which the squatter answered to this assurance proved how little he valued the pledge that the youth in the first revulsion of his feelings was so free to make.

"Neither fear nor favor, but what I call justice has brought me to this judgement," he said. "Do you that which may seem right in your eyes, and believe that the world is wide enough to hold us both, without our crossing each other's path again. If you ar' content, well; if you ar' not content, seek to ease your feelings in your own fashion. I shall not ask to be let up, when you once put me fairly down. And now, Doctor, have I come to your leaf in my accounts. It is time to foot up the small reckoning that has been running on, for some time atwixt us. With you I entered into open and manly faith; in what manner have you kept it?"

The singular felicity with which Ishmael had contrived to shift the responsibility of all that had passed from his own shoulders to those of his prisoners, backed as it was by circumstances that hardly admitted of a very philosophical examination of any mooted point in Ethics, was sufficiently embarrassing to the several individuals, who were so unexpectedly required to answer for a conduct, which, in their simplicity, they had deemed so meritorious. The life of Obed had been so purely theoretic, that his amazement was not the least embarrassing, at a state of things, which might not have proved so very remarkable had he been a little more practised in the ways of the world. The worthy naturalist was not the first by many, who found himself, at the precise moment when he was expecting praise, suddenly arraigned to answer for the very conduct on which he rested all his claims to commendation. Though not a little scandalized at the unexpected turn of the transaction, he was fain to make the best of circumstances, and to bring forth such matter in justification, as first presented itself to his disordered faculties.

"That there did exist a certain compactum, or agreement, between Obed Batt, M.D. and Ishmael Bush, viator, or erratic husbandman," he said, endeavoring to avoid all offense in the use of terms, "I am not disposed to deny. I will admit that it was therein conditioned or stipulated, that a certain journey should be performed conjointly or in company, until so many days had been numbered. But as the said time has fully expired, I presume it fair to infer, that the bargain may now, be said to be obsolete—"

"Ishmael," interrupted the impatient Esther, "make no words with a man who can break your bones as easily as set them, and let the poisoning devil go! He's a cheat, from box to phial. Give him half the Prairie, and take the other half yourself. He an acclimator! I will engage to get the brats acclimated to a fever and ague bottom in a week and not a word shall be uttered, harder to pronounce than the bark of a cherry-tree, with perhaps a drop or two of western comfort. One thing ar' a fact, Ishmael, I like no fellow-travellers who can give a heavy feel to an honest woman's tongue, ay, and that without caring whether her household is in order, or out of order."

The air of settled gloom which had taken possession of the squatter's countenance, lighted, for an instant, with a look of dull drollery as he answered—

"Different people might judge differently, Eester, of the virtue of the man's art. But sin' it is your wish to let him depart, I will not plough the Prairie to make the walking rough. Friend, you ar' at liberty to go into the settlements and there I would advise you to tarry, as men, like me, who make but few contracts do not relish the custom of breaking them so easily."

"And now, Ishmael," resumed his conquering wife, "in order to keep a quiet family, and to smother all heart-burnings atween us, show yonder red-skin and his daughter," pointing to the aged Le Balafré and the widowed Tachechana, "the way to their village, and let us say to them, God bless you, and farewell, in the same breath."

"They ar' the captives of the Pawnee, according to the rules of Indian warfare, and I cannot meddle with his rights."

"Beware the Devil, my man! He's a cheat and a tempter and none can say they ar' safe with his awful delusions before their eyes! Take the advice of one, who has the honor of your name at heart, and send the tawney Jezebel away."

The squatter laid his broad hand on her shoulder and looking her steadily in the eye, he answered, in tones that were both stern and solemn.

"Woman, we have that before us, which calls our thoughts to other matters than the follies you mean. Remember what is to come, and put your silly jealousy to sleep."

"It is true, it is true," murmured his wife, moving back among her daughters, "God forgive me, that I should forget it!"

"And, now, young man; you who have so often come into my clearing, under the pretence of lining the bee into his hole," resumed Ishmael, after a momentary pause, as if to recover the equilibrium of his mind, "with you there is a heavier account to settle. Not satisfied with rummaging my camp, you have stolen a girl who is akin to my wife, and who I had calculated to make, one day, a daughter of my own."

A stronger sensation was produced by this, than by any of the preceding interrogations. All the young men bent their curious eyes on Paul and Ellen, the former of whom seemed in no small mental confusion, while the latter bent her face on her bosom in shame.

"Harkee, friend Ishmael Bush," returned the Bee-hunter, who found that he was expected to answer to the charge of burglary, as well as to that of abduction. "That I did not give the most civil treatment to your pots and pails I am not going to gainsay. If you will name the price you put upon the articles, it is possible the damage may be quietly settled between us, and all hard feelings forgotten. I was not in a church-going humour when we got upon your rock, and it is more than probable there was quite as much kicking as preaching among your wares, but a hole in the best man's coat can be mended by money. As to the matter of Ellen Wade, here, it may not be got over so easily. Different people have different opinions on the subject of matrimony. Some think it is enough to say yes and no to the questions of the magistrate, or of the parson if one happens to be handy, in order to make a quiet house, but I think that when a young woman's mind is fairly bent on going in a certain direction, it will be quite as prudent to let her body follow. Not that I mean to say, Ellen was not altogether forced to what she did, and therefore she is just as innocent, in this matter, as yonder jack-ass, who was made to carry her, and greatly against his will, too, as I am ready to swear he would say himself, if he could speak as loud as he can bray."

"Nelly," resumed the squatter, who paid very little attention to what Paul considered a highly creditable and ingenious vindication. "Nelly, this is a wide and wicked world on which you have been in such a hurry to cast yourself. You have fed and you have slept, in my camp for a year, and I did hope that you had found the free air of the borders, enough to your mind to wish to remain among us."

"Let the girl have her will," muttered Esther, from the rear, "he who might have persuaded her to stay, is sleeping in the cold and naked Prairie, and little hope is left of changing her humour; besides a woman's mind is a wilful thing and not easily turned from its waywardness as you know yourself, my man, or I should not be here the mother of your sons and daughters."

The squatter seemed reluctant to abandon his views on the abashed girl, so easily, and before he answered to the suggestion of his wife, he turned his usual dull look along the line of the curious countenances of his boys, as if to see whether there was not one among them fit to fill the place of the deceased. Paul was not slow to observe the expression, and hitting nigher than usual on the secret thoughts of the other, he believed he had fallen on an expedient which might remove every difficulty.

"It is quite plain, friend Bush," he said, "that there are two opinions in this matter; yours for your sons, and mine for myself. I see but one amicable way of settling this dispute, which is as follows. Do you make a choice among your boys of any you will, and let us walk off together for the matter of a few miles into the Prairies; the one who stays behind, can never trouble any man's house or his fixen, and the one who comes back may make the best of his way he can, in the good-wishes of the young woman."

"Paul!" exclaimed the reproachful, but smothered voice of Ellen.

"Never fear, Nelly," whispered the literal bee-hunter, whose straight-going mind suggested no other motive of uneasiness on the part of his mistress than concern for himself; "I have taken the measure of them all, and you may trust an eye that has seen to line many a bee into his hole!"

"I am not about to set myself up as a ruler of inclinations," observed the squatter. "If the heart of the child is truly in the settlements, let her declare it; she shall have no let or hindrance from me. Speak, Nelly, and let what you say come from your wishes without fear or favor. Would you leave us to go with this young man into the settled countries, or will you tarry and share the little we have to give, but which to you we give so freely?"

Thus called upon to decide, Ellen could no longer hestitate. The glance of her eye was at first timid and furtive. But as the colour flushed her features and her breathing became quick and excited, it was apparent that the native spirit of the girl was gaining the ascendancy over the bashfulness of sex.

"You took me a fatherless, impoverished, and friendless orphan," she said struggling to command her voice, "when others, who live in what may be called affluence compared to your state, chose to forget me, and may heaven in its goodness bless you for it. The little I have done, will never pay you for that one act of kindness. I like not your manner of life; it is different from the ways of my childhood and it is different from my wishes, still, had you not led this sweet and unoffending lady from her friends, I should never have quitted you, until you yourself had said, 'go, and the blessing of God go with you'!"

"The act was not wise but it is repented of; and so far as it can be done, in safety, it shall be repaired. Now, speak freely; will you tarry, or will you go?"

"I have promised the lady," said Ellen dropping her eyes again to the earth, "not to leave her, and after she has received so much wrong from our hands she may have a right to claim that I keep my word."

"Take the cords from the young man," said Ishmael. When the order was obeyed he motioned for all his sons to advance and he placed them in a row before the eyes of Ellen. "Now let there be no trifling, but open your heart. Here ar' all I have to offer, besides a hearty welcome."

The distressed girl turned her abashed look from the countenance of one of the young men to that of another, until her eye met the troubled and working features of Paul. Then nature got the better of forms. She threw herself into the arms of the bee-hunter, and sufficiently proclaimed her choice by sobbing aloud. Ishmael signed to his sons to fall back, and evidently mortified though perhaps not disappointed by the result, he no longer hesitated.

"Take her," he said, "and deal honestly and kindly by her. The girl has that in her which should make her welcome in any man's house, and I should be loth to hear she ever came to harm. And now I have settled with you all, on terms that I hope you will not find hard, but on the contrary just and manly. I have only another question to ask and that is of the Captain; do you choose to profit by my teams in going into the settlements, or not?"

"I hear that some soldiers of my party are looking for me near the villages of the Pawnees," said Middleton, "and I intend to accompany this chief in order to join my men."

"Then the sooner we part the better. Horses are plenty on the bottom. Go, make your choice and leave us in peace."

"That is impossible while the old man who has been a friend of my family near half-a-century is left a prisoner. What has he done that he too is not released?"

"Ask no questions that may lead to deceitful answers," sullenly returned the squatter; "I have dealings of my own with that trapper, that it may not befit an officer of the States to meddle with. Go, while your road is open."

"The man may be giving you honest counsel, and that which it concerns you all to hearken to," observed the old captive who seemed in no uneasiness at the extraordinary condition in which he found himself. "The Siouxes are a numberless and bloody-minded race and no one can say how long it may be, afore they will be out again on the scent of revenge. Therefore I say to you, go, also; and take especial heed in crossing the bottoms that you get not entangled again in the fires, for the honest hunters often burn the grass, at this season, in order that the buffaloes may find a sweeter and a greener pasturage in the spring."

"I should forget not only my gratitude, but my duty to the laws, were I to leave this prisoner in your hands even by his own consent, without knowing the nature of his crime, in which we may have all been his innocent accessaries."

"Will it satisfy you to know that he merits all he will receive?"

"It will at least change my opinion of his character."

"Look then at this," said Ishmael, placing before the eyes of the Captain the bullet that had been found about the person of the dead Asa; "with this morsel of lead did he lay low as fine a boy as ever gave joy to a parent's eyes!"

"I cannot believe that he has done this deed unless in self-defence, or on some justifiable provocation. That he knew of the death of your son I confess, for he pointed out the brake in which the body lay, but that he has wrongfully taken his life nothing but his own acknowledgment shall persuade me to believe."

"I have lived long," commenced the trapper, who found by the general pause that he was expected to vindicate himself from the heavy imputation, "and much evil have I seen in my day. Many are the prowling bears and leaping panthers that I have met fighting for the morsel which has been thrown in their way, and many are the reasoning men that I have looked on striving against each other unto death, in order that human madness might have its hour. For myself, I hope there is no boasting in saying that though my hand has been needed in putting down wickedness and oppression, it has never struck a blow of which its owner will be ashamed to hear, at a reckoning that shall be far mightier than this."

"If my father, has taken life from one of his tribe," said the young Pawnee, whose quick eye had read the meaning of what was passing, in the bullet and in the countenances of the others, "let him give himself up to the friends of the dead, like a warrior. He is too just to need thongs to lead him to judgment."

"Boy, I hope you do me justice. If I had done the foul deed with which they charge me, I should have manhood enough to come and offer my head to the blow of punishment as all good and honest red-men do the same." Then giving his anxious Indian friend a look to reassure him of his innocence, he turned to the rest of his attentive and interested listeners as he continued in English, "I have a short story to tell, and he that believes it will believe the truth, and he that disbelieves it will only lead himself astray, and perhaps his neighbour too. We were all outlying about your camp, friend squatter, as by this time you may begin to suspect, when we found that it contained a wronged and imprisoned lady, with intentions neither more honest nor dishonest than to set her free, as in nature and justice she had a right to be. Seeing that I was more skilled in scouting than the others, while they lay back in the cover, I was sent upon the plain, on the business of the reconnoitrings. You little thought that one was so nigh who saw into all the circumventions of your hunt, but there was I, sometimes flat behind a bush or a tuft of grass, sometimes rolling down a hill into a bottom, and little did you dream that your motions were watched as the panther watches the drinking deer. Lord, squatter, when I was a man in the pride and strength of my days, I have looked in at the tent door of the enemy, and they sleeping, ay, and dreaming too of being at home and in peace. I wish there was time to give you the partic—"

"Proceed with your explanation," interrupted Middleton.

"Ah! and a bloody and wicked sight it was! There I lay in a low bed of grass, as two of the hunters came nigh each other. Their meeting was not cordial, nor such as men who meet in a desert should give each other, but I thought they would have parted in peace, until I saw one put his rifle to the other's back and do, what I call a treacherous and sinful murder. It was a noble and a manly youth, that boy!— Though the powder burnt his coat he stood the shock for more than a minute, before he fell. Then was he brought to his knees and a desperate and manful fight he made to the brake, like a wounded bear seeking a cover."

"And why, in the name of heavenly justice, did you conceal this!" cried Middleton.

"What! think you, Captain, that a man who has spent more than three-score years in the wilderness has not learned the virtue of discretion. What red-warrior runs to tell the sights he has seen, until a fitting time? I took the Doctor to the place in order to see whether his skill might not come in use, and our friend the bee-hunter, being in company, was knowing to the fact that the bushes held the body."

"Ay; it ar' true," said Paul; "but not knowing what private reasons might make the old trapper wish to hush the matter up, I said as little about the thing as possible; which was just nothing at all."

"And who was the perpetrator of this deed?" demanded Middleton.

"If by perpetrator you mean him who did the act, yonder stands the man, and a shame and a disgrace is it to our race that he is of the blood and family of the dead."

"He lies! he lies!" shrieked Abiram. "I did no murder; I gave but blow for blow."

The voice of Ishmael was deep and even awful, as he answered—

"It is enough. Let the old man go. Boys, put the brother of your mother in his place."

"Touch me not!" cried Abiram. "I'll call on God to curse ye if you touch me!"

The wild and disordered gleam of his eye, at first induced the young men to arrest their steps, but when Abner, older and more resolute than the rest, advanced full upon him with a countenance that bespoke the hostile state of his mind, the affrighted criminal turned, and making an abortive effort to fly, fell with his face to the earth, to all appearance perfectly dead. Amid the low exclamations of horror which succeeded, Ishmael made a gesture which commanded his sons to bear the body into a tent.

"Now," he said, turning to those who were strangers in his camp, "nothing is left to be done, but for each to go his own road. I wish you all well; and to you, Ellen, though you may not prize the gift, I say, God bless you."

Middleton, awe-struck by what he believed a manifest judgment of Heaven, made no further resistance but prepared to depart. The arrangements were brief and soon completed. When they were all ready, they took a short and silent leave of the squatter and his family, and then the whole of the singularly constituted party was seen slowly, and silently following the victorious Pawnee, towards his distant villages.

CHAPTER XXXII.

"And I beseech you,
Wrest once the law, to your authority:
To do a great right, do a little wrong."
The Merchant of Venice, IV.i. 214-16.

ISHMAEL awaited long and patiently for the motley train of Hard-Heart to disappear. When his scout reported that the last straggler of the Indians, who had joined their chief so soon as he was at such a distance from the encampment as to excite no jealousy by their numbers, had gone behind the most distant swell of the Prairie, he gave forth the order to strike his tents. The cattle were already in the gears, and the moveables were soon transferred to their usual places in the different vehicles. When all these arrangements were completed, the little wagon, which had so long been the tenement of Inez, was drawn before the tent into which the insensible body of the kidnapper had been borne, and preparations were evidently made for the reception of another Prisoner. Then it was, as Abiram appeared, pale, terrified and tottering beneath a load of detected guilt, that the younger members of the family were first apprised that he still belonged to the class of the living. A general and superstitious impression had spread among them, that his crime had been visited by a terrible retribution from heaven, and they now gazed at him as at a being who belonged rather to another world than as a mortal who like themselves had still to endure the last agony, before the great link of human existence could be broken. The criminal himself appeared to be in a state, in which the most sensitive and startling terror was singularly combined with total physical apathy. The truth was, that while his person had been numbed by the shock his susceptibility to apprehension kept his agitated mind in unrelieved distress. When he found himself in the open air, he looked about him, in order to gather, if possible, some evidences of his future fate, from the countenances of those gathered round. Seeing every where grave but composed features, and meeting in no eye any expression that threatened immediate violence, the miserable man began to revive, and, by the time he was seated in the wagon, his artful faculties were beginning to plot the expedients of parrying the just resentment of his kinsmen, or if these should fail him, the means of escaping from a punishment that his forebodings told him would be terrible.

Throughout the whole of these preparations Ishmael rarely spoke. A gesture, or a glance of the eye, served to indicate his pleasure to his sons, and with these simple methods of communication, all parties appeared content. When the signal was made to proceed, the squatter threw his rifle into the hollow of his arm, and his axe across his shoulder, taking the lead as usual. Esther buried herself in the wagon which contained her daughters; the young men took their customary places among the cattle, or nigh the teams, and the whole proceeded at their ordinary, dull, but unremitted gait.

For the first time, in many a day, the squatter turned his back towards the setting sun. The route he held was in the direction of the settled country, and the manner in which he moved, sufficed to tell his children, who had learned to read their father's determinations in his mien, that their journey on the Prairie was shortly to have an end. Still nothing else transpired for hours, that might denote the existence of any sudden, or violent, revolution in the purposes or feelings of Ishmael. During all that time he marched alone, keeping a few hundred rods in front of his teams, seldom giving any sign of extraordinary excitement. Once or twice, indeed, his huge figure was seen standing on the summit of some distant swell, with his head bent towards the earth, as he leaned on his rifle; but then these moments of intense thought were rare, and of short continuance. The train had long thrown its shadows towards the east, before any material alteration was made in the disposition of their march. Water-courses were waded, plains were passed, and rolling ascents risen and descended, without producing the smallest change. Long practised in the difficulties of that peculiar species of travelling, in which he was engaged, the squatter avoided the more impracticable obstacles of their route by a sort of instinct, invariably inclining to the right or left, in season, as the formation of the land, the presence of trees or the signs of rivers forewarned him of the necessity of such movements.

At length the hour arrived when charity to man and beast required a temporary suspension of labor. Ishmael chose the required spot with his customary sagacity. The regular formation of the country, such as it has been described in the earlier pages of our book, had long been interrupted by a more unequal and broken surface. There were it is true in general the same wide and empty wastes, the same rich and extensive bottoms, and that wild and singular combination of swelling fields and of nakedness which gives that region the appearance of an ancient country, incomprehensibly stripped of its people and their dwellings. But these distinguishing features of the rolling Prairies had long been interrupted by irregular hillocks, occasional masses of rock and broad belts of forest.

Ishmael chose a spring that broke out of the base of a rock some forty or fifty feet in elevation as a place well suited to the wants of his herds. The water moistened a small swale that lay beneath the spot, which yielded in return for the fecund gift, a scanty growth of grass. A solitary willow had taken root in the alluvion, and profiting by its exclusive possession of the soil, the tree had sent up its stem far above the crest of the adjacent rock, whose peaked summit had once been shadowed by its branches. But its loveliness had gone with the mysterious principle of life. As if in mockery of the meagre show of verdure that the spot exhibited, it remained a noble and solemn monument of former fertility. The larger, ragged and fantastick branches still obtruded themselves abroad, while the white and hoary trunk stood naked and tempest-riven. Not a leaf, nor a sign of vegetation was to be seen about it. In all things it proclaimed the frailty of existence, and the fulfilment of time.

Here Ishmael after making the customary signal for the train to approach, threw his vast frame upon the earth and seemed to muse on the deep responsiblity of his present situation. His sons were not long in arriving, for the cattle no sooner scented the food and water than they quickened their pace, and then succeeded the usual bustle and avocations of a halt.

The impression made by the scene of that morning was not so deep, or lasting, on the children of Ishmael and Esther as to induce them to forget the wants of nature. But while the sons were searching among their stores for something substantial to appease their hunger, and the younger fry were wrangling about their simple dishes, the parents of the unnurtured family were differently employed.

When the squatter saw that all, even to the reviving Abiram were busy in administering to their appetites, he gave his downcast partner a glance of his eye and withdrew towards a distant roll of the land, which bounded the view towards the east. The meeting of the pair, in this naked spot was like an interview held above the grave of their murdered son. Ishmael signed to his wife to take a seat beside him on a fragment of rock, and then followed a space during which neither seemed disposed to speak.

"We have journeyed together long, through good and bad," Ishmael at length commenced; "much have we had to try us, and some bitter cups have we been made to swallow, my woman, but nothing like this has ever before lain in my path."

"It is a heavy cross for a poor, misguided and sinful woman to bear!" returned Esther, bowing her head to her knees, and partly concealing her face in her dress. "A heavy and a burthensome weight is this to be laid upon the shoulders of a sister and a Mother!"

"Ay; therein lies the hardship of the case. I had brought my mind to the punishment of that houseless trapper, with no great strivings, for the man has done me few favors, and God forgive me if I suspected him wrongfully of much evil. This is, however, bringing shame in at one door of my cabin in order to drive it out at the other. But shall a son of mine be murdered and he who did it go at large. The boy would never rest!"

"Oh, Ishmael, we pushed the matter far. Had little been said, who would have been the wiser? our consciences might then have been quiet."

"Eest'er," said the husband turning on her a reproachful but still a dull regard, "the hour has been, my woman, when you thought another hand had done this wickedness?"

"I did, I did; the Lord gave me the feeling as a punishment for my sins; but his mercy was not slow in lifting the veil; I looked into the book, Ishmael, and there I found the words of comfort."

"Have you that book at hand, woman; it may happen to advise in such a dreary business."

Esther fumbled in her pocket, and was not long in producing the fragment of a bible, which had been thumbed and smoke-dried till the print was nearly illegible. It was the only article in the nature of a book that was to be found among the chattels of the squatter, and it had been preserved by his wife as a melancholy relick of more prosperous and possibly of more innocent days. She had long been in the habit of resorting to it under the pressure of such circumstances as were palpably beyond human redress though her spirit and resolution rarely needed support under those that admitted of reparation through any of the ordinary means of reprisal. In this manner Esther had made a sort of convenient ally of the word of God, rarely troubling it for counsel, however, except when her own incompetency to avert an evil was too apparent to be disputed. We shall leave casuists to determine how far she resembled any other believers in this particular, and proceed directly with the matter before us.

"There are many awful passages in these pages, Ishmael," she said, when the volume was opened, and the leaves were slowly turning under her finger, "and some there ar' that teach the rules of punishment."

Her husband made a gesture for her to find one of those brief rules of conduct which have been received among all christian nations as the direct mandates of the Creator, and which have been found so just, that even they who deny their high authority admit their wisdom. Ishmael listened with grave attention, as his companion read all those verses which her memory suggested and which were thought applicable to the situation in which they found themselves. He made her show him the words, which he regarded with a sort of strange reverence. A resolution once taken was usually irrevocable in one who was moved with so much difficulty. He put his hand upon the book and closed the pages himself, as much as to apprise his wife that he was satisfied. Esther, who so well knew his character, trembled at the action, and casting a glance at his steady eye, she said—

"And yet, Ishmael, my blood, and the blood of my children is in his veins! cannot mercy be shown?"

"Woman," he answered sternly, "when we believed that miserable old trapper had done this deed, nothing was said of mercy."

Esther made no reply, but folding her arms upon her breast she sat silent and thoughtful for many minutes. Then she once more turned her anxious gaze upon the countenance of her husband, where she found all passion and care apparently buried in the coldest apathy. Satisfied now that the fate of her brother was sealed, and possibly conscious how well he merited the punishment, that was meditated, she no longer thought of mediation. No more words passed between them. Their eyes met, for an instant and then both arose and walked in profound silence, towards the encampment.

The squatter found his children expecting his return in the usual, listless manner with which they awaited all coming events. The cattle were already herded and the horses in their gears, in readiness to proceed, so soon as he should indicate that such was his pleasure. The children were already in their proper vehicle and, in short, nothing delayed the departure but the absence of the parents of the wild brood.

"Abner," said the Father with the deliberation with which all his proceedings were characterized, "take the brother of your mother from the wagon, and let him stand upon the 'arth."

Abiram issued from his place of concealment, trembling it is true, but far from destitute of hopes as to his final success in appeasing the just resentment of his kinsman. After throwing a glance around him, with the vain wish of finding a single countenance in which he might detect a solitary gleam of sympathy, he endeavoured to smother those apprehensions that were by this time reviving in their original violence by forcing a sort of friendly communication between himself and the squatter.

"The beasts are getting jaded, brother," he said "and as we have made so good a march, already, is it not time to 'camp. To my eye, you may go far, before a better place than this is found to pass the night in."

"'Tis well you like it. Your tarry, here, ar' likely to be long. My sons, draw nigh, and listen. Abiram White," he added lifting his cap and speaking with a solemnity and steadiness that rendered even his dull mien imposing, "you have slain my first born and according to the laws of God and Man must you die!"

The kidnapper started at this terrible and sudden sentence, with the terror that one would exhibit who unexpectedly found himself in the grasp of a monster from whose power there was no retreat. Although filled with the most serious forebodings of what might be his lot, his courage had not been equal to looking his danger in the face, and with the deceitful consolation with which timid tempers are apt to conceal their desperate condition from themselves, he had rather courted a treacherous relief in his cunning, than prepared himself for the worst.

"Die!" he repeated in a voice that scarcely issued from his chest. "A man is surely safe among his kinsmen!"

"So thought my boy," returned the squatter, motioning for the team that contained his wife and the girls to proceed, as he very coolly examined the priming of his piece. "By the rifle did you destroy my son; it is fit and just that you meet your end by the same weapon."

Abiram stared about him, with a gaze that bespoke an unsettled reason. He even laughed, as if he would not only persuade himself but others that what he heard was some pleasantry intended to try his nerves. But no where did his frightful merriment meet with an answering echo. All around him was solemn and still. The visages of his nephews were excited, but cold towards him, and that of his former confederate frightfully determined. This very steadiness of mien was a thousand times more alarming and hopeless than any violence could have proved. The latter might possibly have touched his spirit, and awakened resistance, but the former threw him entirely on the feeble resources of himself.

"Brother," he said in a hurried, unnatural whisper, "did I hear you?"

"My words are plain, Abiram White; thou hast done murder, and for the same must thou die."

"Esther! Sister, Sister, will you leave me! Oh! Sister, do you hear my call!"

"I hear one speak from the grave," returned the husky tones of Esther, as the wagon passed the spot where the criminal stood. "It is the voice of my first born calling aloud for justice! God have mercy, God have mercy, on your soul!"

The team slowly pursued its route, and the deserted Abiram now found himself deprived of the smallest vestige of hope. Still he could not summon fortitude to meet his death, and had not his limbs refused to aid him, he would yet have attempted to fly. Then by a sudden revolution from hope to utter despair he fell upon his knees and commenced a prayer in which cries for mercy to God and to his kinsman were wildly and blasphemously mingled. The sons of Ishmael turned away in horror at the disgusting spectacle, and even the stern nature of the squatter began to bend before so abject misery.

"May that which you ask of Him, be granted," he said, "but a father can never forget a murdered child."

He was answered by the most humble appeals for time. A week, a day, an hour were each implored, with an earnestness commensurate to the value they receive when a whole life is compressed into their short duration. The squatter was troubled and at length he yielded in part to the petitions of the criminal. His final purpose was not altered, though he changed the means. "Abner," he said, "mount the rock, and look on every hand, that we may be sure none are nigh."

While his nephew was obeying this order, gleams of reviving hope were seen shooting across the quivering features of the kidnapper. The report was favorable, nothing having life, the retiring teams excepted, was to be seen. A messenger was, however, coming from the latter, in great apparent haste. Ishmael awaited its arrival. He received from the hands of one of his wondering and frighted girls a fragment of that book which Esther had preserved with so much care. The squatter beckoned the child away, and placed the leaves in the hands of the criminal,

"Eester has sent you this," he said, "that in your last moments, you may remember God."

"Bless her, bless her; a good and kind sister has she been to me! But time must be given that I may read, time, my brother, time."

"Time shall not be wanting. You shall be your own executioner, and this miserable office shall pass away from my hands."

Ishmael proceeded to put his new resolution in force. The immediate apprehensions of the kidnapper were quieted by an assurance that he might yet live for days, though his punishment was inevitable. A reprieve, to one abject and wretched as Abiram, temporarily, produced the same effects as a pardon. He was even foremost in assisting in the appalling arrangements, and of all the actors, in that solemn tragedy his voice alone was facetious and jocular.

A thin shelf of the rock projected beneath one of the ragged arms of the willow. It was many feet from the ground, and admirably adapted to the purpose, which in fact, its appearance had suggested. On this little platform the criminal was placed, his arms bound at the elbows behind his back beyond the possibility of liberation, with a proper cord leading from his neck to the limb of the tree. The latter was so placed that when suspended the body could find no foot-hold. The fragment of the bible was placed in his hands, and he was left to seek his consolation as he might from its pages.

"And now, Abiram White," said the squatter when his sons had descended from completing this arrangement, "I give you a last and solemn asking. Death is before you in two shapes. With this rifle can your misery be cut short, or by that cord sooner or later must you meet your end."

"Let me yet live, Oh! Ishmael, you know not how sweet life is, when the last moment draws so nigh!"

"'Tis done," said the squatter, motioning for his assistants to follow the herds and teams. "And now, miserable man, that it may prove a consolation to your end, I forgive you my wrongs, and leave you to your God."

Ishmael turned, and pursued his way across the plain, at his ordinarily sluggish and ponderous gait. Though his head was bent a little towards the earth, his inactive mind did not prompt him to cast a look behind. Once, indeed, he thought he heard his name called in tones that were a little smothered, but they failed to make him pause.

At the spot where he and Esther had conferred, he reached the boundary of the visible horizon from the rock. Here he stopped and ventured a glance in the direction of the place he had just quitted. The sun was near dipping into the plains beyond, and its last rays lighted the naked branches of the willow. He saw the ragged outline of the whole drawn against the glowing heavens, and he even traced the still upright form of the being he had left to his misery. Turning the roll of the swell he proceeded with the feelings of one, who had been suddenly and violently separated from a recent confederate forever.

Within a mile, the squatter overtook his teams. His sons had found a place suited to the encampment for the night, and merely awaited his approach to confirm their choice. Few words were necessary to express his acquiescence. Every thing passed in a silence more general and remarkable than ever. The chidings of Esther were not heard among her young, or if heard, they were more in the tones of softened admonition, than in her usual, upbraiding, key.

No questions or explanations passed between the husband and his wife. It was only as the latter was about to withdraw among her children for the night that the former saw her taking a furtive look at the pan of his rifle. Ishmael bad his sons seek their rest, announcing his intention to look to the safety of the camp in person. When all was still, he walked out upon the Prairie, with a sort of sensation that he found his breathing among the tents too straightened. The night was well adapted to heighten the feelings which had been created by the events of the day.

The wind had risen with the moon, and it was occasionally sweeping heavily over the plain, in a manner that rendered it easy for the sentinel to fancy strange and unearthly sounds were in the blasts. Yielding to the extraordinary impulses of which he was the subject, he cast a glance around, to see that all were slumbering in security, and then he strayed towards the swell of land already mentioned. Here the squatter found himself at a point that commanded a view to the east and to the west. Light fleecy clouds were driving before the moon, which was cold and watery though there were moments, when its placid rays were shed from clear blue fields seeming to soften objects to its own mild loveliness.

For the first time, in a life of so much wild adventure, Ishmael felt a keen sense of solitude. The naked Prairies began to assume the forms of illimitable and dreary wastes, and the rushing of the wind sounded like the whisperings of the dead. It was not long before he thought a shriek was borne past him on a blast. It did not sound like a call from earth, but it swept frightfully through the upper air, mingled with the hoarse acompanyment of the wind. The teeth of the squatter were compressed and his huge hand grasped the rifle, as if it would crush the metal. Then came a lull, a fresher blast, and a cry of horror that seemed to have been uttered at the very portals of his ears. A sort of echo burst involuntarily from his own lips, as men will shout under unnatural excitement, and throwing his rifle across his shoulder he proceeded towards the rock with the strides of a giant.

It was not often that the blood of Ishmael moved at the rate with which the fluid circulates in the veins of ordinary men, but, now he felt it ready to gush from every pore in his body. The animal was aroused, in his most latent energies. Ever as he advanced he heard those shrieks, which sometimes seemed ringing among the clouds, and sometimes passed so nigh, as to appear to brush the earth. At length there came a cry in which there could be no delusion, or to which the imagination could lend no horror. It appeared to fill each cranny of the air, as the visible horizon is often charged to fullness by one dazzling flash of the electric fluid. The name of God was distinctly audible, but it was awfully and blasphemously blended with sounds that may not be repeated. The squatter stopped and for a moment, he covered his ears with his hands. When he withdrew the latter, a low and husky voice at his elbow asked in smothered tones,

"Ishmael, my man, heard ye nothing!"

"Hist!" returned the husband, laying a powerful arm on Esther, without manifesting the smallest surprise at the unlooked for presence of his wife. "Hist, woman, if you have the fear of Heaven, be still!"

A profound silence succeeded. Though the wind rose and fell, as before, its rushing was no longer mingled with those fearful cries. The sounds were imposing and solemn, but it was the solemnity and majesty of nature.

"Let us go on!" said Esther. "All is hushed!"

"Woman, what has brought you here!" demanded her husband, whose blood had returned into its former channels, and whose thoughts had already lost a portion of their excitement.

"Ishmael, he murdered our first born; but it is not meet that the son of my mother should lie upon the ground, like the carrion of a dog!"

"Follow," returned the squatter again grasping his rifle, and striding towards the rock. The distance was still considerable, and their approach, as they drew nigh the place of execution, was moderated by awe. Many minutes had passed before they reached a spot, where they might distinguish the outlines of the dusky objects.

"Where have you put the body?" whispered Esther. "See, here are pick and spade, that a brother of mine may sleep, in the bosom of the earth!"

The moon broke from behind a mass of clouds, and the eye of the woman was enabled to follow the finger of Ishmael. It pointed to a human form swinging, in the wind, beneath the ragged and shining arm of the willow. Esther bent her head and veiled her eyes from the sight. But Ishmael drew nigher and long contemplated his work in awe, though not in compunction. The leaves of the sacred book were scattered on the ground, and even a fragment of the shelf had been displaced by the kidnapper in his agony. But all was now in the stillness of death. The grim and convulsed countenance of the victim, was at times brought full into the light of the moon, and again as the wind lulled, the fatal rope drew a dark line across its bright disk. The squatter raised his rifle, with extreme care and fired. The cord was cut, and the body came lumbering to the earth a heavy and insensible mass.

Until now, Esther had not moved nor spoken. But her hand was not slow to assist in the labor of the hour. The grave was soon dug. It was instantly made to receive its miserable tenant. As the lifeless form descended, Esther, who sustained the head, looked up into the face of her husband, with an expression of anguish, and said —

"Ishmael, my man, it is very terrible. I cannot kiss the corpse of my father's child!"

The squatter laid his broad hand on the bosom of the dead, and said,

"Abiram White, we all have need of mercy, from my soul, do I forgive you. May God in Heaven have pity on your sins."

The woman bowed her face, and imprinted her lips long and fervently on the pallid forehead of her brother. After this came the falling clods and all the solemn sounds of filling a grave. Esther lingered on her knees, and Ishmael stood uncovered while the woman muttered a prayer. All was then finished.

On the following morning the teams and herds of the squatter were seen pursuing their course towards the settlements. As they approached the confines of society, the train was blended among a thousand others. Though some of the numerous descendants of this peculiar pair, were reclaimed from their lawless and semi-barbarous lives, the principals of the family, themselves, were never heard of more.

CHAPTER XXXIII.

—"No leave take I; for I will ride,
As far as land will let me, by your side."

Richard II, I.iii. 251-52.

THE passage of the Pawnee to his village was interrupted by no
scene of violence. His vengeance had been as complete as it was summary. Not even a solitary scout of the Siouxes was left on the hunting
grounds he was obliged to traverse, and of course the journey of
Middleton's party was as peaceful as if made in the bosom of the
States. The marches were timed to meet the weakness of the females.
In short, the victors seemed to have lost every trace of ferocity with
their success, and appeared disposed to consult the most trifling of
the wants of that engrossing people, who were daily encroaching on
their rights, and reducing the red-men of the West, from their state of
proud independance to the condition of fugitives and wanderers.

Our limits will not permit a detail of the triumphal entry of the
conquerors. The exultation of the tribe was proportioned to its previous
despondency. Mothers boasted of the honorable deaths of their sons,
wives proclaimed the honor and pointed to the scars of their husbands, and Indian girls rewarded the younger braves with songs of
triumph. The trophies of their fallen enemies were exhibited, as
conquered standards are displayed in more civilized regions. The
deeds of former warriors were recounted by the aged men and declared
to be eclipsed by the glory of this victory. While, Hard-Heart, himself, so distinguished for his exploits, from boy-hood to that hour, was
unanimously proclaimed and re-proclaimed the worthiest chief and
the stoutest brave that the Wahcondah had ever bestowed on his most
favored children, the Pawnees of the Loup.

Notwithstanding the comparative security in which Middleton
found his recovered treasure, he was not sorry to see his faithful and
sturdy artillerists, standing among the throng, as he entered in the
wild train, and lifting their voices, in a martial shout to greet his
return. The presence of this force, small as it was, removed every
shadow of uneasiness from his mind. It made him master of his movements, gave him dignity and importance in the eyes of his new friends,
and would enable him to overcome the difficulties of the wide region

which still lay between the village of the Pawnees and the nearest fortress of his Countrymen. A lodge was yielded to the exclusive possession of Inez and Ellen, and, even Paul when he saw an armed sentinel in the uniform of the States, pacing before its entrance, was content to stray among the dwellings of the 'redskins' prying with but little reserve into their domestic economy, commenting sometimes jocularly, sometimes gravely and always freely on their different expedients, or endeavoring to make the wondering housewives comprehend his quaint explanations of what he conceived to be the better customs of the whites.

This inquiring and troublesome temper found no imitators among the Indians. The delicacy and reserve of Hard-Heart were communicated to his people. When every attention, that could be suggested by their simple manners and narrow wants, had been fulfilled no intrusive foot presumed to approach the cabins devoted to the service of the strangers. They were left to seek their repose in the manner which most comported with their habits and inclinations. The songs and rejoicings of the tribe, however, ran far into the night, during the deepest hours of which the voice of more than one warrior was heard, recounting from the top of his lodge the deeds of his people and the glory of their triumphs.

Every thing having life, notwithstanding the excesses of the night, was abroad with the appearance of the sun. The expressions of exultation, which had so lately been seen on every countenance, was now changed to one better suited to the feeling of the moment. It was understood by all, that the Pale-faces who had befriended their Chief, were about to take their final leave of the tribe. The soldiers of Middleton in anticipation of his arrival, had bargained with an unsuccessful trader for the use of his boat, which lay in the stream ready to receive its cargo, and nothing remained to complete the arrangements for the long journey.

Middleton did not see this moment arrive, entirely, without distrust. The admiration with which Hard-Heart regarded Inez, had not escaped his jealous eyes, any more than had the lawless wishes of Mahtoree. He knew the consummate manner in which a savage could conceal his designs, and he felt that it would be a culpable weakness to be unprepared for the worst. Secret instructions were therefore given to his men, while the preparations they made were properly masked behind the show of military parade, with which it was intended to signalise their departure.

The conscience of the young soldier reproached him, when he saw the whole tribe accompanying his party to the margin of the stream with unarmed hands and sorrowful countenances. They gathered in a circle around the strangers and their chief and became not only peaceful but deeply interested observers of what was passing. As it was evident that Hard-Heart intended to speak, the former stopped, and manifested their readiness to listen, the trapper performing the office of an interpreter. Then the chief addressed his people, in the usual, metaphorical language of an Indian. He commenced by alluding to the antiquity and renown of his own nation. He spoke of their successes in the hunts and on the war path; of the manner in which they had always known how to defend their rights and to chastise their enemies. After he had said enough to manifest his respect for the greatness of the Loups, and to satisfy the pride of the listeners, he made a sudden transition to the race of whom the strangers were members. He compared their countless numbers to the flights of migratory birds in the season of blossoms, or in the fall of the year. With a delicacy, that none knew better how to practise than an Indian warrior, he made no direct mention of the rapacious temper, that so many of them had betrayed, in their dealings with the red-men. Feeling, that the sentiment of distrust was strongly engrafted in the tempers of his tribe, he rather endeavored to soothe any just resentment they might entertain, by indirect excuses and apologies. He reminded the listeners that even the Pawnee Loups had been obliged to chase many unworthy individuals from their villages. The Wahcondah sometimes veiled his countenance from a red man. No doubt the Great Spirit of the Pale Faces often looked darkly on his children. Such as were abandoned to the worker of Evil, could never be brave or virtuous, let the color of the skin be what it might. He bade his young men look at the hands of the Big knives. They were not empty, like those of hungry beggars. Neither were they filled with goods like those of knavish traders. They were like themselves warriors and they carried arms, which they knew well how to use. They were worthy to be called brothers!

Then he directed the attention of all to the chief of the strangers. He was a son of their Great White Father. He had not come upon the Prairies to frighten the buffaloes from their pastures, or to seek the game of the Indians. Wicked men had robbed him of one of his wives. No doubt she was the most obedient, the meekest, and the loveliest of them all. They had only to open their eyes to see that his words must be true. Now that the White Chief had found his wife he was about to return to his own people in peace. He would tell them that the Pawnees were just, and there would be a line of wampum between the two nations. Let all his people wish the strangers a safe return to their towns. The warriors of the Loups knew, both, how to receive their enemies, and how to clear the briars from the path of their friends.

The heart of Middleton beat quick, as the young Partisan[1] alluded to the charms of Inez, and for an instant he cast an impatient glance at his little line of Artillerists; but the chief, from that moment, appeared to forget he had ever seen so fair a being. His feelings, if he had any on the subject, were veiled behind the cold mask of Indian self-denial. He took each warrior by the hand, not even forgetting the meanest soldier, but his cold and collected eye never wandered, for an instant, towards either of the females. Arrangements had been made for their comfort, with a prodigality and care, that had not failed to excite some surprise in his young men, but in no other particular did he shock their manly pride, by betraying any solicitude in behalf of the weaker sex.

The leave-taking was general and imposing. Each male Pawnee was sedulous to omit no one of the strange warriors in his attentions, and of course the ceremony occupied some time. The only exception, and that was not general, was in the case of Dr. Battius. Not a few of the young men, it is true were indifferent about lavishing civilities on one of so doubtful a profession, but the worthy naturalist found some consolation in the more matured politeness of the old men, who had inferred, that though not of much use in war, the Medicine of the Big knives, might possibly be made serviceable in peace.

When all of Middleton's party had embarked, the trapper lifted a small bundle, which had lain at his feet, during the previous proceedings, and whistling Hector to his side, he was the last to take his seat. The Artillerists gave the usual cheers which were answered by a shout from the tribe, and then the boat was shoved into the current, and began to glide swiftly down its stream.

[1] The Americans and the Indians have adopted several words, which each believes peculiar to the language of the others. Thus "squaw," "papoose" or child, wigwam &c. &c. though it is doubtful whether they belonged at all to any Indian dialect, are much used by both white and red men in their intercourse. Many words are derived from the French, in this species of Prairie nomaic. Partizain, Brave &c., are part of the number. [1832]

A long, and a musing, if not a melancholy, silence succeeded this departure. It was first broken by the trapper, whose regret was not the least visible, in his dejected and sorrowful eye.

"They are a valiant and an honest tribe!" he said; "that will I say boldly in their favor: and second only do I take them to be, to that once mighty but now scattered people, the Delaware of the Hills! Ahs! me; Captain, if you had seen as much good and evil, as I have seen in these nations of red-skins, you would know of how much value, was a brave and simple-minded warrior. I know that some are to be found, who both think and say that an Indian is but little better than the beasts of these naked plains. But it is needful to be honest in one's-self, to be a fitting judge of honesty in others. No doubt, no doubt, they know their enemies, and little do they care to show them, any great confidence, or love."

"It is the way of man," returned the Captain; "and, it is probable they are not wanting in any of his natural qualities."

"No, no, it is little that they want that natur' has had to give. But as little does he know of the temper of a red-skin, who has seen but one Indian, or one tribe, as he knows of the colour of feathers who has only looked upon a crow. Now, friend steersman, just give the boat a sheer towards yonder low, sandy point, and a favor will be granted at a short asking."

"For what?" demanded Middleton, "we are now in the swiftest of the current, and by drawing to the shore we shall lose the force of the stream."

"Your tarry will not be long," returned the old man applying his own hand to the execution of that which he had requested. The oarsmen had seen enough of his influence, with their leader, not to dispute his wishes, and before time was given for further discussion on the subject the bow of the boat had touched the land.

"Captain," resumed the other, untying his little wallet, with great deliberation, and even, in a manner to show, that he found satisfaction in the delay, "I wish to offer you a small matter of trade. No great bargain, mayhap, but still it is the best that one, of whose hand the skill of the rifle has taken leave, and who has become no better than a miserable trapper can offer, before we part."

"Part!" was echoed from every mouth, among those who had so recently shared his dangers, and profited by his care.

"What the devil, old trapper, do you mean to foot it to the settlements, when here is a boat that will float the distance in half the time the Jack Ass the Doctor has given the Pawnee, could trot along the same!"

"Settlements, Boy! It is long sin' I took my leave of the waste and wickedness of the settlements and the village. If I live in a clearing, here it is one of the Lord's making, and I have no hard thoughts, on the matter; but never, again, shall I be seen running wilfully into the danger of immoralities."

"I had not thought of parting," answered Middleton, endeavoring to seek some relief from the uneasiness he felt, by turning his eyes on the sympathizing countenances of his friends, "On the contrary I had hoped and believed that you would have accompanied us below, where, I give you a sacred pledge, nothing shall be wanting to make your days comfortable."

"Yes, lad, yes; you would do your endeavors, but what are the strivings of man against the working of the Devil! Ay, if kind offers and good wishes could have done the thing, I might have been a Congressman or perhaps a Governor, years agone. Your Grand'ther wished the same, and there are them, still living in the Otsego Mountains,* as I hope, who would gladly have given me a palace for my dwelling. But what are riches without content! My time must now be short, at any rate, and I hope it is no mighty sin for one, who has acted his part honestly near ninety winters and summers, to wish to pass the few hours that remain in comfort. If you think that I have done wrong in coming thus far to quit you, again, Captain, I will own the reason of the act, without shame or backwardness. Though I have seen so much of the wilderness it is not to be gainsayed, that my feelings as well as my skin are white. Now, it would not be a fitting spectacle that yonder Pawnee Loups should look upon the weakness of an old warrior, if weakness he should happen to show in parting forever from those he has reason to love, though he may not set his heart so strongly on them, as to wish to go into the settlements in their company."

"Harkee, old trapper," said Paul, clearing his throat with a desperate effort, as if determined to give his voice a clear exit. "I have just one bargain to make, since you talk of trading, which is neither more nor less than this. I offer you as my side of the business, one half of my shanty, nor do I much care if it be the biggest half; the sweetest and the purest honey that can be made of the wild-locust; always enough to eat, with now and then a mouthful of venison or, for that matter a morsel of buffaloe's hump, seeing that I intend to push my acquaintance with the animal, and as good and as tidy cooking as can come from the hands of one like Ellen Wade, here, who will shortly be Nelly some-body-else, and altogether such general treatment as a decent man might be supposed to pay to his best friend or, for that matter to his own father: in return for the same you ar' to give us, at odd moments, some of your ancient traditions, perhaps a little wholesome advice on occasions, in small quantities at a time, and as much of your agreeable company as you please."

"It is well, it is well, boy," returned the old man fumbling at his wallet, "honestly offered and not unthankfully declined. But it cannot be; no, it can never be."

"Venerable venator," said Doctor Battius, "there are obligations which every man owes to society and to human nature. It is time that you should return to your countrymen to deliver up some of those stores of experimental knowledge, that you have doubtless obtained by so long a sojourn in the wilds, which, however, they may be corrupted by preconceived opinions, will prove acceptable bequests to those whom as you say, you must shortly leave forever."

"Friend, Physician," returned the trapper, looking the other steadily in the face, "as it would be no easy matter to judge of the temper of a rattler by considering the fashions of the moose, so it would be hard to speak of the usefulness of one man by thinking too much of the deeds of another. You have your gifts, like others I suppose, and little do I wish to disturb them. But as to me, the Lord has made me for a doer and not a talker, and, therefore, do I consider it no harm to shut my ears to your invitation."

"It is enough," interrupted Middleton. "I have seen and heard so much of this extraordinary man as to know that persuasions will not change his purpose. First we will hear your request, my friend, and then we will consider what may be best done for your advantage here."

"It is a small matter, Captain," returned the old man, succeeding at length in opening his bundle. "A small and trifling matter is it to what I once used to offer in the way of bargain; but then it is the best I have, and, therein, not to be despised. Here are the skins of four beavers that I took, it might be a month afore we met, and here is another from a raccoon, that is of no great matter to-be-sure, but which may serve to make weight atween us."

"And what do you propose to do with them?"

"I offer them in lawful barter. Them knaves, the Siouxes, the Lord forgive me for ever believing it was the Konzas, have stolen the best of my traps, and driven me altogether to make-shift inventions, which might foretell a dreary winter for me, should my time stretch into another season. I wish you therefore to take the skins, and to offer them to some of the trappers you will not fail to meet below in exchange for a few traps, and to send the same into the Pawnee vil-lage in my name. Be careful to have my mark painted on them. A letter N, with a hound's ear, and the lock of a rifle. There is no red-skin who will then dispute my right. For all which trouble I have little more to offer than my thanks, unless my friend the Bee-hunter, here, will accept of the raccoon and take on himself the special charge of the whole matter."

"If I do may I be—" the mouth of Paul was stopped by the hand of Ellen, and he was obliged to swallow the rest of the sentence, which he did with a species of emotion that bore no slight resemblance to the process of strangulation.

"Well, well," returned the old man meekly; "I hope there is no heavy offence in the offer. I know that the skin of a raccoon is of small price, but then it was no mighty labor that I asked in return."

"You entirely mistake the meaning of our friend," interrupted Middleton, who observed that the bee-hunter was looking in every direction but the right one, and that he was utterly unable to make his own vindication. "He did not mean to say that he declined the charge, but merely that he refused all compensation. It is unnecessary, how-ever, to say more of this, it shall be my office to see that the debt we owe is properly discharged and that all your necessities shall be anticipated."

"Anan!" said the old man, looking up enquiringly into the other's face as if to ask an explanation.

"It shall all be as you wish. Lay the skins with my baggage. We will bargain for you as for ourselves."

"Thankee, thankee, Captain. Your Grand'ther was of a free and gen-erous mind. So much so, in truth, that those just people the Dela-wares called him the 'open hand.' I wish now, I was as I used to be, in order that I might send in the Lady a few delicate martens for her tippets and over-coats, just to show you that I know how to give cour-tesy for courtesy. But do not expect the same, for I am too old to give a promise! It will all be just as the Lord shall see fit. I can offer *you* nothing else, for I haven't lived so long in the wilderness not to know the scrupulous ways of Gentlemen."

"Harkee, old trapper," cried the Bee hunter striking his own hand into the open palm which the other had extended, with a report but little below the crack of a rifle. "I have just two things to say. Firstly, that the Captain has told you my meaning better than I can myself, and secondly, that if you want a skin either for your private use, or to send abroad, I have it at your service, and that is the skin of one Paul Hover."

The old man returned the grasp he received, and opened his mouth to the utmost in his extraordinary, silent, laugh.

"You couldn't have given such a squeeze, boy, when the Teton squaws were about you with the knives! Ah! you are in your prime, and in your vigor and happiness, if honesty lies in your path." Then the expression of his rugged features, suddenly changed to a look of seriousness and thought. "Come hither, lad," he said, leading the bee-hunter by a button to the land, and speaking apart in a tone of admonition and confidence. "Much has passed atween us, on the pleasures and respectableness of a life in the woods, or on the borders. I do not, now, mean to say that all you have heard is not true; but different tempers call for different employments. You have taken to your bosom, there, a good and kind child, and it has become your duty to consider her as well as yourself, in setting forth in life. You are a little given to skirting the settlements, but to my poor judgement the girl would be more like a flourishing flower in the sun of a clearing, than in the winds of a Prairie. Therefore forget any thing you may have heard from me, which is nevertheless true, and strive to turn your mind on the ways of the inner country."

Paul could only answer with a squeeze of the hand, that would have brought tears from the eyes of most men, but which produced no other effect on the indurated muscles of the other, than to make him laugh and nod, as if he received the same as a pledge that the bee-hunter would remember his advice. The trapper then turned away from his rough but warm hearted companion, and having called Hector from the boat, he seemed anxious still to utter a few words more.

"Captain," he, at length, resumed, "I know that when a poor man talks of credit, he deals in a delicate word, according to the fashions of the world, and when an old man talks of life, he speaks of that which he may never see. Nevertheless, there is one thing I will say, and that is not so much on my own behalf, as on that of another person. Here is Hector, a good and faithful pup, that has long outlived the time of a dog, and like his master he looks more to comfort now than to any deeds in running. But the creatur' has his feelings as well as a christian. He has consorted latterly with his kinsman, there, in such a sort, as to find great pleasure in his company, and, I will acknowledge that it touches my feelings a little to part the pair so soon. If you will set a value on your hound, I will endeavor to send it to you in the spring, more especially should them same traps come safe to hand, or if you dislike parting with the animal, altogether, I will just ask you for his loan through the winter. I think I can see my pup will not last beyond that time, for I have judgment in these matters, since many is the friend, both hound and red-skin, that I have seen depart in my day, though the Lord has not yet seen fit to order his angels to sound forth my name."

"Take him, take him," cried Middleton. "Take all, or any thing!"

The old man whistled the younger dog to the land, and then he proceeded to the final adieus. Little was said on either side. The trapper took each person solemnly by the hand, and uttered something friendly and kind to all. Middleton was perfectly speechless and was driven to affect busying himself among the baggage, Paul whistled with all his might, and even, Obed, took his leave with an effort that bore the appearance of desperate philosophical resolution. When he had made the circuit of the whole the old man, with his own hands, shoved the boat into the current, wishing God to speed them. Not a word was spoken nor a stroke of the oar given, until the travellers had floated past a knoll that hid the trapper from their view. He was last seen standing on the low point, leaning on his rifle, with Hector crouched at his feet, and the younger dog frisking along the sands, in the playfulness of youth and vigor.

CHAPTER XXXIV.

—"Methought, I heard a voice—"
Macbeth, II. ii. 35.

THE water-courses were at their height, and the boat went down the swift current like a bird. The passage proved prosperous and speedy. In less than a third of the time that would have been necessary for the same journey by land, it was accomplished by the favor of those rapid rivers. Issuing from one stream into another, as the veins of the human body communicate with the larger channels of life, they soon entered the grand artery of the western waters and landed safely, at the very door of the father of Inez.

The joy of Don Augustin, and the embarrassment of the worthy Father Ignatius may be imagined. The former wept and returned thanks to Heaven, the latter returned thanks, and did not weep. The mild provincials were too happy to raise any questions on the character of so joyful a restoration, and, by a sort of general consent it soon came to be an admitted opinion that the bride of Middleton had been kidnapped by a villain and that she was restored to her friends by human agency. There were as respects this belief, certainly a few sceptics, but then they enjoyed their doubts in private, with that species of sublimated and solitary gratification that a miser finds in gazing at his growing, but useless, hoards.

In order to give the worthy priest something to employ his mind, Middleton made him the instrument of uniting Paul and Ellen. The former consented to the ceremony, because he found that all his friends laid great stress on the matter, but shortly after he led his bride into the plains of Kentucky, under the pretence of paying certain customary visits to sundry members of the family of Hover. While there, he took occasion to have the marriage properly solemnized, by a justice of the peace of his acquaintance, in whose ability to forge the nuptial chain he had much more faith than in that of all the gownsmen within the Pale of Rome. Ellen who appeared conscious that some extraordinary preventives might prove necessary to keep one of so erratic a temper, as her partner, within the proper matrimonial boundaries, raised no objections to these double knots, and all parties were content.

The local importance Middleton had acquired by his union with the daughter of so affluent a proprietor as Don Augustin, united to his personal merit, attracted the attention of the Government. He was soon employed in various situations of responsibility and confidence, which both served to elevate his character in the public estimation and to afford the means of patronage. The bee-hunter was among the first of those to whom he saw fit to extend his favor. It was far from difficult to find situations suited to the abilities of Paul in the state of society that existed three and twenty years ago in those regions. The efforts of Middleton and Inez in behalf of her husband were warmly and sagaciously seconded by Ellen, and they succeeded, in process of time, in working a great and beneficial change in his character. He soon became a landholder, then a prosperous cultivator of the soil, and shortly after a town-officer. By that progressive change in fortune, which in the republicks is often seen to be so singularly accompanied by a corresponding improvement in knowledge and self-respect, he went on, from step to step, until his wife enjoyed the maternal delight of seeing her children placed far beyond the danger of returning to that state from which both their parents had issued. Paul is, actually, at this moment, a member of the lower branch of the Legislature of the State where he has long resided, and he is even notorious for making speeches, that have a tendency to put that deliberative body in good humour, and which as they are based on great practical knowledge suited to the condition of the country, possess a merit that is much wanted in many more subtle and fine spun theories that are daily heard in similar assemblies, to issue from the lips of certain instinctive politicians. But all these happy fruits were the results of much care, and of a long period of time. Middleton, who fills, with a credit better suited to the difference in their educations, a seat in a far higher branch of Legislative Authority, is the source from which we have derived most of the intelligence necessary to compose our legend. In addition to what he has related of Paul, and of his own continued happiness, he has added a short narrative of what took place in a subsequent visit to the Prairies, with which, as we conceive it a suitable termination to what has gone before, we shall judge it wise to conclude our labors.

In the autumn of the year that succeeded the season in which the preceding events occurred, the young man, still in the military service, found himself on the waters of the Missouri, at a point not far remote from the Pawnee towns. Released from any immediate calls of duty, and strongly urged to the measure by Paul, who was in his company, he determined to take horse and cross the country, to visit the Partisan and to inquire into the fate of his friend the trapper. As his train was suited to his functions and rank, the journey was effected, with the privations and hardships that are the accompanyments of all travelling in a wild, but, without any of those dangers and alarms that marked his former passage through the same regions. When within a proper distance, he dispatched an Indian runner belonging to a friendly tribe, to announce the approach of himself and party, continuing his route at a deliberate pace, in order that the intelligence might as was customary precede his arrival. To the surprise of the travellers their message was unanswered. Hour succeeded hour, and mile after mile was passed without bringing either the signs of an honorable reception or the more simple assurances of a friendly welcome. At length the cavalcade, at whose head rode Middleton and Paul, descended from the elevated plain, on which they had long been journeying, to a luxuriant bottom, that brought them to the level of the village of the Loups. The sun was beginning to fall, and a sheet of golden light was spread over the placid plain, lending to its even surface, those glorious tints and hues that, the human imagination is apt to conceive, form the embellishment of still more imposing scenes. The verdure of the year yet remained and herds of horses and mules were grazing peacefully in the vast natural pasture, under the keeping of vigilant Pawnee boys. Paul pointed out, among them, the well known form of Asinus, sleek, fat and luxuriating in the fulness of content, as he stood with reclining ears and closed eye-lids, seemingly musing on the exquisite nature of his present indolent enjoyment.

The route of the party led them at no great distance from one of those watchful youths, who was charged with a trust heavy as the principal wealth of his tribe. He heard the trampling of the horses and cast his eye aside, but instead of manifesting curiosity or alarm, his look instantly returned, whence it had been withdrawn, to the spot where the village was known to stand.

"There is something remarkable in all this," muttered Middleton, half offended at what he conceived to be not only a slight to his rank, but offensive to himself, personally; "yonder boy has heard of our approach, or he would not fail to notify his tribe; and yet he scarcely deigns to favor us with a glance. Look to your arms, men, it may be necessary to let these savages feel our strength!"

"Therein, Captain, I think you're in an error," returned Paul. "If honesty is to be met on the Prairies at all, you will find it in our old friend, Hard-Heart; neither is an Indian to be judged of by the rules of a white—see, we are not altogether slighted for here comes a party at last to meet us, though it is a little pitiful as to show and numbers."

Paul was right in both particulars. A groupe of horsemen were, at length, seen wheeling round a little copse and advancing across the plain directly towards them. The advance of this party was slow and dignified. As it drew nigh the Partisan of the Loups was seen at its head, followed by a dozen younger warriors of his tribe. They were all unarmed, nor did they even wear any of those ornaments or feathers, which are considered testimonials of respect to the guest an Indian receives, as well as evidence of his own importance.

The meeting was friendly though a little restrained on both sides. Middleton, jealous of his own consideration no less than of the authority of his government, suspected some undue influence on the part of the agents of the Canadas, and, as he was determined to maintain the authority of which he was the representative, he felt himself constrained to manifest an hauteur that he was far from feeling. It was not so easy to penetrate the motives of the Pawnees. Calm, dignified and yet far from repulsive, they set an example of courtesy blended with reserve, that many a diplomatist of the most polished court might have strove in vain to imitate.

In this manner the two parties continued their course to the town. Middleton had time, during the remainder of the ride, to revolve in his mind, all the probable reasons which his ingenuity could suggest for this strange reception. Although he was accompanied by a regular interpreter, the chiefs made their salutations in a manner that dispensed with his services. Twenty times, the Captain turned his glance on his former friend endeavoring to read the expression of his rigid features. But every effort and all conjectures proved equally futile. The eye of Hard-Heart was fixed, composed, and a little anxious, but as to every other emotion, impenetrable. He neither spoke himself, nor seemed willing to invite discourse in his visiters. It was therefore necessary for Middleton to adopt the patient manners of his companions, and to await the issue for the explanation.

When they entered the town, the whole of its inhabitants were seen collected in an open space where they were arranged with the customary deference to age and rank. The whole formed a large circle, in the centre of which were perhaps a dozen of the principal chiefs.

Hard-Heart waved his hand as he approached, and, as the mass of bodies opened, he rode through, followed by his companions. Then they dismounted, and as the beasts were led apart, the strangers found themselves environed by a thousand, grave, composed but solicitous faces.

Middleton gazed about him, in growing concern, for no cry, no song, no shout, welcomed him among a people, from whom he had so lately parted with regret. His uneasiness, not to say apprehensions, was shared by all his followers. Determination and stern resolution began to assume the place of anxiety in every eye, as each man silently felt for his arms, and assured himself that his several weapons were in a state for service. But there was no answering symptom of hostility on the part of their hosts. Hard-Heart beckoned for Middleton and Paul to follow, leading the way towards the cluster of forms that occupied the centre of the circle. Here the visiters found a solution of all the movements which had given them so much reason for apprehension.

The trapper was placed on a rude seat, which had been made, with studied care to support his frame, in an upright and easy attitude. The first glance of the eye told his former friends that the old man was, at length, called upon to pay the last tribute of nature. His eye was glazed, and apparently as devoid of sight, as of expression. His features were a little more sunken and strongly marked, than formerly, but there all change so far as exterior was concerned, might be said to have ceased. His approaching end was not to be ascribed to any positive malady but had been a gradual and mild decay of the physical powers. Life it is true still lingered in his system, but it was as if at times, entirely ready to depart, and then it would appear to reanimate the sinking form as if reluctant to give up the possession of a tenement that had never been corrupted by vice or undermined by disease. It would have been no violent fancy to have imagined, that the spirit fluttered about the placid lips of the old woodsman, reluctant to depart from a shell that had so long given it an honest and an honourable shelter.

His body was placed so as to let the light of the setting sun, fall full upon the solemn features. His head was bare, the long, thin, locks of gray, fluttering lightly in the evening breeze. His rifle lay upon his knee, and the other accoutrements of the chase were placed at his side, within reach of his hand. Between his feet lay the figure of a hound, with its head crouching to the earth as if it slumbered, and so perfectly easy and natural was its position, that a second glance was necessary to tell Middleton he saw only the skin of Hector stuffed by Indian tenderness and ingenuity, in a manner to represent the living animal. His own dog was playing at a distance, with the child of Tachechana and Mahtoree. The mother herself, stood at hand holding in her arms a second offspring that might boast of a parentage no less honorable than that which belonged to a son of Hard-Heart. Le Balafré was seated nigh the dying trapper, with every mark about his person that the hour of his own departure, also, was not far distant. The rest of those immediately in the centre, were aged men, who had apparently drawn near, in order to observe the manner in which a just and fearless warrior would depart on the greatest of his journeys.

The old man was reaping the rewards of a life so remarkable for temperance and activity, in a tranquil and placid death. His vigor had in a manner endured, to the very last. Decay when it did occur, was rapid, but free from pain. He had hunted with the tribe in the spring, and even throughout most of the summer, when his limbs suddenly refused to perform their customary offices. A sympathysing weakness took possession of all his faculties, and the Pawnees believed that they were going to lose, in this unexpected manner, a sage and counsellor whom they had begun both to love and to respect. But, as we have already said, the immortal occupant seemed unwilling to desert its tenement. The lamp of life often flickered, without becoming extinguished. On the morning of the day on which Middleton arrived, there was a general reviving of the powers of the whole man. His tongue was again heard in wholesome maxims, and his eye, from time to time, recognised the persons of his friends. It merely proved to be a brief and final intercourse with the world on the part of one who had already been considered, as to mental communion, to have taken his leave of it forever.

When he had placed his guests in front of the dying man, Hard-Heart after a pause that proceeded as much from sorrow as decorum, leaned a little forward, and demanded—"Does my Father hear the words of his son?"

"Speak," returned the trapper, in tones that issued from his chest, but which were rendered awfully distinct by the stillness that reigned in the place. "I am about to depart from the village of the Loups, and, shortly shall be beyond the reach of your voice."

"Let the wise chief have no cares for his journey!" continued Hard-Heart, with an earnest solicitude that led him to forget, for the moment, that others were waiting to address his adopted parent. "A hundred Loups shall clear his path from briars."

"Pawnee, I die, as I have lived, a christian man," resumed the trapper with a force of voice, that had the same startling effect on his hearers as is produced by the trumpet, when its blast rises suddenly and freely on the air, after its obstructed sounds have been heard struggling in the distance. "As I came into life, so will I leave it. Horses and arms are not needed to stand in the Presence of the Great Spirit of my people! He knows my colour, and according to my gifts will he judge my deeds."

"My father will tell my young men, how many Mingoes he has struck, and what acts of valour and justice he has done, that they may know how to imitate him."

"A boastful tongue is not heard in the heaven of a white man!" solemnly returned the old man. "What I have done, he has seen. His eyes are always open. That which has been well done will he remember. Wherein I have been wrong, will he not forget to chastise, though he will do the same in mercy. No, my son; a pale-face may not sing his own praises, and hope to have them acceptable before his God!"

A little disappointed, the young partisan stepped modestly back, making way for the recent comers to approach. Middleton took one of the meagre hands of the trapper, and struggling to command his voice, he succeeded in announcing his presence. The old man listened like one, whose thoughts were dwelling on a very different subject, but when the other had succeeded in making him understand that he was present, an expression of joyful recognition passed over his faded features.

"I hope you have not so soon forgotten those whom you so materially served!" Middleton concluded. "It would pain me to think my hold on your memory was so light."

"Little that I have ever seen is forgotten," returned the trapper, "I am at the close of many weary days, but there is not one among them all that I could wish to overlook. I remember you, with the whole of your companions; ay, and your gran'ther, that went before you. I am glad that you have come back upon these plains, for I had need of one, who speaks the English, since little faith can be put in the traders of these regions. Will you do a favor, to an old and dying man?"

"Name it," said Middleton. "It shall be done."

"It is a far journey to send such trifles," resumed the old man, who spoke at short intervals, as strength and breath permitted. "A far and weary journey is the same! But kindnesses and friendships are things not to be forgotten. There is a settlement among the Otsego hills."

"I know the place," interrupted Middleton, observing that he spoke with increasing difficulty. "Proceed to tell me what you would have done."

"Take this rifle, and pouch, and horn, and send them to the person whose name is graven on the plates of the stock.* A trader cut the letters with his knife, for it is long that I have intended to send him such a token of my love."

"It shall be so. Is there more that you could wish?"

"Little else have I to bestow. My traps I give to my Indian son; for honestly and kindly has he kept his faith. Let him stand before me."

Middleton explained to the chief what the trapper had said and relinquished his own place to the other.

"Pawnee," continued the old man, always changing his language to suit the person he addressed, and not unfrequently according to the ideas he expressed, "it is a custom of my people for the Father to leave his blessing with the son, before he shuts his eyes forever. This blessing I give to you. Take it, for the prayers of a Christian man will never make the path of a just warrior to the blessed Prairies, either longer, or more tangled. May the God of a white man look on your deeds with friendly eyes, and may you never commit an act that shall cause him to darken his face. I know not whether we shall ever meet again. There are many traditions concerning the place of good Spirits. It is not for one like me, old and experienced though I am, to set up my opinions against a nation's. You believe in the blessed Prairies, and I have faith in the sayings of my fathers. If both are true, our parting will be final; but if it should prove that the same meaning is hid under different words, we shall yet stand together, Pawnee, before the face of your Wahcondah who will then be no other than my God. There is much to be said in favor of both religions, for each seems suited to its own people, and no doubt it was so intended. I fear I have not altogether followed the gifts of my colour, inasmuch as I find it a little painful to give up forever the use of the rifle, and the comforts of the chase. But then the fault has been my own, seeing that it could not have been His. Ay, Hector," he continued leaning forward a little and feeling for the ears of the hound, "our parting has come at last, dog, and it will be a long hunt. You have been an honest, and a bold and a faithful hound. Pawnee, you cannot slay the pup on my grave, for where a christian dog falls there he lies forever, but you can be kind to him, after I am gone, for the love you bear his Master?"

"The words of my father, are in my ears," returned the young Partisan, making a grave and respectful gesture of assent.

"Do you hear what the chief has promised, dog?" demanded the trapper making an effort to attract the notice of the insensible effigy of his hound. Receiving no answering look, nor hearing any friendly whine, the old man felt for the mouth and endeavored to force his hand between the cold lips. The truth then flashed upon him, although he was far from perceiving the whole extent of the deception. Falling back in his seat, he hung his head like one who felt a severe and unexpected shock. Profiting by this momentary forgetfulness, two young Indians removed the skin, with the same delicacy of feeling that had induced them to attempt the pious fraud.

"The dog is dead!" muttered the trapper, after a pause of many minutes, "a hound has his time as well as a man; and well has he filled his days! Captain," he added making an effort to wave his hand for Middleton. "I am glad you have come, for, though kind, and well meaning according to the gifts of their colour, these Indians are not the sort of men to lay the head of a white man in his grave. I have been thinking too, of this dog at my feet: it will not do to set forth the opinion that a christian can expect to meet his hound, again, still there can be little harm in placing what is left of so faithful a servant nigh the bones of his master?"

"It shall be done as you desire."

"I'm glad you think with me in this matter. In order then to save labor, lay the pup at my feet — or for that matter put him, side by side. A hunter need never be ashamed to be found in company with his dog!"

"I charge myself with your wish."

The old man made a long and, apparently, a musing pause. At times he raised his eyes, wistfully, as if he would again address Middleton, but some innate feeling appeared ever to suppress his words. The other, who observed his hesitation, enquired in a way most likely to encourage him to proceed, whither there was aught else that he could wish to have done.

"I am without kith or kin in the wide world!" the trapper answered. "When I am gone there will be an end of my race. We have never been chiefs; but honest and useful in our way, I hope it cannot be denied we have always proved ourselves. My father lies buried near the sea, and the bones of his son will whiten on the Prairies."

"Name the spot and your remains shall be placed by the side of your father," interrupted Middleton.

"Not so, not so, Captain. Let me sleep where I have lived, beyond the din of the settlements! Still I see no need why the grave of an

honest man should be hid, like a red-skin in his ambushment. I paid
a man in the settlements to make and put a graven stone at the head
of my father's resting-place. It was of the value of twelve beaver-skins;
and cunningly and curiously was it carved! Then it told to all comers
that the body of such a christian lay beneath, and it spoke of his
manner of life, of his years and of his honesty. When we had done
with the Frenchers in the old war, I made a journey to the spot, in
order to see that all was rightly performed, and glad I am to say the
workman had not forgotten his faith."

"And such a stone you would have at your grave?"

"I! no, no, I have no son, but Hard-Heart, and it is little that an
Indian knows of white fashions and usages. Besides I am his debtor,
already, seeing it is so little I have done since I have lived in his tribe.
The rifle might bring the value of such a thing—but then I know it
will give the boy pleasure to hang the piece in his hall, for many is
the deer and the bird that he has seen it destroy. No, no, the gun must
be sent to him whose name is graven on the lock."

"But there is one who would gladly prove his affection in the way
you wish. He who owes you not only his own deliverance from so
many dangers, but who inherits a heavy debt of gratitude from his
ancestors. The stone shall be put at the head of your grave."

The old man extended his meagre hand, and gave the other a
squeeze of thanks.

"I thought you might be willing to do it, but I was backward in
asking the favour," he said, "seeing that you are not of my kin. Put no
boastful words on the same; but just the name, the age, and the time of
the death, with something from the holy book. No more, no more.
My name will then not be altogether lost on 'arth; I need no more."

Middleton intimated his assent, and then followed a pause that was
only interrupted by distant and broken sentences from the dying man.
He appeared now to have closed his accounts with the world, and to
wait merely for the final summons to quit it. Middleton and Hard-
Heart placed themselves on the opposite sides of his seat, and watched
with melancholy solicitude, the variations of his countenance. For
two hours there was no very sensible alteration. The expression of his
faded and time-worn features was that of a calm and dignified repose.
From time to time, he spoke, uttering some brief sentence in the way
of advice, or asking some simple question concerning those in whose
fortunes he still took a friendly interest. During the whole of that
solemn and anxious period each individual of the tribe kept his place,

in the most self-restrained patience. When the old man spoke, all bent their heads to listen; and when his words were uttered they seemed to ponder on their wisdom and usefulness.

As the flame drew nigher to the socket, his voice was hushed, and there were moments when his attendants doubted whether he still belonged to the living. Middleton, who watched each wavering expression of his weather-beaten visage with the interest of a keen observer of human nature softened by the tenderness of personal regard, fancied that he could read the workings of the old man's soul, in the strong lineaments of his countenance. Perhaps what the enlightened soldier took for the delusion of mistaken opinion did actually occur, for who has returned from that unknown world to explain by what forms and in what manner he was introduced into its awful precincts. Without pretending to explain what must ever be a mystery to the quick, we shall simply relate facts as they occurred.

The trapper had remained nearly motionless for an hour. His eyes, alone, had occasionally opened and shut. When opened his gaze seemed fastened on the clouds which hung around the western horizon, reflecting the bright colours and giving form and loveliness to the glorious tints of an American sunset. The hour—the calm beauty of the season—the occasion all conspired to fill the spectators with solemn awe. Suddenly, while musing on the remarkable position in which he was placed, Middleton felt the hand which he held, grasp his own, with incredible power, and the old man, supported on either side by his friends, rose upright to his feet. For a moment, he looked about him, as if to invite all in presence to listen, (the lingering remnant of human frailty) and then, with a fine military elevation of the head, and with a voice that might be heard in every part of that numerous assembly he pronounced the word—

"Here!"

A movement so entirely unexpected, and the air of grandeur and humility which were so strikingly united in the mien of the trapper, together with the clear and uncommon force of his utterance, produced a short period of confusion in the faculties of all present. When Middleton and Hard-Heart, each of whom involuntarily extended a hand to support the form of the old man, turned to him again, they found that the subject of their interest, was removed forever beyond the necessity of their care. They mournfully placed the body in its seat, and Le Balafré arose to announce the termination of the scene, to the tribe. The voice of the old Indian, seemed a sort of echo from that invisible world to which the spirit of the honest trapper had just departed.

"A valiant, a just, and a wise warrior has gone on the path which will lead him to the blessed grounds of his people!" he said. "When the voice of the Wahcondah called him, he was ready to answer. Go: my children; remember the just chiefs of the Pale-faces, and clear your own tracks from briars."

The grave was made beneath the shade of some noble oaks. It has been carefully watched to the present hour by the Pawnees of the Loup, and is often shown, to the traveller and the trader, as a spot where a just white-man sleeps. In due time the stone was placed at its head, with the simple inscription, which the trapper had himself requested. The only liberty taken by Middleton, was to add, *"May no wanton hand ever disturb his remains."*

EXPLANATORY NOTES

1 *the Wahcondah*: the Master of Life; the Supreme Being. According to Orm Överland, *The Making and Meaning of an American Classic: James Fenimore Cooper's 'The Prairie'* (Oslo and New York, 1973), 80–1, Cooper found the word in *Account of an Expedition from Pittsburgh to the Rocky Mountains, performed in the Years 1819 and '20 . . . Under the Command of Major Stephen H. Long* (Philadelphia, 1823), ii, p. lxxii.

comparative desert: a 'Great American Desert', supposed to exist in the trans-Mississippi territory acquired by the Louisiana Purchase, was a widely believed myth of the time.

9 *sole command of the great thoroughfare of the interior*: before the Louisiana Purchase of 1803, both the west bank and the mouth of the Mississippi River were controlled by either Spain or France.

13 *The earth was . . . on the waters*: the source for this description is a passage in *Account of an Expedition*, i. 418–19 (Överland, 75–6). James P. Elliott, however, in his 'Historical Introduction' to the SUNY edition of *The Prairie* (Albany, NY, 1985), points out that 'Cooper's rendition is more imaginative,' pp. xix–xx.

14 *three grand requisites of water, fuel and fodder*: Cooper's source is *Account of an Expedition*, i. 419–20 (Överland, 77).

15 *The figure was colossal*: Överland, pp. 76–7, finds a source for this mirage in *Account of an Expedition*, i. 419.

21 *fixen*: the use of this word and of 'plunder' on p. 22 suggests to Överland, pp. 71–2, that Cooper used James Hall's 'The Missouri Trapper' (*The Port Folio*, No. 275, March 1825), part of his *Letters from the West*, as a source. The words appear in Hall's sketch on p. 219.

24 *buffaloes*: American bison. See Cooper's note, p. 100.

32 *bee-hunter*: a honey gatherer. See Cooper's note, p. 101.

35 *court-house fight*: according to frontier lore, fights would often break out around the court-house in newly settled districts when people gathered for a session of court, a militia drill, or the like.

43 *after examining . . . in perfect stillness*: Cooper describes Indian

behaviour in their encounters with whites both here and elsewhere in *The Prairie* in accordance with a passage he found in *Account of an Expedition*, ii. 372 (Överland, 82).

44 *Weucha*: an authentic Sioux name, which, according to E. Soteris Muszynska-Wallace, 'The Sources of *The Prairie*', *American Literature*, 21 (1949), 195, Cooper found in *History of the Expedition Under the Command of Captains Lewis and Clark . . . Performed during the Years 1804–5–6* (Philadelphia and New York, 1814), i. 57.

45 *milk of the Long-knives*: whisky of the white men. See also Cooper's note, p. 56.

Mahtoree: an authentic Sioux name, that Cooper found in *History of the Expedition*, i. 58 (Muszynska-Wallace, 195).

Great White Father: the President of the United States.

49 *fog*: long or rank grass.

61 *section, or a town, or perhaps a county*: by the Land Ordinance of 1785, the public lands of the United States were divided into townships, each six miles square, and containing thirty-six sections, each one mile square (640 acres). A county is the political unit just below an American state.

63 *Mingo*: Hawkeye's name for a member of the Huron tribe in *The Last of the Mohicans*.

69 *Buffon*: Georges Louis Leclerc, Comte de Buffon (1707–88), French naturalist, who, in his work on natural history, sought to include all scientific knowledge.

Solander: Daniel Carlsson Solander (1736–82), a Swedish-born botanist who moved to England, worked in the British Museum, and with Joseph Banks accompanied Captain James Cook on a voyage to the South Seas in the *Endeavour*, 1768–71.

71 *1805*: if, as Middleton reports on p. 117, 'Lewis is working his way up the river, some hundreds of miles from this', the date must be 1804, since at that time the Lewis and Clark expedition was approaching the Mandan villages in what is now North Dakota. The following autumn they reached the Pacific. Dr Bat's error, suggested by the rest of his sentence, is probably intended to reveal his impracticality and lack of common sense.

78 *Great Bears . . . falls of the Long River*: Grizzly Bears (*ursus horribilis*) at the Great Falls of the Missouri in what is now Montana.

83 *I brought them to the spot myself*: an echo, perhaps, of the closing lines of *The Pioneers*, wherein Leatherstocking, fleeing westward because of the settlers' despoliation of nature, opens the way ironically for those whose depredations he is trying to escape.

84 *accursed Huron ... perch, among the rocks*: an incident in chapter VIII of *The Last of the Mohicans*.

Hori—: Horican, the name Cooper uses for Lake George, New York, in *The Last of the Mohicans*.

95 *Spanish league*: nearly four English miles.

96 *choice morsel ... customary subterranean oven*: Cooper's source for the detail was apparently *Account of an Expedition*, i. 192 ff. (Muszynska-Wallace, 198).

97 *metheglin*: mead, an alcoholic drink made from fermented honey and other ingredients.

111 *Duncan Uncas Middleton*: the grandson of Duncan Heyward and Alice Munro, the hero and heroine of *The Last of the Mohicans*. Other characters in that book mentioned in the ensuing dialogue, p. 113, are Chingachgook ('the Grand Serpent') and his son Uncas (called by the Hurons 'Le Cerf Agile'), the Mohican warriors who are Hawkeye's companions.

115 *beginning with an N. and ending with an L.*: Nathaniel; Natty Bumppo was the trapper's original name.

117 *Lewis*: Meriwether Lewis (1774–1809), a leader, with William Clark (1770–1838), of the expedition President Thomas Jefferson sent to explore the newly acquired Louisiana Territory (1803–6). Other references in *The Prairie* to the Lewis and Clark expedition may be found on pp. 187 and 194.

120 *blister*: a medical treatment designed to raise a blister.

124 *cataplasm*: a poultice.

143 *example of Abraham*: see Genesis 22: 1–18.

151 *Payley, Berkeley, ay even by the immortal Binkerschoef*: William Paley (1743–1805), English churchman and philosopher; George Berkeley (1685–1753), Anglican bishop and philosopher. Binkerschoef is most probably Cornelius van Bynkershoek (1673–1743), Dutch jurist who published many works on important legal questions.

162 *felo de se*: one who ends his own life, or commits an act that leads to his death.

170 *Flapping his sides . . . of this bird*: Cooper thus makes Paul Hover a somewhat mild version of the frontier roarer, a well-known figure in western literature.

Sir William . . . Dieskau: on 8 September 1755 General William Johnson with provincial troops and a body of Indians defeated the French under Baron de Dieskau at Fort Edward, south of Lake George. Hawkeye describes the battle in chapter XIV of *The Last of the Mohicans*.

171 *Delawares nam'd me . . . fashion of my leggings*: thus Cooper accounts for the changing names of his character, Hawkeye in *The Last of the Mohicans* and Leatherstocking in *The Pioneers*. In chapter VII of *The Deerslayer*, however, published fourteen years after *The Prairie*, it is a Huron warrior, the first man that he kills, who names him Hawkeye.

172 *whistle the Kentucky hunters*: 'The Hunters of Kentucky' (1821), written by Samuel Woodworth (1784–1842), was set to music and enjoyed great popularity. It celebrates the role of Kentucky riflemen at the Battle of New Orleans (1815). It is thus an anachronism in a book set in 1804.

179 *Linnæus*: Carolus Linnaeus (1707–78), Swedish botanist for whom is named the system of classifying plants and animals.

184 *Wagh*: the source for this exclamation is *Account of an Expedition*, i. 253 (Muszynska-Wallace, 195).

185 *Alston or Greenough*: Washington Allston (1779–1843), American painter, known for his landscapes and paintings on biblical subjects; Horatio Greenough (1805–52), American sculptor, whose well-known statue of Washington is in the Smithsonian in Washington, DC. He would eventually create *The Rescue*, a frontier group, including an Indian, now at the east entrance of the Capitol in Washington.

186 *short hickory bow . . . tail of the animal depended*: Cooper's source for the bow and quiver is *Account of an Expedition*, i. 290–1 (Överland, 83).

191 *Hard-Heart*: Cooper found the name in *Account of an Expedition*, i. 180 ff., where it is that of an Iowa chief (Muszynska-Wallace, 195.) Cooper's model for the character, however, was Petalesharoo, a chief of the Pawnee Loups, whom Cooper claimed as an acquaintance. See *Letters and Journals of James Fenimore Cooper* ed. James F. Beard (Cambridge, Mass., 1960–8), i. 199.

196 *mistaking a turkey for a horse*: the illusion that Cooper refers to here and the mistake that Dr Bat makes in misperceiving Asinus as a large beast (pp. 69–73) may derive from a passage in *Account of an Expedition*, i. 419 (Muszynska-Wallace, 197–8).

197 *who named the works of His hand*: see Genesis 2: 19–20.

198 *enormous Bison bulls*: Cooper drew on both *Account of an Expedition*, i. 481, and *History of the Expedition*, i. 233, for his description of the buffalo stampede which follows (Muszynska-Wallace, 197).

201 *The ass has spoken, but Balaam is silent*: an allusion to Numbers 22: 22–35.

204 *slaughter this ass*: although Asinus is not killed, the incident recalls the death of David Gamut's colt in chapter V of *The Last of the Mohicans*.

companion who never opened his mouth but to sing: David Gamut, in *The Last of the Mohicans*, a teacher of psalmody who accompanies the other characters throughout the book.

213 *there was a reason that I should bear it*: in *The Pioneers*, Leatherstocking lives in a hut near Templeton with Major Effingham and Oliver Edwards until the lands that rightfully belong to them are restored by Judge Temple, who has held them in trust.

214 *Mahomet's coffin . . . attraction held him in a state of rest*: according to legend, Mahomet's unsupported coffin was suspended in mid-air in a mosque at Medina, where he died. By some Christian writers, it was said to have been made of iron and placed between two magnets.

223 *Menahashah*: 'Long Knife' in the dialect of the Yankton Sioux, a word that Cooper found in *Account of an Expedition*, ii. p. lxxxiv (Muszynska-Wallace, 195).

Washsheomantiqua: Minatare (Gros ventre) word for Spaniard, which Cooper found in *Account of an Expedition*, ii. p. lxxxiv (Överland, 80).

224 *Wahconshecheh* (*bad spirit*): a Yankton Sioux word, which Cooper found in *Account of an Expedition*, ii. p. lxxiii (Muszynska-Wallace, 195).

232 *that night . . . drove us to the caves*: the caves at Glens Falls, New York, where Leatherstocking and his party take refuge from the Hurons in *The Last of the Mohicans*.

245 *Lord will show his might . . . furnace*: see Daniel 3: 13–97.

247 *witnessed in the Eastern hills*: an allusion to the fire that burns Mount Vision in chapters XXXVI–XXXVIII of *The Pioneers*.

249 *courtiers of Ferdinand . . . egg stand on its end*: when, on his return from his first voyage, Columbus was asked by an envious courtier whether other men in Spain might not as easily have made the discovery of the New World, Columbus is said to have replied by asking the company to stand an egg on end. When no one succeeded, he struck it on the table and left it standing on the crushed end, thereby making the point that anyone can perform an act after someone has first shown how it is to be done.

250 *the chief . . . regions of York*: Tamenund, the aged chief of the Delawares in *The Last of the Mohicans*.

257 *under that fresh hide of buffaloe*: Cooper's source for the detail is *History of the Expedition*, i. 121 (Muszynska-Wallace, 196).

261 *The hide was soon drawn . . . collapsing or falling in*: Cooper seems to have drawn material for the description from both *Account of an Expedition*, i. 428–9, and *History of the Expedition*, ii. 400 (Muszynska-Wallace, 199–200).

271 *the hundred lodges . . . wandering Siouxes*: Cooper derived the description of the Indian camp in this and the following paragraph from two illustrations in *Account of an Expedition*: 'Oto Encampment' and 'Moveable Skin Lodges of the Kaskaias' (Överland, 84–7).

278 *a lad, I valued*: Uncas, son of Chingachgook. He is killed by Magua in *The Last of the Mohicans*.

285 *celebrated anathema . . . Tristram Shandy*: see Book III, chapter 11 in Laurence Sterne's *The Life and Opinions of Tristram Shandy, Gentleman*.

286 *expedient of the Pharisees 'in order that they might be seen of men'*: see Matthew 23: 5.

287 *Tachechana*: an authentic Sioux word, which Cooper found in *Account of an Expedition*, ii. p. lxxvi (Överland, 79).

298 *broom-stick jumpers*: those living in a common-law marriage. In American dialect they are said to have 'jumped over the broomstick'.

307 *'river of troubled waters'*: the Missouri, as Cooper makes clear on p. 194.

311 *'waters of the wolves'*: the Loup River, a tributary of the Platte, located in what is now eastern Nebraska.

318 *Babel*: see Genesis 11: 1–9.

323 *I was carried . . . skin of a deer*: a major episode in *The Pioneers*. See chapters XXX–XXXV.

334 *If a red-skin strikes . . . masters of the Prairies*: cf. chapter XXVIII of *The Last of the Mohicans*, where Magua, a Huron warrior, makes a similar appeal in the camp of the Delawares.

343 *'eye must be returned for an eye' and 'a tooth for a tooth'*: see Exodus 21: 23–5; Leviticus 24: 19–20; Deuteronomy 19: 21. Cf. Matthew 5: 38–9.

347 *western comfort*: whisky.

370 *them, still living in the Otsego Mountains*: Oliver and Elizabeth Effingham, who are major characters in *The Pioneers*.

382 *name is graven . . . stock*: Oliver Effingham, who, as Oliver Edwards, is Leatherstocking's companion in *The Pioneers*.

GEORGE ELIOT	Adam Bede
	Daniel Deronda
	Middlemarch
	The Mill on the Floss
	Silas Marner
ELIZABETH GASKELL	Cranford
	The Life of Charlotte Brontë
	Mary Barton
	North and South
	Wives and Daughters
THOMAS HARDY	Far from the Madding Crowd
	Jude the Obscure
	The Mayor of Casterbridge
	A Pair of Blue Eyes
	The Return of the Native
	Tess of the d'Urbervilles
	The Woodlanders
WALTER SCOTT	Ivanhoe
	Rob Roy
	Waverley
MARY SHELLEY	Frankenstein
	The Last Man
ROBERT LOUIS STEVENSON	Kidnapped and Catriona
	The Strange Case of Dr Jekyll and Mr Hyde and Weir of Hermiston
	Treasure Island
BRAM STOKER	Dracula
WILLIAM MAKEPEACE THACKERAY	Barry Lyndon
	Vanity Fair
OSCAR WILDE	Complete Shorter Fiction
	The Picture of Dorian Gray

ANTHONY TROLLOPE

An Autobiography

Ayala's Angel

Barchester Towers

The Belton Estate

The Bertrams

Can You Forgive Her?

The Claverings

Cousin Henry

Doctor Thorne

Doctor Wortle's School

The Duke's Children

Early Short Stories

The Eustace Diamonds

An Eye for an Eye

Framley Parsonage

He Knew He Was Right

Lady Anna

The Last Chronicle of Barset

Later Short Stories

Miss Mackenzie

Mr Scarborough's Family

Orley Farm

Phineas Finn

Phineas Redux

The Prime Minister

Rachel Ray

The Small House at Allington

La Vendée

The Warden

The Way We Live Now

The Oxford World's Classics Website

www.worldsclassics.co.uk

- Information about new titles
- Explore the full range of Oxford World's Classics
- Links to other literary sites and the main OUP webpage
- Imaginative competitions, with bookish prizes
- Peruse *Compass*, the Oxford World's Classics magazine
- Articles by editors
- Extracts from Introductions
- A forum for discussion and feedback on the series
- Special information for teachers and lecturers

www.worldsclassics.co.uk

American Literature

British and Irish Literature

Children's Literature

Classics and Ancient Literature

Colonial Literature

Eastern Literature

European Literature

History

Medieval Literature

Oxford English Drama

Poetry

Philosophy

Politics

Religion

The Oxford Shakespeare

A complete list of Oxford Paperbacks, including Oxford World's Classics, OPUS, Past Masters, Oxford Authors, Oxford Shakespeare, Oxford Drama, and Oxford Paperback Reference, is available in the UK from the Academic Division Publicity Department, Oxford University Press, Great Clarendon Street, Oxford OX2 6DP.

In the USA, complete lists are available from the Paperbacks Marketing Manager, Oxford University Press, 198 Madison Avenue, New York, NY 10016.

Oxford Paperbacks are available from all good bookshops. In case of difficulty, customers in the UK can order direct from Oxford University Press Bookshop, Freepost, 116 High Street, Oxford OX1 4BR, enclosing full payment. Please add 10 per cent of published price for postage and packing.